MW01079403

BIG
GREEK
IDEA
SERIES

James

An Exegetical Guide
for Preaching
and Teaching

BIG
GREEK
IDEA
SERIES

James

An Exegetical Guide
for Preaching
and Teaching

Herbert W. Bateman IV • William C. Varner

KREGEL
ACADEMIC

James: An Exegetical Guide for Preaching and Teaching
© 2022 by Herbert W. Bateman IV and William C. Verner

Published by Kregel Academic, an imprint of Kregel Publications, 2450 Oak Industrial Dr. NE, Grand Rapids, MI 49505-6020.

This book is a title in the Big Greek Idea Series, edited by Herbert W. Bateman IV.

All rights reserved. No part of this book may be reproduced, stored in a retrieval system, or transmitted in any form or by any means—electronic, mechanical, photocopy, recording, or otherwise—without written permission of the publisher, except for brief quotations in printed reviews.

The Hebrew font, NewJerusalemU, and the Greek font, GraecaU, are available from www.linguistsoftware.com/lgku.htm, +1-425-775-1130.

Nestle-Aland, Novum Testamentum Graece, 28th Revised Edition, edited by Barbara and Kurt Aland, Johannes Karavidopoulos, Carlo M. Martini, and Bruce M. Metzger in cooperation with the Institute for New Testament Textual Research, Münster/Westphalia, © 2012 Deutsche Bibelgesellschaft, Stuttgart. Used by permission.

The translation of the New Testament portions used throughout the commentary is the authors' own English rendering of the Greek.

Scripture quotations marked NET are from the NET Bible® copyright ©1996–2017 by Biblical Studies Press, LLC (www.bible.org). Scripture quoted by permission. All rights reserved.

Scripture quotations marked NLT are from the *Holy Bible,* New Living Translation, copyright © 1996, 2004, 2015 by Tyndale House Foundation. Used by permission of Tyndale House Publishers, Inc., Carol Stream, Illinois 60188. All rights reserved.

ISBN 978-0-8254-4542-2

Printed in the United States of America

22 23 24 25 26 / 5 4 3 2 1

Herb dedicates the book to Daniel M. O'Hare,
Aaron C. Peer, and Jeremy Wike.

Will dedicates the work to his past
Greek students at The Master's University.

Contents

Big Greek Idea: Jewish (and probably God-fearing Gentile) followers of Jesus are expected to rejoice in God's working through hardships, to ask God for insight through prayer, to observe universal truths about poverty and wealth, and to discern God's involvement when enticed to do wrong, recognizing that life's good gifts are from God.

Big Greek Idea: Based on a proverb about godly living, God's people are to control their anger and their speech and focus attention on accepting what God says and practicing their faith, especially in helping orphans and widows and not succumbing to the ungodly behavior of nonbelievers.

Big Greek Idea: In the midst of his challenge to believers about partiality and discrimination against the poor, James reveals that the poor are God's rich heirs in his kingdom and are not to be dishonored, and that if people practice partiality, they not only will disobey the Bible, but also will be condemned and judged.

Preface to the Series

The Big Greek Idea Series: An Exegetical Guide for Preaching and Teaching is a grammatical-*like* commentary with interlinear-*like* English translations of the Greek text that provides expositional-*like* commentary to guide pastors and teachers in their sermon and teaching preparations. Every volume of this series has a threefold audience in mind: the busy pastor, the overworked professor of an academic institution, and the student with demanding Greek professors.

WHY PASTORS, PROFESSORS, AND STUDENTS

First and foremost, the Big Greek Idea Series is for the busy *pastor* who desires to use Greek text in sermon preparation. Most preachers who have earned Masters of Divinity degrees and who have taken some NT Greek have not had a lot of exposure in studying books of the NT in Greek. If they were fortunate, they may have studied two NT books in Greek. Furthermore, many preachers who desire to work in the Greek NT do not have the luxury of studying and working in the Greek on their own in any great detail. They need a tool to guide them in their use of NT Greek in their sermon preparation. This series is meant to be that tool.

> THE BIG GREEK IDEA: A GUIDE FOR PREACHING AND TEACHING was ***written for*** three groups of people:
> 1. the busy ***pastor***,
> 2. the overloaded ***professor***,
> 3. and the ***student*** with a demanding New Testament Greek professor.

Second, the Big Greek Idea Series is for the overloaded ***professor*** of an academic institution. Institutional demands are high, and expectations at times appear overwhelming. On the one hand, many academies expect faculty to teach Greek exegesis with minimal time to prepare, forgetting that such courses differ from courses requiring only English language aptitude. On the other hand, students anticipate a great deal of explanation from those who teach them. Often the professor is merely one step ahead of the students. This tool is intended to streamline class preparation and perhaps even serve as a required or recommended textbook to help take a load off the professor.

Finally, the Big Greek Idea Series is for the ***student*** with demanding Greek professors. What a student puts into a course is what a student will get and retain from a course. Students who have professors with great expectations are blessed, though the student may feel cursed (at the time). This tool will provide answers that will impress a professor, but more importantly will provide information that will build confidence in handling the Greek NT. The Big Greek Idea Series will be a tool students will use in ministry long after the course is over.

What Can Be Expected

Each volume of the Big Greek Idea Series features one or more NT books in Greek. It is a series for people who have studied basic NT Greek grammar and intermediate Greek syntax and grammar. Each volume provides an introduction that features information crucial for understanding each NT book while making minimal assumptions about the reader's capabilities to work in the NT Greek text. After the introduction, the volume has three distinct features.

First, each featured NT book is broken into units of thought. The units open with a big Greek idea. Professors sometimes refer to the big Greek idea as the exegetical idea of a passage. The big Greek idea is followed by a structural overview and a simple outline for the unit.

Second, the Nestle-Aland[28] Greek text is broken into independent and dependent clauses that reveal visually the coordination and subordination of thought based upon key structural markers. Verbs and key structural markers are often in bold and always underlined. Under each Greek clause is an original English translation. The interlinear-*like* English translations of the Greek help readers spot the words they know and those they do not.

Finally, each unit closes with an analysis of the clausal outline. It explains our syntactical understanding of clausal relationships; our semantical rendering of all Greek verbs, verbals, and key structural markers; and the interpretive translation of the text. Interspersed throughout this closing section are grammatical, syntactical, semantical, lexical, theological, and text-critical nuggets of information. They are expositional-*like* commentary to enhance an understanding of selected issues that surface in the text.

THE BIG GREEK IDEA: A GUIDE FOR PREACHING AND TEACHING FEATURES

1. Units of Thought
   Big Greek Idea
   Structural Overview
   Outline
2. Clausal Outlines
   Clausal Relationships Visualized
   Structural Markers Identified
   English Translation Provided
3. Explanations
   Syntax Explained
   Semantical Decisions Recognized
   Interpretive Translation Justified
   Expositional Comments Provided

HOW TO USE THE SERIES

The Big Greek Idea Series has the potential for a threefold usage.

First, use it as a grammatical commentary because it is a grammatical-*like* commentary. Every volume represents the early stages of Bible study in NT Greek. Identifying clauses is a first step typically practiced in exegesis. Yet, every independent and dependent Greek clause has a corresponding explanatory discussion that underscores the grammatical, syntactical, and semantical functions of its respective Greek structural markers, which markers are <u>underlined</u> and often in **bold** print for easy interpretation. Unlike computer programs that present an NT Greek text with English translations and parsing capabilities, The Big Greek Idea: A Guide for Preaching and Teaching discusses syntax and semantical options important for exegesis yet, not available with computer programs . . . but I'm sure that too will change.

Second, use it as an interlinear because it has an interlinear-*like* presentation of the Nestle-Aland[28] Greek text with a corresponding English translation. Yet, the Big Greek Idea Series offers far more than a traditional interlinear. The Greek text is presented in a clausal outline format that provides the twenty-first-century reader a visual of the biblical author's flow of thought. More importantly, it causes a person to ***slow down*** and ***look at the text*** more closely.

- What does the text say . . . not what *I* remember about the text?
- What does it mean . . . not what *I* want it to mean?
- What do we need to believe . . . not *my* theological pet peeves?
- How should we then live for God . . . not according to *my* preconceived ideas?

Third, use it as a commentary because interwoven throughout every volume are expositional-*like* nuggets. An "expositional-*like* nugget" is a comment that underscores a grammatical, syntactical, semantical, lexical, theological, or text-critical issue. Typical of any expositional commentary, if time is taken to discuss an issue, it's probably important and warrants some special attention. Similarly, the expositional-like nuggets point the reader to important interpretive issues.

Yet, the Big Greek Idea Series is not meant to replace current commentaries. Commentators generally begin commentary preparation on the clause level, but a publisher's page restriction often makes it difficult to visualize clausal parallels and coordination and subordination of thought. Descriptions are at times ambiguous and perhaps even ignored due to the difficulty in presenting a syntactical situation. The tool used here does no hide ambiguities and difficulties of coordination or subordination of thought because clauses are clearly reproduced and explained for readers to evaluate a contemporary author's decisions. Thus, The Big Greek Idea: A Guide for Preaching and Teaching is meant to complement critical commentaries like Baker's Exegetical Commentary, Word Biblical Commentary, The Anchor Bible, and others.

I trust the Big Greek Idea Series will be a rewarding tool for your use in studying the NT.

HERBERT W. BATEMAN IV
SERIES EDITOR

Acknowledgment of the Authors

English grammar is not the most exciting subject to study and learn, and yet, grammar and syntax are vital skills for interpreting the Bible whether in an English translation or a Greek NT text. Consequently, I'm indebted to several people who throughout my training emphasized the importance of grammar and syntax for interpreting the Bible.

While at Cairn University, Janice Okulski required all her students to create a grammatical diagram for the NIV translation of Philippians, and Dr. MacCorkle expected his students to structurally outline an English translation of Galatians in order to trace Paul's train of thought. Special attention was always given to connecting words like "so that" (= result), "in order that" (= purpose), "therefore" (= inferential), "because" (= reason), and so on. Both professors prepared me for later study in the Greek NT, and I owe a great debt of gratitude to them. Professors Okulski and MacCorkle provided a sound foundation for studying the English Bible, and Dallas Theological Seminary expanded that groundwork when I began working in the NT Greek text.

While at Dallas Theological Seminary, Darrell Bock, Buist Fanning, John Grassmick, and other NT faculty members were instrumental in teaching me skills of translation, syntax, and exegesis. Naturally, skills take time to master, and shortcuts were later developed while teaching others how to learn and work in the NT Greek text. This book *James* and *John's Letters* in the Big Greek Idea Series are two of those shortcuts for assisting people in their study of four of the eight general letters in Greek.

Later as a professor, my pedagogical skills were challenged and eventually sharpened as I was learning how to help students study and learn Greek. Several works resulted from those efforts: *A Workbook for Intermediate Greek: Grammar, Exegesis, and Commentary on 1–3 John* and *Interpreting the General Letters* in Kregel's Handbooks for Greek NT Exegesis. Another benefit that comes with teaching is the students, first teaching them and then getting out of their way so that they can move beyond you and your abilities.

Consequently, I am indebted to three groups of people who have shaped my previous volume in this series, *John's Letters*, as well as this volume, *James*. They are two undergraduate professors from Cairn University, the NT department at Dallas Theological Seminary, and the numerous students whom I have tutored and taught for more than twenty years, especially my teaching assistants while teaching at Grace Seminary: Daniel M. O'Hare, Aaron C. Peer, and Jeremy Wike, to whom I dedicate this volume.

Finally, I am thankful for Will Varner's various contributions to this volume as well as for my wife Cindy Ann Bateman for making it possible for me to complete this volume for the Big Greek Idea Series, as well as for her perpetual support for all the books I have written over the years.

HERBERT W. BATEMAN IV

For years the Letter of James was simply neglected or viewed as somehow inferior to the Pauline correspondence. Martin Luther's pungent comments on what he called "an epistle of straw" are well known. The magisterial commentary by the higher critic Martin Dibelius criticized the disjointed "ethical paraenesis" in James. For more than a century, students of James were best served by the commentary of the evangelical J. B. Mayor. The critical works by such scholars as J. H. Ropes and Dibelius provided excellent observations on the language and style of James but lacked the theological perspective of Mayor. The last forty years, however, have witnessed a new day for Jacobean scholarship with such admirable works as Davids (1982); Johnson (1995); Moo (2000); Witherington (2007); Blomberg et al. (2008); McCartney (2009); McKnight (2011); and Allison (2013). So, is there still a need for another commentary?

Every commentary on James has its strengths, and I trust the one before you displays its strength in its detailed analysis of the grammar and syntax of this short but meaty epistle. For me this volume is the culmination of nearly twenty years of research on this epistle that has led to three commentaries directed at different levels of readers. It has been my delight in this volume to share the stage with another scholar and friend, Herb Bateman. Herb has also devoted himself to the nuts and bolts of how the Greek language works not only through individual words but through words joined together in a clause to convey meaning. I am convinced that there is still a need for such a work as this and I am delighted to lend my cooperation to its gestation and birth.

I have dedicated my past books to various individuals in my life who have touched me positively in several ways. I dedicate this volume to all of my past Greek students at The Master's University.

WILLIAM C. VARNER

Charts and Sidebars

Abbreviations

BIBLE TRANSLATIONS

ASV	American Standard Version
CNT	Comprehensive New Testament
ESV	English Standard Version
KJV	King James Version
NASB	New American Standard Bible
NET	New English Translation. First Beta Edition. Biblical Studies Press, 2001
NIV	New International Version
NJB	New Jerusalem Bible
NLT	New Living Translation
NRSV	New Revised Standard Version

GENERAL ABBREVIATIONS

A.D.	in the year of our Lord
B.C.	Before Christ
B.C.E.	Before the Common Era (equivalent to B.C.)
C.E.	Common Era (equivalent to A.D.)
LXX	Septuagint (the Greek OT)
NT	New Testament
OT	Old Testament

TECHNICAL ABBREVIATIONS

cf.	compare (*confer*)
con.	against (*contra*)
ed(s).	editor(s)
e.g.	for example (*exempli gratia*)
esp.	especially
et al.	and others (*et alii*)
etc.	and others of the same kind (*et cetera*)
i.e.	that is (*id est*)
lit.	literally
n(n).	note(s)
N/a	not available (This is generally used of grammars that do not discuss an introductory or syntactical issue.)

p(p).	page(s)
repr.	reprint
rev.	revised
s.v.	under the word (*sub verbo*)
v(v).	verse(s)

APOCRYPHA AND PSEUDEPIGRAPHA

Tob	Tobit
Did.	The Didache, or Teaching of the Twelve Apostles
Wis	Wisdom of Solomon
Sir	Wisdom of Jesus the Son of Sirach (Ecclesiasticus)
1 Macc	First Maccabees
2 Macc	Second Maccabees
4 Macc	Fourth Maccabees
1 En.	First Enoch

ANCIENT MANUSCRIPTS

P. Oxy.	Oxyrhynchus Papyri

ANCIENT WRITINGS

Aristotle
	Pol.	*Political Theory*

Herodotus
	Hist.	*Histories*

Josephus
	Ant.	*Jewish Antiquities (Antiquitates judaicae)*
	War	*Jewish War (Bellum Judaicum)*
	Life	*The Life (Vita)*

Plato
	Symp.	*Symposium*

Philo, Judaeus
	Mos.	*Life of Moses (De Vita Mosis)*
	Opif.	*On Creation (De Opificio Mundi)*
	Gig.	*On the Giants (De gigantibus)*
	Spec. Leg.	*Special Laws (De Specialibus Legibus)*

Polybius

    Hist.   *Histories*

Most Used Periodical, Reference, and Serial

Adam

Adam, A. K. M. 2013. *James: A Handbook on the Greek Text.* Waco, TX: Baylor University Press.

Baker et al.

Baker, W. R., and T. D. Ellsworth. 2004. *Preaching James.* St. Louis: Chalice.

Bateman[1]

Bateman IV, H. W. 2016. "Review of Robert J. Foster, *The Significance of Exemplars for the Interpretation of the Letter of James.*" *Journal of the Evangelical Theological Society* 59.1: 199–201.

Bateman[2]

Bateman IV, H. W. 2013. *Interpreting the General Letters: An Exegetical Handbook.* Handbooks for New Testament Exegesis. Edited by J. D. Harvey. Grand Rapids: Kregel.

Bateman et al.[1]

Bateman IV, H. W., and S. W. Smith. 2021. *Hebrews: A Commentary for Biblical Preaching and Teaching.* Kerux Commentaries. Grand Rapids: Kregel.

Bateman et al.[2]

Bateman IV, H. W., and A. C. Peer. 2018. *John's Letters: An Exegetical Guide for Preaching and Teaching.* In the Big Greek Idea Series. Grand Rapids: Kregel.

BDAG

Bauer, W., F. W. Danker, W. F. Arndt, and F. W. Gingrich. 2000. *A Greek–English Lexicon of the New Testament and Other Early Christian Literature.* 3rd ed. Chicago and London: University of Chicago Press.

BDF

Blass, F., A. Debrunner, and R. W. Funk. 1961. *A Greek Grammar of the New Testament and Other Early Christian Literature.* Translation and revision of the 9th–10th German edition, by Robert W. Funk. Chicago: University of Chicago Press.

Blomberg et al.

Blomberg, C. L., and M. J. Kamell. 2008. *James.* Zondervan Exegetical Commentary on the New Testament. Grand Rapids: Zondervan.

Davids	Davids, P. 1992. *The Epistle of James.* New International Greek Testament Commentary. Grand Rapids: Eerdmans.
Dibelius	Dibelius, M. 1976. *Commentary on James.* Translated by Michael Williams. Hermeneia. Philadelphia: Fortress Press.
Irons	Irons, C. L. 2016. *A Syntax Guide for Reading the Greek New Testament.* Grand Rapids: Kregel.
Johnson	Johnson, L. T. 1995. *The Letter of James.* Anchor Bible 37A. New York: Doubleday.
LN	Louw, J. P., and E. A. Nida, eds. 1989. *Greek-English Lexicon of the New Testament: Based on Semantic Domains.* 2nd ed. New York: United Bible Societies.
Mayor	Mayor, J. B. 1900. *The Epistle of St. James: The Greek Text with Introduction, Notes, and Comments.* 3rd ed. London: MacMillan & Co.
McCartney	McCartney, D. G. 2009. *James: An Exegetical Commentary on the New Testament.* Grand Rapids: Baker.
Metzger[1]	Metzger, B. M. 1994. *A Textual Commentary on the Greek New Testament.* 2nd ed. Stuttgart, Germany: Biblia–Druck.
Metzger[2]	Metzger, B. M. 1971. *A Textual Commentary on the Greek New Testament.* Stuttgart, Germany: Biblia–Druck.
Montanari	Montanari, F., ed. 2015. *Brill Dictionary of Ancient Greek.* Leiden: Brill.
Moo	Moo, D. J. 2000. *The Letter of James.* Pillar New Testament Commentary. Grand Rapids: Eerdmans.
Moule	Moule, C. F. D. 1984. *An Idiom-Book of the Greek New Testament.* 2nd ed. Cambridge: Cambridge University Press.
Porter	Porter, S. E. 1994. *Idioms of the Greek New Testament.* 2nd ed. Sheffield: JSOT Press.

Robertson[1]	Robertson, A. T. 1934. *A Greek Grammar of the Greek New Testament in the Light of Historical Research*. 3rd ed. New York: George H. Doran Co..
Robertson[2]	Robertson, A. T. 1982. *Word Pictures in the New Testament*. 6 vols. Grand Rapids: Baker.
Spencer	Spencer, A. B. 2020. *A Commentary on James*. Kregel Exegetical Library. Grand Rapids: Kregel.
Trench	Trench, R. C. 1880. *Synonyms of the New Testament*. London: Macmillan and Co.
Turner	Turner, N. 1980. *A Grammar of New Testament Greek*. Edited by J. H. Moulton. Edinburgh: T & T Clark.
Varner[1]	Varner, W. 2017. *James: A Commentary on the Greek Text*. Dallas: Fontes Press.
Varner[2]	Varner, W. 2010. *The Book of James: A New Perspective: A Linguistic Commentary Applying Discourse Analysis*. The Woodlands, TX: Kress Biblical Resources.
W	Wallace, D. B. 1996. *Greek Grammar beyond the Basics: An Exegetical Syntax of the New Testament*. Grand Rapids: Zondervan.
Zerwick	Zerwick, M. 1963. *Biblical Greek: Illustrated by Examples*. Translated by Joseph Smith. SubBi 41. Rome: Pontifical Biblical Institute.
Zerwick et al.	Zerwick, M., and M. Grosvenor. 1981. *A Grammatical Analysis of the New Testament: Unabridged Revised Edition in One Volume*. Rome: Biblical Institute Press.

Introduction

James: An Exegetical Guide for Preaching and Teaching in the Big Greek Idea Series deepens a pastor's or teacher's understanding of James's literary structure, his use of clauses, his syntax, and his writing style with this single intention: to identify the big Greek ideas in James. Tracing the various big Greek ideas in James is possible by recognizing James's thought process evident in the coordination and subordination of the Greek clauses he employs within his letter. Yet, we do not assume that pastors and teachers remember everything learned during their initial study of NT Greek in their college or seminary classes. We strive to define and explain James's use of Greek in ways that help pastors and teachers recall what was once learned, refresh and expand an appreciation for James's letter written in Koine Greek, and underscore the value of engaging the Greek text when preparing to preach and teach James.[1]

We construct the Greek words from James's letter in 203 independent clauses and 155 dependent clauses and arrange them into clausal outlines. Each clause is translated and then explained for interpretive recognition, comprehension, and communication. The clausal outlines represent an early stage in preparing to preach and teach the text.[2] All the clauses

Number of Greek Words in James				
Chapter	NA^{28}	SBL	RP^{2005}	MT
James 1	406	405	409	409
James 2	418	414	425	425
James 3	295	293	300	300
James 4	278	275	270	280
James 5	351	347	345	344
Total	1,748	1,734	1,749	1,758

appear in Greek from the Nestle-Aland^{28} Greek text along with an interpretive translation for easy usage. The clausal outlines make it possible for pastors to visualize the relationship clauses have to one another in order to trace James's flow of thought and ultimately his big idea.

---

1. Naturally, other books move beyond clausal outlines and direct attention to a bigger picture of James, such as W. Varner, *The Book of James: A New Perspective: A Linguistic Commentary Applying Discourse Analysis* (The Woodlands, TX: Kress Biblical Resources, 2010). Yet, clausal observations are always the first step to any discourse analysis or exegetical commentary.
2. For nine steps of exegesis, see Herbert W. Bateman IV, *Interpreting the General Letters: An Exegetical Handbook*, Handbooks for New Testament Exegesis, ed. John D. Harvey (Grand Rapids: Kregel, 2013).

The Clausal Outline

The clausal outlines for James are based on a variety of Greek clauses employed throughout James. By nature, a Greek clause has a subject and a predicate, which may be a verb, a participle, or an infinitive. The clauses may be independent or dependent Greek clauses. Whereas independent clauses can stand alone, dependent clauses have a subordinate relationship to another clause or a relationship within a clause.

Other terminology exists for this same process. Mounce calls it "phrasing," Guthrie calls it "grammatical diagram," and MacDonald calls it "textual transcription."[3] While these other works tend to break sentences into clauses and phrases, *James: An Exegetical Guide for Preaching and Teaching* concentrates on the clause level. As you work your way through the clauses in James, you can expect the following.

1. Every clause reproduces the Greek text in the exact word order of the Nestle-Aland[28] Greek text even when syntax is less than clear. Every attempt is made to make sense of James's syntax regardless of the occasional lack of clarity.

2. Every Greek clause underscores the Greek words deemed as important structural markers. A structural marker is always a verb and sometimes a verbal (participle or infinitive). Other important structural markers are conjunctions, relative and indefinite relative pronouns, and a select number of prepositional phrases that introduce clauses. Structural markers are always underlined and often in bold print.

3. Every Greek structural marker serves to distinguish different types of independent and dependent clauses. The chart below summarizes the types of independent and dependent Greek clauses found in James and the Greek words that often introduce them.

---

3. W. D. Mounce, *A Graded Reader of Biblical Greek* (Grand Rapids: Zondervan, 1996), xvi–xxiii; G. H. Guthrie and J. S. Duvall, *Biblical Greek Exegesis: A Guided Approach to Learning Intermediate and Advanced Greek* (Grand Rapids: Zondervan, 1988), 27–42; W. G. MacDonald, *Greek Enchiridion: A Concise Handbook of Grammar for Translation and Exegesis* (Peabody, MA: Hendrickson, 1979), 145–52.

Types (Classifications) of Independent and Dependent Clauses[4]	
Three Types of Independent Clauses	**Four Types of Dependent Clauses**

Conjunctive clauses are introduced by
 	
   simple connective (καί or δέ),
 	
   contrastive conjunction (δέ, πλήν),
 	
   correlative conjunction (μέν . . . δέ or καί . . . καί)
 	
   explanatory conjunction (γάρ),
 	
   inferential conjunction (ἄρα, διό, οὖν, γάρ),
 	
   transitional conjunction (καί, δέ, οὖν).
	Conjunctive clauses may introduce subordinate adverbial clauses that denote semantical concepts such as time (ὅτε, ὅταν); reason and cause (διό, ὅτι, ἐπεί); purpose and result (ἵνα, ὥστε); comparison (καθώς, ὡς, ὡσεί, ὥσπερ); etc.
	
	Conjunctive clauses may also introduce subordinate substantival subject, direct object, adjectival, appositional, and predicate nominative clauses, most frequently introduced with ὅτι plus an indicative and ἵνα plus a subjunctive.

Prepositional clauses are introduced with a preposition followed by either τοῦτο or τί.
 	
   "for this reason" (**διὰ** τοῦτο; **ἐπὶ** τοῦτο),
 	
   "as a result of this" (**ἐκ** τοῦτο),
 	
   "why" (**εἰς** τί; **διὰ** τί),
 	
   "how" (κατ**ὰ** τί),
 	
   "after this" (μετ**ὰ** τοῦτο),
 	
   "in this" (**ἐν** τοῦτο).
	Pronominal clauses are introduced by
	
	   a relative pronoun (ὅς, ἥ, ὅ),
	
	   a relative adjective (οἷος, *such as*; ὅσος, *as much/many as*),
	
	   a relative adverb (ὅπου, *where*; ὅτε, *when*),
	
	   an indefinite relative pronoun (τις, τι, οἵτινες, ὁποῖος, ὅστις).

	Participial clauses are introduced by participles.
Asyndeton clauses are not introduced by a conjunctive word or phrase.	Infinitival clauses are introduced by infinitives.

4. Every independent Greek clause (the main thought) is placed farthest to the left of the page. A dependent Greek clauses that directly modifies a Greek word in another clause is either placed in parentheses or positioned under (or above if necessary) the word it modifies for easy identification. This positioning of a clause *visualizes* the *subordination* and *coordination* of James's basic grammatical and syntactical relationships, parallelisms, and emphases.

5. Every independent and dependent Greek clause has an interpretive English translation provided under the Greek text. Every translated structural marker is also underlined and often in bold print for easy recognition, use, and evaluation.

4. D. B. Wallace, *Greek Grammar Beyond the Basics* (Grand Rapids: Zondervan, 1996), 656–65.

One to Five Exemplified

An example of what to expect is nicely illustrated with a verse from James 1:2–3.

^{1:2a} Πᾶσαν χαρὰν **ἡγήσασθε**, ἀδελφοί μου,
^{1:2a} **Consider it** pure joy, my brothers,

       |

      ^{1:2b} <u>ὅταν</u> πειρασμοῖς **περιπέσητε** ποικίλοις,
      ^{1:2b} <u>when</u> **you encounter** all types of trials,

         |

           ^{1:3} **γινώσκοντες** (<u>ὅτι</u> τὸ δοκίμιον ὑμῶν τῆς πίστεως **κατεργάζεται** ὑπομονήν)·
           ^{1:3} *because* **you know** (<u>that</u> the testing of your faith **produces** endurance).

1. The order of the Greek sentence is followed.

2. Every Greek clause underscores the Greek words deemed as important structural markers.

3. Every Greek structural marker distinguishes independent and dependent clauses. James **1:2a** is an independent clause with an imperative (ἡγήσασθε) as a major structural marker, **1:2b** is a dependent clause introduced with a conjunction (ὅταν) with its main verb περιπέσητε, and **1:3** is a dependent clause introduced with a participle (γινώσκοντες) along with a conjunctive ὅτι ("that") clause with its main verb κατεργάζεται ("produces"). All structural markers are clearly identified.

4. There are three clauses represented. The **first clause** (1:2a) is an independent asyndeton clause and is placed to the extreme left. The **second clause** (1:2b) is a dependent conjunctive clause introduced with ὅταν ("when") that is functioning adverbially modifying the Greek verb ἡγήσασθε of the independent clause (1:2a). So, the first word of the ὅταν clause is placed below the verb it modifies, ἡγήσασθε. The **final clause** (1:3) is a bit more complex. On the one hand, the entire γινώσκοντες (ὅτι τὸ δοκίμιον ὑμῶν τῆς πίστεως κατεργάζεται ὑπομονήν) is a dependent participial clause that is functioning adverbially modifying the Greek verb ἡγήσασθε. So, the first word of the participial clause (γινώσκοντες) is placed under the verb it modifies, ἡγήσασθε. On the other hand (ὅτι τὸ δοκίμιον ὑμῶν τῆς πίστεως κατεργάζεται ὑπομονήν) in parentheses

is a dependent conjunctive clause introduced with ὅτι that functions substantivally as the direct object of the Greek verbal γινώσκοντες. The entire ὅτι clause is placed in parentheses to visualize the clause's grammatical contribution to the dependent participial clause.

5. Every Greek clause has a corresponding English translation and, as in the Greek, all the translated structural markers are also underscored for easy recognition.

6. Every independent and dependent Greek clause has a corresponding explanatory discussion that underscores the grammatical, syntactical, and semantical functions of its respective structural markers that are <u>underlined</u> and often in **bold** print. So not every word within a clause is discussed. Explanatory discussions focus on the structural markers in order to emphasize James's point.

> **Grammatical Function:** Grammatical function identifies the Greek *structural marker* as to whether it is pronominal, conjunctive, verb, or verbal (participial or infinitval). If the marker is a verb or verbal, it is parsed with an appropriate lexical meaning provided from BDAG. If it is pronominal or conjunctive, a lexical definition is also provided based upon BDAG.

> **Syntactical Function:** Syntactical function first draws attention to the independent or dependent clause's type. If a *dependent clause*, its syntactical function within a sentence is identified, namely, recognizing whether it is substantival, adjectival, or adverbial as well as the word or words the clause modifies.

> **Semantical Function:** Semantical functions are by nature interpretive suggestions whereby a Greek structural marker is explained based upon its literary context. Semantical interpretations employ the categories listed and defined in Wallace's *Greek Grammar Beyond the Basics*, many of which are discussed in critical commentaries and reflected in English Bible translations.[5]

7. Explanatory discussions about James are interspersed with commentary-*like* remarks identified as "nuggets." Numerous text-critical, grammatical, syntactical, structural, theological, and lexical nuggets appear between clausal

---

5. Because Wallace has a wide audience and is used as a textbook in many colleges and seminaries, we have intentionally chosen to employ his categories in the Big Greek Idea Series. Be aware, however, that there are other approaches, e.g., Porter 1994; Fanning 1990; Campbell 2008.

presentations that delve deeper into and expand on issues in order to advance your appreciation for James, his readers, and his message.

8. All independent and dependent clauses are grouped into units of thought. James is presented in this commentary as having eight units of thought (see content listing).

9. Every unit opens with an exegetical or "Big Greek Idea" statement followed by a structural overview that provides a synopsis for the unit's structure and closes with a brief and potential preaching or teaching outline.

10. An interpretive English translation for James and his figures of speech conclude our thoughts for the *James* volume in the Big Greek Idea Series.

All ten expectations are intended to help pastors and teachers to recall and to refresh their previous training in Greek, to expand a person's understanding of Koine Greek, and to encourage personal engagement with the Greek text. Hopefully the process in this book will increase confidence in understanding and appreciating James as plans are made to preach and/or teach this letter.

Yet, *James: An Exegetical Guide for Preaching and Teaching* in the Big Greek Idea Series is not a guide for translation. There are works designed for that task.[6] This book is a grammatical-*like* commentary with interlinear-*like* English translations of the Greek text that provides expositional commentary-*like* comments to guide a pastor and teacher in their sermon and teaching preparations.

But before delving into examining the eight big Greek ideas in James, it may be helpful to pause, define, and illustrate the different types of Greek clauses typically found in James.

INDEPENDENT CLAUSES IN JAMES

Independent Greek clauses are rather important in determining James's main thought in a given sentence. There are *three types of independent clauses* found in the Greek NT: conjunctive, prepositional, and asyndeton. Yet, of the 203 independent clauses, only two types of independent clauses appear in James.

The first type of independent Greek clause in James's letter is the *independent conjunctive clause*. They are introduced by a Greek conjunction (καί, ἀλλά, δέ, γάρ, νῦν, διό, οὖν, οὕτως). Sometimes the Greek conjunction starts the independent

---

6. A. K. M. Adam, *James: A Handbook on the Greek Text* (Waco, TX: Baylor University Press, 2013).

clause. Other times it appears in a post-positive position. The independent conjunctive clause appears quite often in James. There are *at least* ninety-seven identified examples in James. The following are nine representative samples worthy of mention. The conjunction is underlined and the verb is underlined and in **bold** print.

On the one hand, the independent conjunctive clause starts with the conjunction. It is at times the very first word of the clause. The following samples exemplify the most common conjunctions that begin an independent conjunctive clause. They tend to reflect the continuation or linking together of ideas for the sake of an argument. Sometimes James omits a word (called an ellipsis), and we insert the missing word in [*brackets*] and italicized.

1:11b καὶ [ὁ ἥλιος] **ἐξήρανεν** τὸν χόρτον
1:11b and [*the sun*] **dries out** the wild grass

2:18c κἀγώ σοι **δείξω** ἐκ τῶν ἔργων μου τὴν πίστιν.
2:18c and **I will prove** to you my faith by my deeds.

3:5b καὶ μεγάλα **αὐχεῖ**.
3:5b yet, **it** *repeatedly* **boasts** of great *things*.

On the other hand, the conjunction may appear as the second word of the independent clause. It is in the post-positive position. Sometimes the conjunction introduces a transition (1:9; 5:1a). Other times, it draws a conclusion (4:7a; 5:7a). Still other times, it introduces a contrast (2:6a; 4:12d).

1:9 **Καυχάσθω** δὲ ὁ ἀδελφὸς ὁ ταπεινὸς ἐν τῷ ὕψει αὐτοῦ,
1:9 Now, the lowly brother *and sister* **should rather boast** in his exaltation,

2:6a ὑμεῖς δὲ **ἠτιμάσατε** τὸν πτωχόν.
2:6a But you **have dishonored** the poor person.

4:7a **ὑποτάγητε** οὖν τῷ θεῷ,
4:7a Therefore, **submit yourselves** to God,

4:12d σὺ δὲ τίς **εἶ**
4:12d But who **are** you

5:1a Ἄγε νῦν οἱ πλούσιοι, **κλαύσατε**
5:1a Now **listen**, you who are rich, **burst into weeping**

5:7a **Μακροθυμήσατε** οὖν, ἀδελφοί, ἕως τῆς παρουσίας τοῦ κυρίου.
5:7a **Be patient,** therefore, brothers *and sisters*, until the coming of the Lord.

Naturally, these conjunctive clauses are independent because they contain a subject and predicate, present a complete thought, and can stand alone. While it is not evident above, in the pages to follow all independent clauses will be placed farthest to the left of the page because they are independent. Each of the independent clauses above begins with a conjunction that makes some

| **Ellipsis Defined** |
| An ellipsis is the omission of a word or any element of the Greek language that renders a sentence "ungrammatical," yet, the missing element or word is from the context. |

sort of connection with a previous clause or transitions to a new thought. As you can see from the samples above, conjunctions may appear in the post-positive position (1:9a; 2:6a; 4:7a, 12d; 5:1a; 5:7a) but not necessarily (1:11b; 2:18c; 3:5b).

The most frequent independent conjunctive clauses in James are those introduced with καί. Of the ninety-seven conjunctive independent clauses in James, forty-seven begin with καί. James's favored usage is that of a coordinating conjunction rendered as "and" (καί) forty-four times. Yet, καί is also interpreted once as an adversative (3:5b), once as emphatic (2:23a), and once as inferential (5:18a).

And while James's favorite conjunction is καί, eight other Greek conjunctions appear in James: ἀλλά, δέ, ἀντί, γάρ, νῦν (δέ), διό, οὖν, and οὕτως (καί). The following chart not only lists the Greek conjunctions and where they appear in James, it identifies how the conjunction has been interpreted semantically in our interpretive English translation for James.

Conjunctions Introducing Independent Clauses in James			
	καί/κἀγώ	**ἀλλά**	**δέ**
Ascensive The conjunction provides a point of focus "even"			
Connective or Coordinate The conjunction adds an additional element to the discussion "and," "also"	1:5c, 11b, 11c, 11d, 13d, 24b, 24c 2:4b, 6c, 12b, 19b, 19c 3:3c, 6a, 7b, 9b, 14c 4:1b, 2b, [2c], 2d, 2e, [2f], 2g, 3b, 7c, 8b, 8d, 9b, 9c, 10b, 11c 5:2b, 3b, 3c, 4d, 5b, [6b], 11c, 16b, 17b, 17d, 18b, 18c		1:4a, 15c 2:25a 3:18a 5:12a, 14c, 15a, 15b

Conjunctions Introducing Independent Clauses in James								
	καί/κἀγώ	ἀλλά	δέ	ἀντί	γάρ	νῦν (δέ)	διό	οὖν	οὕτως (καί)
Contrastive or Adversative The conjunction provides an opposing thought to the idea to which it is connected "but," "yet"	3:5b	2:18a 3:15	1:6a, 10a, 22a, 25a, 14a 2:6a, 20 3:8a, 17 4:6a, 7b, 12d 5:12b	4:15a					
Emphatic The conjunction intensifies the discussion "indeed"	2:23a "in this way"					4:16a			
Explanatory Following verbs of emotion, the conjunction provides additional information "for" "you see"					1:6c, 7, 11a, 13d, 20, 24a 2:10a, 11a, 13a 3:2a				
Inferential The conjunction signals a conclusion or summary of a discussion "therefore," "thus," "so (also)," "then"	5:18a		1:19b				4:6b	1:21a 4:4b, 7a 5:7a, 16a	1:11e 2:12a, 17a, 26b 3:5a
Transitional The conjunction moves the discussion in a new direction "now"			1:9		3:7a	4:13a 5:1a			

The second type of independent Greek clause is the ***independent prepositional clause***. They are introduced with a Greek preposition (διὰ τοῦτο, εἰς τοῦτο, ἐπὶ τοῦτο, ἐκ τοῦτο, ἐν τοῦτο, μετὰ τοῦτο, εἰς τί, διὰ τί, and κατὰ τί). While independent prepositional clauses appear frequently in John's letters (Bateman et al.[2], 36–37) and Ephesians (Simpson, 28), like Philippians (Moore, 30–34) there are no independent prepositional clauses in James.

The third type of independent Greek clause is the ***independent asyndeton clause***. This independent clause has neither an introductory conjunction nor an opening prepositional phrase. It is a "vivid stylistic feature" for emphasis or rhetorical force (W, 658). Yet it too is an independent clause with only a verb as its structural marker. The independent asyndeton clause is the dominate independent clause in James. There are *at least* 106 identified examples in James. Of these, eight are worthy of mention because they exemplify what to expect when studying James. There is but one structural marker, the verb, which is underlined and in **bold** print. We have grouped our examples into three categories.

First, several of James's independent asyndeton clauses are inquiries. They appear with an interrogative indicative verb (W, 449–50). In James 2:19, the stated verb πιστεύεις is clearly identifiable because it is underlined and in bold print. The indicative probes information about the "what." In James 3:13a, the elliptical indicative verb [ἐστιν] in brackets and italicized, is also underlined. The questions are a rhetorical questions.

> 2:19a σὺ **<u>πιστεύεις</u>** (ὅτι εἶς **<u>ἐστιν</u>** ὁ θεός);
> 2:19a **<u>Do you believe</u>** (that God **<u>is</u>** one)?

> 3:13a Τίς [<u>*ἐστιν*</u>] σοφὸς καὶ ἐπιστήμων ἐν ὑμῖν;
> 3:13a Who [<u>*is*</u>] wise and understanding among you?

Second, most of James's independent asyndeton clauses are mere indicative statements of "assertion or presentations of certainty" (W, 448).

> 1:8 ἀνὴρ δίψυχος [<u>*ἐστιν*</u>] ἀκατάστατος ἐν πάσαις ταῖς ὁδοῖς αὐτοῦ.
> 1:8 A double-minded individual [<u>*is*</u>] unstable in everything he pursues.

> 2:13b **<u>κατακαυχᾶται</u>** ἔλεος κρίσεως.
> 2:13b Mercy **<u>triumphs</u>** over judgment.

> 5:17a Ἠλίας ἄνθρωπος **<u>ἦν</u>** ὁμοιοπαθὴς ἡμῖν.
> 5:17a Elijah **<u>was</u>** a human being with a nature like ours.

Finally, many of James's independent asyndeton clauses are imperatival expectations. Sometimes the imperative is negated (1:16; 5:9a). Other times, it is a mere expectation (2:18d). Still other times, it is a plea for consideration (1:2; 5:7b). The following are three representative examples.

1:16 Μὴ **πλανᾶσθε**, ἀδελφοί μου ἀγαπητοί.
1:16 **Do** not **be deceived**, my beloved brothers *and sisters*.

2:18d **δεῖξόν** μοι τὴν πίστιν σου χωρὶς τῶν ἔργων,
2:18d **Prove** to me your faith apart from your deeds,

5:7b **ἰδοὺ** ὁ γεωργὸς **ἐκδέχεται** τὸν τίμιον καρπὸν τῆς γῆς
5:7b **Consider** *how* the farmer **waits** for the precious fruit of the earth

Once again, these asyndeton clauses are independent clauses because they contain a subject and predicate, present a complete thought, and can stand alone. The asyndeton clauses above have neither an introductory conjunction nor an opening prepositional phrase. They may be categorized as either an inquiry (2:19a; 3:13a), a statement of fact (1:8; 2:13b; 5:17a), or an imperatival expectation or consideration (1:16; 2:18d; 5:7b). All asyndeton clauses, though difficult to visualize above, are placed farthest to the left of the page because they are independent clauses.

In summary, independent clauses are rather important in determining James's main thought of a given sentence. According to our study, James has at least 203 independent clauses. There are ninety-seven independent conjunctive clauses, no prepositional clauses, and 106 independent asyndeton clauses. The chart below identifies where the independent Greek clauses appear in James.

Independent Clauses in James		
Chapter	**Conjunctive Independent Clauses**	**Asyndeton Independent Clauses**
One	4a, 5c, 6a, 6c, 7, 9, 10a, 11a, 11b, 11c, 11d, 11e, 13c, 13d, 14a, 15a, 15c, 19b, 20, 21a, 22a, 24a, 24b, 24c	1a, 1d, 2, 5b, 8, 12a, 13a, 16, 17a, 18b, 19a, 23b, 25d, 26c, 27a
Two	4b, 6a, 6c, 10a, 11a, 12b, 13a, 17a, 18a, 18c, 19c, 20, 23a, 25a	1a, 4a, 5a, 5b, 6b, 7a, 8c, 9b, 11d, 12a, 13b, 14a, 14d, 16c, 18d, 19a, 19b, 19c, 21a, 22a, 24, 26b
Three	2a, 3c, 5a, 5b, 6a, 7a, 7b, 8a, 9b, 12b, 14c, 15c, 17a, 18a	1a, 2c, 3a, 4a, 4d, 5c, 5d, 6b, 8b, 9a, 10a, 10b, 11, 12a, [12b], 13a, 13b, 14b, 15a, [16b], 17b
Four	1b, 2b, 2c, 2d, 2e, 2f, 2g, 3b, 4b, 6a, 6b, 7a, 7b, 7c, 8b, 8d, 9b, 9c, 9e, 10b, 11c, 12d, 13a, 16a	1a, 1c, 2a, 2h, 3a, 4a, 5a, 5b, 8a, 8c, 9a, 9d, 10a, 11a, 11b, 11e, 12a, 14b, 14c, 15a, 16b, 17c

Independent Clauses in James		
Chapter	Conjunctive Independent Clauses	Asyndeton Independent Clauses
Five	1a, 2b, 3b, 3c, 4d, 5b, 6b, 7a, 11c, 12a, 12b, 14c, 15a, 15b, 16a, 16b, 17b, 17d, 18a, 18b, 18c	2a, 3a, 3d, 4a, 5a, 5c, 6a, 6c, 7b, 8a, 8b, 9a, 9c, 10a, 11a, 11b, 13a, 13b, 13c, 13d, 14a, 14b, 15d, 16d, 17a, 20a

Just as there are different types of independent clauses, there are also distinctive types of dependent clauses in James that are worthy of some introduction because they tend to expand James's initial thoughts expressed in his independent clauses.

DEPENDENT CLAUSES IN JAMES

There are **four types of dependent Greek clauses**: (1) Pronominal clauses are introduced by relative pronouns (ὅς, ἥ, ὅ), relative adjective (οἶος, *such as*; ὅσος, *as much/many as*), relative adverbs (ὅπου, *where*; ὅτε, *when*), or indefinite pronouns (τις, τι, οἵτινες, ὁποῖος, ὅστις). (2) Conjunctive clauses are introduced by subordinate Greek conjunctions (ἵνα, ὅτι, ὡς, εἰ, ἐάν, etc.). (3) Participial clauses are introduced by participles. And (4) infinitival clauses are introduced by infinitives with prepositions (e.g., ἀντί, διά, μέτα, εἰς + infinitive) and infinitives that complete "helping" verbs (e.g., δέχομαι, βούλομαι, ὀφείλω, μέλλω, θέλω, etc.). Regardless of their type, dependent clauses generally modify a word or concept in another clause.

Procedurally, *the type of dependent clause* is first identified, and then the relationship of the dependent clause to words in other clauses (i.e., the *syntactical function*) is determined. The syntactical function of a clause may be *adverbial, adjectival,* or *substantival.* Once the syntactical relationship of a dependent clause is determined, it is positioned in the structural outline for easy identification. If *adverbial*, the first word of the dependent clause is positioned under the verb it modifies; if *adjectival*, the first word of the dependent clause is positioned under the noun or pronoun it modifies; if *substantival*, the clause is often placed in parenthesis.

> **Steps for Identifying Dependent Clauses**
>
> 1. Take note of the type of dependent clause it is.
> 2. Be aware of the clause's syntactical function.
> 3. Identify the verb, noun, or pronoun the clause modifies.

The first type of dependent Greek clause is the ***dependent Greek pronominal clause***. There are *at least* thirteen examples of the dependent pronominal clause in James. Pronominal clauses in James are either relative (ὅς, ἥ, ὅ) or indefinite relative (τις, τι, οἵτινες, ὁποῖος, ὅστις) pronominal clauses. Since they are unable to stand alone, they are dependent clauses. Yet, they syntactically function as either a subject or direct object of a clause (substantival) or as a modifier of a noun or pronoun within another clause (adjectival). Naturally, all pronominal clauses begin with a Greek pronoun. The following Greek pronominal clauses are representative of what to expect in James.

On the one hand, there are several forms of the indefinite pronouns in James that function subjectively or adjectivally (W, 347). Two examples appear below whereby the indefinite relative pronoun functions *substantivally*. Yet, one dependent clause is substantival, and the other is adverbial. In James 2:10a, an indefinite relative pronoun ὅστις introduces a subjunctive relative clause: "For **whoever** observes the whole law" (ὅστις γὰρ ὅλον τὸν νόμον τηρήσῃ). It functions grammatically as the subject of the independent clause. Consequently, the indefinite relative clause is placed in parentheses so that you can visualize the substantival relationship of the dependent clause within the independent clause. Again, the indefinite relative pronoun is underlined and its respective verb is underlined and in **bold** print.

2:10a (ὅστις γὰρ ὅλον τὸν νόμον **τηρήσῃ**) . . . **γέγονεν** πάντων ἔνοχος.
2:10a (For whoever **observes** the whole law) . . . **is** accountable for all of it.

In James 4:14a, the indefinite relative pronoun "whoever" (οἵτινες) may be considered the subject of ἐπίστασθε (Adam, 86). Unfortunately, the sentence is long and complex. As a result, some translations do not translate οἵτινες (NET NLT) or they insert "yet" rather than translate οἵτινες (NASB ESV). We, however, address the complexity of the verse by translating "whoever" (οἵτινες) as the subject of the elliptical εἰμί verb, namely, [*you are*]" ([ἐστιν]). So, while οἵτινες is substantival, the dependent relative clause itself functions adverbially modifying "*you* do not know" (οὐκ **ἐπίστασθε**) because the subject "you" is assumed in the verb which "Whoever [*you are*]" is modifying. The very first word of the indefinite relative clause is positioned above ἐπίστασθε ("you know").

4:14a οἵτινες [ἐστιν]
4:14a Whoever [*you are*]
↓
4:14b οὐκ **ἐπίστασθε** τὸ τῆς αὔριον
4:14b **you** do not **know** what will happen tomorrow

On the other hand, two examples appear below whereby the relative clauses function *adjectivally*. In James 1:12b, the entire relative clause "who remains steadfast under a trial" (ὃς **ὑπομένει** πειρασμόν) modifies the object of a prepositional phrase, which is a noun, "man" (ἀνήρ). First, the relative pronoun ὅς agrees in number (singular) and gender (masculine) with "man" (ἀνήρ), the predicate nominative noun in the independent clause. Second, the relative pronoun, "who" (ὅς) appears in the nominative case because it functions as the subject of the relative clause. Third, James's use of "who" (ὅς) triggers a general reference that targets any person. Finally, the very first word of the Greek relative clause is positioned under ἀνήρ ("man"). The relative pronoun is underlined and its respective verb is underlined and in **bold** print.

> ^{1:12a} Μακάριος [ἐστιν] ἀνὴρ
> ^{1:12a} Blessed [_is_] a man
>
> |
>
>   ^{1:12b} <u>ὃς</u> **<u>ὑπομένει</u>** πειρασμόν
>   <u>^{1:12b} who **remains steadfast**</u> under a trial

In James 5:10b, the entire relative clause οἳ ἐλάλησαν ἐν τῷ ὀνόματι κυρίου ("who spoke in the name of the Lord") modifies the noun "prophets" (προφή-τας), which is functioning as the direct object in the independent clause. First, the relative pronoun οἳ agrees in number (plural) and gender (masculine) with "prophets" (προφήτας). Second, the relative pronoun, οἳ ("who") appears in the nominative case because it functions as the subject of the relative clause. Third, James's use of οἳ ("who") triggers a general reference that targets any OT prophet. Fourth, the very first word of the Greek relative clause is positioned below προ-φήτας ("prophets"). Finally, due to space restraints, there is an extended line to visualize the relative clause's dependence on προφήτας ("prophets"). Once again, the relative pronoun is underlined and its respective verb is underlined and in **bold** print.

> ^{5:10a} ὑπόδειγμα **λάβετε**, ἀδελφοί, τῆς κακοπαθείας καὶ τῆς μακροθυμί-ας τοὺς προφήτας
> ^{5:10a} As an example of patient suffering, brothers _and sisters_, **take** the prophets
>
>   ^{5:10b} <u>οἳ</u> **<u>ἐλάλησαν</u>** ἐν τῷ ὀνόματι κυρίου.
>   ^{5:10b} <u>who **spoke**</u> in the name of the Lord.

Again, these relative clauses are dependent clauses because they cannot stand alone. The clauses above are introduced with either a relative or indefinite relative pronoun. They may be categorized as either adjectival (1:12a; 5:10b) or substantival (1:24c; 2:10a). They are either placed under the noun or pronoun they modify or placed in parentheses to visualize their contribution to their respective independent clauses.

The second type of dependent Greek clause is the **_dependent conjunctive clause_**. There are _at least_ seventy-six examples of the dependent conjunctive clause in James. The following are a few representative samples worthy of mention. The

Greek conjunctions are <u>underlined</u> and their respective verbs <u>underlined</u> and in **bold** print for easy recognition.

On the one hand, James displays several simple conjunctive clauses that function adverbially with rather significant interpretive contributions. Three samples are worth examining. In James 2:12c, the comparative conjunction ὡς ("as") introduces a conjunctive dependent clause. The conjunction ὡς modifies the verb ποιεῖτε ("act") in the previous independent clause καὶ οὕτως ποιεῖτε ("and so act"). Since ὡς ("as") introduces a dependent adverbial clause, the entire clause is positioned under the verb so that you can visualize the grammatical function of the dependent conjunctive clause. Again, the conjunction is <u>underlined</u> and its respective verb is <u>underlined</u> and in **bold** print.

> ^{2:12b} <u>καὶ</u> οὕτως **ποιεῖτε**
> ^{2:12b} <u>and</u> so **act**
>
> |
>
> ^{2:12c} <u>ὡς</u> διὰ νόμου ἐλευθερίας **μέλλοντες κρίνεσθαι**.
> ^{2:12c} <u>as</u> those **who are to be judged** under the law of liberty.

In James 3:2b, the conjunction εἴ ("if") introduces a conjunctive dependent clause. The clause is a first-class conditional conjunctive clause that presents something as true for the sake of the argument (W, 690–99). It modifies an elliptical verb [ἐστιν] ("is") in the subequent independent clause οὗτος [ἐστιν] τέλειος ἀνὴρ (this one [is] a perfect man). Since the entire clause is adverbial, the entire clause is positioned above the verb so that you can visualize the grammatical function of the dependent conjunctive clause. Again, the conjunction is <u>underlined</u> and its respective verb is <u>underlined</u> and in **bold** print.

> ^{3:2b} <u>εἴ</u> τις ἐν λόγῳ οὐ **πταίει**,
> ^{3:2b} <u>If</u> anyone **does** not **stumble** in what he says,
>
> |
>
> ^{3:2c} <u>οὗτος</u> [<u>ἐστιν</u>] τέλειος ἀνὴρ
> ^{3:2c} <u>this one</u> [<u>is</u>] a perfect man

In James 5:16c, the conjunction ὅπως ("in order that") introduces a conjunctive dependent clause. The conjunction ὅπως provides a goal for prayer (W, 676). The conjunction ὅπως modifies the verb εὔχεσθε ("pray") in the dependent clause "and pray for one another" (καὶ εὔχεσθε ὑπὲρ ἀλλήλων). Since ὅπως ("in order that") introduces a dependent adverbial clause, the entire clause is positioned below the verb so that you can visualize the grammatical function of the dependent conjunctive clause. Again, the conjunction is <u>underlined</u> and its respective verb is <u>underlined</u> and in **bold** print.

^{5:16b} <u>καὶ</u> **εὔχεσθε** ὑπὲρ ἀλλήλων,
^{5:16b} <u>and</u> **pray** for one another,

|

   ^{5:16c} <u>ὅπως</u> **ἰαθῆτε**.
   ^{5:16c} <u>in order that</u> **you may be healed**.

On the other hand, and more often than not, James's conjunctive clauses are complex. Two multifarious samples are worth examining. In James 1:2, there are two conjunctive clauses. **The first sample** is introduced with the temporal conjunction ὅταν ("when"). The conjunction ὅταν provides the time of the action (W, 677). It modifies an imperative verb ἡγήσασθε ("consider") in the independent clause πᾶσαν χαρὰν ἡγήσασθε, ἀδελφοί μου ("when you encounter all types of trials"). Since ὅταν ("when") introduces a dependent adverbial clause, the entire clause is positioned below the verb so that you can visualize the grammatical function of the dependent conjunctive clause. **The second conjunctive clause** is introduced with the conjunction ὅτι ("that"). However, this conjunctive clause is the direct object for the adverbial participle γινώσκοντες ("because you know") that modifies ἡγήσασθε ("consider"). Semantically, it is an indirect discourse ὅτι that records the content of the verbal γινώσκοντες ("*because* you know") within the dependent adverbial clause (W, 456). Since the entire ὅτι ("that") clause is the direct object of γινώσκοντες, it is placed in parentheses so that you can visualize the syntactical function of the dependent conjunctive clause. Again, the conjunctions are <u>underlined</u> and their respective verbs are <u>underlined</u> and in **bold** print.

   ^{1:2} Πᾶσαν χαρὰν **ἡγήσασθε**, ἀδελφοί μου,
   ^{1:2} **Consider** it pure joy, my brothers *and sisters*,

          |
       ^{1:2b} <u>ὅταν</u> πειρασμοῖς **περιπέσητε** ποικίλοις,
       ^{1:2b} <u>when</u> **you encounter** all types of trials,

          |
       ^{1:3} γινώσκοντες (<u>ὅτι</u> τὸ δοκίμιον ὑμῶν τῆς πίστεως
       κατεργάζεται ὑπομονήν)·
       ^{1:3} *because* you know (<u>that</u> the testing of your faith **produces**
       endurance).

In James 4:17, there are two conjunctive clauses. **The first conjunctive clause** is introduced with the conjunction οὖν ("therefore"; 4:17a). Semantically, it is an inferential conjunction that provides a summary of preceding material (W, 673). The conjunction οὖν modifies ἐστιν ("is") in the independent clause ἁμαρτία αὐτῷ ἐστιν ("it is sin to him"). Since οὖν ("therefore") introduces a dependent adverbial clause, the entire clause is positioned above ἐστιν so that you can visualize the syntactical function of the dependent conjunctive clause. **The second conjunctive clause** is introduced with the conjunction καί ("and"; 4:17b). It is a connective conjunction that adds information to James's summary statement (W, 671). Since the entire καί ("and") clause introduces a dependent adverbial clause, the entire clause is positioned above ἐστιν so that you can visualize its syntactical function. Once again, the conjunctions are <u>underlined</u> and their respective verbs are <u>underlined</u> and in **bold** print.

4:17a **εἰδότι** οὖν καλὸν **ποιεῖν**
4:17a <u>Therefore, **whoever knows to do**</u> the right *thing*

|

4:17b <u>καὶ μὴ **ποιοῦντι**</u> [καλόν],
4:17b <u>and **does** not **do**</u> [*the right thing*],

|

4:17c ἁμαρτία αὐτῷ **ἐστιν**.
4:17c **it is** sin to him.

Typical of dependent clauses, conjunctive dependent clauses are unable to stand alone. They are introduced with a conjunction. While some are substantive and placed in parentheses (1:3), most are adverbial modifying a verb (1:2; 4:17a, b). An adverbial clause is visually adverbial because the first word of the clause appears either immediately above or below the verb it modifies. The conjunction along with its verb are <u>underlined</u> and the verb is also in **bold** print. Dependent conjunctive clauses are extremely important for tracing and explaining James's flow of thought in his letter.

The third type of dependent Greek clauses are the ***dependent participial clauses***. They are declinable verbal adjectives that may function as a noun, adjective, adverb, or verb (W, 613). We refer to them simply as verbals due to their multifaceted usage. There are at least forty-five dependent participial clauses in James. As was the case for the pronominal and conjunctive dependent clauses, participal clauses cannot stand alone. They are dependent. The following examples are representative of dependent participial clauses in James.

Granville Sharp Rule

When the copulative καί *connects two nouns of the same case [viz. nouns (either substantive of adjective, or participles) of personal descriptions, respecting office, dignity, affinity, or connection, and attributes, properties, or qualities, good or ill], if the article* ὁ, *or any of its cases, precedes the first of the said nouns or participles, and is not repeated before the second noun or participle, the latter always relates to the same person that is expressed or described by the first noun or participle: i.e., it denotes a further description of the first-named person . . .* (W, 271). Legitimate examples of the Granville Sharp rule in James can be found in James 1:27; 3:9.

First, there are dependent participial clauses whereby the entire clause *functions as the subject* for an independent clause. There are at least four such clauses in James. We will cite one sample.

In James 4:11b, the dependent substantival participial clause functions as the subject of καταλαλεῖ ("slanders"). The dependent substantival participial clause is placed in parentheses so that you can visualize its function within the independent clause. There is also a construction that *resembles* a Granville Sharp construction (W, 270–72). The Granville Sharp speaks specifically of καί ("and") joining two participles of the same case where the article precedes the first participle but not the second and yet, the article governs both participles. Here in James 4:11b, the particle ἤ ("or") joins two participles of the same case. The article ὁ ("the one") governs two nominative participles καταλαλῶν ("who slanders") and κρίνων ("who condemns") and thereby "the one" is rendered for both participles. But we repeat, however, this *is not* a Granville Sharp construction but one that *resembles* it. Unlike previous clauses, the participles with their article are <u>underlined</u>.

> ⁴:¹¹ᵇ (<u>ὁ **καταλαλῶν**</u> ἀδελφοῦ ἢ <u>**κρίνων**</u> τὸν ἀδελφὸν αὐτοῦ) **καταλαλεῖ** νόμου
> ⁴:¹¹ᵇ (<u>The one who slanders</u> a brother *or sister* or <u>the one who condemns</u> his brother *or sister*), **slanders** the law.

Second, there are dependent participial clauses whereby the entire clause functions as an adjective modifying a noun or pronoun in an independent clause. There are at least twelve woccurrences in James. We will cite one sample. In James 4:12e, the dependent participial clause functions as an adjective modifying τίς ("who") in the independent clause. The adjectival participle agrees in case and number. The article for the participle is placed directly under the indefinite relative pronoun it modifies. Once again, the participle with its article is <u>underlined</u> and in **bold** print.

> ⁴:¹²ᵈ σὺ δὲ τίς **εἶ**
> ⁴:¹²ᵈ But who **are** you
> |
> ⁴:¹²ᵉ <u>ὁ κρίνων</u> τὸν πλησίον;
> ⁴:¹²ᵉ <u>who condemns</u> *your* neighbor?

Third, there are dependent participial clauses where the entire clause *functions as an adverb* modifing a verb in an independent clause. The adverbial participle is the most prominent dependent clause in James, with at least twenty-eight instances. We will cite four representative samples whereby the entire adverbial participle is a unit of thought and thereby the first word of the adverbial clause is placed directly under the verb it modifies. Unlike the substantival and adjectival participles, adverbial participles are <u>underlined</u> and in **bold** because they function as the main verb of their respective dependent clause. Furthermore, Wallace points out that "most adverbial participles belong to one of *eight* semantical categories: temporal, manner, means, cause, condition, concession, purpose, or result (W, 623). So, in James 1:22b, 2:21b, and 5:14d, the first word of the adverbial dependent participial clause is placed under the verb it modifies, the participle is both <u>underlined</u> and in **bold** print, and each reflects one of the eight categories above. In James 1:22b, we have interpreted παραλογιζόμενοι as indicating result, which is evident with our added "*resulting in*" in italics. In James 2:21b, we have interpreted ἀνενέγκας as having temporal force, evident with our added "*when*" in italics. In James 5:14d, we have interpreted ἀλείψαντες as indicating means, evident with our added "*by*" in italics.

1:22a **Γίνεσθε** δὲ ποιηταὶ λόγου καὶ μὴ μόνον ἀκροαταὶ
1:22a <u>But</u> **become** doers of the Word and not hearers only
  |
    1:22b **<u>παραλογιζόμενοι</u>** ἑαυτούς.
    1:22b *resulting in* **deceiving** yourselves.

2:21a Ἀβραὰμ ὁ πατὴρ ἡμῶν οὐκ ἐξ ἔργων **<u>ἐδικαιώθη</u>**
2:21a **<u>Was</u>** not Abraham our father **vindicated** by deeds
                                          |
                      2:21b **<u>ἀνενέγκας</u>** Ἰσαὰκ τὸν υἱὸν
                            αὐτοῦ ἐπὶ τὸ θυσιαστήριον;
                      2:21b *when* **he offered up** his son Isaac
                            on the altar?

5:14c <u>καὶ</u> **προσευξάσθωσαν** ἐπ᾽ αὐτὸν
5:14c <u>and</u> **they should pray** over him,
  |
    5:14d **<u>ἀλείψαντες</u>** αὐτὸν ἐλαίῳ ἐν τῷ ὀνόματι τοῦ κυρίου.
    5:14d *by* **anointing** him with oil in the name of the Lord.

Finally, there are dependent participial clauses whereby "an anarthrous participle can be used with a verb of being (such as εἰμί or ὑπάρχω) to form a finite verbal idea" (W, 647). The construction is typically referred to as a *periphrastic participle*. It functions as the main verb of a clause. Two possible examples exist in James. While James 1:17a is debatable, James 5:15c is not. In James 5:15c, James joins the perfect tense participle "has committed" (πεποιηκώς) with the verb "he was" (ᾖ). It is James's *roundabout* way of saying what could be expressed by a single verb, ποιέω, in the third person singular perfect (W, 649).

5:15c <u>κἂν</u> ἁμαρτίας **<u>ᾖ πεποιηκώς</u>**
5:15c <u>And if</u> **he has committed** sins

The fourth type of dependent Greek clause is the ***dependent infinitival clause***. Infinitives are indeclinable verbal nouns. Although they have tense and voice but no person or mood, they may still function *substantivally* like a noun (e.g., subject, object, apposition) as well as *adverbially* when following a "helping" verb (W, 588–89). There are *at least* twenty-one dependent infinitives. The following are a few representative samples of dependent infinitival clauses worthy of mention. The infinitives below are underlined, in **bold** type, and their respective clauses placed in parentheses for easy identification.

On the one hand, there are five (5) ***substantival infinitives***. They function as either as *indirect object, epexegetical,* or *appositional* (W, 600–607). First, in James 2:14b, the infinitive ἔχειν ("to have") is an indirect discourse after a verb of communications λέγῃ ("claims") (W, 603–4).

²:¹⁴ᵃ Τί [_ἐστιν_] τὸ ὄφελος, ἀδελφοί μου,
²:¹⁴ᵃ What [_is_] the benefit, my brothers *and sisters*,

 |

 ²:¹⁴ᵇ ἐὰν πίστιν **λέγῃ** τις **ἔχειν**
 ²:¹⁴ᵇ if someone **claims to have** faith

 |

 ²:¹⁴ᶜ ἔργα δὲ μὴ **ἔχῃ**;
 ²:¹⁴ᶜ but he **does** not **have** accompanying deeds?

Second, there are two **epexegetical infinitives** that are introduced with εἰς τό (W, 607). Although rare, εἰς τὸ ἀκοῦσαι and εἰς τὸ λαλῆσαι have an epexegetical function that clarify an adjective (W, 611; con. Turner, 4:118). In James 1:19b, "quick" (ταχύς) and "slow" (βραδύς) function as predicate adjectives to the imperative "must be" (ἔστω). The infinitives with respective prepositions "to hear" (εἰς τὸ ἀκοῦσαι) and "to speak" (εἰς τὸ λαλῆσαι) are *epexegetical* in that they clarify their respective predicate adjectives. Although difficult to outline structurally, we have chosen to place the predicate adjectives under the main verb (ἔστω) to visualize how they *complete* the imperative "must be" (ἔστω) and that each predicate adjective is part of the independent clause. The infinitives with εἰς are underlined and in **bold** type.

 ¹:¹⁹ᵇ **ἔστω** δὲ πᾶς ἄνθρωπος
 ¹:¹⁹ᵇ so every person *must* **be**

  |

  ταχὺς **εἰς τὸ ἀκοῦσαι**,
  quick **to hear,**

  |

  βραδὺς **εἰς τὸ λαλῆσαι**,
  slow **to speak,**

  |

βραδὺς εἰς ὀργήν
slow to anger

Third, there are a few infinitives that function substantivally as an **appositional** infinitival dependent clause. In James 1:27b and 27c, two infinitives "to visit" and "to keep" (ἐπισκέπτεσθαι and τηρεῖν) stand in apposition to a noun, namely, "religion" (θρησκεία). Unlike an epexegetical infinitive that *explains* a noun or adjective, an appositional infinitive *defines* them (W, 606). We set off the appositional infinitives with the insertion of "*namely*" and place both infinitives under the noun the infinitives define, "religion" (θρησκεία). However due to spacing, we use an extended line so that the dependent clause is not mistaken as an independent. Once again, the infinitives are underlined and in **bold** print.

1:27a θρησκεία καθαρὰ καὶ ἀμίαντος παρὰ τῷ θεῷ καὶ πατρὶ αὕτη **ἐστίν**,
1:27a This **is** a pure and undefiled religion before God the Father,

> 1:27b **ἐπισκέπτεσθαι** ὀρφανοὺς καὶ χήρας ἐν τῇ θλίψει αὐτῶν,
> 1:27b *namely,* **to visit** orphans and widows in their affliction,
>
> 1:27c ἄσπιλον ἑαυτὸν **τηρεῖν** ἀπὸ τοῦ κόσμου.
> 1:27c *namely,* **to keep** oneself unstained from the world.

On the other hand, there are twelve *adverbial infinitives*. They may indicate *purpose, result, cause,* or function as a *complementary* infinitives. First, there are three purpose infinitives that indicate goal or intention of a verb that essentially answers the question "why" (W, 590–91, 610). In James 5:17c, the genitive article **τοῦ** followed by an infinitive identifies this infinitival clause as answering why pray or giving an intention for praying. We set off the dependent purpose infinitival clause with the insertion of "*in order that*" and place τοῦ directly under the main verb (προσηύξατο) to visualize its contribution to the independent clause. Once again, the infinitive is underlined and in **bold** print.

5:17b καὶ προσευχῇ **προσηύξατο**
5:17b and **he prayed** fervently

> 5:17c **τοῦ** μὴ **βρέξαι**
> 5:17c *in order that* **it might** not **rain**

Second, there are seven *complementary infinitives*. The *complementary infinitive* appears quite often in both independent (2:14d, 20; 3:8a, 10b, 12a, [12b]) and at times in dependent clauses (1:21c). They always appear in James with "helping" verbs like δέχομαι, βούλομαι, ὀφείλω, μέλλω, θέλω (W, 598–99). There are *at least* seven in James, but we will cite two representative samples. In James 1:21c, σῶσαι ("to save") is a complementary infinitive in that it is used with the "helper" verb τὸν δυνάμενον ("*which* is able"). A similar use of "able to save" occurs in James 2:14d. Since it completes the "helping" verb, both the verb and infinitive are underlined and in **bold** print.

1:21a διὸ . . . **δέξασθε** τὸν ἔμφυτον λόγον
1:21a Therefore . . . *then* **accept** with meekness the implanted Word,

1:21c τὸν **δυνάμενον σῶσαι** τὰς ψυχὰς ὑμῶν.
1:21c *which* **is able to save** your souls.

In James 3:10b, **γίνεσθαι** ("to be") is a complementary infinitive in that it is used with the "helper" verb **χρή** ("ought"). Since it completes the "helping" verb, both the verb and infinitive are underlined and in **bold** print.

3:10b οὐ **χρή**, ἀδελφοί μου, ταῦτα οὕτως **γίνεσθαι**.
3:10b My brothers *and sisters*, these things **ought** not **to be** so.

In summary, there are four types of dependent Greek clauses: pronominal, conjunctive, participial, and infinitival. These dependent clauses are extremely important because they provide additional information about the independent clause that helps trace James's flow of thought. The most frequent type of dependent clause in James is the ***dependent conjunctive clause***, with *at least* sixty-nine examples. Another dependent clause commonly found in James is the ***dependent participial clause***, with *at least* forty-three examples.

The following chart lists the types of dependent clauses in James, their syntactical functions, and their semantical categories identified as we have interpreted them.

Syntactical Function	Four Types of Dependent Clauses	
Substantival Clauses	Pronominal	Relative Pronoun Clause: **2:5c**; **5:10b**
		Relative Pronoun Subjective: **4:4b, 11b**
		Relative Adverb: **3:4e**
		Indefinite Relative Pronoun Clause: **1:24c**; **2:10a**; **3:4c**
	Conjunctive	ὅτι Direct Object: **1:3, 7, 13a**; **2:19a, [19c], 20, 22a, [22b], 24d**; **3:1b**; **4:5a**; **5:20a**
		γάρ Appositional: **4:14d**
		καί Appositional: **2:22b**; **4:14f**
	Participial	Subject: **2:11b**; **4:11b, [11c], 12b**
	Infinitival	Indirect object: **1:26**; **2:14b**
		Epexegetical: **1:19b**
		Appositional: **1:27b, c**

Syntactical Function		Four Types of Dependent Clauses
Adjectival Clauses	Pronominal	Relative Pronoun Clause: **1:**12b, 12e; **4:**5; Indefinite Relative Pronoun Clause: **2:**10a
	Conjunctive[7]	ὅτι: **5:**11d οὖν: **4:**17a καί: **3:**6d, 6e; **4:**12c, 13b, 13c, 13d, 14f, 17a
	Participial	Attributive: **1:**21c, 23c; **3:**6c, 9c, 15b; **4:**1d, 12b, [12c], 12e; **5:**1c, 4b, 4c
	Infinitival	none
Adverbial Clauses	Pronominal Conjunctive	Indefinite Relative Pronoun Clause: **4:**14a δέ: **1:**13d, **2:**2b, 3a, 9, 10a, 11b, 14c, 16a, 16d; **3:**14b καί: **2:**3b, 3c, 15b, 25c; **3:**4c; **4:**6d; **5:**15c, 20b ἀλλά: **1:**25d ὡς: **2:**12c γάρ: **1:**13c; **2:**2a, 26a; **3:**16a ὅταν: **1:**2b; **3:**4b διότι: **3:**4c ἕως: **5:**7d ὅτι + Indicative Mood Clauses: **1:**10b, 12c, 23a; **5:**8c ἵνα + Subjunctive Mood Clauses: **1:**4b; **4:**3d; **5:**9b, 12c εἴ (1st class condition): **1:**5a, 26a; **2:**9a, 11b; **3:**2b, 12, 14a; **4:**12d, 11d ἐάν (3rd class condition): **2:**14b, 15a, 17b; **4:**15b; **5:**19a, [19b]
	Participial	Temporal: **1:**12d, 13b, 14b, 15b, 15d, 18a, 26b; **2:**1b, 21a, 21b, 25b, 25c; **5:**16e Means: **1:**6b, 17b, 25b, [25d]; **3:**18b, **5:**7c, 14b Result: **1:**4, 22a; **2:**9c Causal: **1:**3; **3:**1b; **4:**3c Concessive: **3:**4b, [4c] Paraphrastic: **5:**15a
	Infinitival	Complementary: **1:**21c; **2:**14d, 20; **3:**8a, 10b, 12a, 12b Purpose: **1:**27b, 18b; **5:**17c Result: **3:**3b Causal: **4:**2b
Independent	Infinitive	Absolute: **1:**1d

---

7. Technically, examples of a conjunctive clause that functions adjectivally do not exist (at least, to our knowledge). However, the epexegetical and appositional semantic occurrences of ὅτι and ἵνα appear to be the closest facsimile to an adjectival clause and thereby identified in this chart to be *like* an adjective.

James's Style and Vocabulary

Every author of the Greek NT has a writing style that exhibits features readily repeated or perhaps even unique to their letters. Speaking simplistically, the author of Hebrews likes "on the one hand" (μέν) . . . "on the other hand" (δέ) constructions and the use of the Greek period, Peter idiomatically employs Greek imperatival participles, John favors the use of dependent substantival participles in his letters, Jude favors the use of adjectival Greek participles, and the adverbial Greek participle abounds in Paul. Peter, Jude, Paul, and the author of Hebrews, are at times difficult to read due to their complex writing styles. They often appeal to the OT by either direct quotation or allusion. John and James, on the other hand, seldom quote the OT. Yet, James frequently alludes to the sayings of Jesus in Matthew. Although other stylistic issues could be listed for each of these authors, James exhibits several stylistic features worth highlighting. One of the classic commentators on James offered the following general opinion about the author's style: "If we are asked to characterize in a few words the more general qualities of St. James' style, as they impress themselves on the attentive reader, perhaps these would be best summed up in the terms, energy, vivacity, and, as conducive to both, vividness of representation" (Mayor, cclvii). No one familiar with the Greek text of James would disagree with Mayor's remark about the way our author employs the Greek language in this letter.

James's Style

First, James employs a more literary Greek than some of the other NT authors. Occasionally this leads to the question of how a Galilean could be expected to use a more literary Greek. The arguments of Sevenster, Hengel, and more recent scholars have established the point that there is nothing in James that a first-century Galilean who had any contact with the world around him would not be expected to know.[8]

Nazareth, although a small town, was only a couple of miles north of the ancient *Via Maris*, the most important international highway in the Middle East, and one of the most important thoroughfares in the entire ancient world! Recent excavations at Sepphoris, just two miles distant from Nazareth in the other direction, reveal that this town was a thoroughly Hellenistic center where Gentile Roman/Greeks with their theater and mosaics of pagan scenes coexisted with a

---

8. J. N. Sevenster, *Do You Know Greek? How Much Greek Could the First Jewish Christians Have Known?* NovTSup 19 (Leiden: Brill, 1968); M. Hengel, *Judaism and Hellenism: Studies in Their Encounter in Palestine during the Early Hellenistic Period*, trans. J. Bowden (Philadelphia: Fortress Press, 1974); and S. E. Porter, "Jesus and the Use of Greek in Galilee," in *Studying the Historical Jesus: Evaluations of the State of Current Research*, eds. B. D. Chilton and C. A. Evans, New Testament Tools and Studies 19 (Leiden: Brill, 1994), 123–54.

flourishing Jewish culture. Nazareth existed in the hub of a very thorough Hellenistic milieu. While difficult to conclude anything about literary knowledge and abilities, literacy rates were quite low. Based upon literary studies of the Greco-Roman world, it seems that James may have spoken his letter to a trained Jewish scribe (or an amanuensis) who in turn transcribed the letter on behalf of James (Bateman[2], 49–51).

Second, while certainly not with the literary flourish of some Attic writers, James's writing style displays some interesting rhetorical features. As evident above, James is known for simple sentences with few subordinate clauses that are combined with a large use of **asyndeton** (lack of conjunctions). This pales in comparison with the large number of complex sentences utilized by the author of the letter to the Hebrews (Bateman et al.[1], 71 n. 1). Such a comparison is quite justified since both works share a common hortatory thrust. The clipped style of James would strike horror in an Attic rhetorician, but it is that very forceful, direct style that has endeared James to so many readers.

Yet, James's simple and straightforward style is anything but pedantic and boring. James can employ such tropes as **alliteration** (the use of π- in 1:2, 11, 17, 22) and **wordplay** (the use of ἔργων over against ἀργή [ἀ + ἔργων] in 2:20). Although obviously it is a written document, this colorful and rhetorically vibrant message seems more like an impassioned homily than the polished deliverance of an Attic Greek rhetorician. The epistle also features a number of examples of **alliterations** (on the sound *p*: 1:2, 3, 11, 17, 22; 3:2; on *m*: 3:5; on *d*: 1:1, 6, 21; 2:16; 3:8; on *d* and *p*: 1:21; on *l*: 1:4; 3:4; on *k*: 1:26f; 2:3; 4:8) (Turner, 117); as well as **parataxis**, where the conjunction καί is very frequent in the linking of sentences (1:11, 24; 4:7–11; 5:2–3, 4, 14–15, 17–18, etc., about 32 times). Mayor (cclvi) gives these statistics: 140 sentences without finite subordinate verbs; forty-two sentences with a single subordinate clause; seven sentences only with two subordinate clauses; three with more than two. This literary feature is sometimes referred to as characteristically Semitic.

It is important to recognize another literary feature in the book: namely, its heavily **hortatory** character. James's language is strongly marked by a large number of asyndeton clauses with **imperatival** verb forms. James delivers these exhortations by a total of fifty-five imperative verbs (both in the second and third persons) plus four imperatival future forms, nearly sixty commands within a total of 109 verses! These imperatives comprise a higher ratio to total words (3.375 percent) than in any other NT book. James's fondness for the imperative mood, as compared with other NT authors, can be visually demonstrated by the following chart.

Ratio of Imperatives to Total Words in Each NT Book			
Book	Imperatives	Total Words	Percentage Imperatives
Matt.	351	18,346	1.913%
Mark	169	11,304	1.495%
Luke	314	19,482	1.612%
John	139	15,635	0.889%
Acts	136	18,450	0.737%
Rom.	69	7,111	0.970%
1 Cor.	103	6,829	1.508%
2 Cor.	27	4,477	0.603%
Gal.	22	2,230	0.987%
Eph.	40	2,422	1.652%
Phil.	26	1,629	1.596%
Col.	34	1,582	2.149%
1 Thess.	21	1,481	1.418%
2 Thess.	9	823	1.418%
1 Tim.	45	1,591	2.828%
2 Tim.	34	1,238	2.746%
Titus	14	659	2.124%
Philem.	4	335	1.194%
Heb.	36	4,953	0.727%
James	**59**	**1,748**	**3.375%**
1 Peter	42	1,684	2.494%
2 Peter	7	1,099	0.637%
1 John	13	2,141	0.607%
2 John	3	245	1.224%
3 John	2	219	0.913%
Jude	5	461	1.085%
Rev.	96	9,851	0.975%

Unlike other NT letters in which the hortatory sections are largely separate from the indicative sections (e.g., Rom. 1–11/12–16; Eph. 1–3/4–6, and Col. 1–2/3–4), these imperatives appear evenly throughout the five chapters of James. This distribution demonstrates the pervasive hortatory nature of the document. The rhetoric of exhortation found in James, however, does not consist of random or unconnected commands, because these imperatives are usually accompanied by explanations or reasons. James uses participles (1:3, 14, 22; 2:9, 25; 3:1), γάρ clauses (1:6c, 7a, 11a, 13c, 20, 24a; 2:11a, 13a, 26a; 3:2a, 16a; 4:14d), and ὅτι clauses (1:12c, 23a; 3:1b; 4:4a; 5:8c, 11d) in connection with these exhortations. The commands are also often connected to purpose clauses (1:3; 5:8) and sometimes occur in the context of an implied argument signified by the use of οὖν (4:4b, 7a; 5:7a, 16a), διό (1:21a; 4:6), or οὕτως (1:11e; 2:12a, 17a; 2:26b; 3:5a). The discourse is thus heavily hortatory in whatever final form is utilized to convey these exhortations.[9]

> **Historical Nugget:** What is Attic Greek? Attic Greek is the dialect of the language that was spoken in the ancient region of Attica, centering around the city of Athens. This dialect is often called Classical Greek and was the language of the Greek world in the centuries preceding the conquests of Alexander the Great. Attic Greek was the predecessor and basis of Hellenistic or Koine Greek, which is the language of the Septuagint and the NT. Attic Greek is the standard form of the language taught in universities today as "Ancient Greek."

Third, one commentator has characterized the Greek style of James as exhibiting a particular "energy." J. B. Mayor (277), to whom I am indebted for some of the following points, observes that James writes with that "energy" and "forcibly" with the style of one who is absolutely convinced of the truth and of the importance of his message. There is a great economy in his words with little or no circumlocution. Yet, he often displays a poetic imagination (such as his description of the tongue in chapter 3). His tirades against sin (5:1–6) can be compared to the most powerful of the OT prophetic diatribes. These attacks can be softened but not blunted by the gentler influence of that wisdom that is from above (3:13–18). In its rugged abruptness and brevity of its phrases, however, James's language is almost unique among the writings of the NT. Note the biting **irony** in the words he uses to confront those who trust only in an orthodox creed: σὺ πιστεύεις ὅτι εἷς θεός ἐστιν; καλῶς ποιεῖς· καὶ τὰ δαιμόνια πιστεύουσιν καὶ φρίσσουσιν ("Do you believe that God is one? You are doing well. The demons even believe that God is one, and they shudder!" 2:19). The well-known irony utilized by Paul in 2 Corinthians is the only real comparison with the linguistic energy of James. For example, in James 5:1–6 the tarnishing of precious metals witnesses to the defrauding of the day laborer and it eats as a canker at the very heart of these landed oppressors of the poor. While we may still be uncertain of its exact meaning, who can resist the linguistic energy in the abrupt yet, powerful end to the passage: κατεδικάσατε, ἐφονεύσατε τὸν δίκαιον. οὐκ ἀντιτάσσεται ὑμῖν? ("You have condemned; you have murdered the righteous person. Does he not oppose you?" 5:6). Perhaps this almost contradictory combination of simplicity of language along with profundity of style is what has contributed to making this epistle such a favorite among lay Christian readers.

---

9. The above material on imperatives is adapted from Varner, *The Book of James*, 50–51.

James's Vocabulary

What strikes the Greek beginner who translates James is the larger vocabulary of the book. If we recognize the higher register of his Greek, the larger vocabulary makes perfect sense. Probably more than any writer after the writers of the Synoptics, James constantly uses examples and illustrations from nature and the mercantile arts. Such efforts demand a specialized vocabulary, but that does not mean that the vocabulary is somehow higher in its literary style! Different and even rare lexical words need only imply that the subjects discussed are simply different. The rare vocabulary in James can best be illustrated by the large number of words that are unique to the letter. The following chart identifies fifty-three *hapax legomena* in James, plus one proper name, Ἰώβ, in James 5:11.

	James	*Hapax Legomenon*	Lexical Form	Lexical Meaning
		Hapax Legomena in James		
1	1:5	ἁπλῶς	ἁπλῶς	"sincerely" BDAG, s.v., p. 104
2	1:6	ἀνεμιζομένῳ	ἀνεμίζω	"be driven by the wind" BDAG, s.v., p. 77
3	1:6	ῥιπιζομένῳ	ῥιπίζω	"toss about" BDAG, s.v., p. 906
4	1:11	εὐπρέπεια	εὐπρέπεια	"beauty" BDAG, s.v., p. 410
5	1:11	μαρανθήσεται	μαραίνω	"wither away" BDAG, s.v., p. 616
6	1:13	ἀπείραστός	ἀπείραστός	"without temptation" BDAG, s.v., p. 100
7	1:14	ἐξελκόμενος	ἐξέλκω	"drag away" BDAG, s.v., p. 347
8	1:17	παραλλαγὴ	παραλλαγή	"variation" BDAG, s.v., p. 768
9	1:17	τροπῆς	τροπή	"turning, change" BDAG, s.v., p. 1016
10	1:17	ἀποσκίασμα	ἀποσκίασμα	"shadow" BDAG, s.v., p. 120
11	1:21	ῥυπαρίαν	ῥυπαρία	"impurity" BDAG, s.v., p. 908
12	1:21	ἔμφυτον	ἔμφυτος	"implanted" BDAG, s.v., p. 326

	James	*Hapax Legomenon*	Lexical Form	Lexical Meaning
				Hapax Legomena in James
13	1:25	ἐπιλησμονῆς	ἐπιλησμονή	"forgetfulness" BDAG, s.v., p. 375
14	1:25	ποιήσει	ποίησις	"doing" BDAG, s.v., p. 842
15	1:26	θρησκὸς	θρησκός	"religious" BDAG, s.v., p. 459
16	2:2	χρυσοδακτύλιος	χρυσοδα- κτύλιος	"with gold ring on finger" BDAG, s.v., p. 1093
17	2:9	προσωπολη- μπτεῖτε	προσωπολη- μπτέω	"show partiality" BDAG, s.v., p. 887
18	2:13	ἀνέλεος	ἀνέλεος	"merciless" BDAG, s.v., p. 77
19	2:15	ἐφημέρου	ἐφήμερος	"daily" BDAG, s.v., p. 418
20	2:16	ἐπιτήδεια	ἐπιτήδειος	"necessary" BDAG, s.v., p. 383
21	2:19	φρίσσουσιν	φρίσσω	"shudder" BDAG, s.v., p. 1065
22	3:5	αὐχεῖ	αὐχέω	"boast" BDAG, s.v., p. 154
23	3:5	ὕλην	ὕλη	"forest" BDAG, s.v., p. 1027
24	3:6	τροχὸν	τροχός	"wheel, cycle" BDAG, s.v., p. 1017
25	3:7	ἐναλίων	ἐνάλιος	"belonging to the sea" BDAG, s.v., p. 330
26	3:8	θανατηφόρου	θανατηφόρος	"deadly" BDAG, s.v., p. 442
27	3:9	ὁμοίωσιν	ὁμοίωσις	"likeness" BDAG, s.v., p. 708
28	3:10	χρή	χρή	"it is necessary" BDAG, s.v. p. 1089
29	3:11	βρύει	βρύω	"pour forth" BDAG, s.v., p. 184
30	3:12	ἁλυκὸν	ἁλυκός	"salty" BDAG, s.v., p. 48

		Hapax Legomena in James		
	James	*Hapax Legomenon*	**Lexical Form**	**Lexical Meaning**
31	3:13	ἐπιστήμων	ἐπιστήμων	"understanding" BDAG, s.v., p. 381
32	3:15	δαιμονιώδης	δαιμονιώδης	"demonic" BDAG, s.v., p. 210
33	3:17	εὐπειθής	εὐπειθής	"open to reason" BDAG, s.v., p. 410
34	3:17	ἀδιάκριτος	ἀδιάκριτος	"impartial" BDAG, s.v., p. 19
35	4:4	φιλία	φιλία	"love, friendship" BDAG, s.v., p. 1057
36	4:5	κενῶς	κενῶς	"in vain" BDAG, s.v., p. 540
37	4:5	κατῴκισεν	κατοικίζω	"cause to dwell" BDAG, s.v., p. 535
38	4:9	ταλαιπωρήσατε	ταλαιπωρέω	"be miserable" BDAG, s.v., p. 988
39	4:9	γέλως	γέλως	"laughter" BDAG, s.v., p. 191
40	4:9	μετατραπήτω	μετατρέπω	"turn" BDAG, s.v., p. 642
41	4:9	κατήφειαν	κατήφεια	"gloom" BDAG, s.v., p. 533
42	4:12	νομοθέτης	νομοθέτης	"lawgiver" BDAG, s.v., p. 676
43	5:1	ὀλολύζοντες	ὀλολύζω	"cry out" BDAG, s.v., p. 704
44	5:2	σέσηπεν	σήπω	"to decay" BDAG, s.v., p. 922
45	5:2	σητόβρωτα	σητόβρωτος	"moth-eaten" BDAG, s.v., p. 922
46	5:3	κατίωται	κατιόω	"become rusty" BDAG, s.v., p. 534
47	5:4	ἀμησάντων	ἀμάω	"mow fields" BDAG, s.v., p. 52
48	5:4	βοαὶ	βοή	"a cry, a shout" BDAG, s.v., p. 180

	James	*Hapax Legomenon*	Lexical Form	Lexical Meaning
49	5:5	ἐτρυφήσατε	τρυφάω	"live for pleasure" BDAG, s.v. p. 1018
50	5:7	πρόϊμον	πρόϊμος	"early (rain)" BDAG, s.v., p. 870
51	5:7	ὄψιμον	ὄψιμος	"late (rain)" BDAG, s.v., p. 746
52	5:10	κακοπαθείας	κακοπάθεια	"suffering" BDAG, s.v., p. 500
53	5:11	πολύσπλαγχνός	πολύσπλαγ-χνός	"compassionate" BDAG, s.v., p. 850

Hapax Legomena in James

In addition to these true *hapax legomena*, there are another eight words that appear only twice in James: ἀκατάστατος ("unstable," 1:8; "restless," 3:8); ἀποκυ-έω ("to give birth," 1:15, 18); δίψυχος ("double-minded," 1:8; 4:8); ἔοικα ("to be like," 1:6, 23); μετάγω ("to guide," 3:3, 4); πικρός ("bitter," 3:11, 14); φλογίζω ("to set on fire," 3:6); χαλιναγωγέω ("to bridle," 1:26; 3:2). Observation: Half of these occur in chapter 3.

Naturally, all English translations reflect interpretations. Consequently, numerous interpretive decisions are reflected throughout this volume in the Big Greek Idea Series. So, when comparing our explanations with English translations and commentaries, remember to think critically. We take no offense if you differ with us. We do, however, take offense if you just accept at face value our interpretive interactions and renderings. Please engage and wrestle with James and have fun.

James

The Letter from James can be viewed as a type of encyclical authored by the leader of the Jerusalem church and sent to believing Jewish assemblies in the Diaspora (1:1). This letter, however, is also a powerful message to all believers whatever their ethnic background. That is why James addresses his audience so often by the familial term "brothers *and sisters*" (ἀδελφοί; 1:2) or "beloved brothers *and sisters*" (ἀδελφοί μου ἀγαπητοί; 1:16).[1]

James is also a very practical book. Throughout this letter the author calls us to be "perfect" or "whole" or "mature" people. The way we do that is to follow the wisdom that comes from above (1:4–5; 3:17) and reject the wisdom that is from below (3:15–16). If we want to have it both ways, he charges us with being "double-minded" friends of the world and thus enemies of God (1:8; 4:8).

How does James get that overall message across in five chapters? The following summary of the letter is based on its "exhorting" character. The central points in 3:13–18 and 4:1–10 express the main subject, namely to follow divine wisdom, and then convey the strongest exhortations regarding acting according to that wisdom. These sections are the "thematic peak" and the "hortatory peak" of the letter. The following sections are either addressed to the "brothers *and sisters*" or to a group who are condemned (4:13 and 5:1). Each group is then given an imperative command or asked a rhetorical question.

These commands are to be joyful in trials (1:2–15); to not be deceived about God's goodness (1:16–18); to become a good hearer/doer of the Word (1:19–27); to not show favoritism (2:1–13); to show your faith by your works (2:14–26); to be consistent in your speech (3:1–12); to follow the wisdom of God (3:13–18); to become a friend of God (4:1–10); to not speak against one another (4:11–12); to not plan presumptuously (4:13–17); to exhort the rich to treat the poor justly (5:1–6); to wait patiently for the Lord's coming (5:7–11); to not swear but pray (5:12–18); and to convert the erring brother or sisters (5:19–20).

Because Jesus is mentioned by name only twice in James (1:1; 2:1), some critics consider it as lacking in a strong "Christian" theme. One should also notice, however, the references to the coming of the "Lord"—a clear reference to Jesus's second coming. The observant reader can also recognize over two dozen quotations and allusions to teachings by Jesus recorded in the Synoptic Gospels. See, for example, the clear allusion in 5:12 to Jesus's strong teaching about "oaths"

---

1. "Brothers" (ἀδελφοί) is generic and rendered "brothers and sisters."

in Matthew 5:33–37. When readers recognize the prevalence of Jesus's teaching throughout this letter, a valid conclusion is that James is actually one of the most thoroughly Christian books because it is so saturated with the teachings of the "Christ." It could perhaps even qualify to be called the "Fifth Gospel."

Finally, according to James, faith is the guiding force behind all the actions a believer performs, whether it is the avoidance of partiality or the correct use of the tongue. In everything we do, faith without deeds is dead (2:17). All of this behavior gives expression to the perfect "law of liberty," the law of love (1:25; 2:12). Perfection, rightly understood as spiritual wholeness and maturity (1:3–4), emerges as the heartbeat of the letter's spirituality. Every perfect gift comes from God, and the perfect law of love becomes the guiding principle of every action. James echoes and expands his older brother's summary of what God expects from us: "love God and love others" (Matt. 22:37–40).

James 1:1–18

Big Greek Idea: Jewish (and probably God-fearing Gentile) followers of Jesus are expected to rejoice in God's working through hardships, to ask God for insight through prayer, to observe universal truths about poverty and wealth, and to discern God's involvement when enticed to do wrong, recognizing that life's good gifts are from God.

Structural Overview: Admittedly, James 1:1 stands separately as a literary unit (Varner[2], 41–44); nevertheless, we include it as opening James's letter as part of God's working through personal hardships (vv. 1–4) before James moves to seeking God through prayer concerning personal hardships (vv. 5–8). James then redirects his discussion to observing a universal truth about economic situations between the poor and the wealthy (vv. 9–11), and discerning God's involvement when facing personal enticements and the reception of good gifts (vv. 12–18; cf. Baker et al., 1–18).

Outline:

> Rejoice in God's Working through Personal Hardships (1:1–4).
> Ask for God's Insight through Prayer (1:5–8).
> Observe a Universal Truth about Social Economic Situations (1:9–11).
> Discern God's Involvement in Personal Enticements (1:12–18).

Rejoice in God's Working through Personal Hardships (James 1:1–4)[1]

Clausal Outline for James 1:1–4

[1:1a] **Ἰάκωβος** θεοῦ καὶ κυρίου Ἰησοῦ Χριστοῦ δοῦλος
[1:1a] **James**, a slave of God and of the Lord Jesus Christ

[1:1b] *ταῖς δώδεκα φυλαῖς*
[1:1b] **to the twelve tribes**

|
[1:1c] **ταῖς** ἐν τῇ διασπορᾷ
[1:1c] **who** are in the Diaspora

---

1.   Although presented as part of a larger discourse with its own big Greek idea, these four verses may be preached as a separate unit with the following big idea: After greeting his readers, James exhorts them to look for the good when facing personal hardships because they serve to develop a strengthened and refined person. See a suggested sermon entitled "Smiling through Tears" that may be preached in three points: "Smile—You Will Have Tough Times," "Smile—You Can Persevere," and "Smile—You Will Grow Up" (see Baker et al., 19–23).

^{1:1d} **χαίρειν**.
^{1:1d} **Greetings.**

^{1:2a} Πᾶσαν χαρὰν **ἡγήσασθε**, ἀδελφοί μου,
^{1:2a} **Consider it** pure joy, my brothers *and sisters,*

> ^{1:2b} <u>ὅταν</u> πειρασμοῖς **περιπέσητε** ποικίλοις,
> ^{1:2b} <u>whenever</u> **you encounter** all types of trials,

> ^{1:3} **γινώσκοντες** (<u>ὅτι</u> τὸ δοκίμιον ὑμῶν τῆς πίστεως **κατεργάζεται** ὑπομονήν)·
> ^{1:3} *because* **you know** (<u>that</u> the testing of your faith **produces** endurance).

^{1:4a} ἡ <u>δὲ</u> ὑπομονὴ ἔργον τέλειον **ἐχέτω**,
^{1:4a} <u>And</u> endurance **should bring about** its perfect work,

> ^{1:4b} <u>ἵνα</u> **ἦτε** τέλειοι καὶ ὁλόκληροι,
> ^{1:4b} <u>in order that</u> **you may be** perfect and complete,

> > ^{1:4c} ἐν μηδενὶ **λειπόμενοι**.
> > ^{1:4c} *resulting in* **lacking** in nothing.

SYNTAX EXPLAINED FOR JAMES 1:1–4

^{1:1a} Ἰάκωβος: The proper noun Ἰάκωβος is the transliterated and Graecized form of the OT Hebrew name "Jacob" (Gen. 27:36). It was a common name appearing among three leaders in the early church: James the brother of John, James the Apostle, and James the brother of Jesus (BDAG, s.v. "Ἰάκωβος" 4, p. 464). The Latin is also a transliteration from the Greek (*Iakōbos*). The English "James" probably developed from a variant medieval spelling of the Latin *Iakōmos*. **Syntactically,** Ἰάκωβος is a nominative absolute that is the subject of an assumed verb like λέγει or γράφει (W, 49–51; Adam, 1). The James referred to here was the uterine brother of Jesus (1 Cor. 15:7; Gal. 1:19; 2:9, 12). Although initially skeptical of his brother's Messianic role (John 7:3–5), James would later become, along with Peter and John, one of the three original pillars of the earliest church (Acts 15; Gal. 2:9). The combination of simplicity and authority that is found in this superscription suggests that this name can only refer to James, the "brother of the Lord," who alone in the early church could expect such immediate recognition.

Lexical Nugget: What is the meaning of the word δοῦλος? The noun denotes literal ownership by another person (BDAG, s.v. "δοῦλος" 1, p. 260), but in the LXX it often indicates a special relationship between God and a person defined in terms of service. The term was applied to leaders who mediated between God and his people, such as Joshua (Josh. 24:30), David (2 Sam. 7:8, 25, 29), and Moses (Ps. 104:26), and was often used of prophets as messengers of the Lord (Amos 3:7; Joel 3:2; Jonah 1:9; Zech. 1:6). In the NT *it also appears as a title for Christians who minister publicly,* either in the expression "slave of Jesus Christ" (Rom. 1:1; Phil. 1:1; 2 Peter 1:1) or "slave of Christ" (Gal. 1:10).

1:1b ταῖς δώδεκα φυλαῖς: "To the twelve tribes" (ταῖς δώδεκα φυλαῖς) is a phrase. **Syntactically,** "to the twelve tribes" (ταῖς δώδεκα φυλαῖς) is in the dative case because it is the indirect object of an assumed verb like λέγει or γράφει. **Semantically,** "to the twelve tribes" (ταῖς δώδεκα φυλαῖς) is the normal mode for addressees in ancient letters and is thereby a dative of recipient (W, 148–49). James, in his role at the center of the Jerusalem church, is writing a Diaspora encyclical letter to believing Jewish communities, as he did also in Acts 15:23–31 to believing Gentiles.

Semantical Nugget: Is the expression "twelve tribes in the Diaspora" to be taken literally? The location of the "twelve tribes" is *in* the Diaspora—the lands outside the land of Israel. *Diaspora* refers to Jews scattered abroad, which first occurred with the Assyrian dispersion of Jews (722 B.C.) followed by the Babylonian dispersion (586 B.C.; cf. Bateman[2], 49). While some commentators identify "the twelve tribes" as a reference to the church, this approach ignores the literal meaning of διασπορά in John 7:35 and Acts 26:7. Thus the meaning of "*the* twelve tribes" and "*the* Diaspora" describes Jewish (and probably God-fearing Gentile) believers living outside the land of Israel. The latter is the probable meaning of the genitive form in 1 Peter 1:1.

1:1c ταῖς ἐν τῇ διασπορᾷ: The "who are in the Diaspora" (ταῖς ἐν τῇ διασπορᾷ) is a phrase. **Syntactically,** "who are in the Diaspora" (ταῖς ἐν τῇ διασπορᾷ) is an attributive phrase modifying "to the twelve tribes" (ταῖς δώδεκα φυλαῖς but more specifically "tribes" [φυλαῖς]). **Semantically,** the article ταῖς is used as a relative pronoun ("who," NASB; "which," KJV), a usage appearing often in the NT and also occasionally in James (2:7). The Greek word διασπορᾷ refers to "the place in which the dispersed are found" (BDAG, s.v. "διασπορά" 2, p. 236). While some translations render τῇ διασπορᾷ as "to the Dispersion" (NRSV ESV), "to the dispersed" (NASB), or "scattered" (KJV NIV NLT), the better rendering is "to the Diaspora" that "resonances with the letter's Judaic environment" (Adam, 3).

1:1d χαίρειν: This structural marker is a present active infinitive of χαίρω that means "greetings" (NASB ESV NIV NET etc.; BDAG, s.v. "χαίρω" 2b, p. 1075). **Syntactically**, the infinitive stands apart from the syntax of the sender and addressee and is the standard form in the salutation of a letter attested since the classical Greek period. **Semantically**, this use of the present tense infinitive is an "infinitive absolute." A word like λέγει was intentionally suppressed so the infinitive χαίρειν would function here as an infinitive in indirect discourse that often follows a verb like λέγει. This yields the following sense: "James tells (those in the Diaspora) to feel greeted." The imperative singular of the word (χαῖρε) is used for a greeting directed to Jesus (Matt. 26:49; 27:29) and the imperative plural (χαίρετε) is used by the resurrected Jesus directed to his disciples (Matt. 28:9). Although the infinitive form of the word here does not appear in other NT letter salutations, in the only other letter that we have from James, also an encyclical letter, he utilizes this same word for the greeting (Acts 15:23; cf. Adam, 3).

1:2a ἡγήσασθε: This structural marker is a second person plural aorist middle imperative of ἡγέομαι that conveys the idea of an intellectual process and may be rendered "think," "consider," or "regard" (BDAG, s.v. "ἡγέομαι" 2, p. 434). **Syntactically**, it functions as a command in the main verb of this independent asyndeton clause. **Semantically**, it is an aorist tense and is an imperative of command (W, 485–86). Aorist imperatives are accompanied by a limiting circumstance within which the specific command is to be obeyed. While it may be rendered "consider" (NASB NRSV NIV NET) or "count" (KJV ASV ESV), we render the imperative as "consider it pure joy *whenever you encounter trials.*"

> **Lexical Nugget:** What does James mean when he uses the verb ἡγέομαι? The verb appears in the NT in two senses: "regard" and "lead" (BDAG, s.v. "ἡγέομαι" 2, p. 434). The meaning of "regard" or "consider" is consistent with its other occurrences in the Epistles (except Heb. 13:7, 17, 24). In Philippians 2:3, we are to *regard* one another as higher than ourselves (ἀλλήλους ἡγούμενοι ὑπερέχοντας ἑαυτῶν), and in 2:6, Jesus did not *regard* equality with God as something to be grasped: οὐχ ἁρπαγμὸν ἡγήσατο τὸ εἶναι ἴσα θεῷ (cf. Moore, 127). Thus, it denotes some sort of mental judgment, such as "regarding" (1 Thess. 5:13; 2 Thess. 3:15) or "reckoning" (Phil. 2:25; 3:7, 8; Heb. 10:29; 11:26). In every use of ἡγέομαι in the indicative and imperative there is the element of a value judgment. James does not say that trial *is* all joy, but he asks us to *consider* it "pure joy" (lit. "all that joy"; BDF, §275.3) or "with full liberty" (Zerwick, §188), which means to look at the trial as capable of being turned to our highest good.

1:2b ὅταν . . . περιπέσητε: The structural marker περιπέσητε is a second person plural aorist active subjunctive of περιπίπτω that may be rendered "fall into" or "become involved in" uncomfortable circumstances (BDAG, s.v. "περιπί-πτω" 2b, p. 804). **Syntactically**, it is part of a dependent participial clause introduced by ὅταν that modifies "consider" (ἡγήσασθε). **Semantically**, when the subjunctive of περιπίπτω is combined with the adverb ὅταν, it is a temporal clause that does not convey general time (*when*; KJV ASV NASB ESV NET NLT; Zerwick et al., 691) but implies "at all times" (*whenever*; NRSV NIV; cf. Adam, 5). The aorist tense, περιπέσητε, views the action of encountering trials as a whole. Its meaning is illustrated by its use in Luke 10:30: λῃσταῖς περιέ-πεσεν, "he fell among [or 'encountered'] bandits" (cf. Bock, II, 1029).

> **Semantical Nugget:** What kind of "trials" are meant by the word πειρα-σμοῖς? This noun is largely confined to biblical usage (BDAG, s.v. "πει-ρασμός" 1, p. 793), and along with the cognate verb πειράζω, is used for various kinds of testing, but especially of man by God and God by man. A πειρασμός usually refers to a test of humans by God. The noun is here used of *outward* trials, and examples of such are in Paul's description of his own sufferings (1 Cor. 4:9–13; 2 Cor. 11:23–29). The *inner* trial ("temptation") is expressed in 1:13 by the verb πειράζω. In 1:2, the noun brings out the externality of the "trial" rather than the internal temptation arising from "your own desires" (ἰδίας ἐπιθυμία) in 1:14.

1:3 γινώσκοντες: This structural marker is a nominative plural masculine present active participle of γινώσκω that conveys the idea of coming to the knowledge of something and is often rendered "know" (BDAG, s.v. "γινώσκω" 6c, p. 200). **Syntactically**, it introduces a dependent participial clause that modifies "consider" (ἡγήσασθε). **Semantically**, it is a customary present participle of cause (W, 521–22). Although some commentators consider γινώσκοντες as a command and thereby rendered "and know" (McCartney, 85), many others consider γινώσκοντες as providing the reason for the readers' commended attitude—that their ability to perceive trials as joy comes from a conviction that adversity strengthens character: "because you know" (NRSV NIV NET; cf. Irons, 533) or "for you know" (ESV). This appeal to a shared knowledge is a common feature of ethical admonition in the NT (Rom. 6:6; Heb. 10:34; 2 Peter 3:3). The participle also introduces the rhetorical figure known in Latin as a *gradatio*, in which one clause builds on another to a climax by the use of repetition of clauses and by keywords. It ascends through 1:4 when it reaches the top "step."

ὅτι: This structural marker is a conjunction translated here as "that" (BDAG, s.v. "ὅτι" 1c, p. 732). **Syntactically**, it introduces a dependent conjunctive clause. The entire ὅτι clause functions as the direct object of the causal participle "because you know" (γινώσκοντες). The clause is placed in parentheses in the structural outline in order to visualize the clause's contribution to the dependent clause. **Semantically**, it introduces an indirect quotation so the ὅτι is translated "that" (KJV ASV NASB NRSV NIV ESV NET etc.; W, 454–55; Adam, 5) and thereby provides the content of what his readers know, namely, that testing measures the genuineness of faith.

> **Lexical and Grammatical Nugget:** What is meant by the *testing* of our faith? The words τὸ δοκίμιον ("the testing") involve the process of measuring the genuineness of one's faith (BDAG, s.v. "δοκίμιον" 1, p. 256). The noun appears in the NT only here and in the parallel expression in 1 Peter 1:7: ἵνα τὸ δοκίμιον ὑμῶν τῆς πίστεως. The genitive πίστεως receives the action implied in the verbal head noun δοκίμιον and thus is an objective genitive (W, 116–19). This is the first of fourteen occurrences of the term πίστις in James. In 2:22–24, it recalls the example of Abraham, who became the classic exemplar of one who had his faith tested (cf. Foster, 59–103).

κατεργάζεται: This Greek word is a third person singular present middle/passive indicative of κατεργάζομαι that may be rendered as "bring about," "produce," "create" or "to cause a state or condition" (BDAG, s.v. "κατεργάζεται" 2, p. 531). **Syntactically**, it functions as the main verb in this dependent ὅτι clause that serves as a direct object of γινώσκοντες. The entire ὅτι clause provides the content of what was known (γινώσκοντες). **Semantically**, this verb in its same form occurs also in 1:20 as one of the new readings adopted in NA[28]. The word prepares the reader for the use of the cognate noun ἔργον in the next verse.

> **Semantical Nugget:** The translation of ὑπομονήν as "endurance" is to be preferred over "patience" (conveyed more by μακροθυμία). Endurance is a quality subject to testing elsewhere in the NT (Luke 8:15; 21:19; Rom. 2:7; 8:25; 15:4–5; 2 Cor. 1:6; Col. 1:11; Heb. 12:1). It will be seen in the example of Job (5:11), as well as in the statements utilizing the verb form in 1:12 and 5:11. The overall meaning of 1:3 is that testing our faith will determine whether it is genuine or not. What is genuine will then produce endurance.

1:4a δέ: This structural marker is a conjunction meaning "and" (BDAG, s.v. "δέ" 2, p. 213). **Syntactically**, it introduces an independent conjunctive clause used to link segments of thoughts together. It appears in a post-positive position. **Semantically**, it may serve as a contrast: "but" (KJV; BDAG, s.v. "δέ" 4, p. 213) or even left untranslated (NIV), but it seems more reasonable to present δέ as a marker linking narrative segments and rendered as "and" (ASV NASB NRSV NET ESV CNT) or "so" (NLT).

ἐχέτω: This Greek word is a third person singular present active imperative of ἔχω that may be rendered "to have" or "include in itself," "bring about," or "cause"

(BDAG, s.v. "ἔχω" 8, p. 422). **Syntactically**, it is the main verb of this independent asyndeton clause. **Semantically**, the present tense is a customary present that indicates something that should bring about "endurance" (NASB NET NLT), "patience" (KJV), or "steadfastness" (ESV). While we render ἐχέτω as "should bring about," it is often rendered as "let it have" (cf. W, 521–22; Adam, 6).

1:4b ἵνα: This structural marker is a conjunction, which may be rendered as "that" or "in order that" as an objective marker (BDAG, s.v. "ἵνα" 1aα, p. 475). **Syntactically**, it introduces a dependent conjunctive clause that functions adverbially modifying "should bring about" (ἐχέτω): "*in order that* you may be perfect and complete" (ἵνα ἦτε τέλειοι καὶ ὁλόκληροι). **Semantically**, it is considered as purpose: "in order that" or "that" (KJV ASV ESV; cf. W, 472–73; Adam, 6). The entire clause provides the purpose of James's request for endurance, namely, that his readers might attain maturity. Admittedly, however, it is difficult to discern the difference from a result clause, "so that" (NASB NIV NET) and may be considered a purpose–result (cf. W, 473–74).

ἦτε: This Greek word is a second person plural present active subjunctive of εἰμί that seems to be in reference to one's condition and may be rendered "be" (BDAG, s.v. "εἰμί" 3c, p. 284). **Syntactically**, it is the main verb of this dependent conjunctive clause. "May be" (ἦτε) is subjunctive because ἵνα takes its verb in the subjunctive voice. **Semantically**, it is a customary present and is the clearest attempt by James to express an overall general-purpose statement (to be mature and whole) anywhere in the book.

> **Grammatical and Semantical Nugget:** How can believers be "perfect"? The adjective τέλειον (see also 1:17, 25; 3:2), expresses the idea to be "finished, complete, or mature" (see "perfect love" in 1 John 4:18). Here it is the effect of endurance that is "perfect." Note James's statement in 2:22 about Abraham: "from deeds [ἔργον] his faith [πίστις] was perfected [ἐτελειώθη]." In the combination τέλειοι καὶ ὁλόκληροι, the term "perfect" shifts from the action to the person: "*you* are the perfect work." The adjective ὁλόκληρος ("complete") has the nuance of "wholeness" or "soundness" in contrast to disease (Acts 3:16). As τέλειος can also mean "complete," so ὁλόκληρος means "complete with no part missing."

1:4c λειπόμενοι: This structural marker is a nominative plural masculine present middle participle of λείπω that may be rendered "fall short," "be inferior," or "lack" (BDAG, s.v. "λείπω" 1a, p. 590). **Syntactically**, it introduces a dependent participial clause that modifies "may be" (ἦτε). The participle is then followed by a prepositional phrase "in nothing" (ἐν μηδενί). **Semantically**, it expresses the result of allowing trials to perfect us or make us mature (W, 638) and is rendered "lacking" (ASV NASB NIV ESV), "deficient" (NET), "needing" (NLT).

While it may appear redundant, it actually makes explicit what is implicit in ὁλόκληρος—that to be whole means to lack nothing. The "lacking" here has nothing to do with material realities (as the verb is used in 2:15) but rather deals with moral and spiritual realities. This concluding clause helps to define the essence of "perfection"—namely, being mature and whole and complete.

ASK FOR GOD'S INSIGHT THROUGH PRAYER (JAMES 1:5–8)[2]

CLAUSAL OUTLINE FOR JAMES 1:5–8

1:5a Εἰ δέ τις ὑμῶν **λείπεται** σοφίας,
1:5a <u>Now,</u> <u>if</u> any one of you **is lacking** wisdom,

|

1:5b **αἰτείτω** παρὰ τοῦ διδόντος θεοῦ πᾶσιν ἁπλῶς καὶ μὴ ὀνειδίζοντος,
1:5b **he should ask** from God, the one who gives without reservation and does not reproach,

1:5c <u>καὶ</u> **δοθήσεται** αὐτῷ.
1:5c <u>and</u> **it will be given** to him.

1:6a **αἰτείτω** δὲ ἐν πίστει,
1:6a <u>But</u> **he should ask** in faith,

|

1:6b μηδὲν **διακρινόμενος**,
1:6b <u>by</u> **doubting** nothing,

1:6c ὁ γὰρ διακρινόμενος **ἔοικεν** κλύδωνι θαλάσσης ἀνεμιζομένῳ καὶ ῥιπιζομένῳ.
1:6c <u>for</u> the one who doubts **is like** a wave of the sea tossed and turned by the wind.

1:7 μὴ γὰρ **οἰέσθω** ὁ ἄνθρωπος ἐκεῖνος (<u>ὅτι</u> **λήμψεταί** τι παρὰ τοῦ κυρίου).
1:7 <u>For</u> that person **should** not **expect** (<u>that</u> **he will receive** anything from the Lord).

1:8 ἀνὴρ δίψυχος [*ἐστιν*] ἀκατάστατος ἐν πάσαις ταῖς ὁδοῖς αὐτοῦ.
1:8 A double-minded individual [*is*] unstable in everything he pursues.

---

2.   Although presented as part of a larger discourse with its own big Greek idea, these four verses may be preached as a separate unit with the following big idea: James exhorts his readers that if they feel they lack insight, they are to ask God in confidence that they will receive wisdom to face life's situations.

Syntax Explained for James 1:5–8

[1:5a] δέ: This structural marker is a conjunction meaning "now" (BDAG, s.v. "δέ" 2, p. 213). **Syntactically**, it introduces a dependent conjunctive clause and links two segments of thought together. It appears in the post-positive position. **Semantically**, it may serve as a contrast: "but" (ASV NASB NET; BDAG, s.v. "δέ" 4, p. 213) or even left untranslated (KJV NRSV NIV ESV NLT CNT), but it seems reasonable to present δέ as a marker that moves to provide more information about a person who may feel deficient in their understanding and best be rendered "now" (cf. Adam, 7).

εἰ: This Greek word is a conjunction meaning "if" (BDAG, s.v. "εἰ" 1aβ, p. 277). **Syntactically**, it is a significant part of this dependent conjunctive clause introduced with δέ because it identifies the clause as adverbial: "*if* any one of you is lacking wisdom" (εἰ δέ τις ὑμῶν λείπεται σοφίας). The clause is adverbial modifying "he should ask" (αἰτείτω) and appears above the verb αἰτείτω to visualize its dependence on the subsequent clause. **Semantically**, "if" (εἰ) introduces a first–class conditional clause and is the protasis of the conditional sentence (W, 682–89). James is assuming that his readers are lacking wisdom to be true for the sake of his argument (W, 690–94; Adam, 7). The protasis extends through σοφίας and assumes the reality of the various conditions.

λείπεται: This Greek word is a third person singular present middle indicative of λείπω that conveys the idea of leaving something behind and may be rendered "be/do without," "lack," "be in need or want (of)" (BDAG, s.v. "λείπω" 1b, p. 590). **Syntactically**, it functions as the main verb in the protasis of the conditional εἰ sentence. **Semantically**, the present tense is an iterative present (W, 520–21) that reflects an off-and-on sense of lacking wisdom and picks up the λείπεται from the previous verse (1:4c).

> **Semantical Nugget:** What is "wisdom" (σοφίας) in James? James and other biblical authors espouse a practical definition of σοφία as they seek to *describe* rather than *define* the word. James describes wise behavior as "pure, then it is peaceable, gentle, open to reason, full of mercy and good fruits, impartial, sincere" (3:17). Wisdom is a characteristic of heart and mind needed for the right conduct of life. As in OT wisdom literature, wisdom is the principal thing and has the same prominence for James as faith for Paul, love for John, and hope for Peter. The greatest example of a request for wisdom is Solomon (1 Kings 3:9–12). See also Proverbs 2:3 and James 3:17: ἡ ἄνωθεν σοφία ("the wisdom that comes from above").

[1:5b] αἰτείτω: This structural marker is a third person present active imperative of αἰτέω that conveys the idea of claiming an answer and is often rendered "ask"

(BDAG, s.v. "αἰτέω," 30). **Syntactically**, αἰτείτω functions as the predicate in the independent asyndeton clause. It is the apodosis of the preceding conditional protasis in the first-class εἰ conditional sentence. "The imp. may be (James 1:5) the apodosis of an expressed condition and the implied protasis of another conclusion"—namely, the imperative αἰτείτω in 1:6 (Robertson[1], 1023). **Semantically**, it is an imperative command (W, 485–86). The translation "should ask" (NIV NET) is better than the traditional "let him ask" (KJV ASV NASB ESV; W, 485–86; Adam, 3) because it avoids the idea of permission associated with the English word "let." Others translate the verb as a strict imperative, "ask" (NRSV NLT), which also eliminates any idea of permission. The present tense of the command is customary present and conveys a pattern of behavior, namely, to ask on a regular basis.

τοῦ διδόντος: This articular (διδόντος) Greek word is a genitive singular masculine present active participle of δίδωμι that conveys the idea to give something out and may be rendered as "give," "bestow," or "grant" (BDAG, "δίδωμι" 2, p. 242). **Syntactically**, the participle is an attributive participle in the genitive case because it modifies θεοῦ which is the object of the preposition παρὰ. The article τοῦ preceding the διδόντος is in the first attributive position modifying θεοῦ. One would expect that an article plus the participle would follow the noun (in the second attributive position) and describe what God does for those who are the recipients of his giving, as is the case with the following participle, ὀνειδίζοντος. This unexpected order is also found in 2 Peter 3:2 and Matthew 25:34. **Semantically**, the present tense may be rendered as iterative where God is described as giving over and over again, but we consider the present tense as a customary present that describes God's habitual giving (W, 521–22; cf. McCartney, 89). James may wish to lend greater prominence to God's manner of giving by the initial placement of the participle. Although it may sound redundant, the sense of this construction may be expressed as follows: "Ask from the giving God, *who gives* to all without reservation."

Lexical Nugget: How should ἁπλῶς best be translated? This adverb occurs only here in the NT and signifies simplicity as opposed to complexity. The adjective ἁπλοῦς, "single-fold" (Matt. 6:22), and the noun ἁπλότης are more common in the NT (2 Cor. 8:2; 9:11, 13; Rom. 12:8). BDAG (s.v. "ἁπλοῦς," p. 793) defines this *hapax legomenon* only as "without reservation" and cites patristic sources such as *Shepherd of Hermas* 27.4: "give without hesitation to those in need." This meaning fits with James's call for singleness and his aversion to doubleness throughout the discourse (cf. Adam, 7). In other words, God's willingness to give "without hesitation" contrasts vividly with the unanswered prayers of the person who prays "with hesitation."

ὀνειδίζοντος: This Greek word is a genitive singular masculine present active participle of ὀνειδίζω, which means "reproach," "revile," or "mock" or "to find fault in a way that demeans another" (BDAG, s.v. "ὀνειδίζω" 1, p. 710). **Syntactically**, it is an attributive particple modifying θεοῦ. It parallels the previous participle διδόντος but with the added negative particle μή. It is a kind of verbal extortion, with the purpose of obtaining something from another. But here God gives without reproach. **Semantically**, the present tense is a customary present (W, 521–22) that speaks about a habitual practice. Its meaning as "rebuke" or "reproach" is in both the LXX (Prov. 25:8–9) and in the NT (Matt. 5:11; Rom. 15:3; 1 Peter 4:14). This is not intended to mean that God never reproaches someone (Mark 16:14: ὠνείδισεν τὴν ἀπιστίαν αὐτῶν), but that where there is repentance, he freely gives and forgives whatever may have been a person's past sins.

1:5c κaί: This structural marker is a conjunction meaning "and" (BDAG, s.v. "καί" 1bα, p. 494). **Syntactically**, it introduces an independent conjunctive clause. **Semantically**, translations render καί as a coordinating conjunction that joins two independent clauses: "and" (KJV NASB NRSV ESV NET NIV CNT).

δοθήσεται: This Greek word is a third person singular future passive indicative of δίδωμι that may be rendered "give" or "grant" as an expression of generosity (BDAG, s.v. "δίδωμι" 1, p. 242). **Syntactically**, it is the main verb of this independent conjunctive clause. The subject is unexpressed as what will be given to the one who asks in faith. **Semantically**, the future tense is a predictive future (W, 568). Following the participle διδόντος in the previous conditional clause, this future form of the same root declares that what has been requested will be given. The same form of the verb with the same sense is found in Matthew 7:7 (αἰτεῖτε καὶ δοθήσεται ὑμῖν), which makes this verse one of James's adapted *logia* of Jesus.

1:6a δέ: This structural marker is a conjunction meaning "but" (BDAG, s.v. "δέ" 4d, p. 213). **Syntactically**, it introduces an independent conjunctive clause and appears in a post-positive position "*but* he should ask in faith" (αἰτείτω δὲ ἐν πίστει). **Semantically**, it is a marker of contrast: "but" (e.g., KJV NASB ESV NIV NET etc.). It is a "mild adversative" that "lets the reader know that another part of the picture is in view" (Davids, 73). Believers who have a need are to ask God, *but* they are to do so in faith.

αἰτείτω: This Greek word is a third person singular present active imperative of αἰτέω that may be rendered "ask" or more specifically, "to ask for, with a claim on receipt of an answer" (BDAG, s.v. "αἰτέω," p. 30). **Syntactically**, the imperative is the main verb of this independent conjunctive clause. James recalls the third person present imperative αἰτείτω in 1:5. **Semantically**, the present tense is an iterative present (W, 520–21) expressing requests made on-and-off on a need basis. While some translations render "when he asks," (NIV NLT), there is no temporal force indicated in the text to warrant the rendering. The translation "should ask" above or "must ask" (NASB NET) is preferred over the traditional "let him ask" (KJV ASV ESV). For another use of αἰτείτω, see 4:3a, where there is also a limitation on the prayer that is sure of an answer.

> **Grammatical Nugget:** What is the relation of αἰτείτω to the previous verse? This third person imperative verb introduces a clause that is the apodosis of the preceding conditional protasis in the first-class conditional sentence. The translation "should ask" rather than the traditional "let him ask" avoids the idea of permission associated with the English word "let." The greatest example of this request is Solomon (1 Kings 3:9–12; see also Prov. 2:3 and James 3:17: ἡ ἄνωθεν σοφία).

1:6b διακρινόμενος: This structural marker is a nominative singular masculine present middle participle of διακρίνω that may be rendered "be at odds with oneself," "doubt," or "waver" (BDAG, s.v. "διακρίνω" 6, p. 231). **Syntactically**, it introduces a dependent participial clause that modifies αἰτείτω. **Semantically**, it is a participle of manner explaining how to ask, namely, with no hesitation (W, 627–28). The particle "nothing" (BDAG, s.v. "μηδέν" 2b, p. 647) is often rendered "without" (NASB NET), "with no" (RSV ESV), or "nothing" (KJV ASV). However to capture the semantical force of the clause, we render the dependent clause as "by doubting nothing." The tense is an iterative present (W, 520–21) whereby James expects believers to make it a repeated practice to ask of God for wisdom whenever the need arises.

> **Semantical Nugget:** What does it mean "to doubt"? The verbal διακρινό-μενος used for "doubting" has not been found in writings earlier than the NT. It is sometimes used of quarrelling (Acts 11:2; Jude 22), and of internal division and is contrasted with faith (Matt. 21:21; Mark 11:23; Rom. 4:20; 14:23; Acts 10:20; James 2:4). This meaning is confined to the NT and later Christian writings. The active voice of the verb also appears in the sense of *distinguishing* (Matt. 16:3; Acts 15:9; 1 Cor. 11:29—not distinguishing the body of Christ from common food—and 14:29—discerning of spirits). The force of the word as "doubting" can be illustrated by the attitudes expressed in James 4:4 ("whoever is a friend of the world is an enemy of God") and by Matthew 6:24 ("no one is able to serve two masters").

1:6c γάρ: This structural marker is a conjunction meaning "for" or "you see" (BDAG, s.v. "γάρ" 1b, p. 189). **Syntactically**, it introduces an independent conjunctive clause that further supports the previous clause: "by doubting nothing" (cf. Adam, 8). **Semantically**, it provides the reason for why a person should ask in faith without wavering or doubting and is rendered as "for" (KJV ASV NASB NRSV ESV CNT; cf. W, 658).

ἔοικεν: This Greek word is a third person perfect active indicative of ἔοικα that may be rendered "be like" or "resemble" (BDAG, s.v. "ἔοικα," 355). **Syntactically**, "is like" (ἔοικεν) is the main verb of this independent conjunctive clause with "the one who doubts" (ὁ . . . διακρινόμενος) as its subject. The substantival participle suggests uncertainty that may be rendered "to be at odds with oneself," "doubt," or "waver" (BDAG, s.v. "διακρίνω" 6, p. 231). **Semantically**, it is a perfect with present force (W, 579–80) and rendered "is like" (KJV ASV NASB NRSV NIV NET ESV). It is found in the NT only here and in 1:23, both times in the same form and semantics. It conveys the timeless state of affairs of the respective analogies. It describes the unstable person who doubts God regularly as similiar to the instability of nature, namely, waves that are set in motion by the wind that "tosses" (ἀνεμιζομένῳ; BDAG, s.v. "ἀνεμίζω," p. 77) and "blows and tosses" waves here and there (ῥιπιζομένῳ; BDAG, s.v. "ῥιπίζω," p. 906).

> **Grammatical and Semantical Nugget:** How does James employ an analogy from nature? The expression "wave of the sea" (κλύδωνι θαλάσσης) in extrabiblical literature can also mean "rough seas" (Philo, *Opif.* 58; Josephus, *Ant.* 9.10.210). The two adjectival participles ἀνεμιζομένῳ and ῥιπιζομένῳ are descriptive participles that modify the dative noun κλύδωνι (cf. W, 518–19). The first dative participle does not appear in Greek literature and may have been coined by James. The second dative participle ῥιπιζομένῳ means literally "turned" and was used by Greek writers of the action of wind on the sea (e.g., Philo, *Gig.* 11), and is a colorful word found only here in the NT. The word "wind" is supplied in every English version consulted. A fondness for analogies from nature is characteristic of James (1:11, 17; 3:3–12; 5:3–4, 7).

1:7 γάρ: This structural marker is a conjunction that means "for" or "you see" (BDAG, s.v. "γάρ" 1b, p. 189). **Syntactically**, it introduces an independent conjunctive clause and appears in a post-positive position: "*For* that person should not expect . . ." (μὴ γὰρ **οἰέσθω** ὁ ἄνθρωπος ἐκεῖνος . . .). Yet, there is close continuity with the preceding independent clause that further underscores James's point (Adam, 9). **Semantically**, it provides the reason for why a person who doubts should not expect God to answer prayers and is rendered as "for" (KJV ASV NASB NRSV ESV CNT; cf. W, 658). A similar use appears in 1:6c.

μὴ . . . οἰέσθω: This negated Greek word is a third person singular present middle imperative of οἴομαι that conveys the idea that something is "true but with a component of tentativeness" and may be rendered "think," "suppose," or "expect" to be true (BDAG, s.v. "οἴομαι," p. 701). **Syntactically,** οἰέσθω is the main verb of this independent conjunctive clause. **Semantically,** the negated (μή) verb (οἰέσθω) is a customary present. It is one of three appearances in the NT (John 21:25 and Phil. 1:17). The present tense imperative is a customary present that conveys the idea that "you should not continually expect" (BDF, § 336.3; cf. W, 724–25). The verb appeared often both in earlier and contemporary Greek literature (Job 11:2; 1 Macc 5:61; P. Oxy. 1666, 2), usually with the idea of wrong judgment or conceit.

ὅτι: This structural marker is a conjunction meaning "that" (BDAG, s.v. "ὅτι" 1c, p. 731). **Syntactically,** it introduces a substantival dependent conjunctive clause: "*that* he will receive anything from the Lord" (ὅτι λήμψεταί τι παρὰ τοῦ κυρίου). The entire ὅτι clause functions as the direct object of the verb: "expect" (οἴομαι). The clause is placed in parentheses in order to visualize its contribution to the independent clause. **Semantically,** ὅτι is an indirect discourse: "that" (cf. KJV NASB ESV NET etc.). The entire ὅτι clause provides the content of the negated verb of mental perception: "should not expect" (μὴ οἴομαι; W, 456). Yet, the specifics are found in the next verb.

λήμψεταί: This Greek word is a third person singular future middle indicative of λαμβάνω that conveys the idea of being a receiver and may be rendered "receive," "get," or "obtain" (BDAG, s.v. "λαμβάνω" 10c, p. 585). **Syntactically,** it is the main verb of this dependent ὅτι clause. **Semantically,** it is a predictive future: "will receive" (NASB ESV NET cf. KJV ASV) or "expect to receive" (NRSV NIV NLT; cf. W, 568). The entire sentence probably alludes to another of Jesus's sayings on prayer: "for everyone who asks, receives" (Matt. 7:8; Luke 11:10).

Theological Nugget: How does James describe prayer in this verse? The prepositional phrase "from the Lord" (παρὰ τοῦ κυρίου) matches "from God" in 1:5b (παρὰ τοῦ . . . θεοῦ). Here and later (4:15a; 5:10b, 11c, 11d), the word κυρίου is used of God, but it is used specifically of Jesus in 1:1a and 2:1a, and probably also in 5:8c, 14d, 15b. This entire primary clause declares that such a wavering "person" (ἄνθρωπος) should never even suppose (μὴ . . . οἰέσθω) that he or she will receive anything from the Lord in prayer. James begins and ends his letter with references to prayer (1:5–7; 5:13–18). NT letters often contained both, even if they are doxological prayers (Rom. 1:8–10; 16:25–27; 1 Cor. 1:3–4; 16:22–24; 1 Thess. 1:2–3; 5:23–25).

1:8 [ἐστιν] This structural marker is a third person singular present active indicative from the verb εἰμί that means "is" (BDAG, s.v. "εἰμί" 2a, p. 283). **Syntactically,** the bracketed [ἐστιν] is an ellipsis that serves as the main verb of an independent asyndeton clause. The subject of the verb is "man" (ἀνήρ), a generic noun for "individual" (cf. Bateman[1], 146–48). There is a switch from the use of ἄνθρωπος in 1:7 to ἀνήρ here in 1:8. James uses ἀνήρ with a characterizing adjective like μακάριος (1:12a), χρυσοδακτύλιος (2:2a), or τέλειος (3:2c), while ἄνθρωπος is employed with a general adjective like ἐκεῖνος and πᾶς (1:7, 19b). The individual in this verse is described as "double-minded" (δίψυχος; adj.). **Semantically**, it serves as an equative verb that reveals a close connection to or identifies the double-minded "individual" (= ἀνήρ; nom.) as "unstable" (ἀκατάστατος; pred. nom.; cf. Adam, 11).

Semantical Nugget: What is a "double-minded" person? English versions usually translate δίψυχος as "double-minded," with Tyndale rendering it as "waveringe mynded." This is the first appearance of this adjective in Greek literature, and it is used in the NT only here and in 4:8d. While δίψυχος may have been invented by James, the practice conveyed by the word was not novel to the reader of Israel's Scriptures. The concept of "doubleness" is found in Psalm 12:2 as well as in 1 Chronicles 12:33 and 1 Kings 18:21. Although introduced by James, the word was quickly taken up by other writers, since it appears more than forty times in *Shepherd of Hermas*, as well as three times in *1 Clement* 11.2; 23:3 and *2 Clement* 11.2, while Didache condemns being double-souled with a cognate verb (οὐ διψυχήσεις).

Text-Critical Nugget: The most recent critical texts (NA[28] and UBS[5]) place a comma after δίψυχος and read the rest of the verse as a further elaboration of the person mentioned in 1:6–7. "He is a double-minded man, unstable in all his ways." The verse/clause does not contain an expressed verb and requires that the readers supply either a copulative verb or both a pronoun and a copulative verb. On the other hand, Westcott-Hort's punctuation of the text with no intervening comma considers ἀνὴρ δίψυχος as the subject of λήμψεται. We recommend that it be read as a primary clause/sentence that is independent in structure from the previous verse. Then by including the understood copula and by removing any partial stop following δίψυχος, the complete sentence would translate: "A double-minded man *is* unstable in all his ways."

Punctuation should be preferred for additional reasons. (1) Verse 8 read this way sounds like a concise aphoristic saying. James will often round off one of his paragraphs by adding such a stand-alone aphorism that illustrates his main point. This suggestion would better explain the sudden switch to the masculine ἀνήρ in 1:8 from the more generic ἄνθρωπος in 1:7. (2) The initial English versions (Tyndale, Geneva, KJV, and Douay) preferred this approach to the verse by recognizing a full stop before 1:8 and inserting no comma after "a double-minded man." (3) Support from antiquity for reading 1:8 as an independent clause is in the fourth-century manuscript B (Vaticanus), which indicates a full stop before 1:8. Thus, 1:8 should stand by itself as the concluding judgment on the man who prays while still doubting the effectuality of his prayer. Expressed as one independent clause, 1:8 should read: "A double-minded man is unstable in everything he pursues" (ἀνὴρ δίψυχος ἀκατάστατος ἐν πάσαις ταῖς ὁδοῖς αὐτοῦ).

OBSERVE A UNIVERSAL TRUTH ABOUT SOCIAL ECONOMIC SITUATIONS (JAMES 1:9–11)[3]

CLAUSAL OUTLINE FOR JAMES 1:9–11

1:9 **Καυχάσθω** δὲ ὁ ἀδελφὸς ὁ ταπεινὸς ἐν τῷ ὕψει αὐτοῦ,
1:9 Now, the lowly brother *and sister* **should rather boast** in his exaltation,

1:10a ὁ δὲ πλούσιος [*καυχάσθω*] ἐν τῇ ταπεινώσει αὐτοῦ,
1:10a but the rich [*should rather boast*] in his humiliation,

1:10b ὅτι ὡς ἄνθος χόρτου **παρελεύσεται**.
1:10b because like a flower of *wild* grass **he will pass away**.

1:11a **ἀνέτειλεν** γὰρ ὁ ἥλιος σὺν τῷ καύσωνι
1:11a For *you see* the sun **rises** *along* with its scorching heat

1:11b καὶ [*ὁ ἥλιος*] **ἐξήρανεν** τὸν χόρτον
1:11b and [*the sun*] **dries out** the wild grass,

1:11c καὶ τὸ ἄνθος αὐτοῦ **ἐξέπεσεν**
1:11c and the flower [*of the wild grass*] **falls** *to the ground*,

1:11d καὶ ἡ εὐπρέπεια τοῦ προσώπου αὐτοῦ **ἀπώλετο**;
1:11d and its beautiful appearance [*of the wild grass's flower*] **perishes**;

1:11e οὕτως καὶ ὁ πλούσιος ἐν ταῖς πορείαις αὐτοῦ **μαρανθήσεται**.
1:11e so also the rich man **will fade away** in the midst of his pursuits.

SYNTAX EXPLAINED FOR JAMES 1:9–11

1:9 δέ: This structural marker is a conjunction that may be rendered "now" (BDAG, s.v. "δέ" 2, p. 213). **Syntactically**, it introduces an independent conjunctive

---

3. Although presented as part of a larger discourse with its own big Greek idea, these three verses may be preached as a separate unit with the following big idea: James underscores a universal truth about the poor who boast in God and the rich who should be more humble due to the perishable nature of their wealth.

clause and appears in a post-positive position. **Semantically**, δέ may be considered as a transitional conjunction "now" (NET NASB) that may be described as a conjunction that indicates further development of James's argument (W, 674; Adam, 11). Despite our semantical rendering, many versions leave δέ untranslated (cf. KJV NRSV NIV ESV NLT CNT).

καυχάσθω: This Greek word is a third person singular present middle imperative of καυχάομαι that conveys the idea of taking pride in something and may be rendered as "boast," "glory," "pride oneself," or "brag" (BDAG, s.v. "καυχάομαι" 1, p. 536). **Syntactically**, it is the main verb of this independent conjunctive clause. **Semantically**, the aorist imperative is a request (W, 487–88). The verb has been rendered by different words and expressions, from the more literal "boast" (ESV NRSV NLT CSB) to "rejoice" (KJV), "glory" (NASB), and "take pride" (NAB NET NIV). BDAG (p. 536) defines the word as "take pride in something" with the context deciding whether the action is viewed as good (here and Phil. 3:3) or bad (Gal. 6:13). James will turn to the subject of *inappropriate* boasting in 3:14b and 4:16a. James's readers are to take pride in their high position.

> **Lexical Nugget:** What kind of humility/lowliness is conveyed by the noun ταπεινός? The traits embodied in the word group ταπεινός/ταπεινοφροσύνη were not particularly admired by ancient Greeks. "The instances are few and exceptional in which ταπεινός signifies anything for them which is not groveling, slavish, and mean-spirited" (Trench, 149). In contrast, the NT references draw upon the self-designation of Jesus in Matthew 11:29: ("I am gentle and humble in heart" (πραΰς εἰμι καὶ ταπεινὸς τῇ καρδίᾳ). Lowliness of heart becomes one of the distinguishing Christian virtues. If we choose "meekness" as the translation, it should be remembered that meekness does not equate with weakness (BDAG, s.v. "ταπεινός," p. 989).

1:10a δέ: This structural marker is a conjunction meaning "but" (BDAG, s.v. "δέ" 4a p. 213). **Syntactically**, it introduces an independent conjunctive clause and implies a development from what precedes in 1:9. The conjunction is in the post-positive position: "*but* the rich [*should rather boast*] in his humiliation" (ὁ δὲ πλούσιος [καυχάσθω] ἐν τῇ ταπεινώσει αὐτοῦ). **Semantically**, it is a marker of contrast: "but" (e.g., KJV NIV NET etc.). James contrasts lowly believers who are to boast in their exaltation in Jesus with the rich who should boast in humiliation (cf. Adam, 11). Yet, there are translations that consider the word as "and" (ASV NASB1995 NRSV ESV NLT; cf. BDAG, s.v. "δέ" 2, p. 213) as though James is merely adding something to his argument. The former, however, seems more in keeping with James's style of introducing contrasts (cf. 1:6a).

[καυχάσθω]: This Greek word is a third person singular present middle imperative of καυχάομαι conveys the idea of taking pride in something and may be rendered as "boast," "glory," "pride oneself," or "brag" (BDAG, s.v. "καυχάομαι" 1, p. 536). **Syntactically,** the bracketed [καυχάσθω] is an ellipsis understood from 1:9. It serves as the main verb of this independent conjunctive clause. **Semantically,** the aorist imperative is a request (W, 487–88). James's readers are to differ from the rich who should be humble.

1:10b ὅτι: This structural marker is a conjunction meaning "because" (BDAG, s.v. "ὅτι" 4a, p. 732). **Syntactically,** it introduces a dependent conjunctive clause: "*because* like a flower of the grass he will pass away" (ὅτι ὡς ἄνθος χόρτου παρελεύσεται). The clause is placed under the elliptical verb "should rather boast" (καυχάσθω) to visualize its contribution to the independent clause. **Semantically,** it is causal: "because" (cf. KJV NASB NET etc.). The entire ὅτι clause provides the reason why the rich should be a bit more humble (W, 460–61).

παρελεύσεται: This Greek word is a third person singular future middle indicative of παρέρχομαι that conveys the idea of coming to an end and so no longer being there and may be rendered may be translated "pass away" or "disappear" (BDAG, s.v. "παρέρχομαι" 3, p. 776). **Syntactically,** it is the main verb for this dependent conjunctive clause. **Semantically,** the future tense is a predictive future, but its subject is difficult to determine. Is it the rich man or his wealth that will disappear? The closest possible antecedent is the rich man, but larger semantic issues can take precedence. These words effectively announce in what the "humbling" of the rich consists, and in which he should "boast." It should be noted that the verbs παρελεύσεται in 1:10b and μαρανθήσεται in 1:11 are not used of eternal punishment in other biblical passages. In light of all these factors, it is best to take "it will pass away" as referring to a person's wealth rather than to the person.

Semantical Nugget: What is conveyed by the colorful language from nature in these verses? The vivid imagery requires a vivid vocabulary to communicate it. There is one *hapax legomenon* in this passage (εὐπρέπεια), and two words that appear only once elsewhere (ἄνθος, 1 Peter 1:24; πορεία, Luke 13:22). Another word (καύσων) occurs only once in Matthew (20:12) and once in Luke (12:55). This analogy from nature suggests fragility and transience. The noun χόρτος is used of field plants such as hay and ἄνθος and is used of a flower or bloom. The terms suggest fragile wildflowers of the field that are exposed to the sun. The elegance of the KJV rendering of the fourth clause in 1:11 should not be ignored because of its quaint beauty: "and the grace of the fashion of it perisheth."

1:11a γάρ: This structural marker is a conjunction meaning "for" or "you see" (BDAG, s.v. "γάρ" 1b, p. 189). **Syntactically,** it introduces an independent conjunctive clause and appears in a post-positive position: "*For you see* the sun rises along with its scorching heat" (ἀνέτειλεν γὰρ ὁ ἥλιος σὺν τῷ καύσωνι). **Semantically,** it provides concluding material that supports verse 10 and is rendered as "for" (KJV ASV NASB NRSV ESV CNT; cf. W, 658). The entire clause parallels Isaiah 40:7 without the affirmation of the eternity of God's Word (Adam, 12). The clause introduces a mini-parable and should be read as a whole as an extended sentence with its four clauses that further describe the sun and its withering effects: the sun rises "*along* with (σύν) its scorching heat" (σύν; cf. BDF, §221), the sun "withers the wild grass," the "flower of the wild grass falls to the ground," and the "beautiful appearance of the wild grass's flower perishes."

ἀνέτειλεν: This Greek word is a third person singular aorist active indicative of ἀνατέλλω that conveys the idea of something moving upward above the horizon and may be rendered "rise," "spring up," or "dawn" (BDAG, s.v. "ἀνατέλλω" 2a, p. 73). **Syntactically,** it is the main verb of the first of four independent conjunctive clauses in this verse, all of which are parallel to one another. The subject of the verb is the sun (ὁ ἥλιος) that rises on the horizon. **Semantically,** the aorist tense is the first of four "gnomic (proverbial) aorist[s]" (Zerwick et al. 692; Irons, 534) in that it describes a universal reality about the upward rise of the sun on the horizon (W, 562).

1:11b καί: This structural marker is a conjunction meaning "and" (BDAG, s.v. "καί" 1bα, p. 494). **Syntactically,** it introduces an independent conjunctive clause. **Semantically,** translations render καί as a coordinating conjunction that joins two independent clauses: "and" (KJV NASB NRSV ESV NET NIV CNT).

ἐξήρανεν: This Greek word is a third person singular aorist active indicative of ξηραίνω that conveys the sapping of flowing water in something, causing dryness, and may be rendered "to dry," "to dry up," or "to cause dryness" (BDAG, s.v. "ξηραίνω" 1a, p. 684). **Syntactically,** the verb is the main verb of the second of four parallel independent conjunctive clauses in verse 11. The assumed subject carried over from the previous clause is "the sun" (ὁ ἥλιος). It is the sun that dries out the "wild grass" (BDAG, s.v. "χόρτος," p. 1087). **Semantically,** the tense is a "gnomic (proverbial) aorist" in that it conveys a universal reality about wild grass (W, 562; Zerwick et al. 692; Irons, 534).

1:11c καί: This structural marker is a conjunction meaning "and" (BDAG, s.v. "καί" 1bα, p. 494). **Syntactically,** it introduces an independent conjunctive clause. **Semantically,** translations render καί as a coordinating conjunction that joins two independent clauses: "and" (KJV NASB CNT).

ἐξέπεσεν: This Greek word is a third person singular aorist active indicative of ἐκπίπτω that means "fall" (BDAG, s.v. "ἐκπίπτω" 1, p. 308a). **Syntactically**, it is the main verb of the third of four parallel clauses in verse 11. This verb describes "the flowers" (BDAG, s.v. "ἄνθος" 1, p. 80) *of wild grass* that fall to the ground. "Its" (αὐτοῦ) is anaphoric in that it refers to the wild grass mentioned in the previous clause. **Semantically**, the aorist tense is a gnomic (proverbial) aorist that conveys a universal reality about wild grass (W, 562; Zerwick et al. 692; Irons, 534).

1:11d καί: This structural marker is a conjunction meaning "and" (BDAG, s.v. "καί" 1bα, p. 494). **Syntactically**, it introduces an independent conjunctive clause. **Semantically**, translations render καί as a coordinating conjunction that joins two independent clauses: "and" (KJV NASB NRSV ESV NET NIV CNT).

ἀπώλετο: This Greek word is a third person singular aorist middle indicative of ἀπόλλυμι that may be rendered "perish" or "fading beauty" (BDAG, s.v. "ἀπόλλυμι" 1bβ, p. 116). **Syntactically**, it is the main verb of the final of four parallel independent conjunctive clauses in verse 11. This verb describes "the beautiful appearance" (BDAG, s.v. "εὐπρέπεια," p. 410; s.v. "πρόσωπον" 4, p. 888) *of the flowers of wild grass* that fall to the ground. "Its" (αὐτοῦ) is anaphoric in that it refers to the flower of the wild grass mentioned in the previous clause. **Semantically**, the aorist tense is a gnomic (proverbial) aorist that conveys a universal reality about wild grass (W, 562; Zerwick et al. 692; Irons, 534).

> **Grammatical Nugget:** What is the significance of the analogy drawn from nature? James utilizes in 1:10 the future tense when the rich man "will pass away" and in 1:11 he describes with the future tense that the rich man "will fade away." Between these two future tense forms, he employs a string of aorist verbs to describe the relationship in nature between the sun's shining and the earth's vegetation. The gnomic aorist verbs do not refer to an event that occurred in past time but rather to events that occur during many occasions and thus are not bound to any past occurrence. Most examples of the gnomic aorist are used to describe processes of nature. The present tense is still the best translation, as long as we do not think that the Greek present tense is equivalent to a gnomic aorist.

1:11e οὕτως καί: These structural markers are conjunctions. The first οὕτως, is a conjunction that may be rendered as "thus," "so," or "in this manner" (BDAG, s.v. "οὕτως" 1b, p. 742). The second Greek word is a conjunction often rendered "also" or "likewise" (BDAG, s.v. "καί" 2a, p. 495). **Syntactically**, they introduce an independent conjunctive clause. While οὕτως is identified as an adverbial comparative conjunction that connects ideas or in this case connecting examples together (W, 675, 761–62), καί is an adjectival conjunction that is rendered "also" (ESV NET). **Semantically**, they draw a consequential conclusion to James's four previous parallel clauses and are rendered "so also" (KJV ASV NASB ESV NET) or as other translations have suggested, "in the same way" (NIV NLT).

μαρανθήσεται: This Greek word is a third person singular future passive indicative of μαραίνω that conveys the idea of disappearing gradually and may be rendered "die out," "fade," "disappear," or "wither" (BDAG, s.v. "μαραίνω," p. 616). **Syntactically**, it is the main verb of this independent conjunctive clause introduced with the consequential adverb οὕτως. **Semantically**, this future passive form is translated as active: "will fade away" (NASB1995 NIV NLT; cf. ESV CNT) or "will wither away" (NRSV NET). The verb parallels the previous future middle verb παρελεύσεται that ends verse 10.

DISCERN GOD'S INVOLVEMENT IN PERSONAL ENTICEMENTS (JAMES 1:12–18)[4]

CLAUSAL OUTLINE FOR JAMES 1:12–18

1:12a Μακάριος [**ἐστιν**] ἀνὴρ
1:12a Blessed [**is**] the person

|
1:12b ὃς **ὑπομένει** πειρασμόν,
1:12b who **remains steadfast** under a trial,

|
1:12d **δόκιμος** γενόμενος
1:12d *after* **he has** stood the test

|
1:12c ὅτι . . . **λήμψεται** τὸν στέφανον τῆς ζωῆς,
1:12c because . . . **he will receive** the crown of life,

|
1:12e ὃν **ἐπηγγείλατο** τοῖς
ἀγαπῶσιν αὐτόν.
1:12e which **he has promised**
to those who love him.

1:13a μηδεὶς . . . **λεγέτω** (ὅτι Ἀπὸ θεοῦ **πειράζομαι**)·
1:13a **Let** no one **say** . . . , ("**I am being tempted** by God"),

---

4. Although presented as part of a larger discourse with its own big Greek idea, these seven verses may be preached as a separate unit with the following big idea: After describing a blessed person, James exhorts people not to think that God entices them to do wrong but rather that all good gifts are God given. See a suggested sermon entitled "Serving through Temptation" that may be preached in two points: "Tempted to Blame God" and "Being Tempted to Excuse Ourselves" (see Baker et al., 23–30).

|
1:13b **πειραζόμενος**
1:13b *when* **he is tempted**

1:13c ὁ γὰρ θεὸς ἀπείραστός **ἐστιν** κακῶν,
1:13c *for you see*, God cannot **be** tempted with evil things,

|
1:13d **πειράζει** δὲ αὐτὸς οὐδένα.
1:13d and he himself **tempts** no one.

1:14a ἕκαστος δὲ **πειράζεται** ὑπὸ τῆς ἰδίας ἐπιθυμίας
1:14a But each person **is tempted** by his own desire

|
1:14b **ἐξελκόμενος** καὶ δελεαζόμενος·
1:14b *when* **he is lured** and **enticed**

1:15a εἶτα ἡ ἐπιθυμία . . . **τίκτει** ἁμαρτίαν,
1:15a Then desire . . . **gives birth** to sin

|
1:15b **συλλαβοῦσα**
1:15b *when desire* **has conceived**

1:15c ἡ δὲ ἁμαρτία . . . **ἀποκύει** θάνατον.
1:15c and sin . . . **gives birth** to death.

|
1:15d **ἀποτελεσθεῖσα**
1:15d *when* *sin* **is fully grown**

1:16 Μὴ **πλανᾶσθε**, ἀδελφοί μου ἀγαπητοί.
1:16 **Do** not **be deceived**, my beloved brothers *and sisters*.

1:17a πᾶσα δόσις ἀγαθὴ καὶ πᾶν δώρημα τέλειον ἄνωθέν **ἐστιν**
1:17a Every good act of giving and every complete gift **is** from above

1:17b **καταβαῖνον** ἀπὸ τοῦ πατρὸς τῶν φώτων,
1:17b *by continually* **coming down** from the Father of the lights

|
1:17c παρ᾽ ᾧ οὐκ **ἔνι** παραλλαγὴ ἢ τροπῆς ἀποσκίασμα
1:17c with whom **there is** no variation or shadow due to change.

1:18a **βουληθεὶς**
1:18a *When God* **decided**,

1:18b **ἀπεκύησεν** ἡμᾶς λόγῳ ἀληθείας
1:18b **he gave birth** to us by the Word of Truth,

1:18c **εἰς τὸ εἶναι** ἡμᾶς ἀπαρχήν τινα τῶν αὐτοῦ κτισμάτων.
1:18c **so that we should** be a first portion of his created beings.

SYNTAX EXPLAINED FOR JAMES 1:12–18

1:12a [ἐστιν]: This structural marker is a third singular present active indicative from the verb εἰμί that means "is" (BDAG, s.v. "εἰμί" 2a, p. 283). **Syntactically**, [ἐστιν] is in brackets because it is an ellipsis that serves as the main verb of the independent asyndeton clause. The subject of the verb is "Blessed" (μακάριος) and "man" (ἀνήρ) is the predicate nominative; ἀνήρ is generic for an individual and rendered as "the one" (Bateman1, 146–48). **Semantically**, it is an equative verb that reveals a close connection to or identifies a man as blessed.

> **Semantical Nugget:** What is meant by the Greek word μακάριος? A *macarism* (Greek for the Latin "beatitude") is pronounced on the one who endures trial. Μακάριος ἀνήρ ("blessed is a man *and woman*") occurs six times in the LXX Psalms (1:1; 31:2; 33:9; 39:5; 83:6; 111:1) and twice in Proverbs (8:34; 28:14). Some translations prefer the translation "happy" but in the OT the term is applied to a person in a right relationship with God (Deut. 33:29; Pss. 1:1; 2:12; 32:1), and so the translation "blessed" is to be preferred. The same singular *macarism* (μακάριος ἀνήρ) occurs also in Romans 4:8, a quotation from Psalm 31:2, but does not appear elsewhere in the NT. James adapts the same form of the blessing employed by Jesus in the Gospels (Matt. 5:3–12; Luke 6:20–26). The plural adjective μακάριος appears twenty-six times in the NT and describes in Revelation 14:13; 19:9; 22:14 the blessedness of believers in death.

> **Text-Critical Nugget:** Should ὁ κύριος or ὁ θεός be added in James 1:12? The earlier and better witnesses (P[23] ℵ A B Ψ 81 206* 323 it[ff] cop[sa]), following a Jewish tendency to suppress the divine name, support the reading ἐπηγγείλατο in 1:12 without a subject being expressed. Later witnesses complete what seemed to be a lacuna by adding either κύριος (C 1829) or ὁ κύριος (K L P most minuscules syr) or ὁ θεός (33[vid] 322 323 463 547 945 1241 1739 2492 vg syr eth) as the subject of the verb. It is difficult to imagine why a later scribe would omit the divine name, and the fact that there is evidence of three different efforts to supply a name supports the absence of the name as the original reading (cf. Metzger[1], 608; Metzger[2], 679).

^{1:12b} ὅς: This structural marker is a masculine singular nominative from the relative pronoun ὅς that means "who" (BDAG, s.v. "ὅς" 1bα, p. 725). **Syntactically**, it introduces a dependent substantival relative clause. The entire relative clause functions adjectivally modifying "the one" (ἀνήρ, lit. "man"). The relative pronoun is masculine singular because it agrees in number and gender with "man" (ἀνήρ). The relative pronoun is in the nominative case and thereby the subject of its verb "remains steadfast under trial" (ὑπομένει πειρασμόν).

ὑπομένει: This Greek word is a third person singular present active indicative of ὑπομένω that conveys the idea of a person who maintains a belief or course of action in the face of opposition and may be rendered as "hold out," "endure," or "remain steadfast" (BDAG, s.v. "ὑπομένω" 2, p. 1039). **Syntactically**, it serves as the main verb of a dependent relative clause introduced by ὅς, which in turn relates to the ἀνήρ earlier in the verse and functions as the subject of the verb. **Semantically**, the present tense is a customary present that infers a habitual event, namely, being "steadfast." This is the first of six occurrences of the πειρα-word group in these four verses that bind together the overall section with 1:2. The verb is best rendered by "endures" or "remains steadfast." This same blessing for enduring trial is mentioned again in 5:11 of Job (and the prophets) who was tested and endured. It is not the one who experiences the trial, but the one who patiently endures the trial who is pronounced "blessed."

^{1:12c} ὅτι: This structural marker is a conjunction that may be rendered as "because" or "for" (BDAG, s.v. "ὅτι" 4a–b, p. 732). **Syntactically,** it introduces a dependent conjunctive clause: *"because . . . he will receive the crown of life"* (ὅτι . . . λήμψεται τὸν στέφανον τῆς ζωῆς). The entire ὅτι clause functions adverbially to the verb: "remains steadfast" (ὑπομένει) and is thereby placed under the verb. **Semantically**, it functions as a marker of causality and may be rendered as "because" (NIV NET) or "for" (KJV ASV NASB ESV CNT). And yet, some translations provide no translation for ὅτι (NRSV NLT).

λήμψεται: This Greek word is a third person singular future middle indicative of λαμβάνω and conveys a person who is a receiver and may be rendered "receive," "get," or "obtain" (BDAG, s.v. "λαμβάνω" 10b, p. 585). **Syntactically**, it functions as the main verb in the dependent conjunctive clause. **Semantically**, the future tense is predictive: "will receive" (NASB NRSV ESV NET NLT CNT) or "shall receive" (Tyndale KJV ASV). The verb points to an eschatological fulfillment of receiving a reward for those who succeed in passing divine testing.

^{1:12d} γενόμενος: This structural marker is a nominative singular masculine aorist middle participle of γίνομαι that may be rendered "become something" or "to experience a change in nature and so indicate entry into a new condition" (BDAG, s.v. "γίνομαι" 5b, p. 198). **Syntactically**, the participle is the main

verb of the dependent participial clause. It is adverbial and modifies the verb "receive" (λήμψεται) and placed above the verb. **Semantically**, the participle has a temporal force that is followed by a predicate adjective δόκιμος (W, 310, 312). Although γενόμενος may be understood as conditional ("*if* he stands the test"; cf. W, 632–33) or causal ("because he stands the test"; cf. Adam, 14), it is better translated as temporal ("*when* he is approved"; cf. KJV ASV ESV NET; "*afterward*," NLT) because it points to the *testing* nuance of the πειρα-word group rather than the *tempting* aspect, which clearly is its meaning in 1:13. Saying that one *has stood the test* or that he *has been approved* is another way of saying that he *endures*. The aorist tense of the participle indicates action prior to the main verb λήμψεται (W, 623–25).

> **Lexical Nugget:** What is conveyed by the noun στέφανον? The word is used in the NT for the wreath of victory in the Greek games (1 Cor. 9:25, 2 Tim. 2:5; BDAG, s.v. "στέφανος," pp. 943–44). In Proverbs 1:9 the instruction of father and mother "shall be a crown (στέφανον) of grace unto your head" (also 4:9). The noun διάδημα was more commonly used in a royal sense, as in Revelation 19:12: "and upon his head were many diadems (διαδήματα)."

1:12e ὅν: This structural marker is a masculine singular accusative from the relative pronoun ὅς that means "which" (BDAG, s.v. "ὅς" 1bα, p. 725). **Syntactically**, it introduces a dependent substantival relative clause. The entire relative clause modifies "the crown" (τὸν στέφανον) and thereby is placed under τὸν στέφανον. The relative pronoun is masculine singular because it agrees in number and gender with "the crown" (τὸν στέφανον). The relative pronoun is in the accusative case and thereby the direct object of its verb: "he has promised" (ἐπηγγείλατο).

ἐπηγγείλατο: This Greek word is a third person singular aorist middle indicative of ἐπαγγέλλομαι that conveys the idea of declaring to do something with the implication to carry out what is stated and may be rendered as "promise" or "offer" (BDAG, s.v. "ἐπαγγέλλομαι" 1b, p. 356). **Syntactically**, it is the main verb of this dependent relative clause introduced by ὅν. The relative pronoun relates back to στέφανον, but is in the accusative because it is the direct object of ἐπηγγείλατο. **Semantically**, the aorist tense is a constative aorist that describes the event as a whole (W, 557–58). Apart from Revelation 2:10, which was written later, we do not find the precise words τὸν στέφανον τῆς ζωῆς in any other specific scriptural passage. This may be an allusion to a *logion* of Jesus that is not preserved in which he made such a promise.

τοῖς ἀγαπῶσιν. This articular verbal τοῖς ἀγαπῶσιν is a dative plural masculine present active participle of ἀγαπάω that may be rendered "cherish," "have affection for," or "love" extended to a broad range of individuals (BDAG, s.v. "ἀγαπάω" 1aα, p. 5). **Syntactically**, it functions as a substantival participle in the dative case serving as the indirect object of ἐπηγγείλατο (Adam, 14). **Semantically**, the present tense is customary, indicating God's constant affection to all those who love "him" (αὐτόν).

1:13a λεγέτω: This structural marker is a third person singular present active imperative of λέγω that means "utter in words," "say," "tell," or "give expression to" orally or in written form (BDAG, s.v. "λέγω" 1, p. 588). **Syntactically**, it is the main verb of this independent asyndeton clause. **Semantically**, the present tense of the imperative with a negative ("no one," μηδείς) conveys a command: "Let no one say" (NASB1995 ESV; cf. KJV ASV) or "no one should say" (NIV NRSV). It conveys an ongoing process but there is no lessening of the imperatival force in the third person (W, 485–86).

ὅτι: This structural marker is a conjunction meaning "that" (BDAG, s.v. "ὅτι" 1c, p. 731). **Syntactically**, it introduces a substantival dependent conjunctive clause: *that* I am being tempted by God" (ὅτι Ἀπὸ θεοῦ πειράζομαι). The entire ὅτι clause functions as the direct object of the verb: "let no one . . . say" (μηδείς . . . λεγέτω). The clause is placed in parentheses in order to visualize its contribution to the independent clause. **Semantically**, it can introduce both a direct and an indirect quotation. Here it introduces a direct quotation so the ὅτι is not translated and functions like an initial quotation mark. This use is sometimes referred to as "ὅτι *recitativum*" (W, 454–55). So, the entire ὅτι clause provides the content of the negated verb of saying: "let no one . . . say" (μηδείς . . . λεγέτω). Yet, the specifics are found in the next verb.

πειράζομαι: This Greek word is a first person singular present passive indicative of πειράζω that means "tempt" or "to entice to improper behavior" (BDAG, s.v. "πειράζω" 4, p. 793). **Syntactically**, it serves as the main verb within this dependent conjunctive clause. **Semantically**, it functions as a "direct quotation." The present tense is customary present that conveys a pattern of behavior. People are to make it a practice not to blame God for their trials. We might expect the preposition ὑπό at this point, but the ἀπό expresses a remoter source, compared with the personal agency conveyed by ὑπό (W, 433).

> **Semantical Nugget:** What is meant by the cognate words πειραζόμενος, πειράζομαι, ἀπείραστός, and πειράζει? While James has employed the noun πειρασμός twice (1:2b, 12b), he now uses the verb πειράζω four times in 1:13a, 13b, 13d, 14a and the adjective once. The verb πειράζω can mean "put to the test," i.e., "to discover the nature or character of something" (BDAG, s.v. "πειράζω" 2, p. 792) or, as it is used here, "to tempt," i.e., "to entice to improper behavior" (BDAG, 4, p. 793). In the

LXX its "religious" uses indicate a trial of virtue by means of affliction or adversity, or even by Satan's intervention (Job 1:9). God tested Abraham by asking him to sacrifice Isaac (Gen. 22:1–2), and he tested his people in the wilderness (Exod. 15:25). These trials are tests by which Yahweh assesses the quality of his servants (see Exod. 16:4). Though a trial is ordered by God for our good, the inner solicitation to evil aroused by the outer trial is from ourselves. The noun πειρασμός denotes the objective *trial*, while the verb πειράζομαι denotes a more subjective *temptation*.

1:13b πειραζόμενος: This structural marker is a nominative singular masculine present passive participle of πειράζω that conveys the idea of enticing someone into unacceptable behavior and is often rendered "tempt" (BDAG, s.v. "πειράζω" 4, p. 793). **Syntactically**, it introduces a dependent participial clause that modifies the negated (μηδεὶς) subject of λεγέτω: "let no one say." **Semantically**, it is a temporal participle: "*when* he is tempted" (KJV ASV NASB NIV ESV NET CNT; cf. NRSV NLT; Zerwick et al., 692; Irons, 534). The tense of the participle is customary and speaks of a person who persists in blaming or habitually accusing God for his or her being tempted to sin.

1:13c γάρ: This structural marker is a conjunction meaning "for" or "you see" (BDAG, s.v. "γάρ" 1b, p. 189). **Syntactically**, it introduces a dependent conjunctive clause and appears in a post-positive position. The entire γάρ clause functions adverbially and modifies "say" (λεγέτω) and thereby is placed under λεγέτω. **Semantically**, it introduces the first of a twofold reason why God is unable to be tempted (Davids, 82).

ἐστιν: This Greek word is a third person singular present active indicative from the verb εἰμί that means "be" or "to take place as a phenomenon or event" (BDAG, s.v. "εἰμί" 5, p. 283). **Syntactically**, ἐστιν serves as the main verb of the dependent conjunctive clause. The subject of the verb is the nominative "God" (θεός) and "tempted" (ἀπείραστός: lit. *without* temptation) as the predicate adjective. **Semantically**, ἐστιν serves as an equative verb that explains identity or in this case what is impossible with God: "God cannot be tempted" (KJV ASV NASB NRSV NIV ESV NET) or some might say "inexperienced in evil" or "alien to evil" (BDF, §182).

1:13d δέ: This structural marker is a conjunction meaning "and" (BDAG, s.v. "δέ" 1, p. 213). **Syntactically**, it introduces a conjunctive independent clause and appears in a post-positive position: "*and* he himself tempts no one" (πειράζει δὲ αὐτὸς οὐδένα). **Semantically**, it is a coordinating conjunction that offers an additonal rationale for rejecting the idea that God tempts people: "*and* he himself tempts no one" (πειράζει δὲ αὐτὸς οὐδένα) (cf. Adam, 16). It links two clauses together: "God cannot be tempted" and "God tempts no one."

πειράζει: This Greek word is a third person singular present active indicative of πειράζω that means "tempt" or "to entice to improper behavior" (BDAG, s.v. "πειράζω" 4, p. 793). **Syntactically**, it is the main verb of this dependent conjunctive clause in 1:13d. The direct object of πειράζει is the accusative οὐδένα. **Semantically**, the present tense is customary that reflects a pattern of behavior, namely, it is God's practice not to tempt people. Yet, James's statement appears to conflict with OT statements where God does test/tempt his followers (see Gen. 22:1).

> **Lexical Nugget:** The semantic field of πειράζει and the entire word group includes both concepts of testing and tempting (BDAG, s.v. "πειράζω" 4, p. 793). James utilizes that shared semantic field by moving from one shade of the meaning (testing for a good purpose) in 1:2–4, 12 to the other shade of meaning (enticement for an evil purpose) in 1:13–15. This semantic shift is possible because the arrangement of the chapter is influenced by word linkage. Thus 1:12 and 1:13–16 are linked by the words πειρασμός and πειράζω rather than by their semantic equivalence. God is immediately behind the idea of a "test," but while he is ultimately behind all things as a providential ruler, he is not the immediate seducer to sin. The one who is that seducer is Satan/the devil and has been described by those terms in the Chronicler's handling of David's sin (cf. 1 Chron. 21:1 with 2 Sam. 21:1). While Satan/the devil is not mentioned by name in this passage, his role as a solicitor to evil should not be discounted. The "devil" is mentioned later in that very role (James 4:7b).

1:14a δέ: This structural marker is a conjunction meaning "but" (BDAG, s.v. "δέ" 4, p. 213). **Syntactically**, it introduces an independent conjunctive clause, implies a development from what precedes in verse 13 about being tempted, and appears in the post-positive position: "*but* each person is tempted by his own desire" (ἕκαστος δὲ πειράζεται ὑπὸ τῆς ἰδίας ἐπιθυμίας). **Semantically**, it is a marker of contrast: "but" (e.g., KJV NASB ESV NIV NET etc.). In contrast to blaming God for temptation, James suggests we need only look at ourselves. It contrasts an incorrect way of thinking with a correct one.

πειράζεται: This Greek word is a third person singular present passive indicative of πειράζω that conveys the idea of enticing to improper behavior and may be rendered "tempt" (BDAG, s.v. "πειράζω" 4, p. 793). **Syntactically**, it serves as the main verb of the independent conjunctive clause of 1:14 and its subject is "each person" (ἕκαστος). **Semantically**, the present tense is customary that reflects a pattern of behavior, namely, it is God's practice not to tempt people (see v. 13d).

> **Lexical Nugget:** What is meant by ἐπιθυμίας? The noun basically means desire, and by itself is neutral, gaining its moral sense from the worth of the object desired. In the LXX, ἐπιθυμία and ἐπιθυμέω are defined by their object. The Decalogue forbids any ἐπιθυμία for a neighbor's wife or property (Exod. 20:17; Deut. 5:21). Yet, the ἐπιθυμία of a righteous person is acceptable (Prov. 10:24). Its use for sexual desire, however, enables the term easily to move into the meaning of "lust" (BDAG, s.v. "ἐπιθυμία" 2, p. 372). If God is not the source of temptation, James then points deep within our inner persons: our own desires.

1:14b ἐξελκόμενος: This structural marker is a nominative singular masculine present passive participle of ἐξέλκω that means "drag away" (BDAG, s.v. "ἐξέλκω," p. 347). **Syntactically**, it introduces a dependent participial clause. The entire clause is adverbial modifying "is tempted" (πειράζεται). The entire participial clause is placed under "is tempted" (πειράζεται). **Semantically**, it is a temporal participle: "*when* he is lured" (ESV NET), "*when* he is drawn away" (KJV ASV), "*when* he is dragged away" (NIV; cf. NRSV), or "*when* he is carried away" (NASB CNT). The present tense conveys action concurrent with the main verb πειράζεται. This colorful verb is another *hapax legomenon* in James.

> **Semantical Nugget:** What meaning is conveyed by the participles ἐξελκόμενος and δελεαζόμενος? The first verbal, from ἐξέλκω, is another *hapax legomenon* in James, while the verb δελεάζω is used elsewhere only in 2 Peter 2:14, also in a metaphorical sense of the snare of false teachers. These are fishing and hunting terms applied to the snares of temptation. The desire, like a creature, is drawn out (ἐξελκόμενος) of its "normal" sphere and then seduced (δελεαζόμενος) by the bait.

δελεαζόμενος: This Greek word is a nominative singular masculine present passive participle of δελεάζω that may be rendered "lure" or "entice" (BDAG, s.v. "δελεάζω," p. 217). **Syntactically**, it is the second participle of this dependent participial clause modifying "is tempted" (πειράζεται). **Semantically**, it is also a temporal participle: "*when* he is enticed." Yet, translations (like ours) tend to merely add "and" with an assumption of temporal force: "*and* enticed" (KJV ASV NASB NRSV ESV NIV NET CNT). The present tense conveys action concurrent with the main verb πειράζεται.

1:15a εἶτα: This structural marker is an adverb that appears sixteen times in the NT but only here in James and that conveys the idea of "being next in order of time" and may be rendered "then" or "next" (BDAG, s.v. "εἶτα" 1, p. 295).

Syntactically, it introduces an independent conjunctive clause and is rendered "then" (KJV ASV NASB NRSV ESV NIV NET CNT).

τίκτει: This Greek word is a third person singular present active indicative of τίκτω that means "bring forth," "produce," or "cause to come into being" (BDAG, s.v. "τίκτω" 2, p. 1004). **Syntactically**, it is the main verb of the first of two independent conjunctive clauses in 1:15. **Semantically**, the present tense is customary present indicating a pattern of behavior (W, 521–22). Of the eighteen examples of the verb in the NT, it is used most often of physical birth (e.g., Matt. 1:21), and once of the "birth" of plants (Heb. 6:7). The verb's only metaphorical usage is in this verse.

1:15b συλλαβοῦσα: This structural marker is a nominative singular feminine aorist active participle of συλλαμβάνω that conveys the idea of becoming pregnant and is often rendered "conceive" (BDAG, s.v. "συλλαμβάνω" 3, p. 955). **Syntactically**, it identifies the clause in a dependent participial clause that modifies "τίκτει" (gives birth) and is placed immediately below τίκτει. **Semantically**, the participle is temporal: *when* it (= desire) is conceived (ASV NASB NRSV ESV NET; cf. NIV). The tense looks at the action as a whole and precedes the action of the main verb τίκτει. This verb appears sixteen times in the NT, but only five times with the meaning of "conceive" (Luke 1:24, 31, 36; 2:21) and only here in a metaphorical sense.

> **Structural Nugget:** The verse has a rhetorical balance with two independent clauses connected by δέ, with each clause having an articular subject followed by a participle plus a verb and direct object.
>
> | ἡ | ἐπιθυμία | συλλαβοῦσα | τίκτει | ἁμαρτίαν, |
> | ἡ δέ | ἁμαρτία | ἀποτελεσθεῖσα | ἀποκύει | θάνατον. |

1:15c δέ: This structural marker is a coordinating conjunction meaning "and" (BDAG, s.v. "δέ" 1, p. 213). **Syntactically**, it introduces an independent asyndeton clause and appears in a post-positive position: "*and* sin . . . gives birth" (ἡ δὲ ἁμαρτία . . . ἀποκύει θάνατον). **Semantically**, it is a conjunction that connects two independent clauses about the birth of sin. It introduces James's progression from "desire" (ἡ ἐπιθυμία) in the first independent clause to "death" (θάνατον) in the second independent clause (cf. Adam, 17).

ἀποκύει: This Greek word is a third person singular present active indicative of ἀποκυέω that means literally "give birth to" (BDAG, s.v. "ἀποκυέω" b, p. 114) but can also be used metaphorically. **Syntactically**, it is the main verb of the second independent conjunctive clause with "desire" (ἐπιθυμία) as the subject. **Semantically**, the present tense is a customary present suggesting something that is a pattern: a desire (ἐπιθυμία) for things forbidden or simply inordinate (BDAG, s.v. "ἐπιθυμία" 2, p. 372). There is more than one birth here, and it is better to view the analogy as describing the birth of both a child (sin) and a grandchild (death). James's purpose is not a technical analysis of sin's process, but an attempt to place the blame on the sinner for yielding to wrong desire. The verb will be used again of God in 1:18. Two different words are used in this verse of the actual "birth" event—τίκτει and ἀποκύει—but what distinguishes them is not the intent. James often creatively employs synonyms for language variety.

1:15d ἀποτελεσθεῖσα: This structural marker is a nominative singular feminine aorist passive participle of ἀποτελέω and may be rendered "bring to completion," "finish," or "bring an activity to an end" (BDAG, s.v. "ἀποτελέω" 1, p. 123). **Syntactically**, it introduces a dependent participial clause that modifies the verb "gives birth" (ἀποκύει) and is placed immediately below ἀποκύει. **Semantically**, it is a temporal participle: *"when sin is fully grown"* (ESV NET NLT CNT) or *"when it is fully grown"* (NRSV NIV; cf. ASV; cf. Irons, 534). The aorist tense is a constative aorist that looks at the action as a whole and precedes the action of the main verb ἀποκύει. There are seven participles in 1:13–15, comprising the most intense concentration of participles in the book. The four vivid temporal participles in verses 14 and 15 colorfully convey the sequential drama of the analogy in 1:14–15 ("lured," "enticed," "conceived," "finished").

> **Lexical Nugget:** Is there an intended difference in meaning between the verbs τίκτει and ἀποκύει? While the verb τίκτω literally means "to give birth" (Matt. 1:21; John 16:21; Rev. 12:4), it had also been used metaphorically in the LXX (Prov. 10:23). The verb ἀποκύει means literally "give birth to" (BDAG, s.v. "τίκτω" 2, p. 1004), but as mentioned it can also be used metaphorically. There is more than one birth here, and it is best to view the analogy as describing the birth of both a child (sin) and a grandchild (death). The second verb is used again of God in 1:18. While these are two different words for the actual "birth" event, efforts to find what distinguishes them are strained. James will creatively use synonyms simply for language variety (see 1:17).

1:16 μὴ πλανᾶσθε: This (negated) structural marker is a second person plural present passive imperative of πλανάω that conveys the idea of people who are mistaken in judgment and deceive themselves and may be rendered as "go astray," "be misled," or "wander about aimlessly" (BDAG, s.v. "πλανάω" 2bγ, p. 822). **Syntactically**, it is the main verb of the independent asyndeton clause accompanied by "my brothers" (μου ἀδελφοί). "Brothers" (ἀδελφοί) is generic and rendered "brothers *and sisters*" (NET NLT; cf. Bateman[2], 146–48). This imperative begins a new section in James (KJV ASV NASB NRSV NIV ESV NET NLT CNT). **Semantically**, the present imperative is an imperative of request (W, 487–88). James is appealing to his readers to avoid being deceived or misled.

> **Lexical Nugget:** What is the specific meaning of the verb πλανᾶσθε? The verb πλανάω means to wander or to go astray (Matt. 18:12–13), and it is used in that sense also in 5:19. In the passive, it can mean "to be led astray" (Deut. 11:28) or "to be deceived/in error" (Deut. 4:19; Luke 21:8). This negated present imperative appears elsewhere in the NT in 1 Corinthians 6:9; 15:33; and Galatians 6:7. In each example the writer is calling attention to a decisive statement about God in the form of a proverbial saying. These admonitions refer not to intellectual error about divine ways, but to an error that strikes at the heart of faith itself. This is the case here, since what follows are statements about God's goodness.

1:17a ἐστιν: This structural marker is a third person singular present active indicative from the verb εἰμί meaning "be" or "comes" where the emphasis is on the point of derivation or origin (BDAG, s.v. "εἰμί" 8, p. 285). **Syntactically**, it is the main verb of the independent clause. The subjects of the verb are two nominal phrases joined by "and" (καί): "every good act of giving and every complete gift" (πᾶσα δόσις ἀγαθὴ καὶ πᾶν δώρημα τέλειον; but *cf.* Irons, 534). **Semantically**, it is a gnomic present: "comes" (KJV ASV). Yet, the more common translation is "is" (cf. KJV NASB ESV NIV NET NLT CNT etc.). In either case, it presents a gnomic truth about gifts coming from God (W, 523). God's gifts that he gives are *always* perfect.

1:17b καταβαῖνον: This structural marker is a nominative singular neuter present active participle of καταβαίνω that indicates a place from which something comes or goes down and may be rendered "come," "go," or "climb down" (BDAG, s.v. "καταβαίνω" 1aα, p. 514). **Syntactically**, the challenge here is to determine if the verb ἐστιν is related directly to the adverb ἄνωθέν that precedes it or to the participle καταβαῖνον that follows it. On the one hand, the latter choice makes the participle periphrastic ("is coming down"), and the first choice makes the participle simply adverbial ("is from above, coming down"). The similar use of the copula-adverb-participle in 3:14 (ἔστιν αὕτη ἡ σοφία ἄνωθεν κατερχομένη) points to the periphrastic use, although the word order there is different (cf. W, 647–48). On the other hand, Moule writes that "it need not be periphrastic at all" (Moule, 17). Moule's view is preferred, and two options are possible. First, one could repeat the "is" and add an "and" to make better sense ("the gift is from above *and is* coming down"). Second, one could render as "comes" and **semantically** render the participle as a customary present tense participle of means: "*by continually* coming down" (W, 521–22). The choice here is based more on a smooth translation rather than on some clear grammatical "rule." James's point is the dependability of continuous gifts coming from God.

> **Lexical Nugget:** Is there a difference between the nouns δόσις and δώρη-μα? Some commentators, heeding cautions about the abuse of synonyms, conclude that the terms are synonymous (Moo, 77; Blomberg et al., 73). These words rarely appear in the NT, with δόσις only in Matthew 6:1 and Philippians 4:15. While δόσις describes human actions of giving and receiving, it can also refer to gift-giving by God in the LXX (Sir. 26:14; 34:18). The second word for "gift," δώρημα, occurs elsewhere in the NT only in Romans 5:16 but is used in the LXX twenty-one times. The two words here in James 1:17 are describing divine gifts (BDAG, s.v. "δόσις," p. 259; "δώρημα" p. 266). A general observation is that nouns ending in -σις express the action of the verbal root while nouns ending in -μα stress the result of the action implied in the verbal root.

1:17c οὐκ ἔνι: This negated (οὐκ) structural marker is a short form of the third person singular present active indicative ἔνεστιν that conveys the idea of existing in a certain context derived from ἔνειμι and may be rendered "there is" (BDAG, s.v. "ἔνι," p. 334; s.v. "ἔνεστιν," p. 336). **Syntactically**, it is the negated verb of the independent relative clause (παρ' ᾧ, "with whom"). The negative form οὐκ ἔνι appears elsewhere only in negative constructions like this one (1 Cor. 6:5; Gal. 3:28; Col. 3:11). **Semantically**, the present tense is customary: "there is no" (NASB ESV NET NLT), "can be no" (ASV), or "there is no possibility of" (Adam, 19). It conveys a pattern of behavior about the dependability of God: he doesn't change (NIV NLT).

> **Text-Critical Nugget:** What is the correct reading ἔνι or ἐστίν in James 1:17? The rare form ἔνι, a present form of the verb ἔνεστιν, is replaced by the more common form ἐστίν in the uncials ℵ and P. This is a clear example of later scribal "correction" to a more "acceptable" form. The can-on of *"prefer the more difficult reading"* advises the retention of the *more difficult* reading ἔνι. This shorter form appears elsewhere in the NT in 1 Corinthians 6:5; Galatians 3:28; and Colossians 3:11, and only in nega-tive expressions as it does here (BDAG, s.v. "ἔνι," p. 337).

> **Semantical Nugget:** Is there a Greek philosophical background to the expression παραλλαγὴ ἢ τροπῆς ἀποσκίασμα? In this elegant expres-sion, the *hapax legomenon* παραλλαγὴ signifies "change" or "alteration" (BDAG, s.v. "παραλλαγή," p. 768). The noun τροπὴ occurs frequently in astronomical contexts (Deut. 33:14; Job 38:33; Wis 7:18; BDAG, s.v. "τρο-πή," p. 1016). The noun ἀποσκίασμα literally means "shadow" (BDAG, s.v. "ἀποσκίασμα," p. 120), and here it is the shadow cast by the alteration

of a heavenly light. James desires his readers to become whole and complete persons (1:4). Therefore, the God who has gifted "us" to become his spiritual creation by the Word of Truth (1:18) is also himself undivided and complete! It is not necessary to see this as a Stoical expression since the purpose of James is more ethical than metaphysical.

1:18a βουληθείς: This structural marker is a nominative singular masculine aorist passive participle of βούλομαι that means "intend," "plan," or "will," more specifically of God who plans a course of action (BDAG, s.v. "βούλομαι" 2b, p. 182). **Syntactically**, it introduces a dependent participial clause modifying "he gave birth" (ἀπεκύησεν) and is thereby adverbial. While the use of βουληθείς is not irregular, the passive voice and the verb's being fronted prior to the main verb merit reflection. The participle form of βούλομαι appears thirteen times in the NT, but apart from 1:18 it is in the present middle form βουλόμενος in its various cases (e.g., Mark 15:15; Acts 12:4; 22:30; 23:28; 27:43; 2 Cor. 1:17; Heb. 6:17; 2 Pet. 3:9). **Semantically**, the participle's form in 1:18 does not appear in the LXX, but Philo employs it twenty times regarding the divine will, and always in a temporal sense. Typical of these uses is in his work, *Virtues* 188: "For when God decided [βουληθείς] to establish this in us out of his own exceeding mercy . . . ." Most English versions translate the participle here in an "instrumental" sense. Typical are the KJV, ESV, and CNT: "Of his own will;" or the CSB: "By his own choice" (cf. NET). However, since the only other use of βουληθείς in Judeo-Christian literature is in a temporal sense, a temporal rather than instrumental translation is preferred: "when he decided" (cf. Adam, 20). A clearly instrumental dative later in the verse conveys that the divine Word is the means by which he gave birth to us. Therefore, we should render the verse: "*When he decided*, he gave birth to us *by* the Word of Truth [λόγῳ ἀληθείας]." The aorist tense portrays action prior to the main verb ἀπεκύησεν. Just as the Maker of the lights was sovereign in his creation of his natural "children" in the heavens, so he is also sovereign in the timing of the creation of his supernatural "children" on earth.

Semantical Nugget: What is meant by the expression ἀπαρχήν τινα τῶν αὐτοῦ κτισμάτων? In the LXX, the word ἀπαρχήν translates different Hebrew terms for the offering to God of the first animals or vegetation from field or flock (Exod. 22:29; 25:2–3; Lev. 2:12; Num. 15:20–21; Deut. 18:4). In Exodus 23:19, it is defined as the "first produce of the earth." In the NT the term is used as a figure for the pledge of the Spirit (Rom. 8:23); for the first one to rise from the dead (1 Cor. 15:20, 23); for the founding of the early Christian communities (Rom. 16:5; 1 Cor. 16:15); for the elect in heaven (Rev. 14:4); and for the remnant of believing Israel (Rom. 11:16). Since James is writing specifically to Jewish believers, the first fruits refer to the initial Jewish messianic community. These Jewish believers in Jesus as Messiah (2:1) are the first installment of the later harvest that would eventually include the many Gentile believers in the body of the Messiah (see also Rom. 8:19–23).

1:18b ἀπεκύησεν: This structural marker is a third person singular aorist active indicative of ἀποκυέω that means "give birth to" (BDAG, s.v. "ἀποκυέω" b, p. 114). **Syntactically**, it is the main verb of the independent asyndeton clause with the subject embedded in the verb: "he gave birth" (NRSV NIV NET NLT; cf. KJV) or "he brought forth" (ASV NASB1995 ESV CNT). **Semantically**, the aorist tense is a constative aorist (W, 557). It explains the event as a whole. James follows the mention of "the Word" here with a reference to the "implanted Word" which "saves your souls" in 1:21. Therefore, the "truthful message" (descriptive genitive ἀληθείας) is the message that contains the truth about the Messiah (2:1).

1:18c εἰς τὸ εἶναι: This articular structural marker (τὸ εἶναι) is a present active infinitive of εἰμί that conveys the idea of showing how something is to be understood and thereby a representation of something. It is often rendered "to be" (BDAG, s.v. "εἰμί" 2cα, p. 283). **Syntactically**, the entire statement, εἰς τὸ εἶναι, introduces a dependent infinitive clause that modifies the verb "he gave birth" (ἀπεκύησεν). The clause is placed under ἀπεκύησεν to visualize its dependence. **Semantically**, the present active infinitive with εἰς τό plus the accusative subject of the infinitive ἡμᾶς introduces a purpose infinitive clause (W, 591–92; BDF, §402.2; Adam, 21). It conveys God's purpose for "we" believers.

JAMES 1:19–27

Big Greek Idea: Based on a proverb about godly living, God's people are to control their anger and their speech and focus attention on accepting what God says and practicing their faith, especially with regard to helping orphans and widows and not succumbing to the ungodly behavior of nonbelievers.

Structural Overview: James opens with a proverbial guideline about an expectation to control anger (vv. 19–21). He then transitions to an exhortation to accept and put into practice what the Bible says in order to receive God's blessing (vv. 22–24). James closes with a final exhortation to talk less and do more (vv. 25–27).

Outline:

> Godly Living Involves Controlling Anger (1:19–21).
> Godly Living Involves Accepting and Putting into Practice His Expectations (1:22–24).
> Godly Living Involves Talking Less and Doing More (1:25–27).

GODLY LIVING INVOLVES CONTROLLING ANGER (JAMES 1:19–21)

CLAUSAL OUTLINE FOR JAMES 1:19–21

1:19a **Ἴστε**, ἀδελφοί μου ἀγαπητοί·
1:19a **Know this**, my beloved brothers *and sisters*;

1:19b **ἔστω** δὲ πᾶς ἄνθρωπος
1:19b <u>so</u> every person *must* **be**
    |
    ταχὺς <u>εἰς τὸ</u> **ἀκοῦσαι**,
    quick **to hear**
    |
    βραδὺς <u>εἰς τὸ</u> **λαλῆσαι**,
    slow **to speak**,
    |
    βραδὺς εἰς ὀργήν
    slow to anger;

1:20 ὀργὴ <u>γὰρ</u> ἀνδρὸς δικαιοσύνην θεοῦ οὐ **ἐργάζεται**.
1:20 <u>for *you see*</u> a man's anger **does** not **produce** the righteousness of God.

    1:21b **ἀποθέμενοι** πᾶσαν ῥυπαρίαν καὶ περισσείαν κακίας
    1:21b **put away** all filthiness and rampant wickedness

1:21a δὶο . . . **δέξασθε** τὸν ἔμφυτον λόγον

1:21a Therefore . . . *then* **accept** with meekness the implanted Word,

1:21c τὸν **δυνάμενον σῶσαι** τὰς ψυχὰς ὑμῶν.

1:21c *which* **is able to save** your souls.

SYNTAX EXPLAINED FOR JAMES 1:19–21

1:19a Ἴστε: This structural marker is a second person plural perfect active imperative of οἶδα that may be rendered "understand," "recognize," "come to know," "experience," or "to have information about" (BDAG, s.v. "οἶδα" 1i, p. 694). **Syntactically**, it is a command that functions as the main verb of this independent asyndeton clause and governs the entire unit of thought. **Semantically**, this form of the word can be either a perfect imperative or a perfect indicative second person plural. In either case, it is a rare form, appearing only twice elsewhere in the NT (Eph. 5:5; Heb. 12:17). Most commentators have preferred the imperative (Davids, 91; Blomberg et al., 85; McCartney, 114–15) and say that James is calling attention to what follows. Those favoring an indicative say that James is appealing to the readers' knowledge of what he has just written. The imperative is preferred, as witnessed by the above translation, for the following reasons. (1) It is consistent with the style of James, who uses the imperative more than any other NT writer, especially when opening a new paragraph. (2) James makes his appeal to his readers' knowledge elsewhere in the form of a rhetorical question (4:4: οὐκ οἴδατε—"do you not know?" and 2:20: θέλεις δὲ γνῶναι—"do you wish to understand?"), not with an indicative statement. (3) The other two occurrences of the form (Eph. 5:5; Heb. 12:17) are indicative, but each is introduced by a causal γάρ, which is not the case here with its absolute, stand-alone appeal for the readers to know what follows. (4) In the other uses of "beloved brothers *and sisters*," James calls attention to what follows, which is more consistent with the imperative usage (1:16; 2:5). (5) In these passages James is fond of using what linguists call a "meta-comment"—an orienter that is not necessary to the sentence but calls attention to what is about to be said ("do not be deceived," "listen"; see also "above all things" in 5:12). The verb functions to call attention to the imperative ἔστω that is then followed by three infinitives.

Text-Critical Nugget: Instead of the abrupt Ἴστε opening in 1:19, the Byzantine family of manuscripts and the Textus Receptus connect the following ἔστω δέ (dropping δέ) more closely with 1:18 by substituting ὥστε, which is supported by a variety of later witnesses (Κ Π Ψ 614 *Byz* syr^p). The reading adopted as the text, however, is strongly supported by both Alexandrian and Western witnesses (‭א‬ᶜ B C 81 1739 it vg). Furthermore, it is the more difficult reading because the later reading looks like a scribal attempt to smooth out what was considered as a rarely used form followed by an awkward word order. These variants comprise a clear example of the Byzantine scribal effort to smooth over some of the perceived roughness of the Greek (Metzger[1], 609; Metzger[2], 680; Davids, 91).

1:19b δέ: This structural marker is a conjunction meaning "so" (BDAG, s.v. "δέ" 2, p. 213). **Syntactically**, it introduces an independent conjunctive clause and appears in a post-positive position. **Semantically**, δέ may serve as a contrast: "but" (ASV NASB1995 CNT), left untranslated (NET ESV NRSV NIV NLT), or viewed as a marker linking a narrative segment "so" as a summary of the previous clause (cf. Adam, 23) and the perspective presented above.

ἔστω: This Greek word is a third person singular present active imperative of εἰμι that means "to be" or "to be in close connection with" (BDAG, s.v. "εἰμί" 2, p. 283). **Syntactically**, it serves as the main verb of this independent conjunctive clause. **Semantically**, the third person imperative is as strong in force as any of the second person imperatives in the book ("must be"). Any translation that leaves an impression of permission and not of a command reflects an English phenomenon of the verb "let" and does not reflect the Greek imperatival force. It is this imperative ἔστω that serves to introduce what the readers must do or be as indicated in the following εἰς plus infinitives dependent clauses.

Semantical Nugget: What is the contextual significance of the triad of commands in 1:19? The adjectives ("quick" and "slow") and the infinitives that complete the imperative ἔστω convey the imperatival commands in the following paragraph rather than the initial imperative Ἴστε, which only calls attention to them. The three commands, "every person must be quick to hear, slow to speak, slow to anger," are then developed in the entire passage through 1:27. The subject of being "quick to hear" is developed in 1:22–25; "slow to speak" is developed in 1:27; "slow to anger" is developed in 1:20–21. This triad also introduces three prominent themes in the book, which are: (1) becoming swift to hear and do; (2) becoming slow to speak; and (3) becoming slow to anger. McCartney (115) rightly notes that verse 19 "reads like a typical proverb that corresponds to other proverbs (15:1; Eccl. 5:1–2; 7:9; Sir 5:11)."

εἰς τὸ ἀκοῦσαι: This articular Greek word (τὸ ἀκοῦσαι) is the aorist active infinitive of ἀκούω that conveys the idea of hearing something from somebody and is often rendered "hear" (BDAG, "ἀκούω" 1bβ, p. 37). **Syntactically**, it is a dependent infinitival clause introduced with the preposition "to"

(BDAG, "εἰς" 1bβ, p. 289). The preposition εἰς that precedes τὸ ἀκοῦσαι is key. Every person (ἄνθρωπος) must be quick *with reference to* hearing and slow *with reference to* anger (BDF, §402.2). **Semantically**, the entire statement, εἰς τὸ ἀκοῦσαι, has an epexegetical function that further explains the adjective "quick" (ταχὺς) that precedes it (W, 607). So the adjective "quick" (ταχύς) and the infinitive "to hear" (ἀκοῦσαι) complete the imperative "be" (ἔστω) and convey the expected imperatival commands in the paragraph rather than the initial imperative Ἴστε, which only calls attention to them.

εἰς τὸ λαλῆσαι: This articular Greek word (τὸ λαλῆσαι) is the aorist active infinitive of λαλέω that may be rendered "talk," "speak," or "express oneself" (BDAG, s.v. "λαλέω" 1aβ, p. 582a–b). **Syntactically**, it is a dependent infinitival clause introduced with the preposition "to" (BDAG, "εἰς" 1bβ, p. 289). The preposition εἰς that precedes τὸ λαλῆσαι is the key. Every person (ἄνθρωπος) must be slow *with reference to* speaking and *with reference to* anger (BDF, §402.2). **Semantically**, the entire statement, εἰς τὸ λαλῆσαι, has an epexegetical function that further explains the adjective "slow" (βραδὺς) that precedes it (W, 607). So the adjective "slow" (βραδὺς) and the infinitive "to speak" (τὸ λαλῆσαι) complete the imperative "be" (ἔστω) and convey the expected imperatival commands in the paragraph rather than the initial imperative Ἴστε, which only calls attention to them.

1:20 γάρ: This structural marker is a conjunction meaning "for" or "you see" (BDAG, s.v. "γάρ" 1b, p. 189). **Syntactically**, it introduces an independent conjunctive clause and appears in a post-positive position: "*For you see* a man's anger does not produce the righteousness of God" (ὀργὴ γὰρ ἀνδρὸς δικαιοσύνην θεοῦ οὐ ἐργάζεται). **Semantically**, it provides concluding material that supports verse 9 and is rendered as "for" (KJV ASV NASB NRSV ESV NET CNT; cf. W, 658).

ἐργάζεται: This Greek word is a third person singular present middle indicative of ἐργάζομαι that conveys the idea of achieving or accomplishing something and may be rendered "do," "accomplish," or "carry out" (BDAG, s.v. "ἐργάζομαι" 2, p. 389). **Syntactically**, it is the main verb of this independent conjunctive clause. Its direct object is "righteousness" (δικαιοσύ-νην). **Semantically**, the present tense is customary present and indicates a pattern of behavior (W, 521). It is best to translate the verb as "produce," as in 2 Corinthians 7:10, where it alternates with κατεργάζεσθαι ("to produce"). The translation "produce righteousness" makes it difficult to think that James could be referring to God's gift of a righteous standing—the sense in which Paul most often uses the noun δικαιοσύνη (e.g. Rom. 1:17; 3:22, 26; etc.). James uses the phrase "produce righteousness" with the meaning it normally has in the Bible: to do what God requires of his people. Jesus used the word "righteousness" this way when he called on his followers to exhibit a "righteousness" that exceeds that of the Pharisees (Matt. 5:20; see also Matt. 5:6, 10; 6:33). We may compare this idea with the phrase δίκαιοι ἐνώπιον τοῦ Θεοῦ in Luke 1:6 (Zechariah and Elizabeth), in Acts 4:19; 8:21; and in 1 Peter 3:4. To do righteousness is simply to do what pleases God.

1:21a διό: This structural marker is a conjunction meaning "therefore" (BDAG s.v. "διό," p. 250). **Syntactically**, it introduces an independent conjunctive clause: *"therefore . . . accept the implanted Word"* (διὸ . . . δέξασθε τὸν ἔμφυτον λόγον). It is a further application of the warnings in 1:19–20. **Semantically**, it is an inferential conjunction that is rendered "therefore" (NASB NRSV NIV ESV CNT; Zerwick et al., 693) or "so" (NET NLT). It draws a conclusion about refraining from anger and the production of God's righteousness (Davids, 93). It introduces an imperative commanding the reader about receiving God's Word.

δέξασθε: This Greek word is a second person plural aorist middle imperative of δέχομαι that conveys the idea of approval or conviction by acceptance and may be rendered as "approve" or "accept" (BDAG, s.v. "δέχομαι" 5, p. 221). **Syntactically**, it is the main verb of this independent clause in the sentence that comprises 1:21. Its direct object is the phrase τὸν ἔμφυτον λόγον. It is preferable to take the phrase ἐν πραΰτητι with the second person aorist middle imperative verb (δέχομαι) that follows it. There is good reason, therefore, that the placing of the comma in the Greek text should be moved to before ἐν πραΰτητι. **Semantically**, the aorist imperative is a specific command concerning conduct. The aorist tense is an ingressive aorist that reflects a sense of urgency to begin a certain action (W, 719) that translations have rendered "accept" (NIV NLT), "receive" (KJV ASV NASB ESV CNT), or in a less urgent sense "welcome" (NRSV NET). Thus, the specific and urgent command is to "accept" or have a teachable attitude in which to receive or welcome what the Bible has to say (Adam, 25).

1:21b ἀποθέμενοι: This structural marker is a nominative plural masculine present middle participle of ἀποτίθημι that may be rendered "take off," "lay aside," or "rid oneself of something" figuratively speaking (BDAG, s.v. "ἀποτίθημι" 1b, p. 123). The verb ἀποτίθημι is used for removing clothes in Acts 7:58, and this imagery in the verb is applied metaphorically elsewhere in the NT for the "stripping off" of a non-Christian lifestyle from the walk of a believer (Rom. 13:12; Eph. 4:22, 25; Col. 3:8; Heb. 12:1; 1 Peter 2:1). **Syntactically**, it functions as the main verb in a dependent participial clause modifying *"then* accept" (δέξασθε) and placed above δέξασθε. **Semantically**, it may be considered as an attendant circumstance participle taking on its mood as an imperative δέξασθε and rendered "put away" (ESV NET; cf. KJV NRSV NIV NLT). The idea is to "put away" and *"then* accept" (Adam, 24). Yet, it may also be considered a participle of means "*by* putting off" (cf. ASV NASB). Our translation assumes the mood of the imperative δέξασθε in the independent clause, as is normal with adverbial attendant circumstance participles (W, 640–45). The aorist participle functions as a constative aorist, viewing the action as a whole.

> **Syntactical Nugget:** Where should the comma go in this verse, after κα-κίας or after πραΰτητι? Most critical texts place the comma after the πραΰτητι, so that the phrase is related to the participle ἀποθέμενοι by indicating the way in which we are to put off anger (i.e., "put away wickedness with meekness"). English versions do not usually translate ἐν πραΰτητι with the previous clause. The NA²⁸/UBS⁵ texts remove the comma and leave the decision to the reader. Perhaps the earlier editors were uncomfortable with placing a prepositional phrase like ἐν πραΰτητι before the imperative δέξασθε in the following clause. James does this again in 2:1 when he places ἐν προσωπολημψίαις before the imperative ἔχετε! The fronting of the phrase, rather than being ungrammatical, actually lends a greater prominence to the attitude required when we receive the Word, namely, with humility rather than anger.

1:21c τὸν δυνάμενον: This articular (τόν) structural marker is a nominative singular neuter present middle participle of δύναμαι that my be rendered "can," "am able," or "be capable" (BDAG, s.v. "δύναμαι" a, 261). **Syntactically**, it is an attributive participle modifying λόγον and introduces a dependent participial clause: "*which is able* to save your souls" (τὸν δυνάμενον σῶσαι τὰς ψυχὰς ὑμῶν). The location of the article indicates that the construction is in the second attributive position (W, 306–7), thus functioning adjectivally by modifying τὸν ἔμφυτον λόγον. **Semantically**, the verbal conveys the power of the "implanted Word" (τὸν ἔμφυτον λόγον). God's implanted Word in us has power.

σῶσαι: This Greek word is an aorist active infinitive of σῴζω that conceptually speaks of preserving a person from eternal death and is often rendered "save" (BDAG, s.v. "σῴζω" 2αγ, p. 982). **Syntactically**, the infinitive is functioning adverbially as part of the main verb of the dependent participial clause: "which is able *to save* your souls" (τὸν δυνάμενον σῶσαι τὰς ψυχὰς ὑμῶν). Its direct object is "your souls" (τὰς ψυχὰς ὑμῶν). **Semantically**, it is a complementary (supplementary) adverbial infinitive that completes the adjectival participle, "which is able" (τὸν δυνάμενον; cf. W, 598–99). The aorist tense is a constative aorist that speaks of the action as a whole as it speaks of preserving a person from eternal death and is rendered as "to save" (KJV ASV NASB NRSV ESV NET NLT CNT; cf. NIV). The entire expression states that the Word that has been implanted by the gracious God in the soul of the

believer is able to save his soul. The expression "save your souls" does not refer to the initial experience of salvation, but to the continuous (imperfective
aspect of δυνάμενον) work of restoring and rescuing the inner life of believers. This is obvious when one recognizes that James is addressing "brothers
and sisters" (1:19) who have already been "birthed" through a supernatural
Word from God (1:18).

> **Theological Nugget:** What is meant by "save your souls"? This expres-
> sion σῶσαι τὰς ψυχὰς ὑμῶν does not refer to the initial experience of
> salvation, as in the popular exhortation that we should "save souls." The
> expression refers to the implied ongoing contrast between soul and body.
> This perspective is also found in 5:20, which promises that one who res-
> cues a brother will "save his soul from death." The "soul" may thus be used
> as a metonymy for the entire person (BDAG, s.v. "ψυχή" 3, p. 1099), a
> usage common in James and in both testaments (LXX Exod. 1:5: "seventy
> souls"; Acts 2:41: "about three thousand souls").

GODLY LIVING INVOLVES ACCEPTING AND PUTTING INTO PRACTICE HIS EXPECTATIONS (JAMES 1:22–24)

CLAUSAL OUTLINE FOR JAMES 1:22–24

1:22a **Γίνεσθε** δὲ ποιηταὶ λόγου καὶ μὴ μόνον ἀκροαταὶ
1:22a But **become** doers of the Word and not hearers only

|
    1:22b **παραλογιζόμενοι** ἑαυτούς.
    1:22b *resulting in* **deceiving** yourselves.

      1:23a ὅτι **εἴ** τις ἀκροατὴς λόγου **ἐστὶν** καὶ οὐ ποιητής,
      1:23a Because **if** anyone **is** a hearer of the Word and not a doer,

    |
1:23b οὗτος **ἔοικεν** ἀνδρὶ
1:23b this one **is like** a man

        |
        1:23c **κατανοοῦντι** τὸ πρόσωπον τῆς γενέσεως αὐτοῦ ἐν
        ἐσόπτρῳ.
        1:23c **who looks intently** at his natural face in a mirror.

1:24a **κατενόησεν** γὰρ ἑαυτὸν
1:24a For *you see* he **looks at** himself

1:24b καὶ **ἀπελήλυθεν**
1:24b and he **goes away**

1:24c <u>καὶ</u> εὐθέως **ἐπελάθετο** (ὁποῖος **ἦν**)
1:24c <u>and</u> at once <u>he **forgets**</u> (what *kind of person* <u>he **was**</u>).

SYNTAX EXPLAINED FOR JAMES 1:22–25

1:22a δέ: This structural marker is a conjunction meaning "but" (BDAG, s.v. "δέ" 4a, p. 213). **Syntactically**, it introduces an independent conjunctive clause and appears in a post-positive position: "*but* become doers of the Word and not hearers only" (Γίνεσθε δὲ ποιηταὶ λόγου καὶ μὴ μόνον ἀκροαταί). It implies a development from what precedes in verse 21 about the implanted Word of God. **Semantically**, it is a marker of contrast: "but" (e.g., KJV NASB ESV NET etc.). In contrast to blaming God for temptation, James suggests we need only look at ourselves. This term introduces a contrast to being a person who merely listens to or reads "God's Word" (= Bible).

γίνεσθε: This Greek word is a second person plural present middle imperative of γίνομαι that conveys experiencing a change in nature and so indicates entry into a new condition: *become something* and may be rendered "become" (BDAG, s.v. "γίνομαι" 5, p. 198). **Syntactically**, it is the main verb of the independent conjunctive clause with an understood "you" as its subject and ποιηταὶ as its predicate nominative. Here it means not simply "be" as possessing a characteristic (BDAG, s.v. "γίνομαι" 7, p. 199) but rather the more dynamic nuance of "becoming" or "become." **Semantically**, the imperfective aspect of the present tense further supports this dynamic idea of process (W, 722). It is an ongoing process of a change of attitude (Adam, 26). This is consistent with the imperatival function of the verb in 3:1: "Do not many of you become (γίνεσθε) teachers." It is also the way James uses the verb in 1:12d, 25b; 2:4b, 10a, 11d. The issue in 1:22 is one of *becoming* rather than *being*—namely, turning profession into action.

> **Grammatical and Semantical Nugget:** What is meant by "doers" and "hearers" of the Word? This noun plus genitive construction, ποιηταὶ λόγου, is a clear example of an "objective genitive" in which the genitive word receives the action of the verbal idea contained in its head noun. The construction is unpacked as "those who do the Word." The same idea is in Matthew 7:24: "Everyone who hears these words [λόγους] of mine and does [ποιεῖ] them" (see also Luke 6:46, 11:28; and John 13:17). The word ποιητής occurs only six times in NT, four of which are in James in this verse(1:23a, 25c; 4:11e). A similar sense is "those who do the Law" (οἱ ποιηταὶ νόμου) in Romans 2:13. Semantic parallels are found in a number of Jesus's sayings, including Matthew 7:24–27 and Luke 11:28. The noun ἀκροαταί could be rendered literally

as "auditor" and appears three times in this paragraph. Note the similar construction in Romans 2:13: "not the hearers [ἀκροαταί] of the law are righteous before God but the doers [ποιηταί] of the law will be declared righteous." The "Word" is not just the Torah but refers back to the "Word of Truth" that was the theme of 1:18–21.

1:22b παραλογιζόμενοι: This structural marker is a nominative plural masculine present middle participle of παραλογίζομαι that may be rendered "deceive," "delude," or "deceive oneself" (BDAG, s.v. "παραλογίζομαι" v, p. 768). **Syntactically**, it introduces a dependent participial clause. The clause functions adverbially modifying the imperative "become" (γίνεσθε) and is placed under that verb to visualize the clause's dependence. **Semantically**, it is a participle of result: "*resulting in* deceiving yourselves" (W, 637–39). It expresses the result that takes place when one hears but does not act upon what he heard by obeying it: self-deception.

Lexical Nugget: What is meant by "deceiving yourselves"? In the LXX, the verb appears in 1 Samuel 28:12 where the woman of Endor says to Saul: "Why have you deceived [παραλογίσω] me?" This verb elsewhere in the NT is only in Colossians 2:4: "so that no one fraudulently deceives [παραλογίζηται] you." The same idea is found here—namely, that those who hear but fail to do are also "deceiving themselves" into thinking that some sort of passive reception of the message is enough. The result is that they are "defrauding themselves" by missing the path to maturity through doing the Word.

1:23a ὅτι: This structural marker is a conjunction meaning "because" (BDAG, s.v. "ὅτι" 4a, p. 732). **Syntactically**, it introduces a dependent conjunctive clause. The entire clause is adverbial modifying "is like" (ἔοικεν) and placed above the verb ἔοικεν to visualize the entire clause's dependence. The ὅτι clause serves to loosely link together James's discussion (BDF, §456). **Semantically**, it is causal introducing a reason: "*Because* if anyone is . . ." (W, 460–61) though translations render the ὅτι as "*for* if anyone is . . ." (KJV ASV NASB NRSV ESV NET NLT CNT).

εἴ: This Greek word is a conjunction meaning "if" (BDAG, s.v. "εἴ" 1aα, p. 277). **Syntactically**, it introduces a dependent conjunctive clause within a ὅτι clause. This imbedded conjunctive clause introduces the protasis of a conditional clause (W, 682–89). **Semantically**, this clause is a first-class conditional clause that assumes the reality of the protasis for the sake of the argument (W, 690–94). The assumption is that someone is listening to God's Word (= the Bible) but not following what the Bible says. The repeated words of 1:22 emphasize James's point.

ἐστὶν: This Greek word is a third person singular present active indicative of εἰμί that describes a special connection between the subject and predicate nominative and often rendered "is" (BDAG, s.v. "εἰμί" 2b, p. 284). **Syntactically**, it is the main verb of the dependent conjunctive clause. The indefinite pronoun "anyone" (τις) is the subject of the present active indicative verb ἐστὶν in the protasis and "hearer" (ἀκροατὴς) is the predicate nominative. **Semantically**, it is a stative verb. The expression "hearer of the Word" (ἀκροατὴς λόγου) is another example of a noun plus objective genitive construction (cf. ποιηταὶ λόγου in 1:22). The emphasis here is that it describes a person's situation as a non-doer. There is a parallel in thought with Jesus's condemnation of those who only listen to his words (Matt. 7:24–27), but James does not utilize Jesus's parable of the two houses. The assumption of such a person's hearing and not doing in the protasis of the clause leads to James's own effective parable in the apodosis.

1:23b ἔοικεν: This structural marker is a third person singular perfect active indicative of ἔοικα that may be rendered "be like" or "resemble" (BDAG, s.v. "ἔοικα," p. 355). **Syntactically**, it is the main verb in an independent asyndeton clause and the apodosis of a first–class conditional clause with οὗτος as its subject. **Semantically**, the perfect tense is stative and could be called "gnomic" because of its parabolic association (W, 580–81). James has previously used this same form, ἔοικεν, in 1:6c when he had introduced another parable about nature, the only times the form appears in the NT (only twice also in the LXX: Job 6:3, 25). He will also apply the parable with the same demonstrative pronoun in 1:25 with the opposite point when it refers to the "hearer and doer" who will be blessed and is a characteristic of his style (see also 1:26, 27; 3:2, 10).

1:23c κατανοοῦντι: This structural marker is a dative singular masculine present active participle of κατανοέω that conveys the idea of looking at something in a reflective manner and may be rendered as "consider" or "contemplate" (BDAG, s.v. "κατανοέω" 2, p. 522). **Syntactically**, it introduces a dependent participial clause that modifies "man" (ἀνδρί; or "person" in general). The entire clause is placed under ἀνδρί. A similar occurrence appeared in verse 6. Here, James uses ἀνήρ with descriptive words like "blessed" (μακάριος; 1:12), "looks" or "gazes" (κατανοῶν; 1:23), "gold ring" (χρυσοδακτύλιος; 2:2), and "perfect" (τέλειος; 3:2), and utilizes "man" (ἄνθρωπος) with more general expressions like "that" (ἐκεῖνος), "all" (πᾶς), and "no one" (οὐδείς). **Semantically**, the present tense functions as a customary present, denoting a habitual pattern of behavior or an ongoing state (cf. 1:25; W, 521).

Semantical Nugget: What is meant by τὸ πρόσωπον τῆς γενέσεως αὐτοῦ? This expression is literally "the face of his birth," and is used to contrast the reflection of a face in the mirror that belongs to this passing life. For the word γενέσεως as meaning "birth," see the LXX of Genesis 31:13; Ruth 2:11; and Matthew 1:18. The noun is used, as in 3:6d, in the sense of "nature," to mean the created world (including man) as distinguished from God, and with a suggestion of its temporal character. The reflection of the character is being shaped here by that contrasting look into the Word which he is about to mention.

Lexical Nugget: What is the precise meaning of ἐσόπτρῳ? The "mirror" made out of polished metal was referred to quite often in secular literature, especially in the papyri. In the LXX it appears only twice in wisdom books (Wis 7:26; Sir 12:11). The noun appears in the NT in 1 Corinthians 13:12, where imperfect knowledge gained through reflection is contrasted with the perfect knowledge of the reality. In 2 Corinthians 3:18 the cognate verb (κατοπτριζόμενοι: "reflecting as in a mirror") alludes to the glory in the face of Moses.

1:24a γάρ: This structural marker is a conjunction meaning "for" or "you see" (BDAG, s.v. "γάρ" 1b, p. 189). **Syntactically**, it introduces an independent conjunctive clause and appears in a post-positive position: *"for* he looks at himself" (κατενόησεν γὰρ ἑαυτόν). **Semantically**, γάρ, while providing continuity with the previous verse, also provides an explanation about a person who merely reads or hears what God says in the Bible.

κατενόησεν: This Greek word is a third person singular aorist active indicative of κατανοέω that conveys the idea of looking at something in a reflective manner and may be rendered "consider," "contemplate" (BDAG, s.v. "κατανοέω" 2, p. 522). **Syntactically**, it is the first of three main verbs in the clause of which the man (or "person" in general) mentioned in the previous verse is the referent. Thus, the verb's third person subject is "he." **Semantically**, the aorist tense here and later is gnomic (W, 562; Irons, 535) or "omnitemporal" (Porter, 38). It conveys an historical truth as a whole about any person who might see him-/herself in a mirror and contemplate his/her image.

Grammatical Nugget: James displays a skillful variety of different verb tenses that vividly highlight the forgetful actions of the mirror-gazer in 1:24. He looks (κατενόησεν—aorist tense) at himself; he departs (ἀπελήλυθεν—perfect tense), and then at once forgets (ἐπελάθετο—aorist tense) what he looked like. Some commentators see this as an example of stylistic variety (Moo, 125; Davids, 98). Another approach is to recognize the function of the perfect tense form as conveying greater prominence for this action in the narrative. What James wants the reader to focus on is the state of a forgetful looker's having departed from his gazing in the mirror. James's fondness for using the perfect tense in this stative role while being juxtaposed with an aorist is also seen in 2:10: "For whoever keeps [aorist τηρήσῃ] the whole law, yet, stumbles [aorist πταίσῃ] in one point, he has become [perfect γέγονεν] guilty of all." This man "took cognizance of himself," and then "has gone away and immediately forgot what kind [of person] he was." He saw, he went off, he forgot. His hearing gained him nothing as far as the real power of the Word is concerned.

1:24b καί: This structural marker is a conjunction meaning "and" (BDAG, s.v. "καί" 1bα, p. 494). **Syntactically,** it introduces an independent conjunctive clause. **Semantically,** translations render καί as a coordinating conjunction that joins two independent clauses: "and" (KJV NASB NRSV ESV NET NIV CNT).

ἀπελήλυθεν: This Greek word is a third person singular perfect active indicative of ἀπέρχομαι that may be rendered "go away" or "depart" with no indication of destination (BDAG, s.v. "ἀπέρχομαι" 1a, p. 102). **Syntactically,** it serves as the main verb of an independent clause with an assumed "he" of the person (lit. "man") mentioned in the previous verse as the subject. **Semantically,** the perfect tense is gnomic in that it speaks of a generic or proverbial occurrence (W, 580–81; BDF, §344; cf. Zerwick et al., 693; Irons, 535) about any person who might see him/herself in a mirror and then leaves the mirror. It is often rendered in the present tense (W, 574): "goes away" (ESV NIV NET CNT; cf. KJV ASV NRSV) or "walk away" (NLT).

1:24c καί: This structural marker is a conjunction meaning "and" (BDAG, s.v. "καί" 1bα, p. 494). **Syntactically,** it introduces an independent conjunctive clause. **Semantically,** translations render καί as a coordinating conjunction that joins two independent clauses: "and" (KJV NASB NRSV ESV NET NIV CNT).

ἐπελάθετο: This Greek word is a third person singular aorist middle indicative of ἐπιλανθάνομαι that means "forget" or more specifically "not have remembrance of something about the past character of a person" (BDAG, s.v. "ἐπιλανθάνομαι" 1, p. 374). **Syntactically,** it serves as the main verb of an independent conjunctive clause with an assumed subject "he" of the person (lit. "man") mentioned in the previous verse. **Semantically,** the aorist tense here is gnomic aorist (W, 561) or "omnitemporal" (Porter, 38). It conveys a historical truth as a whole about any person who might see him-/herself in a mirror and then what he/she saw in the mirror.

Syntactical Nugget: The triple compound clauses have special uses of the verb tenses. James's verbs vividly highlight the forgetful actions of the mirror-gazer in 1:24. They look (κατενόησεν—aorist tense) at themselves, depart (ἀπελήλυθεν—perfect tense), and then at once forget (ἐπελάθετο—aorist tense) what they looked like. There is a change in tense from the aorist to the perfect and back to the aorist. Many of the standard grammars and many commentators refer to the "gnomic aorist" (see W, 562) and suggest a similar function for the perfect (W, 581). Some explain the purpose in using different tense forms as an example of stylistic variety (Davids, 98). Porter, on the other hand, prefers the category "omnitemporal" for these aorists that grammaticalize the "perfective" aspect. The perfective aspect of the aorist is used to describe a natural process (James 1:11), conceiving the process as complete. Porter (40) describes the stative aspect of the perfect tense form as describing a "state of affairs." This is the best approach to understanding James's use of the perfect tense in this passage, particularly when one recognizes the function of the perfect tense as bringing to greater prominence this action in the narrative. In other words, what James wants the reader to focus on is the state of the forgetful *looker* as he has departed from his gazing in the mirror. James's fondness for using the perfect tense in this stative role while juxtaposed with an aorist can also be seen in 2:10: "For whoever keeps [aorist τηρήσῃ] the whole law, yet, stumbles [aorist πταίσῃ] in one point, he has become [perfect γέγονεν] guilty of all." This man "took cognizance of himself," and then "has gone away and immediately forgot what kind [of man] he was." This is what made him a hearer only: he saw, went off, and forgot. His hearing netted him nothing as far as the real purpose and the power of the Bible are concerned.

ἦν. This Greek word is an imperfect active indicative third person singular of εἰμί that means "to be" (BDAG, s.v. "εἰμί" 1, p. 283). **Syntactically**, it is the main verb in the clausal complement to "he forgets" (ἐπελάθετο). The clause is place in parentheses to visualize its contribution to the independent conjunctive clause with "what kind of person" (ὁποῖος) as the predicate nominative for ἦν. **Semantically**, the imperfect of εἰμί is stative and may be rendered "what he was like" (NRSV ESV; cf. NLT) or "what *kind of person* he was" (NASB NET; cf. KJV ASV).

Godly Living Involves Talking Less and Doing More (James 1:25–27)

Clausal Outline for James 1:25–27

1:25a (ὁ δὲ **παρακύψας** εἰς νόμον τέλειον τὸν τῆς ἐλευθερίας καὶ **παραμείνας**)

1:25a (But **the one who looks carefully** into the perfect law of liberty and **continues in it**),

|

1:25b οὐκ ἀκροατὴς ἐπιλησμονῆς **γενόμενος**

1:25b *by* not **relating** to a forgetful hearer

|

1:25c ἀλλὰ [*γενόμενος*] ποιητὴς ἔργου,

1:25c but [*by relating*] to one who does the deed,

1:25d οὗτος μακάριος ἐν τῇ ποιήσει αὐτοῦ **ἔσται**.

1:25d this one **will be** blessed in his doing.

1:26a Εἴ τις **δοκεῖ** θρησκὸς **εἶναι**

1:26a If anyone **thinks he is** religious

| |

1:26b μὴ **χαλιναγωγῶν** γλῶσσαν αὐτοῦ ἀλλὰ **ἀπατῶν** καρδίαν αὐτοῦ,

1:26b *while* not **bridling** his tongue but **deceiving** his heart,

|

1:26c τούτου μάταιος [*ἐστίν*] ἡ θρησκεία.

1:26c this *person's* religion [*is*] worthless.

1:27a θρησκεία καθαρὰ καὶ ἀμίαντος παρὰ τῷ θεῷ καὶ πατρὶ αὕτη **ἐστίν**,

1:27a This **is** a pure and undefiled religion before God the Father,

1:27b **ἐπισκέπτεσθαι** ὀρφανοὺς καὶ χήρας ἐν τῇ θλίψει αὐτῶν,

1:27b *namely,* **to visit** orphans and widows in their affliction,

|

1:27c ἄσπιλον ἑαυτὸν **τηρεῖν** ἀπὸ τοῦ κόσμου.

1:27c *namely,* **to keep** oneself unstained from the world.

Syntax Explained for James 1:25–27

1:25a δέ: This structural marker is a conjunction meaning "but" (BDAG, s.v. "δέ" 4, p. 213). **Syntactically**, it introduces a dependent conjunctive clause that implies a development from the behavior in verse 23. The conjunction is in the post-positive position: "*but* the one who looks carefully into the perfect law of liberty" (ὁ δὲ παρακύψας εἰς νόμον τέλειον τὸν τῆς ἐλευθερίας). **Semantically**, δέ is a marker of contrast: "but" (e.g., KJV NASB ESV NIV NET etc.). It provides an adversative to an incorrect way of behaving (v. 24), giving a correct or positive way of living.

> **Grammatical Nugget:** Why is verse 25 so long? This sentence is probably the closest that James ever comes to what is called a classical "periodic sentence" (BDF, §464). The three aorist participles (παρακύψας, παραμείνας, γενόμενος) in the opening clause complex set up the future tense (ἔσται) in the last clause. While not containing the normal features of a conditional clause, the sentence functions that way because the participles form the protasis to which the future tense responds as the apodosis.

ὁ . . . παρακύψας: This articular (ὁ) Greek word is a nominative singular masculine aorist active participle of παρακύπτω that means "look (in, into)" or "try to find out something intellectually" (BDAG, s.v. "παρακύπτω" 2, p. 767). **Syntactically**, it is a dependent participial clause that is functioning as the subject of the following ἔσται (Adam, 29; Irons, 535). It is placed in parentheses to visualize its contribution to the clause. "This one" (οὗτος) in the subsequent clause serves to resume the topic. **Semantically**, the aorist participle functions as a constative aorist, viewing the action of looking in a mirror as a whole.

> **Semantical Nugget:** How does James utilize his own beatitude? The comparison between two types of hearers is brought into sharp relief by the use of the demonstrative pronoun οὗτος in 1:23b and 1:25d. In 1:23b the conditional clause proposes a forgetful hearer and then adds: "this one" is like a person who forgets what he looks like in the mirror. On the other hand (δέ), 1:25d describes a hearer who obeys and then concludes with the important beatitude: "this one" will be blessed in his deed (ἐν τῇ ποιήσει αὐτοῦ). The noun ποιήσει rhetorically balances the cognate noun ποιηταί in 1:22a. It is also possible to see another inclusio at work with the two *macarisms*, or beatitudes: μακάριος initiating a new section in 1:12 and ending one here in 1:25d.

καί: This Greek word is a coordinating conjunction meaning "and" (BDAG, s.v. "καί" 1bα, p. 494). **Syntactically**, it continues James's dependent conjunctive clause. **Semantically**, translations render καί as a coordinating conjunction that link together two participles: "and" (KJV NASB NRSV ESV NET NIV CNT). It shows both continuity and development of thought concerning one person who looks and continues.

παραμείνας: This Greek word is a nominative singular masculine aorist active participle of παραμένω that means "continue in an occupation or office," or "continue in an official capacity" (BDAG, s.v. "παραμένω" 2, p. 769). **Syntactically**, it also is a substantival participle functioning along with παρακύψας as the subject of the following ἔσται. The construction, "the one who looks . . . and continues" (ὁ δὲ παρακύψας . . . καὶ παραμείνας) is a Granville Sharp construction where the article "the" (ὁ) governs both participles and thereby speaks of one person not two. Thus, both participials appear in the single clause and are placed in parentheses to visualize their close lexical connection. **Semantically**, the aorist participle functions as a constative aorist, viewing the action as a whole as it pertains to continue to do what God says and is rendered "perseveres" (NRSV ESV CNT), "abides" (NASB1995), or "continues" (KJV NIV).

> **Lexical Nugget:** While some think that James is contrasting two types of "looking"—namely, a casual glance in the mirror with a studied peering into the Word—such fine distinctions between the meanings of these two verbs, with the verb κατανοέω in 1:23, 24 apparently conveying a more casual glance and the participle form of παρακύπτω conveying a more intent gaze, misunderstand the real purpose of the intended analogy. Other appearances of the first verb, κατανοέω, simply do not imply any less serious "glance" (Acts 11:6; 27:39; Rom. 4:19; esp. Heb. 3:1; 10:24). The contrast in this parable is not between the ways the two verbs look at their respective objects. The real difference between the two is that the first person forgets what he saw, and the second person perseveres (παραμείνας) in his looking and does not forget what he saw. When one gives careful attention to what the Word teaches by not forgetting what it teaches, then this person will be blessed both in his hearing and his doing. The blessed one is he who does not forget what he has heard and who obeys the Word. The person condemned is he who does not allow the Word to affect his "doing."

1:25b γενόμενος: This structural marker is a nominative singular masculine aorist middle participle of γίνομαι that means "belong to" or "to be closely related to someone or something" (BDAG, s.v. "γίνομαι" 9, p. 198). **Syntactically**, it introduces a dependent participial clause: "*by relating* not to a forgetful hearer" (οὐκ ἀκροατὴς ἐπιλησμονῆς γενόμενος). **Semantically**, since this participle follows the main verb, it expresses manner (W, 627–28). In this clause "by relating" is negated with οὐκ: "by not relating." This subordinate clause, anchored by the participle γενόμενος, serves like a modern "parenthesis" in the verse, clarifying what he means by looking into the law and continuing to do so. The aorist participle functions as a constative aorist, viewing the action as a whole (W, 557), namely, it summarizes the idea of a person who forgets.

1:25c ἀλλά [γενόμενος]: This structural marker is a conjunction meaning "but" (BDAG s.v. "ἀλλά" 2, p. 45). **Syntactically**, it introduces a dependent conjunctive clause with an assumed or elliptical verb ["by relating"] [γενόμενος] from the preceding clause. **Semantically**, the conjunction functions to offer a contrast to the person who forgets, namely, one who listens, and it affects his life.

1:25d ἔσται: This structural marker is a third person singular future middle indicative of εἰμί that means "to be" (BDAG, s.v. "εἰμί" 2a, p. 283). **Syntactically**, it is the main verb of an independent asyndeton clause. "This one" (οὗτος) is a resumptive demonstrative pronoun that resumes the topic introduced with two participles: "the one who looks . . . and continues" (ὁ δὲ **παρακύψας** . . . καὶ παραμείνας; v. 25a). **Semantically**, the future tense may be considered a gnomic future to indicate the likelihood that a *generic* event will take place (W, 571), but due to its rare occurrence, most render it as a predictive future: "he will" (NASB NRSV NIV ESV NET etc.). The comparison between the two different types of hearers is brought into sharp relief by the effective use of the demonstrative pronoun οὗτος in 1:23 and 1:25. The use of this pronoun to emphasize the apodosis after a relative, a condition, or a participle, has been noted as a characteristic of the writer's style elsewhere in 1:25 and 3:2. In 1:23 the conditional clause proposes a forgetful hearer and then adds: "this one" is like a person who forgets what he looks like in the mirror. On the other hand (δέ), 1:25 describes a hearer who obeys and then concludes with the important beatitude: "this one" will be blessed in his deed (ἐν τῇ ποιήσει αὐτοῦ).

> **Structural Nugget:** Is there any significance to the presence of "doers" (ποιηταὶ) in verse 22 and "doing" (ποιήσει) in verse 25? The final word of the inclusio, the noun "doing" (ποιήσει), answers to the cognate noun "doers" (ποιηταί) in 1:22a. It is also possible to see another inclusio at work with the two *macarisms*, or beatitudes: μακάριος initiating a new section in 1:12 and ending one here in 1:25.

1:26a εἰ: This structural marker is a conjunction meaning "if" used in combination with an indefinite pronoun "anyone" (τις) (BDAG, s.v. "εἰ" 7, p. 279). **Syntactically**, this combination "if anyone" introduces the protasis of a dependent conjunctive clause: "*if* anyone thinks he is religious" (εἰ τις δοκεῖ θρησκὸς εἶναι) with an adjoined dependent participial clause "*while* not bridling his tongue but deceiving his heart" (μὴ χαλιναγωγῶν γλῶσσαν αὐτοῦ ἀλλὰ ἀπατῶν καρδίαν αὐτοῦ). The entire εἰ clause with the adjoined participial clause modifies the elliptical "is" [ἐστίν] and is placed immediately above [ἐστίν] to visualize its dependence. **Semantically**, εἰ introduces a first-class conditional clause that assumes the reality of the protasis for the sake of the argument (W, 682–94; Adam, 40), an assumption clarified with the clause's verb, δοκεῖ.

δοκεῖ: This Greek word is a third person singular present active indicative of δοκέω that conveys considering something as probable and may be rendered "think," "believe," "suppose," or "consider" (BDAG, s.v. "δοκέω" 1b, p. 254). **Syntactically**, it is the main verb of the dependent conjunctive clause. The subject is τις, which is part of the protasis of the "εἰ" conditional clause. **Semantically**, the present tense is customary or possibly iterative that points out a pattern of behavior (W, 521–22). In this case, it is the habit of religious people to say things without thinking or without any sort of control. This is a continuation of the theme of self-deception referred to in 1:22. The verb is often used in the NT for a false opinion, as it is here (Matt. 3:9; 6:7; 26:53; Mark 6:49; Luke 8:18; 12:51; 13:2; 19:11; 24:37; John 5:39; Acts 12:9).

> **Lexical Nugget:** How does James describe a "religious" person? The predicate adjective θρησκός is a NT *hapax legomenon* which does not appear in previous Greek literature (BDAG, s.v. "θρησκός," p. 459). The cognate noun θρησκεία appears later in this verse and in 1:27. It is best translated as "religious," and denotes a relationship with the Deity, but there is more to be considered in the cognate noun in 1:27. The term here refers to religious observance—rites and rituals, prayer and fasting, the elements of worship and devotional practice—while the term θρησκεία in 1:27 refers to religion in its more cultic aspects (Acts 26:5), something reinforced by the further use of the term ἄσπιλος ("unstained" or "spotless") in the same verse.

εἶναι: This Greek word is a present active infinitive of εἰμί that may be rendered "to be" or "is" (BDAG, s.v. "εἰμί" 2b, p. 283). **Syntactically**, it is an infinitive that is part of the main verb "he thinks" (δοκεῖ) in this dependent conjunctive clause. The verb δοκέω is often followed by an infinitive (W, 598–99). **Semantically**, it functions as a complementary infinitive and serves as a good example of indirect discourse (W, 603–5). In other words, imagine that the "direct discourse" spoken by this hypothetical person is: "I am religious."

1:26b μὴ χαλιναγωγῶν: This negated (μή) structural marker is a nominative plural masculine present active participle of χαλιναγωγέω that figuratively means "bridle" or "hold in check" (BDAG, s.v. "χαλιναγωγέω," p. 1076). **Syntactically**, it introduces a dependent participial clause that modifies "thinks" (δοκεῖ) and is placed under δοκεῖ to visualize the clause's dependence. **Semantically**, it is probably temporal, conveying the temporal sense of *"while* he is not bridling his tongue" (Blomberg et al., 93), or possibly manner: *"by* not bridling his tongue." The present tense functions as a customary present, denoting regular action or a pattern of behavior (W, 521–22). The colorful word apparently is the first known usage of the verb and occurs again in relation to the tongue in 3:2.

> **Lexical Nugget:** What is significant about the verb "to bridle"? The colorful participle χαλιναγωγῶν apparently is the first known usage of the verb and occurs again in relation to the tongue in 3:2d. The present participle is probably temporal, conveying the sense of "while he is not bridling his tongue." Some, however, see it as concessive, with the sense being "although not bridling his tongue" (Dibelius, 121). A good paraphrastic rendering of the verb might be "a tongue as loose as an unbridled horse."

ἀπατῶν: This Greek word is a nominative plural masculine present active participle of ἀπατάω that may be rendered "deceive" or "mislead oneself" (BDAG, s.v. "ἀπατάω" 1, p. 98). **Syntactically**, it is parallel to *"while* not bridling" (μὴ χαλιναγωγῶν) and so could also be temporal (as above), but its contribution to the dependent conjunctive clause is evident with the adversative "but" (ἀλλά) preceding it and we chose to place it on the same line. **Semantically**, it functions as a concessive participle that conveys something contrary to the main verb: "he thinks he is" (δοκεῖ . . . εἶναι; cf. Adam, 31; W, 634). This concessive function is underscored with the adversative conjunction ἀλλά, "but". The present tense functions as a customary present, denoting regular action or an ongoing state of habitual behavior, namely, self-deception.

> **Lexical Nugget:** The theme of self-deception has been running through the chapter (1:6–7, 14, 16, 22). This stress on the self-deception of the "heart"—the first of five references to this inner seat (3:14a; 4:8d; 5:5c, 8b)—is a reminder that the ethical James is no mere moralist, since he always traces both the behavioral problems and their solutions to that which is within us, not just in a change of our outward actions (cf. 1:15–17; 4:1–3).

1:26c [ἐστίν]: This structural marker is a third singular present active indicative from the verb εἰμί that conveys the idea of being in close connection (with) and may be rendered simply as "is" (BDAG, s.v. "εἰμί" 2a, p. 283). **Syntactically**, [ἐστίν] in brackets underscores it being an ellipsis that serves as the main verb of the independent asyndeton clause. Since the pronoun is more definite, the subject of the verb is "this person's religion" (τούτου μάταιος) and "worthless" (ἡ θρησκεία) is the predicate nominative (cf. W, 40–43). **Semantically**, [ἐστιν] serves as an equative verb that reveals a close connection between religion and worthlessness.

1:27a ἐστίν: This structural marker is a third person singular present active indicative of εἰμί that conveys the idea of being in close connection (with) and may be rendered simply as "is" (BDAG, s.v. "εἰμί" 2a, p. 283). **Syntactically**, it is the main verb of the independent asyndeton clause with "this" (αὕτη) as its subject because it is more definite than "religion" (θρησκεία) and thereby θρησκεία is the predicate nominative (W, 40–43). "Religion" (θρησκεία) is modified with two adjectives "pure and undefiled," which is an example of the Granville Sharp Rule (W, 274). While it may seem awkward in English to find the verb at the end of the sentence, it is not unusual in Greek. **Semantically**, the tense is stative.

> **Semantical Nugget:** How does James utilize sacrificial language? This verse uses a number of terms associated with Jewish purity laws. The term καθαρός describes ceremonial/cultic objects and persons fit to approach the deity (Gen. 7:3; 8:20; Lev. 4:12; 7:19; 11:32; 15:13; see also Luke 11:41; Rom. 14:20; Titus 1:15; Heb. 10:22). The adjective ἀμίαντος has similar associations, since μιαίνω is used in the LXX for making someone or something ritually impure (Lev. 5:3; 11:24; 18:24) and carries the sense of moral or religious purity in the NT (Heb. 7:26; 13:4; 1 Peter 1:4). James does not apply these terms as examples of Jewish ritual purity but subverts these cultic associations by applying the terms to ethical behavior.

1:27b ἐπισκέπτεσθαι: This structural marker is a present middle infinitive of ἐπισκέπτομαι that conveys the idea of going to see a person with helpful intent and may be rendered as "visit" (BDAG, s.v. "ἐπισκέπτομαι" 2, p. 378). **Syntactically**, it is a dependent infinitival clause that modifies "this" (αὕτη), and the entire clause is placed under αὕτη to visualize its dependence. **Semantically**, some commentators view ἐπισκέπτεσθαι as functioning epexegetically modifying "this" (αὕτη; cf. Adam, 32). Others consider it as functioning appositionally by modifying "religion" (θρησκεία; cf. W, 606). Since εἰμί is an equative verb in the independent clause (v. 27a), "to visit" may modify either "this" (αὕτη) or "religion" (θρησκεία). We visualize the infinitive as appositional with a further clarification of "religion" (θρησκεία) and render it as "*namely, to seek.*" The present tense functions as a customary present, denoting regular action, namely, a pattern of behavior that involves helping orphans and widows. James begins his definition of true religion by turning toward the internal concerns in the community of the faithful.

> **Semantical Nugget:** How does James define "orphans" and "widows" in social terms? James singles out as special objects for compassionate care the often-impoverished orphans and widows, an important theme in the Torah (Exod. 22:20–21; 23:9; Lev. 19:9–10; 19:33; Deut. 10:17–19), the prophets (Isa. 3:5, 14–15; Jer. 22:3; Hos. 12:8–9; Amos 2:6–8; 3:2; Micah

3:1–4; Mal. 3:5), the writings (Prov. 19:17; 21:3; 31:9); and in other NT examples (Acts 6:1–6; 1 Tim. 5:3–16). By placing the assistance of the disadvantaged at the heart of true religion, James prepares the reader for his rebuke of those who favor rich over poor in 2:1–7, his insistence on helping the needy in 2:14–16, and his condemnation of the oppressive rich landowners in 5:1–6. To visit orphans and widows may be literally to go and spend time with them (Matt. 25:36, 43), but such "visiting" also is for the purpose of making provision for their needs (cf. Spencer, 105). The word "visit" in both Testaments involves tangible actions as well as presence, especially when God is the "visitor" (Gen. 21:1; 50:24–25; Exod. 3:16; 4:31; Luke 1:68; 7:16).

1:27c τηρεῖν: This structural marker is a present active infinitive of τηρέω that conveys the idea of continuing in a state or condition and may be rendered as "keep," "hold," "reserve," or "preserve" (BDAG, s.v. "τηρέω" 2b, 1002b–c). **Syntactically**, it is a dependent infinitival clause that modifies "this" (αὕτη), and the entire clause is also placed under αὕτη to visualize its dependence and viewed as parallel to the first infinitive "to visit" (ἐπισκέπτεσθαι). **Semantically**, some commentators identify τηρεῖν as functioning epexegetically to "this" (αὕτη; Adam, 32). Yet, we favor an appositional function to "religion" (θρησκεία) and rendered "*namely*, to keep." As it was with the previous infinitive, it is possible to view "to keep" as appositional to either "this" (αὕτη) or "religion" (θρησκεία) because εἰμί is an equative verb in the independent clause (v. 27a). We visualize the infinitive as appositional and as a further clarification of "religion" (θρησκεία). The present tense functions as a customary present, denoting regular or habitual action in remaining unstained by worldly behavior (W, 521–22). The clause anchored by the infinitive τηρεῖν turns outward from the community toward being "*free* from the world" (ἀπὸ τοῦ κόσμου; BDF, §182.3; Irons, 535), namely, free from the dangers found in the ungodly behavior of the external world.

Lexical Nugget: What does "world" (κόσμος) mean in James? In John's letters, κόσμος is often used as a figure of speech for people (1 John 3:1, 13; 4:3–5, 14) and behavior (1 John 2:15–17; 5:4–5, 19). This is James's first use of the term κόσμος, and it appears in binary opposition to God (παρὰ τῷ θεῷ / ἀπὸ τοῦ κόσμου), the way it functions later in the letter (2:5b; 3:6b; 4:4b). It is clear that "to keep oneself unstained from the world" has nothing to do with ritual observance and everything to do with moral attitudes and behavior.

JAMES 2:1–13

Big Greek Idea: In the midst of his challenge to believers about partiality and discrimination against the poor, James reveals that the poor are God's rich heirs in his kingdom and are not to be dishonored, and that if people practice partiality, they not only will disobey the Bible, but also will be condemned and judged.

Structural Overview: In this passage, James expands a theme about hearing and obeying Scripture introduced in 1:22–25 essentially to expose hypocrisy of the rich among followers of Jesus, using a hypothetical example meant to condemn favoritism (cf. Baker et al., 46; Spencer, 115). The inconsistent practice of "partiality" is the focus of this section evident in the repetition of the word "partiality" (vv. 1, 9), a parable (vv. 2–4), and an adapted saying of Jesus (vv. 5–6) that is immediately followed by an application of God's royal law (vv. 8–13; cf. Varner[2], 81). First, James challenges partiality and acts of discrimination by the rich over the poor among those who are expressing faith in Jesus (vv. 1–4). Then James highlights that it is the poor who are God's rich heirs in his kingdom and when they are dishonored and oppressed the name of Jesus is dishonored (vv. 5–7). Finally, James reveals from Scripture God's desired treatment of all people and his subsequent condemnation and judgment of any partiality among those who claim to believe in and to obey the Bible (vv. 8–13).

Outline:[1]
> Partiality and Discrimination among Christians Are Challenged (2:1–4).
> God's Rich Heirs of His Kingdom Are Not to Be Dishonored (2:5–7).
> Partiality Is Divinely Condemned and Judged (2:8–13).

PARTIALITY AND DISCRIMINATION AMONG CHRISTIANS ARE CHALLENGED (JAMES 2:1–4)

CLAUSAL OUTLINE FOR JAMES 2:1–4

2:1a Ἀδελφοί μου **μὴ** ... **ἔχετε** τὴν πίστιν τοῦ κυρίου ἡμῶν Ἰησοῦ Χριστοῦ τῆς δόξης

2:1a My brothers *and sisters you must* not ... **hold** to the faith of our glorious Lord Jesus Christ

2:1b ἐν **προσωπολημψίαις**

2:1b while committing acts of partiality

---

1. Although the verse notation in Baker is incorrect (2:1–13 and not 2:1–17), a suggested sermon entitled "Love and the Unlovely" may be preached in four points: "A Royal Crime" (2:1–7), "A Royal Command" (2:8–9), "Be Obedient" (2:10–11), and "Be Merciful" (2:12–13) (see Baker et al., 55–62). For a description of who may make up the poor today, see A. B. Spencer, *A Commentary on James*, Kregel Exegetical Library (Grand Rapids: Kregel), 157–60.

2:2a **ἐὰν** γὰρ **εἰσέλθῃ** εἰς συναγωγὴν ὑμῶν ἀνὴρ χρυσοδακτύλιος ἐν ἐσθῆτι λαμπρᾷ

2:2a For ***suppose*** a man **enters** into your synagogue wearing a gold ring in fine clothing

|

2:2b **εἰσέλθῃ** δὲ καὶ πτωχὸς ἐν ῥυπαρᾷ ἐσθῆτι,

2:2b and [*suppose*] a poor man in shabby clothing also **enters**,

|

2:3a **ἐπιβλέψητε** δὲ ἐπὶ τὸν φοροῦντα τὴν ἐσθῆτα τὴν λαμπρὰν

2:3a and [*suppose*] **you pay attention** to the one who wears the fine clothing

|

2:3b καὶ **εἴπητε**·σὺ **κάθου** ὧδε καλῶς,

2:3b and [*suppose*] you **say** [*to the rich man*], "You **sit** here in a good place,"

|

2:3c καὶ τῷ πτωχῷ **εἴπητε**·σὺ **στῆθι** ἐκεῖ ἢ **κάθου** ὑπὸ τὸ ὑποπόδιόν μου,

2:3c and [*suppose*] **you say** to the poor man, "You **stand** over there," or "Sit down at my feet,"

|

2:4a οὐ **διεκρίθητε** ἐν ἑαυτοῖς

2:4a *have you* not **made discriminations** among yourselves,

2:4b καὶ **ἐγένεσθε** κριταὶ διαλογισμῶν πονηρῶν;

2:4b and *have you* [*not*] **become** judges with evil thoughts?

SYNTAX EXPLAINED FOR JAMES 2:1–4

2:1 μὴ . . . ἔχετε: This negated (μή) structural marker is a second person plural present active imperative of ἔχω that means "have" and is understood here as to experience or "have" an inner emotion (BDAG, s.v. "ἔχω" 7aβ, p. 421) or to be in some state or condition (BDAG, s.v. "ἔχω" 10b, p. 422). **Syntactically**, this negated verb is the main verb in the independent asyndeton clause. **Semantically**, the present tense functions as a customary present, denoting regular action or an ongoing state about faith (W, 521–22). Yet, the form ἔχετε can be either imperative or indicative. At least one version (NRSV; cf. NLT) views it as indicative and translates it as a question ("do you really believe?"). This would imply a negative response and also involves a bit of rhetorical sarcasm by James. James is certainly not averse to asking his readers confrontational rhetorical questions (2:5, 6, 7, 14, 16, 20, 21, 25), but those questions are not in the same form as here (ἀδελφοί plus a present imperative verb). Consistent with other paragraph openings accompanied by ἀδελφοί, it is best to take the verb here as an imperative (KJV ASV NASB NRSV NIV etc., see 1:2, 16; 3:1a; 4:11a; 5:7a, 12a, 20a; Davids, 105; McCartney, 134–35). The present tense does not imply that James is telling his readers to stop practicing partiality (Adam, 33). While the present imperative with μή *could* refer to the cessation of an activity in progress, it can also convey a "general precept." This usage "makes no comment about whether the action is going on or not" (W, 724–25). A tendential sense may express the idea well: "Do not *try* to combine faith in Christ with (whatever the sin)."

ἐν προσωπολημψίαις: "While committing acts of partiality" is a phrase and not a clause. **Syntactically**, the phrase is functioning adverbially modifying the main verb ἔχετε ("hold") of the independent clause. Although the phrase is not a clause it is rather important due to its semantical emphasis. **Semantically**, the preposition ἐν is "a marker of a time period" and thereby has a *temporal force* (BDAG, s.v. "ἐν" 10, p. 329): "while showing partiality" (Irons, 535) or as we have rendered it "while committing acts of partiality." The object of the preposition is plural in form and probably refers to "acts of partiality." Hence a permissible translation is: "while committing acts of partiality" in contrast to most translations that consider ἐν as though a preposition of sphere "in . . . our glorious Lord . . ." (NASB NRSV NIV NET NLT; cf. ESV). The noun "partiality" (προσωπολημψίαις) appears here for the first time in Greek literature (like δίψυχος in 1:8) and appears also in Romans 2:11; Ephesians 6:9; and Colossians 3:25. Along with the cognate verb προσωπολημπτέω (only in James 2:9) and the personal noun προσωπολήμπτης (only in Acts 10:34), this word group represents the expression πρόσωπον λαμβάνειν in the LXX, which in turn is an attempt to render the Hebrew "to show favor" (נָשָׂא פָּנִים; lit. "to raise the face," see Lev. 19:15; Mal. 1:8). This conveys the literal idea of "receiving" or "regarding" the "face" of someone when making a judgment. The broader semantic theme of showing partiality is often mentioned in judicial contexts (see LXX: Lev. 19:15: οὐ λήμψῃ πρόσωπον; cf. Adam, 33; Davids, 107–8). James's use of the noun is either an allusion to Leviticus 19:15 or at least a prominent NT echo of that verse.

Grammatical Nugget: Is τὴν πίστιν τοῦ κυρίου ἡμῶν Ἰησοῦ Χριστοῦ an objective genitive ("faith *in* Christ") or subjective genitive ("the faith *of* Christ")? Recent English translations usually view it as an objective genitive expressed by "faith *in* our Lord . . ." Older English versions render it as "*the* faith *of* our Lord . . ." Later in the chapter, James does employ the noun to refer to an individual's faith, but the specific object of that faith is not mentioned in those verses (2:14, 17, 18, 20, 22, 24, 26). The article τήν before πίστιν should cause us to return to the older versions for the translation/interpretation of Ἰησοῦ Χριστοῦ as a subjective genitive: "the faith *of* . . . Jesus Christ." Thus, the translation of the arthrous head noun τὴν πίστιν combined with the imperative ἔχετε would be: "My brothers and sisters do not *hold to the faith of our glorious Lord Jesus Christ*, while showing acts of partiality." "The faith of Jesus" is *the* faith that is displayed by the Jesus *logion* in 2:5b and also by the "royal law" of 2:8a, which law was reaffirmed by Jesus in Matthew 22:39. It is *the faith that comes from Jesus* that would never show such partiality exhibited by the behavior that is about to be exemplified in 2:2–4. Therefore, the following context also supports the presence of a subjective genitive in 2:1.

2:2a ἐὰν γάρ: In this twofold structural marker, ἐάν is a conjunction meaning "if " (NET ESV NASB NRSV KJV) or "suppose" (NIV NLT; cf. BDAG, s.v. "ἐάν" 1cγ, p. 268). The second word, γάρ, is a conjunction in the post-positive position meaning "for" or "you see" (BDAG, s.v. "γάρ" 2, p. 189). **Syntactically**, ἐάν and γάρ introduce a dependent conjunctive clause. The entire dependent clause, "for if . . . he enters" or "for suppose . . . he enters" (ἐὰν ... εἰσέλθῃ), functions adverbially. It modifies the verb "made discriminations" (διεκρίθητε). The conjunctions ἐάν and γάρ introduce several contrasting examples to communicate a rather significant point about prejudice. **Semantically**, ἐάν is a third-class conditional clause that introduces an elaborate protasis (2:2–3) of which 2:4 is its corresponding apodosis (W, 696–99). We should read all five subjunctive clauses as part of one large protasis rather than break them up into separate sentences (cf. Irons, 535). The γάρ introduces an illustration (Zerwick et. al., 694). Together, ἐὰν γάρ raises a hypothetical situation. James is not necessarily describing a scene that he has witnessed or heard that has taken place in his readers' assemblies. The scene that is portrayed in their "synagogue" *may* have taken place, but it is not necessarily a scene that actually *has* taken place.

εἰσέλθῃ: This Greek word is a third person singular aorist active subjunctive of εἰσέρχομαι that means "enter" or more specifically "move into a structural area" like a synagogue (BDAG, s.v. "εἰσέρχομαι" 1aγ, p. 294). The verb is in the subjunctive because ἐάν takes its verb in the subjunctive (W, 469–70). **Syntactically**, it is the main verb of the dependent conjunctive clause and is the first part of the protasis in this third-class ἐάν conditional sentence (W, 469–71; Irons, 535). **Semantically**, the aorist tense is a constative aorist and views the action of a rich man entering an assembly as a whole (W, 557–58; Adam, 35).

Lexical Nugget: What is meant by συναγωγὴν ὑμῶν? In its 228 LXX occurrences the noun never (in the canonical books) has the meaning that it later acquires clearly by NT times. It was during the time between the testaments that συνάγωγη began to acquire the technical meaning of a building set apart for worship and the reading of the Torah, a "synagogue." This συνάγωγη has congregants who hold to the faith of Jesus the Messiah

(2:1). This building is not synonymous with the "church" (ἐκκλησία) in 5:14, which refers to the body of people. The context is Jewish, and the use of the word elsewhere in the NT affirms that it is a worship center for Jewish believers. This is the only place in the NT where this specific term is used for gatherings of Jesus-followers, although a similar cognate noun (ἐπισυναγωγή) is used in a parallel function in Hebrews 10:25 (cf. Bateman et al.[2], 282). This illustrates the Jewish-Christian nature of the letter and may also exemplify continuity between Torah-based communities and Jesus-based communities in these early days of the movement. When in 5:14 we read of the ministry of the elders from the "assembly" (τοὺς πρεσβυτέρους τῆς ἐκκλησίας), the word is consistent with its usage elsewhere in the NT—namely, the ἐκκλησία is the *gathering* of believers, while the term συνάγωγη is used for their gathering *place*.

2:2b δέ: This structural marker is a conjunction meaning "and" (BDAG, s.v. "δέ" 1, p. 213). **Syntactically**, it introduces a dependent conjunctive clause and appears in a post-positive position. **Semantically**, it is a marker connecting a series of closely related information; more specifically, James provides additional information about prejudice, which is evident in the rest of the clause.

καί: The Greek word καί is a conjunction meaning "also" and is not intended to coordinate or connect clauses (BDAG, s.v. "καί" 2a, p. 44). **Syntactically**, it is part of the dependent conjunctive clause, but it *does not* introduce an independent conjunctive clause. **Semantically**, it is adjunctive: "also" (KJV ESV NIV NASB; W, 671). Yet, some translations do not translate it (NET NLT). Nevertheless, it underscores the parallel between the rich and the poor who may enter a synagogue.

εἰσέλθη: This Greek word is a third person singular aorist active subjunctive of εἰσέρχομαι that means "enter" or more specifically "move into a structural area" like a synagogue (BDAG, s.v. "εἰσέρχομαι" 1aγ, p. 294). The verb is in the subjunctive because ἐάν takes its verb in the subjunctive (W, 469–70). **Syntactically**, it is the main verb in this dependent conjunctive clause and serves as the second verb of the protasis in the ἐάν third-class conditional sentence. Even though ἐάν is not repeated, the subjunctive mood indicates that this second verb is also part of the third-class ἐάν conditional protasis (cf. Adam, 36; Irons, 535). **Semantically**, the aorist tense is constative and views the action of a poor man entering an assembly as a whole (W, 557–58).

2:3a δέ: This structural marker is a conjunction meaning "and" (BDAG, s.v. "δέ" 1, p. 213). **Syntactically**, it introduces a dependent conjunctive clause and appears in a post-positive position. **Semantically**, it is a marker connecting closely related information expressed in the verb.

ἐπιβλέψητε: This Greek word is a second person plural aorist subjunctive of ἐπιβλέπω that means to "pay special attention" (NASB NIV) or "show special respect" with an implication of flattery or reverence (BDAG, s.v. "ἐπιβλέπω" 2, p. 368). The verb is in the subjunctive because ἐάν takes its verb in the subjunctive (W, 469–70; Zerwick et al., 694). **Syntactically**, it is the main verb in this dependent conjunctive clause and serves as the third subjunctive verb that continues the elaborate protasis (2:2–3) of which 2:4 is its corresponding apodosis with a shift to the second person. Even though ἐάν is not repeated, the subjunctive mood indicates that this third verb is also part of the third-class ἐάν conditional protasis (cf. Adam, 36; Irons, 535). **Semantically**, the aorist tense is a constative aorist that describes an event about a person looking favorably on the rich as a whole (W, 557–58). The verb is used in the Psalms for looking on someone favorably (LXX: Pss. 12:4; 24:16; 32:13; 68:17; 73:20). This is the sense in its only other NT uses (Luke 1:48; 9:38). Here the favorable look is based solely on the outward appearance of the rich man.

τὸν φοροῦντα: This articular (τόν) Greek word is an accusative neuter singular present active participle of φορέω that means "*bear* (in contrast to φέρω) *constantly/regularly,* hence *wear* clothing" (BDAG, s.v. "φορέω" 1, p. 1064). **Syntactically**, it is a substantival participle in a dependent clause serving (with the article τόν) as the object of the preposition ἐπί. **Semantically**, the present tense functions as a customary present, denoting regular action or an ongoing state (W, 521–22). Here the extended definition in "is finely dressed" (NET) or "wears fine clothing" (ESV NIV NASB NRSV) portrays the participle as describing the habitually worn "bright clothing" (τὴν ἐσθῆτα τὴν λαμπρὰν) as a figure of speech portraying a rich person.

²:³ᵇ καί: This structural marker is a conjunction meaning "and" (BDAG, s.v. "καί" 1bα, p. 494). **Syntactically**, it introduces a dependent conjunctive clause. **Semantically**, it is a coordinating connective: "and" (NET ESV NASB NRSV etc.). James's conjunctive clauses provide additional information about prejudice, which is evident in the rest of the clause.

εἴπητε: This Greek word is a second person plural aorist active subjunctive of λέγω that means "say" or "express oneself orally" (BDAG, s.v. "λέγω" 1, p. 588). The verb is in the subjunctive because the earlier ἐάν takes its verb in the subjunctive (W, 469–70). **Syntactically**, it is the main verb in this dependent conjunctive clause and serves as the fourth subjunctive verb in this complex protasis of a third-class ἐάν conditional sentence that began in verse 2. Even though ἐάν is not repeated, the subjunctive mood indicates that this fourth verb is also part of the third-class ἐάν conditional protasis (cf. Adam, 37; Irons, 535). **Semantically**, the aorist tense is a constative aorist that describes an event as a whole (W, 557–58). The verb introduces the hypothetical direct speech of the imaginary person whose behavior is being condemned for showing favoritism or prejudice.

κάθου: This verb is the second person singular present middle imperative of κάθημαι that means "sit" or "take a seated position" (BDAG, s.v. "κάθημαι" 3, p. 491; cf. BDF, §100). **Syntactically**, it is the main verb in this dependent conjunctive clause and serves as the first command in an embedded quotation in this fourth clause of the protasis in this third-class ἐάν conditional sentence that began in verse 2. **Semantically**, the present tense functions as a customary present, denoting regular action or an ongoing state (W, 521–22). The rich man, whom we might refer to as Mr. "Goldfinger," is presented as one who is regularly ushered to sit "here in a good place" (ὧδε καλῶς). The presence of καλῶς gives the impression that the aorist imperative κάθου is a command of polite address extended to a superior (W, 487–88; Adam, 37). The main verbs of 2:3 are actually plural in form, following the plurality of the opening address in 2:1. In the illustration, the singular verbs refer to one person who would show favoritism and thereby direct people to their seats in accord with their social status.

> **Text-Critical Nugget:** Should the text read "stand or sit there" (στῆθι ἢ κάθου ἐκεῖ) or "stand there or sit" (στῆθι ἐκεῖ ἢ κάθου) in James 2:3? The first variant adjusts the text so that there are only two places mentioned in the verse: "here" (with reference to the position of the speaker) and "there" (under the footstool); and this reading is accepted by the NA[28]. The NA[27] reading (ἐκεῖ ἢ κάθου), however, has good testimony from Codices A and Ψ and is adopted by the *Tyndale House GNT* (see also Metzger[1], 609; Metzger[2], 680).

2:3c καί: This structural marker is a conjunction meaning "and" (BDAG, s.v. "καί" 1bα, p. 494). **Syntactically**, it introduces a dependent conjunctive clause. **Semantically**, it is a coordinating connective: "and" (NET NASB NRSV etc.). James's conjunctive clauses provide additional information about prejudice, which is evident in the rest of the clause.

εἴπητε: This Greek word is a second person plural aorist active subjunctive of λέγω that means "say" or "express oneself orally" (BDAG, s.v. "λέγω" 1, p. 588). This second appearance of the verb is also in the subjunctive because ἐάν takes its verb in the subjunctive (W, 469–70). **Syntactically**, it is the main verb in this dependent conjunctive clause and serves as the fifth subjunctive verb in this complex protasis of a third-class ἐάν conditional sentence that began in verse 2 (cf. Adam, 37; Irons, 535). Even though ἐάν is not repeated, the subjunctive mood serves as a signpost that this fifth verb is also part of the third-class ἐάν conditional protasis. **Semantically**, the aorist tense is a constative aorist that describes an event as a whole (W, 557–58). This second appearance of the verb also introduces the hypothetical direct speech of the imaginary person whose behavior is being condemned for showing favoritism or prejudice.

στῆθι: This Greek word is a second person singular aorist active imperative of ἵστημι that means here "be in a stationary position" or "stand still" (BDAG, s.v. "ἵστημι" 1, p. 482). **Syntactically**, it is the first verb of an embedded quotation in the fifth clause of the protasis of a third-class ἐάν conditional sentence that began in verse 2. **Semantically**, the aorist tense is a constative aorist that views the action as a whole (W, 557–58). The aorist imperative without the presence of καλῶς gives the impression that the aorist imperative στῆθι is merely a command (W, 485–86; Adam, 37) to the poor person in contrast with the command in the previous clause directed to the rich person.

κάθου: This Greek word is a second singular present middle imperative of κάθημαι that means "sit" or "take a seated position" of honor (BDAG, s.v. "κάθημαι" 3, p. 491; cf. BDF, §100). **Syntactically**, it is the second verb of an embedded quotation in the fifth clause of the protasis of a third-class ἐάν conditional sentence that began in verse 2. **Semantically**, the present tense functions as a customary present, denoting regular action (W, 521–22). The poor man is presented as one who is regularly directed to sit "on the floor" (NET NLT; cf. NIV), "at my feet" (NRSV ESV; cf. NIV) or "by my footstool" (KJV ASV NASB).

> **Grammatical Nugget:** What is the significance of the conditional sentence begun in this verse? James 2:2–3 composes an elaborate protasis of a conditional clause, of which 2:4 is its corresponding apodosis. The intensity of the five subjunctive verbs is increased by two embedded clause-quotations in 2:3 conveying by direct discourse the directions to the rich person and to the poor person about their respective seating assignments. The subjunctive clauses are part of one large protasis rather than broken up into separate sentences. This is a third-class conditional sentence, where the initial condition simply projects some action or event for hypothetical consideration (W, 469–71). James is again raising a hypothetical situation and is not necessarily describing a scene that he has witnessed or that he has heard to have taken place in believers assemblies. The scene that is portrayed in their "synagogue" *may* have taken place, but it is not necessarily a scene that actually *has* taken place.

2:4a οὐ διεκρίθητε: This negated (οὐ) structural marker is a second person plural aorist passive indicative of διακρίνω that means "make a distinction" or "differentiate" (BDAG, s.v. "διακρίνω" 6, p. 231). **Syntactically**, it is the main verb of an independent asyndeton clause in verse 4. It is the first verb in the apodosis of the ἐάν conditional sentence that began in verse 2. **Semantically**, the indicative mood is an interrogative indicative with the negative particle οὐ that expects a positive answer (W, 449–50; Adam, 38; Zerwick et al., 694): *"have you not made distinctions* among yourselves" (οὐ διεκρίθητε ἐν ἑαυ- τοῖς; cf. NASB NRSV ESV NET; cf. ASV) or perhaps *"have you not discrimi- nated* among yourselves" (NIV; cf. KJV). The answer is "yes." The aorist tense is a constative aorist and views the action as a whole (W, 557–58; cf. Zerwick, §257). The divisiveness displayed here reflects an overall divided attitude to- ward the rich and the poor, instead of a whole and "perfect" attitude that treats each in one consistent way. This is the same verb used in 1:6 of doubting in prayer (διακρινόμενος), and the divisiveness conveyed is characteristic of the unstable "double-souled man" (1:8).

> **Grammatical Nugget:** What is the significance of the question οὐ διεκρίθη- τε? The apodosis of the conditional clause is actually a question that (with the negative particle οὐ) expects a positive answer. The question is asked: "Have you not made distinctions among yourselves . . . ?" The answer is expected: "Yes, we have." On a literal level, the passive verb διεκρίθητε expresses an internal dividedness, in the sense of trying to live by two standards at once and thus being "divided in opinion" (Matt. 21:21; Mark 11:23; Acts 10:20; Rom. 4:20; 14:23). At the same time, the active sense of the verb ("to make distinctions/discriminate") is conveyed in Matthew 16:3; Acts 11:12; 15:9.

2:4b καί: This structural marker is a conjunction meaning "and" (BDAG, s.v. "καί" 1bα, p. 494). **Syntactically**, it introduces an independent conjunctive clause. **Semantically**, it is a coordinating connective: "and" (NET ESV NASB NRSV etc.). James's conjunctive clauses provide additional information about preju- dice, which is evident in the following clause.

ἐγένεσθε: This Greek word is a second person plural aorist middle indicative of γίνομαι meaning "become" (BDAG, s.v. "γίνομαι" 7, p. 199). **Syntacti- cally**, it is the main verb of this independent conjunctive clause and serves as the second verb in the apodosis of the ἐάν conditional sentence that began in verse 2. **Semantically**, the indicative mood here is an interrogative indica- tive that expects a positive answer (W, 449–50): and *have you become* judges with evil thoughts (καὶ ἐγένεσθε κριταὶ διαλογισμῶν πονηρῶν). The aorist tense is a constative aorist that views the action as a whole (W, 557–58). By asking this question, James declares that that they had become judges with evil thoughts (κριταὶ διαλογισμῶν πονηρῶν).[2] The noun κριταί is a predi- cate nominative completing the equative verb (W, 40–43; Adam, 39).

---

2.   James uses a number of rhetorical questions in chapter 2. For a chart identifying the "Sequence of Questions and Statements in James 2," see Spencer, *A Commentary on James*, 122.

God's Rich Heirs of His Kingdom Are
Not to Be Dishonored (James 2:5–7)

Clausal Outline for James 2:5–7

2:5a **Ἀκούσατε**, ἀδελφοί μου ἀγαπητοί·
2:5a **Listen**, my beloved brothers *and sisters*,

2:5b <u>οὐχ</u> ὁ θεὸς **ἐξελέξατο** τοὺς πτωχοὺς τῷ κόσμῳ πλουσίους ἐν πίστει καὶ κληρονόμους τῆς βασιλείας
2:5b **has** <u>not</u> God **chosen** those considered poor *in* the world to be rich *with respect to* faith and heirs of the kingdom

2:5c ἧς **ἐπηγγείλατο** τοῖς **ἀγαπῶσιν** αὐτόν;
2:5c that **he promised** to **those who love** him?

2:6a ὑμεῖς <u>δὲ</u> **ἠτιμάσατε** τὸν πτωχόν.
2:6a <u>But</u> you **have dishonored** the poor person.

2:6b <u>οὐχ</u> οἱ πλούσιοι **καταδυναστεύουσιν** ὑμῶν
2:6b **Do** <u>not</u> the rich **oppress** you,

2:6c <u>καὶ</u> αὐτοὶ **ἕλκουσιν** ὑμᾶς εἰς κριτήρια;
2:6c <u>and</u> **do they** [*not*] **drag** you into courts?

2:7a <u>οὐκ</u> αὐτοὶ **βλασφημοῦσιν** τὸ καλὸν ὄνομα
2:7a **Do they** <u>not</u> **blaspheme** that honorable name

2:7b τὸ **ἐπικληθὲν** ἐφ᾽ ὑμᾶς;
2:7b which **has been pronounced** over you?

Syntax Explained for James 2:5–7

2:5a Ἀκούσατε: This structural marker is a second person plural aorist active imperative from ἀκούω that means "hear" or in the imperative "listen" or "pay attention to by listening" (BDAG, s.v. "ἀκούω" 4, p. 38). It is important to remember that this letter would have been read to a group of people made up of both men and women. **Syntactically**, it is the main verb in this independent asyndeton clause. **Semantically**, the imperative is a polite request of a leader in the form of a plea (W, 485–86). In the LXX the imperative of ἀκούω is used to mark the importance of what follows in the law (Deut. 6:3–4; 9:1), in the prophets (Isa. 1:10; Amos 3:1; Mic. 1:2), and in the writings (Ps. 119:149; Prov.

1:8). It is also used in Matthew 13:18; Mark 7:14; Luke 18:6; and Acts 22:1 to direct attention to a following principle of fundamental importance. This is the last of three times that James will accompany one of these imperatives with ἀγαπητοί (see 1:16, 19a). The aorist tense here and the following aorists are constative and view the action as a whole (W, 557–58). The common characteristic in each of these occurrences is that a principle is stressed that the readers know but are neglecting to do or to recognize.

2:5b οὐχ . . . ἐξελέξατο: This negated (οὐχ) structural marker is a third person singular aorist middle indicative of ἐκλέγομαι meaning "choose" (BDAG, s.v. "ἐκλέγομαι" 2cγ, p. 305). **Syntactically**, it is the main verb in this independent asyndeton clause with ὁ θεός as its subject and τοὺς πτωχούς as its direct object. **Semantically**, the indicative mood, with the negative particle οὐχ, expects a positive answer (W, 449–50; Adam, 39): "*has not* God *chosen* those considered poor *in* the world . . ." (οὐχ ὁ θεὸς ἐξελέξατο τοὺς πτωχοὺς τῷ κόσμῳ . . .). The answer is "yes." Thus, James's rhetorical point is that God has chosen the poor. The aorist tense is constative and views the action as a whole (W, 557–58) concerning God choosing.

> **Grammatical Nugget:** What is the significance of the particles οὐχ and οὐκ here and in verses 6–7? These clauses contain three rhetorical questions, which also provide a link with the rhetorical questions asked at the end of 2:4. After the hypothetical scene in 2:2–3, James makes his point by means of these questions, each of which is conveyed with the negative particle οὐχ/οὐκ that indicates that James expects a positive answer (Porter, 278–79). The rhetorical effect of these questions is that of conveying three declarative statements, which James expects his readers to then affirm. Those question-declarations are (1) that God *has* chosen those that are poor by the world's standards to become rich heirs in his kingdom, 2:5; (2) that the rich usually dishonor the poor and often oppress them, 2:6; and (3) that by doing so, ironically the rich dishonor the name that is honored by the poor, 2:7.

2:5c ἧς: This Greek structural marker is a relative pronoun meaning "that" (BDAG, s.v. "ὅς" 1a, p. 725). **Syntactically**, it introduces a dependent relative clause. As a general rule, the relative pronoun agrees in gender and number with the noun or pronoun to which it refers (i.e., its antecedent; W, 336–39). In this case, ἧς is a feminine genitive that refers back to its antecedent βασιλείας ("kingdom"; Adam, 40). The entire clause is placed under the noun it modifies "of the kingdom" (τῆς βασιλείας) to visualize its dependence.

ἐπηγγείλατο: This Greek word is a third person singular aorist middle indicative of ἐπαγγέλλομαι that means "promise," "offer," or "declare to do something" (BDAG, s.v. "ἐπαγγέλλομαι" 1b, p. 356). **Syntactically**, it is the main verb in this dependent relative clause with ἧς serving as the subject of the clause. **Semantically**, the aorist tense is a constative aorist that views the action as a whole (W, 557–58). The "poor who are rich in faith" are inheritors of a kingdom not received by the normal channels of inheritance. The kingdom here is thought of as still in the future.

τοῖς ἀγαπῶσιν: This articular (τοῖς) Greek word is a dative plural masculine present active participle of ἀγαπάω that conceptually speaks of a warm regard for and interest in God and may be rendered as "cherish," "have affection for," or "love" (BDAG, s.v. "ἀγαπάω" 1aβ, p. 5). **Syntactically**, τοῖς ἀγαπῶσιν is a substantival participle that is the indirect object of the verb ἐπηγγείλατο. **Semantically**, the present tense functions as a customary present, denoting a pattern of behavior (W, 521–22). Those who make it a practice to exhibit love toward God are recipients of God's promise. Thus, the "rich poor" are heirs through a promise given to those who love him. Later in this section, that "royal law" will be expressed in terms of Leviticus 19:18 and its use by Jesus in Matthew 22:37–39. The regular practice of loving one's neighbor is stressed in Leviticus and Matthew, but here James underscores a pattern of love directed to God as commanded in Deuteronomy 6:5. Already James has mentioned through the very same words in 1:12 that God promised the crown of life "to those who love him" (ἐπηγγείλατο τοῖς ἀγαπῶσιν αὐτόν). Thus, the twofold command of love to God and love to mankind is evident in James's message.

2:6a δέ: This Greek structural marker is a conjunction meaning "but" (BDAG, s.v. "δέ" 5a, p. 213). **Syntactically**, it introduces an independent conjunctive clause and appears in a post-positive position. **Semantically**, it is a conjunction that serves as a marker of contrast: "but" (NET ESV NIV NASB NRSV NLT; etc.). It indicates a development from 2:5 that stresses the teaching of Jesus. More specifically, it provides contrastive information about God's perspective for the poor and those who are prejudiced against "the poor" (τὸν πτωχόν; collective sg., BDF, §139).

ἠτιμάσατε: This Greek word is a second person plural aorist active indicative of ἀτιμάζω that conveys the idea of depriving someone of honor or respect and is often rendered "dishonor" or "insult" (BDAG, s.v. "ἀτιμάζω,"148d; cf. Zerwick et al., 694). **Syntactically**, it is the main verb of this independent conjunctive clause with τὸν πτωχόν as the direct object. **Semantically**, the aorist tense is a constative aorist that views the action as a whole (W, 557–58) concerning the wealthy's disrespect or dishonoring of the poor: "you have dishonored" (ASV NASB NRSV ESV NET CNT) or "you have insulted" (NIV). The fronting of the pronoun ὑμεῖς further intensifies the charge. The two groups of the rich and the poor figure prominently at other locations in his book (1:9–11; 5:1–6) as well as here in 2:1–7.

> **Semantical Nugget:** What is the ancient significance of "dishonoring" the poor? It is widely acknowledged that *honor* and *shame* are two of the most pivotal values of the Mediterranean world (cf. D. DeSilva, *Honor, Patronage, Kinship, & Purity*). These values are illustrated in the synagogue context with the poor man dishonored while the rich man is honored. The divine standard, however, is communicated both in the Jesus *logion* of 2:5 and later in the "royal law" of 2:8. These statements actually subvert the so-called accepted societal norms and reveal the countercultural nature of James's ethical values for the community of those who follow Jesus as Messiah.

2:6b οὐχ . . . καταδυναστεύουσιν: This negated (οὐχ) structural marker is the third person plural present active indicative of καταδυναστεύω typically rendered as "oppress," "exploit," or "dominate" (BDAG, s.v. "καταδυναστεύω," p. 516). **Syntactically**, it is the main verb in this independent asyndeton clause with ὑμῶν as its direct object. The pronoun appears in the genitive because this verb takes the genitive direct object (W, 171–73; Adam, 40; Irons, 536; BDAG, "σύ" 1aγ, p. 950). **Semantically**, the indicative mood here, with the negative particle οὐχ, expects a positive answer (W, 449–50): "*Do not* the rich *oppress* you" (οὐχ οἱ πλούσιοι καταδυναστεύουσιν ὑμῶν). The answer is "yes." Thus, James's rhetorical point is that the rich (οἱ πλούσιοι; collective pl.) oppress the poor. The present tense functions as an iterative present since the rich practice time and again many acts of oppression (W, 520–21). James employs two vivid verbs (with ἕλκουσιν) to describe how the rich dishonor the poor in this context. The verb καταδυναστεύω conveys the sense of oppression or exploitation by abuse of power and is used frequently in the LXX for the oppression of the poor by the rich and powerful (Ezek. 18:12, 22:29; Amos 4:1; Zech. 7:10; cf. Davids, 112). The powerful man condemned in Leviticus 19:15 is in the LXX referred to by the cognate noun δυνάστης.

2:6c καί: This structural marker is a conjunction meaning "and" (BDAG, s.v. "καί" 1b, p. 494). **Syntactically**, it introduces an independent conjunctive clause: "and" (NET ESV NASB NRSV etc.). **Semantically**, it is a coordinating conjunction: "and" (NET ESV NASB etc.) that underscores another form of mistreatment of the poor.

ἕλκουσιν: This Greek word is a third person plural present active indicative of ἕλκω that means "draw" or "drag" (ESV NASB NASV NLT; cf. NET NIV) or "compel an unwilling person" (BDAG, s.v. "ἕλκω" 1, p. 318). **Syntactically**, it is the main verb of this independent conjunctive clause with πλούσιοι as its subject. The direct object is an expected accusative form of ὑμᾶς (W, 179–81).

Semantically, the present tense functions as an iterative present that describes the rich who time and again drag the poor to court (W, 520–21). This verb appears in Acts for those who often threatened to bring a form of their own perverted legal action against believers (Acts 4:1; 16:19; 21:30).

> **Semantical Nugget:** How were believers "dragged into court"? The verb ἕλκω is used for those who attempted "to drag" Paul away in Acts 16:19 and 21:30 (BDAG, s.v. "ἕλκω," p. 318). Wealthy Sadducees had also done this with Peter and John (Acts 4:1). Paul had once dragged (σύρω) men and women before the Sanhedrin (Acts 8:3; 22:4) and had even tried to make them blaspheme (Acts 26:11). This judgment seat is also called a κρινήσιν in Exodus 21:6; Daniel 7:9; 1 Corinthians 6:2, 4. Paul suffered what he had earlier inflicted on others (Acts 13:50). Jesus had indeed foretold that this fate would befall his disciples before the courts of Jews and Gentiles (Matt. 10:17–23). The appearance here of the noun κριτήρια actually supports that "legal proceedings" were taking place earlier in 1:2–4.

2:7a οὐκ … βλασφημοῦσιν: This negated (οὐκ) structural marker is a third person plural present active indicative of βλασφημέω that may be rendered "slander," "revile," or "defame" (BDAG, s.v. "βλασφημέω" bε, p. 178). **Syntactically**, it is the main verb of this independent asyndeton clause with "that honorable name" (τὸ καλὸν ὄνομα) as its direct object. **Semantically**, the indicative mood here, with the negative particle οὐκ, expects a positive answer (W, 449–50): "*Do they not blaspheme* that honorable name" (*οὐκ αὐτοὶ βλασφημοῦσιν* τὸ καλὸν ὄνομα). The answer is "yes." Thus, James's rhetorical point is that the rich blaspheme God's name. The present tense functions as an iterative present that describes the rich who time and again blaspheme (W, 520–21). Blasphemy in general is injurious speech, but here in its religious context, it is speaking disrespectfully of God or sacred things (Acts 13:45; 18:6; 26:11; 1 Cor. 12:3; 1 Tim. 1:13).

2:7b τὸ ἐπικληθέν: This articular (τό) Greek word is an accusative neuter singular aorist passive participle of ἐπικαλέω, that means "call," "give a surname," or "address someone by a special term" (BDAG, s.v. "ἐπικαλέω" 2, p. 373). **Syntactically**, τὸ ἐπικληθέν is a substantival participle that modifies τὸ καλὸν ὄνομα as part of the direct object of βλασφημοῦσιν. **Semantically**, the aorist participle functions as a constative aorist that views the action of God's name having been pronounced upon believers as a whole (W, 557–58). James's use of the aorist participle suggests that he is deliberately alluding to the time when the name was received. The passive reflects something belonging to God and reminiscing "to call a name upon someone" in the LXX that indicates possession, often by God (Amos 9:12; Deut. 28:10; 2 Chron. 7:14; Isa. 43:7; Jer. 14:9; cf. Irons, 536).

Semantical Nugget: What was the "honorable name" called over believers? The "name" mentioned may have been the title "Christian" since it had recently been used of the believers in Antioch (Acts 11:26) and communicated the idea of a "Messianist" (see Acts 26:28). James, however, could refer to the naming of believers at their baptism, indicating their new owner by taking on his "name" (Davids, 114). Whatever its original context, "Christian" soon came to be a name that was worn by believers with honor (1 Peter 4:16; Did. 12:4). At the "Jerusalem Council," James at one point quoted the prophecy in Amos 9:12 where the LXX uses the same language to describe Yahweh's naming of Gentiles as their new owner, when they are brought into the eschatological kingdom (Acts 15:17—ἐφ᾽ οὓς ἐπικέκληται τὸ ὄνομά μου; "upon whom my name is called").

PARTIALITY IS DIVINELY CONDEMNED AND JUDGED (JAMES 2:8–13)

CLAUSAL OUTLINE FOR JAMES 2:8–13

2:8a Εἰ μέντοι νόμον **τελεῖτε** βασιλικὸν κατὰ τὴν γραφήν·
2:8a If **you** really **are obeying** the royal law according to the Scripture,

2:8b **ἀγαπήσεις** τὸν πλησίον σου ὡς σεαυτόν,
2:8b **_You shall love_** your neighbor as yourself

2:8c καλῶς **ποιεῖτε**·
2:8c **you are doing** well;

2:9a εἰ δὲ **προσωπολημπτεῖτε**,
2:9a but if **you are showing partiality**,

2:9b ἁμαρτίαν **ἐργάζεσθε**
2:9b **you are committing** sin

2:9c **ἐλεγχόμενοι** ὑπὸ τοῦ νόμου ὡς παραβάται.
2:9c _and as a result_ **convicted** by the law as transgressors.

2:10a (ὅστις γὰρ ὅλον τὸν νόμον **τηρήσῃ**) . . . **γέγονεν** πάντων ἔνοχος.
2:10a (For whoever **observes** the whole law) . . . **is** accountable for all of it.

2:10b **πταίσῃ** δὲ ἐν ἑνί,
2:10b but he **stumbles** in one point,

2:11a (ὁ γὰρ **εἰπών**, Μὴ μοιχεύσῃς), **εἶπεν** καί, Μὴ φονεύσῃς·
2:11a (**For he who said**, "Do not **commit adultery**"), **said** also "**Do** not **murder**."

2:11b εἰ δὲ οὐ **μοιχεύεις**,
2:11b Now if you **do** not *commit* **adultery**

|

        2:11c **φονεύεις** δέ,
        2:11c yet **you commit murder**,

|

2:11d **γέγονας** παραβάτης νόμου.
2:11d **you have become** a transgressor of the law.

2:12a οὕτως **λαλεῖτε**
2:12a So **speak**

2:12b καὶ οὕτως **ποιεῖτε**
2:12b and so **act**

|

        2:12c ὡς διὰ νόμου ἐλευθερίας **μέλλοντες κρίνεσθαι**.
        2:12c as those **who are to be judged** under the law of liberty.

2:13a ἡ γὰρ κρίσις [**ἐστιν**] ἀνέλεος τῷ μὴ ποιήσαντι ἔλεος·
2:13a For judgment [**is**] merciless to one who has shown no mercy.

2:13b **κατακαυχᾶται** ἔλεος κρίσεως.
2:13b Mercy **triumphs** over judgment.

SYNTAX EXPLAINED FOR JAMES 2:8–13

2:8a εἰ: This structural marker is a conjunction meaning "if" (BDAG, s.v. "εἰ" 1aα, p. 277). **Syntactically**, it introduces a dependent conjunctive clause: "*if* you are really obeying the royal law" (εἰ μέντοι νόμον τελεῖτε βασιλικόν). The clause functions adverbially modifying "you are doing" (ποιεῖτε). The entire clause appears above the verb τελεῖτε to visualize its grammatical dependence on the subsequent clause. **Semantically**, it introduces a first-class conditional clause and is the protasis of James's assumption. James assumes something to be true for the sake of an argument (W, 450; Adam, 42), an assumption clarified with the clause's verb, τελεῖτε.

τελεῖτε: This Greek word is a second person plural present active indicative of τελέω that conveys the idea of carrying out an obligation or demand and may be rendered as "carry out," "accomplish," "perform," "fulfill," and "keep it" (BDAG, s.v. "τελέω" 2, p. 997). **Syntactically**, it is the main verb of this dependent conjunctive clause with νόμον as its direct object. **Semantically**, the present tense functions as a customary present (W, 521–22). It describes a person who "really" (μέντοι) makes it a practice to keep the "royal law" (νόμον . . . βασιλικόν) but is often rendered "fulfill" (KJV ASV NRSV ESV NET; cf. NASB). We, however, prefer "obey" (NLT) in that it more pointedly underscores the idea of carrying out an obligation. This is the only time τελέω appears in James, although it is used elsewhere to express the fulfilling or keeping of the νόμος (Luke 2:39; Rom. 2:27).

2:8b ἀγαπήσεις: This structural marker is a second person singular future active indicative of ἀγαπάω that conceptually conveys the idea to have a warm regard for and interest in another and may be rendered as "cherish," "have affection for," or "love" (BDAG, s.v. "ἀγαπάω" 1aα, p. 5). **Syntactically**, it is the main verb of an independent asyndeton clause with τὸν πλησίον as its direct object. We have chosen to visualize the entire OT quotation as in apposition to "according to the Scripture" (κατὰ τὴν γραφήν) and thereby placed it under γραφήν to visualize its relationship to γραφήν. **Semantically**, the future tense has an imperatival force of command typically used with OT quotes (W, 569–70; Adam, 44). The citation from Leviticus 19:15 is the "royal" or "kingly" law mentioned earlier. Jesus the King cited this verse in response to a question about what is the greatest commandment in the law (Matt. 22:34–40; Mark 12:28–31; Luke 10:25–27). But Jesus also included the great command to love the Lord God as part of his response (Deut. 6:5). How could James omit this command in his application of the royal law to the problem of partiality? A reading of the context indicates that he does not omit it. In 2:5c, he mentioned that the kingdom is promised "to those who love him." Thus, love for God and for neighbor are joined together both by Jesus and also by James in this chapter.

Semantical Nugget: How is this quotation a "royal law"? The adjective βασιλικόν is used of a king's official or "royal" robe (LXX Esther 8:15) and also in the graphic scene about Herod (Acts 12:21). The previous reference to "kingdom" (2:5) indicates that a rendering connecting it to royalty is appropriate. It is "kingly" because its source is the king and it is the law of his kingdom. This reference to "law" here and elsewhere in James is not restricted to the Mosaic law. When James speaks of the OT "law" and its commandments, he simply uses νόμον (2:10–11). When he is referring to the Jesus-shaped understanding of that "law," he qualifies νόμος, as in 1:25a and 2:12c: "the law of liberty." Here the term "law" is equally qualified, and in this case the specific "law" was mentioned by both Moses and by Jesus! This is the kingdom that the believing poor will inherit, and it is also an allusion to the beatitude in Matthew 5:3 and Luke 6:20. This language also recalls the "faith of our glorious Lord Jesus Christ" in 2:1a, whose name has been called over those same believing poor in 2:7b. Thus, when "our glorious" messianic king cited Leviticus 19:18 as part of his program of kingdom values, it was transformed into the "kingly" law.

^{2:8c} ποιεῖτε: This structural marker is a second person plural present active indicative of ποιέω that conveys the idea of carrying out an obligation of a moral or social nature and may be rendered as "do," "keep," "carry out," "practice," or "commit" (BDAG, s.v. "ποιέω" 3d, p. 840). **Syntactically**, it is the main verb of the independent asyndeton clause. It is the apodosis in the "if" (εἰ) conditional sentence with ἁμαρτίαν as its direct object. **Semantically**, the present tense functions as a customary present of a person whose life reflects a habitual well-being (W, 521–22), provided that person is obeying the Law. Because James uses it in an ironic sense in 2:19, is irony his intention here? This expression used elsewhere means simply "you are doing well" (Mark 7:37; Acts 10:33; 1 Cor. 7:37; 2 Peter 1:19; 3 John 6). Furthermore, irony misses the effective rhetorical use of the adverb. In 2:3, James quotes one of the leaders of the synagogue as saying to the wealthy attendee, "You sit here in a good place [καλῶς]." In other words, you are doing *well* to love your neighbor as yourself instead of seating the rich man *well*.

^{2:9a} εἰ δέ: These are two structural markers. The first, εἰ, is a conjunction meaning "if" (BDAG, s.v. "εἰ" 6h, p. 278). The second, δέ, is also a conjunction that offers a contrast: "but" or "on the other hand" (BDAG, s.v. "δέ" 4d, p. 213; cf. BDF, §450.1). **Syntactically**, εἰ and δέ introduce a dependent conjunctive clause. The clause functions adverbially modifying the verb "you are committing" (ἐργάζεσθε). The entire clause is placed above ἐργάζεσθε to show its dependence. **Semantically**, εἰ along with δέ is in a first-class conditional clause: "*if on the other hand* you show prejudice" or "*but if* you show prejudice" (NET ESV NASB NRSV NLT KJV). It is the protasis of James's assumption. James assumes something to be true for the sake of an argument (W, 450; Adam, 44), an assumption clarified with the clause's verb, προσωπολημπτεῖτε.

προσωπολημπτεῖτε: This Greek word is a second person plural present active indicative of προσωπολημπτέω that may be rendered "show partiality" (BDAG, s.v. "προσωπολημπτέω," p. 887). **Syntactically**, this is the main verb in the dependent conjunctive clause. It is the protasis of this first-class εἰ conditional sentence. **Semantically**, the present tense is customary present that underscores people who are habitually living out a form of prejudice (W, 521–22; Adam, 44). The verb is a *hapax legomenon*, perhaps coined by James. Yet, it is part of the word group he uses in 2:1b (προσωπολημψίαις). The noun does appear three times in Paul's writings, where it indicates that there is no partiality with God (Rom. 2:11; Eph. 6:9; Col. 3:25). In a similar context, the noun προσωπολήμπτης appears in Acts 10:34. The allusion to Leviticus 19:15 is even more obvious here than in 2:1. In the context of this law of love, Leviticus adds, "Do not practice wickedness in judgment. Do not accept the appearance of the poor man nor be astounded at the appearance of the powerful man. In justice, you will judge your neighbor" (Lev. 19:15).

2:9b ἐργάζεσθε: This structural marker is a second person plural present middle indicative of ἐργάζομαι that may be rendered as "do *something*," "accomplish *something*," "carry out *something*" (BDAG, s.v. "ἐργάζομαι," 2a, p. 389). **Syntactically**, it is the main verb in the independent asyndeton clause. It is the apodosis in the "if" (εἰ) conditional sentence, with ἁμαρτίαν ("sin") as its direct object. **Semantically**, the present tense functions as a customary present drawing attention to a person who has a pattern of sinful behavior (W, 521–22). James's two uses of the verb ἐργάζομαι are both negative. In 1:20, he asserts that human anger does not "accomplish" the righteousness of God, and here the "working" of a sin opposes righteous judgment. His use of the verb ἐργάζομαι may appear unexpected ("accomplishing sin"?) but is appropriate to his later discussion of the "works" in 2:13ff contrasted with the "works" of faith done by Abraham and Rahab in 2:21–25.

2:9c ἐλεγχόμενοι: This Greek word is a nominative plural masculine present passive participle of ἐλέγχω that conveys the idea of bringing a person to the point of recognizing wrongdoing and may be rendered as "convict" or "convince" (BDAG, s.v. "ἐλέγχω" 2, p. 315). **Syntactically**, it introduces a dependent clause. The entire clause is placed under the verb "you are committing" (ἐργάζεσθε) to show its relationship to the independent clause. **Semantically**, the participle expresses a logical result or outcome of committing sin (W, 637–39; Adam, 44). The present tense functions as a customary present that describes a conviction that occurs regularly (W, 521–22). The result of one's crime of prejudice is conviction! The verb ἐλέγχω can mean to reprove someone (Luke 3:19) or to expose them (John 3:20) or convict someone of something (John 8:46). The passive voice "are convicted" with ὑπὸ τοῦ νόμου indicates the thing by which they "are convicted" (KJV NASB NRSV NIV ESV NET; see 1 Cor. 14:24). The law itself both exposes and convicts a person of the sin of discrimination.

> **Lexical Nugget:** What is meant by the noun παραβάται? The noun παραβάται is related to παράβασις, an "overstepping" or "transgression" as in Romans 2:23 (BDAG, s.v. "παράβατης," p. 759). The noun does not appear in the canonical books of the LXX, but the concept is related to παράβασις, which involves a very serious "overstepping" or "transgression" of the law (Ps. 100:3). By "working" (ἐργάζεσθε) this sin they cross over God's established boundaries. The word is found in the NT outside of Paul (Rom. 2:25, 27; Gal. 2:18) only here in James 2:9 and 11. It may be that James also is speaking of the new law of 2:8, since one cannot fulfill this "supreme law" and still discriminate against the poor, as is brought out in the next verse. James, however, would probably not acknowledge that there must be a choice made between either the Levitical law or Jesus's law, since he viewed them both as one piece.

^{2:10a} γάρ: This structural marker is a conjunction meaning "for" (BDAG, s.v. "γάρ" 1d, p. 189). **Syntactically**, it introduces an independent conjunctive clause and appears in a post-positive position. **Semantically**, it serves as a marker where the general statement in the previous verses is confirmed by more specific information about being convicted of prejudice and thereby violators of the Mosaic law (cf. Adam, 45).

ὅστις . . . τηρήσῃ: This structural marker, ὅστις, appears here with its respective verb. Whereas ὅστις is a generic (indefinite) relative pronoun (BDAG, "ὅστις" 1d, p. 729), τηρήσῃ is a verb that is the third person singular aorist active subjunctive of τηρέω that conveys the idea of persisting in something and is often rendered "keep," "observe," "fulfill," or "pay attention to" (BDAG, s.v. "τηρέω" 3, p. 1002). The presence of the indefinite ὅστις or the relative ὅς plus a subjunctive without ἄν or ἐάν is an exception (see Mark 3:29; John 4:14; Gal. 5:10). **Syntactically**, ὅστις introduces a dependent relative clause with τηρήσῃ as the main verb of the clause with "whoever" (ὅστις) as its subject and "the law" (τὸν νόμον) as the direct object. The entire clause, "whoever obeys the law," is placed in parentheses to visualize its function as the subject of the verb γέγονεν with "the law" (τὸν νόμον) as its direct object (cf. W, 343–45; Adam, 45). **Semantically**, the aorist tense is a constative aorist that describes any person's obedience of the law as a whole (W, 557–58). When ὅστις takes the subjunctive, it is usually joined with ἄν, as in Matthew 10:33; 12:50; Luke 10:35; John 2:5; 14:13; Acts 3:23; and Galatians 5:10. The verb τηρέω is used like the Hebrew "guard" (שָׁמַר) in reference to a command, the idea being guarding something against violation. The placement of the adjective ὅλον before τὸν νόμον conveys the following idea: "whoever keeps the law as a whole."

γέγονεν: This Greek word is a third person singular perfect active indicative of γίνομαι that conveys the idea of coming into a certain state or possessing certain characteristics and may be rendered "be," "prove to be," "turn out to be," or "to come" (BDAG, s.v. "γίνομαι" 7, p. 199). **Syntactically**, it is the main verb of the independent conjunctive clause with the relative clause "whoever observes the whole law" (ὅστις . . . ὅλον τὸν νόμον τηρήσῃ) as its subject. **Semantically**, the perfect tense is a proleptic perfect (W, 581; Irons, 536; BDF, §344). The verb γίνομαι describes the entrance into a state of being a violator, transgressor, or sinner pertaining to keeping the law.

Lexical Nugget: What is the meaning of ἔνοχος? The adjective basically means "subject to/liable to," but has a wide range of applications (BDAG, s.v. "ἔνοχος" 2, p. 338). It can mean liable to a penalty, as in Matthew 26:66. In the NT, it can also mean subject to slavery (Heb. 2:15) or responsible for the body and blood of the Lord (1 Cor. 11:27). The punishment with ἔνοχος is usually in the genitive (Matt. 26:66; Mark 3:29; 14:64), but also in the dative

(Matt. 5:21). Πάντων is equivalent to ὅλον τὸν νόμον. Some passages in rabbinical writings agree with the teaching in this verse, especially *Shemot Rabbah* xxv: "The Sabbath weighs against all the precepts." In other words, if you break the Sabbath law, you have broken all of them.

2:10b δέ: This structural marker is a conjunction meaning "but" (BDAG, s.v. "δέ" 4a, p. 213). **Syntactically**, it introduces an independent conjunctive clause that is parenthetical to the previous clause about a hypothetical person who is accountable to the law (cf. Adam, 47). **Semantically**, it is contrastive: "but" (NRSV ESV NET), "yet" (KJV ASV NASB NIV), or "except" (NLT).

πταίσῃ: This Greek word is a third person singular aorist active subjunctive of πταίω that means "to lose one's footing," "stumble," or "trip" (BDAG, s.v. "πταίω" 1, p. 894). **Syntactically**, it is the main verb of this dependent conjunctive clause. The entire clause functions as a parenthetical contrast and contributes to the subject of the verb γέγονεν, namely, a hypothetical person who is accountable to the law. **Semantically**, the aorist tense is a constative aorist that describes an event of stumbling (cf. ASV NASB NIV), "failing" (NRSV ESV NET), or "offending" (KJV) as a whole (W, 557–58).

Lexical Nugget: What is the meaning of the verb πταίσῃ? The verb πταίω refers to a literal stumbling (BDAG, s.v. "πταίω" 1, p. 894), but this meaning lent itself easily to moral stumbling (Philo, *Leg.* 3.66). In the indicative it appears again in 3:2b where it describes stumbling with the tongue. See its figurative use in Romans 11:11. The picture here is that of a παραβάτης ("transgressor") stumbling over a border marking the way, which is consistent with the famous expression in Jewish rabbinic writings about making a "hedge" or "fence" around the Torah (*m. Avot* 1.1).

2:11a γάρ: This structural marker is a conjunction meaning "for" (BDAG, s.v. "γάρ" 1d, p. 189). **Syntactically**, it introduces a complex independent conjunctive clause and appears in a post-positive position. **Semantically**, it serves to add more information about the expectation to obey the entire law (cf. Adam, 45).

ὁ . . . εἰπών: This articular (ὁ) Greek word is a nominative singular masculine aorist active participle of λέγω that means "say" or "tell" (BDAG, s.v. "λέγω" 1a, p. 288). **Syntactically**, it is a substantival participle functioning as the subject of the following εἶπεν. **Semantically**, the aorist tense is a constative aorist that describes an act of speaking as a whole (W, 557–58) and is rendered "he who said" (NASB NIV ESV NET CNT), "God who said" (NLT), or "the one who said" (NRSV). The participle serves as a circumlocution for God, following a Jewish practice of not directly uttering the name of the Lord (*Yahweh*) unless it was necessary. The citation formula introducing the two precepts is different from James's usual way of referencing OT passages. He normally introduces these as γραφή (2:8a, 23a; 4:5a), but here he uses a masculine article and participle. The aorist participle suggests the definitive speaking of the Lord on Sinai: "The one who said . . . said also."

μὴ μοιχεύσῃς: This negated (μή) Greek word is a second person singular aorist active subjunctive of μοιχεύω that is rendered as "commit adultery" with reference to both sexes (BDAG, s.v. "μοιχεύω" a, p. 657). **Syntactically**, it is the main verb of an OT quote that is an independent conjunctive clause, which actually functions as the direct object of εἰπών, telling what God said the clause is placed in parentheses to visualize the substantival relationship to εἰπών. **Semantically**, the combination of aorist tense with the subjunctive is a prohibitive subjunctive (W, 469). James reverses the order of God's commands whereby the seventh command precedes the sixth. See LXX Exodus 20:13, 15; Luke 18:20; and Romans 13:9. The usual order originally given in Exodus 20 is found in Deuteronomy 5:17–18; Matthew 5:21, 27; and 19:18.

εἶπεν: This Greek word is a third person singular aorist active indicative of λέγω meaning "say" or "tell" (BDAG, s.v. "λέγω" 1η, p. 289). **Syntactically**, it is the main verb of this complex independent conjunctive γάρ clause. The substantival ὁ . . . εἰπών is the subject of εἶπεν. **Semantically**, the aorist is constative. The verb recalls the oral speech of God from Mount Sinai (Exod. 19ff.).

μὴ φονεύσῃς: This negated (μή) Greek word is a second person singular aorist active subjunctive of φονεύω that may be rendered "murder" or "kill" (BDAG, s.v. "φονεύω," p. 1063). **Syntactically**, it is the main verb of an OT quote that is an independent conjunctive clause. It actually functions as the direct object of εἶπεν, telling what God said. **Semantically**, the combination of aorist tense with the subjunctive mood is a prohibitive subjunctive (W, 469). The verb appears only in citations of the Sinai command, except for Matthew 23:31, 35; and James 5:6. See above for the order of the commands in this verse.

2:11b εἰ: This structural marker is a conjunction meaning "if" (BDAG, s.v. "εἰ" 1aβ, p. 277). **Syntactically**, it introduces two dependent conjunctive clauses: "*if* you do not commit adultery" (εἰ . . . οὐ μοιχεύεις) and "yet you commit murder" (φονεύεις δέ). Together, these clauses modify "you have become" (γέγονας) and appear above the verb γέγονας to visualize their grammatical dependence on the subsequent clause. **Semantically**, "if" (εἰ) introduces a first-class conditional clause that assumes the reality of the condition and the protasis of the clause (W, 686–94; Adam, 46). In this case, James's assumption is clarified with the clause's verb, μοιχεύεις.

δέ: This Greek word is a conjunction meaning "now" (BDAG, s.v. "δέ" 2, p. 213). **Syntactically**, it is the second conjunction introducing this dependent conjunctive clause. It appears in the post-positive position. **Semantically**, δέ is often left untranslated (NIV ESV CNT), but it seems reasonable to present δέ as a marker that provides more information about a person who may feel deficient in their understanding that is best rendered "now" (KJV ASV NASB NRSV NET; cf. Adam, 46).

οὐ μοιχεύεις: This negated (μή) Greek word is a second person singular present active indicative of μοιχεύω that is rendered "commit adultery" (BDAG, s.v. "μοιχεύω" a, p. 657). **Syntactically**, it is the main verb of this dependent conjunctive clause and the protasis of this first-class εἰ conditional sentence (W, 684–94). **Semantically**, the present tense is customary and implies someone's ability to abstain from habitual acts of adultery (μή μοιχεύεις; W, 521–22; Adam 46). This is the second time that James directly cites the OT from Exodus 20:14 (see 2:8 for the first time). The shift from the μή plus subjunctive to the οὐ plus indicative indicates a shift from direct quotation in 2:11a to the indirect quotation in the conditional clause of 2:11b.

2:11c δέ: This structural marker is a conjunction meaning "but" (BDAG, s.v. "δέ" 4a, p. 213). **Syntactically**, it introduces a dependent conjunctive clause and appears in a post-positive position. **Semantically**, δέ is a marker of contrast: "but" (ASV NASB NRSV NIV ESV NET CNT NLT) or "yet" (KJV). It contrasts someone who practices self-control in one area but loses it in another.

φονεύεις: This Greek word is a second person singular present active indicative of φονεύω that may be rendered "murder" or "kill" (BDAG, "φονεύω," p. 1063). **Syntactically**, it is the main verb of this dependent conjunctive clause and the protasis of this first-class εἰ conditional sentence (W, 684–94). **Semantically**, the present tense is customary present that implies several acts of murder (W, 521–22; Adam, 46). James is referring to Exodus 20:13. James later couples these two commands when he accuses the readers of "murder" in 4:2 and follows up calling them "adulteresses" in 4:4!

Grammatical and Text-Critical Nugget: Why is the order of the commandments different than in Exodus 20? For the order of the seventh commandment preceding the sixth, see LXX Exodus 20:13, 15; Luke 18:20; and Romans 13:9. The usual order given in Exodus 20 is found in Deuteronomy 5:17–18; Matthew 5:21, 27; and 19:18. A handful of uncials (C, Ψ) and minuscules (614, 630, 945, 1241, 1505, 1739, 1852, 2464) seek to conform James's aorist subjunctives to future indicatives (οὐ μοιχεύεις and οὐ φονεύεις) that are found in the LXX of Exodus 20:13–15. This reflects an effort to change the indirect discourse found here (ὁ γὰρ εἰπῶν and εἶπεν καί) to convey the direct discourse of the LXX. The order in the text reflects the NA and also the TH readings. For a chart on "James 2:11 Compared to Similar Biblical References," see Spencer, 136.

2:11d γέγονας: This structural marker is a second person singular perfect active indicative of γίνομαι that conveys the idea of coming into a certain state or possessing a certain characteristic and may be rendered "be," "prove to be," or "turn out to be" (BDAG, "γίνομαι" 7, p. 199). **Syntactically**, it is the main verb of this independent asyndeton clause, which is the apodosis for the first-class conditional εἰ clause (W, 684–94), with παραβάτης as its predicate nominative. **Semantically**, the perfect tense is an intensive perfect, "frequently with stative verbs," that emphasizes the result or present produced from a past action (W, 574–76). The tense also has in view the current state of the transgressor and is rendered "you have become" (NASB NRSB NIV ESV NET CNT) or "you are become" (KJV ASV). So, if a person refrains from breaking one law but breaks another, he or she is still "a transgressor of the law." For the use of the perfect tense of γίνομαι following different tenses in both verses, see the comments on 1:24. The "stative" aspect of the perfect verb places into greater prominence the state of affairs in which the lawbreaker is found—he or she *is* a guilty transgressor.

2:12a οὕτως: This structural marker is a conjunction that may be rendered as "thus," "so," or "in this manner" (BDAG, s.v. "οὕτως" 1b, p. 742). **Syntactically**, it introduces an independent conjunctive clause that may function as a "redundant comparative conjunction" connecting together two statements (Adam, 47; cf. W, 675, 761–62). **Semantically**, it adds emphasis to the exhortation to follow (Adam, 47). It is most frequently rendered "so" (KJV ASV NASB NRSV ESV NLT CNT). Yet, some translations provide no rendering for οὕτως (NIV NET).

λαλεῖτε: This structural marker is a second person plural present active imperative of λαλέω that conveys the idea of a person expressing oneself and may be rendered as "talk" or "speak" (BDAG, s.v. "λαλέω" 2αβ, p. 582). **Syntactically**, it is the main verb of this independent conjunctive clause. **Semantically**, the present tense imperative is an imperative of command (W, 585–86) whereby the action of speaking is habitual (W, 521–22). It is typically used for general precepts for habits, in this case patterns of speaking, that should characterize a person's attitude and behavior (W, 721; cf. Adam, 47).

2:12b καί οὕτως: These are two structural markers. The first is a conjunction meaning "and" (BDAG, s.v. "καί" 1bζ, p. 494). The second is a conjunction that may be rendered as "thus," "so," or "in this manner" (BDAG, s.v. "οὕτως" 1b, p. 742). **Syntactically**, καί οὕτως introduces an independent conjunctive clause. While οὕτως is identified as an adverbial conjunction, it is more of a connector of ideas or in this case connecting another example about the outworkings of the law (W, 675, 761–62). **Semantically**, καί οὕτως indicates a result that comes from the preceding clause. As coordinating conjunctions, they are rendered as "and so" (KJV ASV NASB NRSV ESV CNT). Yet, some translations provide no rendering for the second occurrence of οὕτως (NIV NET NLT).

ποιεῖτε: This Greek word is a second person plural present active imperative of ποιέω that conveys the idea of carrying out an obligation of a moral or social nature and may be rendered "do," "keep," "carry out," "practice," or "commit" (BDAG, s.v. "ποιέω" 3d, p. 840). **Syntactically**, it is the main verb of this independent conjunctive clause. **Semantically**, the present tense imperative is an imperative of command (W, 585–86) whereby the action of speaking is habitual (W, 521–22). It is typically used for general precepts for habits, in this case patterns of speaking, that should characterize a person's attitude and behavior (W, 721; cf. Adam, 47). Together, the two present tense imperatives in verse 12 underscore the character of a person's attitude: "You must keep on speaking and acting in every respect." The exhortations insist on the right regulation of speech (3:1–12), as well as correct behavior (2:14–26).

2:12c ὡς: This structural marker is a comparative conjunction often rendered "as" (BDAG, s.v. "ὡς" 1bα, p. 1103). **Syntactically**, it introduces a dependent conjunctive clause that modifies both οὕτως clauses with their respective imperatives "speak" (λαλεῖτε) and "do" (ποιεῖτε) even though the structural outline visualizes a modifying of only "do" (ποιεῖτε). **Semantically**, it underscores the manner in which one's speech and actions are to be done with a fixed goal in mind due to the presence of μέλλοντες.

μέλλοντες: This Greek word is a nominative plural masculine present active participle of μέλλω that conveys something that is inevitable or destined to occur (BDAG, s.v. "μέλλω" 2a, p. 628). **Syntactically**, it is the main verb of this dependent conjunctive clause introduced by ὡς. **Semantically**, the present tense functions as a futuristic present to describe a future event that expresses immediacy or certainty (W, 535–36): "those who will" (NET; cf. KJV NLT) or "those who are" (NASB NRSV NIV ESV CNT; cf. ASV). While the present μέλλοντες ("about to") provides an eschatological frame of reference (see 5:8–9; Adam, 47), it is possible that μέλλω followed by an infinitive is "in a weakened sense [a form that] serves simply as a periphrasis for the future" (cf. BDAG, s.v. "μέλλω" 1cβ, p. 627).

κρίνεσθαι: This Greek word is a present passive infinitive of κρίνω that conveys the idea of being handed over for judicial punishment or engaged in a judicial process and may be rendered "judge," "decide," or "condemn" (BDAG, s.v. "κρίνω" 5ba, p. 568). **Syntactically**, it is part of the main verb of this dependent conjunctive clause. **Semantically**, it is a complementary infinitive to the participle μέλλοντες (W, 755). While the passive voice indicates a judgment that will be imposed upon people, the agent doing the judgment may be understood to be God (W, 437–38). Whenever that judgment takes place, readers should recognize that those who have wrongly judged others (2:1–4) will themselves give an account.

> **Semantical Nugget:** What is the "law of liberty"? The "perfect law of liberty" (1:25), the "law of liberty" (2:12c), the "royal law" (2:8a), the "law" (2:9c, 11d), and the "whole law" (2:10) are not different "laws" but are in continuity with each other as *the law* as it is expounded by Jesus. James wishes us to view the wholeness of the entire law, and it is truly revealed in many aspects and characteristics. It is, however, given by the one lawgiver in heaven, conveyed by his servant lawgiver on Sinai, and then fulfilled through his messianic law-interpreter on the hills of Galilee.

2:13a γάρ: This structural marker is a conjunction meaning "for" (BDAG, s.v. "γάρ" 1d, p. 189). **Syntactically**, it introduces an independent conjunctive clause and appears in a post-positive position. **Semantically**, γάρ serves as another marker where the general statement in the previous verses is confirmed by more specific information about the expectation of a future judgment (cf. Adam, 49).

[ἔστιν]: This Greek word is a third person singular present active indicative from the verb εἰμί meaning "is" (BDAG, s.v. "εἰμί" 2a, p. 283). **Syntactically,** the bracketed [ἔστιν] is an ellipsis, and the main verb of this independent conjunctive clause. The subject of the verb is "the judgment" (ἡ . . . κρίσις), and "merciless" (ἀνέλεος) is the predicate adjective (W, 40–46; 146–48). This is an aphorism (general truth) that is negative in tone: "judgment is merciless." **Semantically**, [ἔστιν] serves as an equative verb that reveals a close connection between the two concepts or describes judgment as being without mercy: "judgment *is* merciless" (NET) or "judgment *is* without mercy" (ASV ESV). It is possible, however, to consider the ellipsis verb as future: "the judgment *will be* merciless" (NASB) or "judgment *will be* without mercy" (NRSV CNT; cf. NIV NLT). Both options are possible for the ellipsis (Adam, 48).

μὴ ποιήσαντι: This negated (μή) Greek word is a dative masculine singular aorist active participle of ποιέω that conveys the idea of carrying out an obligation of a moral or social nature and is frequently rendered "practice" (BDAG, s.v. "ποιέω" 3b, p. 840). **Syntactically**, it "belongs to the larger category of indirect object" (W, 143) within this independent conjunctive clause.

Semantically, the dative participle is a dative of disadvantage (W, 142–44). It expresses the disadvantage of being a person who refuses to extend mercy to others (cf. Matt. 18:21–35). The aorist participle functions as a constative aorist, viewing the action as a whole (W, 557–58), namely, God's judgment.

> **Lexical Nugget:** What is meant by ἔλεος? Mercy as a moral virtue is widely attested in Jewish wisdom writings (Sir 27:30–28:7; Tob 14:9). When the canonical LXX translates the Hebrew word חֶסֶד as ἔλεος, it conveys the expression of God's loving-kindness, grace, and love toward his human creations, especially conveyed through his covenant with Israel (Pss. 5:8; 6:5; 39:11; 47:10). The focus in James, however, is not on God's mercy to his people, but mercy shown to one another. This horizontal focus of "doing mercy" also recalls many OT references combining the verb "do" (עָשָׂה) with the noun "mercy" (חֶסֶד). This combination is translated in the LXX with ποιεῖν and ἔλεος. See Joshua 2:12: "Swear to me before the Lord your God, 'I will show you mercy [ποιῶ ... ἔλεος / חֶסֶד],' and that you will 'show mercy' (ποιήσετε ... ἔλεος /חֶסֶד) to my father's house." James draws on the Hebraic חֶסֶד concept of "steadfast love" as reflected in covenant relationships. Jesus also communicates this same idea by a cognate expression in Matthew 6:2: Ὅταν οὖν ποιῇς ἐλεημοσύνην (see also Matt. 5:7; 6:14; 7:1; 18:21–25; 25:41–46).

2:13b κατακαυχᾶται: This structural marker is a third person singular present middle indicative of κατακαυχάομαι that conveys a cause for boasting because of advantage in power and may be rendered "triumph over" (BDAG, s.v. "κατακαυχάομαι" 2, p. 517). **Syntactically**, it is the main verb of an independent asyndeton clause with ἔλεος as its subject. This second aphorism (general truth) is more positive in tone: "Mercy triumphs over judgment." The absence of a connecting conjunction heightens the stand-alone nature of this aphorism that is specifically applied to partiality. The compound verb used here is also found in 1:9; 3:14 and Romans 11:18. **Semantically**, the present tense of this middle voice (W, 428–30) functions as a customary present giving emphasis to a pattern of mercy's triumphing over judgment (W, 521–22). James concludes 2:1–13, his exhortation on partiality, with two parallel indicative clauses, the first introduced by γάρ (2:13a), and the second standing alone (2:13b). The subtle shift from the second person used in 2:12 to the third person used in 2:13 indicates the role of these two statements as general aphorisms that apply to the problem he has been discussing.

JAMES 2:14–26

Big Greek Idea: Indifference toward people in need reflects a lifeless faith similar to that of demons in contrast to a genuine faith vindicated with deeds as in the cases of Abraham and Rahab.

Structural Overview: While James continues to expand his theme of hearing and doing Scripture introduced in 1:22–25, he also continues the theme of discrimination (2:1) and the poor (2:5) (cf. Varner[2], 102). In this unit (vv. 14–26), James underscores his faith/action theme. First, by way of another set of hypothetical examples (cf. 1:22–25; 2:2–4), James challenges people who claim to have faith and yet, exhibit indifferent and callous responses toward the poor as an indication of dead faith (vv. 14–17).[1] James then challenges a person's deedless faith as real faith with a sense of sarcasm about demonic belief in God (vv. 18–19). Finally, James contrasts dead faith with two OT exemplars, Abraham and Rahab, whereby he argues their deeds vindicated their faith as a pattern of genuine faith (vv. 20–26).

Outline:[2]

> Indifference toward the Needy Exposes Lifeless Faith (2:14–17).
> Faith Assertions in God Are Universal and Meaningless (2:18–19).
> Action Vindicates Real Faith (2:20–26).

INDIFFERENCE TOWARD THE NEEDY EXPOSES LIFELESS FAITH (JAMES 2:14–17)

CLAUSAL OUTLINE FOR JAMES 2:14–17

2:14a Τί [ἐστιν] τὸ ὄφελος, ἀδελφοί μου,
2:14a What [*is*] the benefit, my brothers *and sisters*,

> 2:14b ἐὰν πίστιν **λέγῃ** τις **ἔχειν**
> 2:14b if someone **claims to have** faith

> 2:14c ἔργα δὲ μὴ **ἔχῃ**
> 2:14c but he **does** not **have** accompanying deeds?

2:14d μὴ **δύναται** ἡ πίστις **σῶσαι** αὐτόν
2:14d Is that kind of faith **able to save** him?

---

1. While some may consider "dead faith" as a weaker form of faith (Hodges, 62–63), it blunts the severity of James's attack here and again in verse 26 (Varner[2], 107; cf. Spencer, 142).
2. A suggested sermon entitled "Show Me Your Faith" may be preached in four points: "Words Are Not Enough (2:14–17)," "Belief Is Not Enough (2:18–20)," "Goodness Is Not Enough (2:21–26)," and "God's Grace Is Enough (2:21–26)" (see Baker et al., 73–79).

²:¹⁵ᵃ ἐὰν ἀδελφὸς ἢ ἀδελφὴ γυμνοὶ **ὑπάρχωσιν**
²:¹⁵ᵃ <u>If</u> a brother or sister **is** poorly clothed

|

²:¹⁵ᵇ καὶ **λειπόμενοι ὦσιν** τῆς ἐφημέρου τροφῆς
²:¹⁵ᵇ <u>and</u> **is lacking** in daily food,

|

²:¹⁶ᵃ **εἴπῃ** δέ τις αὐτοῖς ἐξ ὑμῶν·
²:¹⁶ᵃ <u>and</u> one of you **says** to them

    |

    ²:¹⁶ᵇ (**ὑπάγετε** ἐν εἰρήνῃ,
    ²:¹⁶ᵇ (**Go** in peace,

        |

    ²:¹⁶ᶜ **θερμαίνεσθε** καὶ **χορτάζεσθε**,)
    ²:¹⁶ᶜ <u>keep yourself</u> **warm** and **filled**)

|

²:¹⁶ᵈ μὴ **δῶτε** δὲ αὐτοῖς τὰ ἐπιτήδεια τοῦ σώματος,
²:¹⁶ᵈ <u>and yet without</u> **giving** them the things needed for the body,

|

²:¹⁶ᵉ τί [*ἐστιν*] τὸ ὄφελος;
²:¹⁶ᵉ <u>what</u> [*is*] the benefit?

²:¹⁷ᵃ <u>οὕτως καὶ</u> ἡ πίστις νεκρά **ἐστιν** καθ᾽ ἑαυτήν,
²:¹⁷ᵃ <u>So also</u>, that kind of faith . . . **is** dead by itself.

              |

      ²:¹⁷ᵇ <u>ἐὰν</u> [*ἐστιν*] μὴ **ἔχῃ** ἔργα,
      ²:¹⁷ᵇ <u>if</u> [*it is*] <u>not</u> **accompanied** by actions.

SYNTAX EXPLAINED FOR JAMES 2:14–17

²:¹⁴ᵃ [*ἐστιν*]: This structural marker is a third person singular present active indicative from the verb εἰμί meaning "is" (BDAG, s.v. "εἰμί" 2a, p. 283). **Syntactically**, the bracketed [ἔστιν] is an ellipsis and the main verb of the independent asyndeton clause. Its subject is "the good" (τὸ ὄφελος), and the interrogative pronoun "what" (τί) is the predicate adjective (W, 40–46). Τί appears for the first time here in James's letter and introduces a rhetorical question with no expressed verb, as also in 2:16a, and later in 3:13a, 13b; 4:12d–e; and 5:13c (twice). James has asked rhetorical questions in 2:5, 6, and 7, and such questions continue as part of his rhetorical strategy, particularly in this section (2:16, 20, 21, 25). **Semantically**, [ἔστιν] serves as an equative verb in this apodosis for the following ἐάν clause. It reveals a question equivalent to the American idiom: "What's the use" (Adam, 49) or "What is the benefit" (cf. KJV ASV). However, most render the clause: "What good is it" (NASB ESV NET NLT etc.; Irons, 536).

Lexical Nugget: What is the meaning of ὄφελος and how does James use this term? This noun appears only once in the LXX (Job 15:3), and occurs outside James in the NT only in 1 Corinthians 15:32, where Paul asks, "If from human motives I fought with wild beasts at Ephesus, what does it benefit me [τί μοι τὸ ὄφελος]?" The verb ὀφείλω appears often in the NT, and Matthew 16:26 provides an interesting parallel to the use of the noun here: "For what shall a person be benefited [τί γὰρ ὠφεληθήσεται ἄνθρωπος] if he gains the whole world and loses his soul?" James will again use this question to end 2:16, and thus it serves as an inclusio to "bookend" his point about the necessary alliance of faith and works.

2:14b ἐάν: This structural marker is a conjunction meaning "if" (NET ESV NASB NRSV) or "suppose" (BDAG, s.v. "ἐάν" 1cγ, p. 268). **Syntactically**, it introduces a dependent conjunctive clause. The entire dependent clause, "if someone claims to have faith" (ἐὰν πίστιν λέγῃ τις ἔχειν) functions adverbially and placed below [ἐστιν] to visualize its dependence. **Semantically**, it is a third-class conditional clause that introduces a hypothetical situation for the sake of the discussion (W, 696–99; Adam, 49). So once again, the hypothetical situation is not necessarily describing a scene that James has witnessed or heard that has taken place. The scene that is portrayed" *may* have taken place, but it is not necessarily a scene that actually *has* taken place.

λέγῃ: This Greek word is a third person singular present active subjunctive of λέγω that conveys the idea of expressing oneself orally or in written form and may be rendered "utter in words," "say," "tell," or "give expression to" (BDAG, s.v. "λέγω" 1aγ, p. 588). **Syntactically**, it is the main verb of the dependent conjunctive clause. As part of the protasis it is in the subjunctive mood because ἐάν takes its respective verb in the subjunctive (W, 469–70). The subject of λέγῃ is the indefinite pronoun τις ("someone") (BDAG, s.v. "τις" 1aα ⸃, p. 1008). **Semantically**, the present tense functions as a customary present. It describes a person who speaks regularly of his or her faith (W, 521–22): "if someone *claims*" (NIV NET) or "if someone *says*" (KJV ASV NASB NRSV ESV NLT CNT). This clause charges the imagined person to have a faith that is not accompanied by appropriate deeds. It is important to notice the reported speech of this imagined person. He does not necessarily have faith; he "claims" or "says" (λέγῃ) that he has faith.

ἔχειν: This Greek word is a present active infinitive of ἔχω that conveys the idea of possessing something and may be rendered as "have" or "own" (BDAG, s.v. "ἔχω" 1aα, p. 420). **Syntactically**, it is the direct object of this dependent conjunctive for a proposed person who speaks (λέγῃ). **Semantically**, it is an infinitive of indirect discourse. The present tense functions as a customary present that describes a person who regularly speaks of his or her faith (W, 521–22). It gives voice to the imagined person who later engages with James as a debate opponent (see W, 604–3). That interlocutor is directly quoted in the parable of 2:18–19 and is directly addressed by the second person vocative in 2:20 as "O vain person." This interpersonal dynamic, so vividly portrayed through the diatribe format, progressively increases in intensity throughout the section.

2:14c δέ: This structural marker is a conjunction meaning "but" (BDAG, s.v. "δέ" 4a, p. 213). **Syntactically**, it introduces a dependent conjunctive clause and appears in a post-positive position. **Semantically**, it is a marker of contrast: "but" (ASV NASB NRSV NIV ESV NET CNT NLT) even though it is possible to render δέ as "and" (KJV). We, however, see it as a contrast between what is spoken versus what is practiced.

μὴ ἔχῃ: This negated (μή) Greek word is a third person singular present active subjunctive of ἔχω that conveys the idea of possessing something and may be rendered as "have" or "own" (BDAG, s.v. "ἔχω" 1aα, p. 420). **Syntactically**, it is the main verb of this dependent conjunctive clause. As the second part of this third-class conditional ἐάν clause, the verb is in the subjunctive because ἐάν takes its respective verbs in the subjunctive (W, 469–70). **Semantically**, the negated (μή) present tense is again a customary present that describes a person who lacks any deeds regularly (W, 521–22). We render ἔργα as "deeds" or "actions" since the English word "works" carries a good deal of baggage from the discussions in the Reformation over meritorious religious "works." As will be seen, James and Paul are using this important term in different but very important ways. This translation of "deeds" will at least help to avoid confusion with Paul's teaching on "works of the law."

2:14d μὴ δύναται: This negated (μή) structural marker is a third person singular present middle indicative of δύναμαι that conveys capability and may be rendered "can," "be able," or "be capable" (BDAG, s.v. "δύναμαι" aα; p. 262). **Syntactically**, it is the main verb of this independent asyndeton clause with πίστις as its subject. It concludes the question of 2:14a–c. The negater μή in this last clause of the rhetorical question expects a negative answer (Adam, 49; Zerwick et al. 695). **Semantically**, the present tense of this middle voice (W, 428–30) is a customary present with the focus on faith that continually lacks any visible deed. This rhetorical question brings into doubt the nature of a faith professed but not accompanied by the appropriate actions.

Grammatical Nugget: How does James ask his question with the article before πίστις? The first πίστιν is anarthrous (without an article) and signals a new subject from that in 2:1–13. The negative particle μή in the second clause/question indicates an expected negative reply (Porter, 277–79). The article ἡ before πίστις serves an anaphoric function, referring back to the type of deficient faith that was described in the earlier conditional sentence (W, 219; cf. McCartney, 155–56). In other words, the sense conveyed is: "No. That kind of faith cannot save the person who says that he has it." The importance of this translation lies in not leaving an impression that James is saying that faith does not save. This misunderstanding could possibly arise from the KJV rendering ("can faith save him?") and possibly contributed to the supposed contradiction between James and other NT writers. James will repeat this anaphoric use of the article when he ties together the argument of this subsection in 2:17: "So also that kind of faith (ἡ πίστις), if it is not accompanied by actions, is dead by itself."

σῶσαι: This Greek word is an aorist active infinitive of σῴζω that conveys the idea of saving or preserving from transcendent danger or destruction and may be rendered "save" or "preserve from eternal death" (BDAG, s.v. "σῴζω" 2, 2αγ, p. 982–93). **Syntactically**, it is the main verb of the independent asyndeton clause with πίστις as its subject and αὐτόν as its direct object. It concludes the question of 2:14. **Semantically**, it is a complementary infinitive that completes the verb δύναται (W, 598–99; Adam, 50). The aorist tense is a constative aorist that describes a hypothetical situation as a whole (W, 557–58) about salvation, namely, is it possible that faith without deeds is able to save? While most render the clause as "Can that faith save him" (NASB ESV; cf. NLT), "Can such faith save him" (NIV CNT), or "Can this faith save him" (NET), we render it as "Is that kind of faith able to save him" to accentuate the infinitive.

Theological Nugget: What does "able to save" (δύναται . . . σῶσαι) mean here? The reference to salvation echoes other passages in James. It is the "Word of Truth" (1:18) implanted by God that is "able to save your souls" (1:21), but that takes place only if you are "doers of the Word and not hearers only" (1:22–25). It is God who both saves and destroys (4:12), and it is the concerned brother or sister who saves the wanderer (5:20). So, it is true that the right kind of faith does save (5:15a–b)! In keeping with James's eschatological emphasis elsewhere in the letter, the saving refers to final salvation, especially since δύναται ("is able") implies a future event (Dibelius, 152; Davids, 120).

2:15a ἐάν: This structural marker is a conjunction meaning "if " (BDAG, s.v. "ἐάν" 1cγ, p. 268). **Syntactically**, it introduces a complex dependent conjunctive clause. The entire clause, "if a brother or sister [is] poorly clothed" (ἐὰν ἀδελφὸς ἢ ἀδελφὴ [ἐστιν] γυμνοὶ ὑπάρχωσιν) functions adverbially and placed above the verb [ἐστιν] in the subsequent clause (2:16e) to visualize its dependence. **Semantically**, it is a third-class conditional clause that introduces a hypothetical situation for the sake of the discussion (W, 696–99; Adam, 50). So again, the hypothetical situation is not necessarily describing a scene that James has witnessed or heard that has taken place in their assemblies. The scene that is portrayed in their "synagogue" *may* have taken place, but it is not necessarily a scene that actually *has* taken place.

ὑπάρχωσιν: This Greek word is a third person plural present active subjunctive of ὑπάρχω that conveys the idea of being in a state or circumstance and may be rendered as "be" but "is" is a widely used substitute (BDAG, s.v. "ὑπάρχω" 2, p. 1030; cf. BDF, §414.1). **Syntactically**, it is the main verb of this dependent conjunctive clause. The verb is in the subjunctive mood because ἐάν takes its verb in the subjunctive (W, 469–70; Adam, 50) in the protasis. Its subject is ἀδελφὸς ἢ ἀδελφή (BDF, §135.4). **Semantically**, the present tense is a customary present that describes a person who lives in an ongoing state of poverty as it concerns the lack of clothing (W, 521–22) or "being poorly clothed" (cf. ESV NET). James again utilizes a conditional sentence as he proposes a possible scenario in 2:15–16. His fondness for parables, already seen in 1:22–25 and in 2:2–4, is illustrated again by introducing people who, like the poor person in 2:2, are inadequately dressed.

> **Lexical Nugget:** What is the specific meaning of γυμνοί? In the ancient world people were considered "naked" (γυμνοί) if they did not have clothing adequate for a public appearance and thus the word has been rendered by some translations as though these people were possibly literally "naked" (KJV ASV NRSV; cf. Zerwick et al. 695). Most translations, however, rightfully render γυμνοί as a hyperbole: "poorly clothed" (ESV NET; cf. BDAG, s.v. "γυμνός," p. 208) or "without clothing" (NASB NIV CNT). The word was used of the fisherman Peter at work in John 21:7. These people in 2:15 are lacking appropriate public clothing. The term is associated with poverty (Rev. 3:17) and shame (LXX Gen. 3:10; Rev. 3:18). The naked ones, therefore, are people who are most in need of assistance (cf. Spencer, 140–41).

2:15b καί: This structural marker is a conjunction meaning "and" (BDAG, s.v. "καί" 1b, p. 494). **Syntactically**, it introduces a dependent conjunctive clause. **Semantically**, it is a coordinating conjunction that links together two clauses within a protasis. It is often rendered "and" (NET ESV NASB NRSV etc.) and adds another description of the poor.

λειπόμενοι: This Greek word is a nominative plural masculine present middle participle of λείπω that conveys the idea of leaving behind and may be rendered "fall short" or "lack" (BDAG, s.v. "λείπω" 1b, p. 590). **Syntactically**, it is part of the main verb in this dependent conjunctive clause and part of the protasis for the third-class conditional clause. The entire clause is placed above the verb [ἐστιν] in the subsequent independent clause (2:16e) to visualize its dependence. Although Wallace prefers to label λειπόμενοι as a "predicate participle" and cites Hebrews 4:12 (Ζῶν γὰρ ὁ λόγος) as an example, Hebrews does not have a form of εἰμί (W, 619; cf. Adam, 50). So Wallace's description of λειπόμενοι must change if the following ὦσιν is accepted as being in the original text (cf. NA²⁸, supported by ℵ, B, and C) as we have so accepted. **Semantically**, the present tense is a customary present that describes a person who lives in an ongoing state of poverty as it concerned the lack of food (W, 521–22). The verb describes those whose need is so obvious that to refuse them is to betray the very nature of religious "faith" (Sir 4:1–6; 34:20–22). The verse again echoes a Jesus *logion* in Matthew 25:36: "I was naked (γυμνὸς) and you clothed me."

ὦσιν: This Greek word is a third person plural present active subjunctive of εἰμί that may be rendered "to be" (BDAG, s.v. "εἰμί" 11b, p. 285). **Syntactically**, it is part of the main verb in this independent conjunctive clause and part of the protasis for the third-class conditional clause. The verb is in the subjunctive mood because ἐάν takes its verb in the subjunctive (W, 469–70). The NA²⁸ adds ὦσιν following the present participle λειπόμενοι, which as a "verbal adjective," parallels the earlier adjective γυμνοί. **Semantically**, it is a periphrastic construction. The present tense verb is a customary present that is part of James's description of a person who lives in an ongoing state of poverty as it concerned the lack of food (W, 521–22). The expression ἐφημέρου τροφῆς ("necessary food" or "daily food") is the direct object genitive following the participle λειπόμενοι.

2:16a δέ: This structural marker is a conjunction meaning "and" (BDAG, s.v. "δέ" 1, p. 213). **Syntactically**, it introduces a dependent conjunctive clause. **Semantically**, it is a marker that connects a series of closely related hypothetical information. Thus, it develops the discussion of the dependent adverbial ἐάν conditional clause: "and" (KJV ASV NRSV ESV NET NLT).

εἴπῃ: This Greek word is a third person singular aorist active subjunctive of λέγω that conveys the idea of expressing oneself orally or in written form to someone and may be rendered "say" or "tell" (BDAG, s.v. "λέγω" 1bγ, p. 588). **Syntactically**, it is the main verb of this compound protasis of the conditional sentence. The verb is in the subjunctive mood because ἐάν takes its verb in the subjunctive (W, 469–70). The indefinite pronoun τις is the subject. The indefinite pronoun τις with the prepositional phrase ἐξ ὑμῶν is rendered "one of you" (BDAG, s.v. "τις" 1aαℵ, p. 1007; cf. KJV ASV NASB NRSV ESV NET; cf. NIV). **Semantically**, the aorist is ingressive, stressing the beginning of the action (W, 558–59).

Grammatical Nugget: How does the structure of this sentence convey the message? The subjunctive third person verb ϵἴπῃ relates to the original ἐάν in 2:15a. Also repeated is the indefinite pronoun "someone" (BDAG, s.v. "τις" 1aαℵ, p. 1007). The description of the indifferent response to the needy one portrays this guilty person as part of the community James is addressing. He or she is "from among you" (ἐξ ὑμῶν). The serious callousness conveyed by this heartless response is magnified by the fact that it is spoken by someone in the disadvantaged person's believing community.

2:16b ὑπάγετε: This structural marker is a second person plural present active imperative of ὑπάγω that conveys the idea of leaving someone's presence and may be rendered "go away" or "go" (BDAG, s.v. "ὑπάγω" 1, p. 1028). **Syntactically**, it introduces a dependent direct object clause that modifies "someone says" (ϵἴπῃ . . . τις). We have chosen to place the entire clause under τις to visualize its relationship with the previous clause because it is the reported speech of "someone" (τις) who says (ϵἴπῃ). **Semantically**, the imperative present tense verb conveys a general command that may or may not have taken place (W, 722). In this case, it is a command that conveys the idea of moving along (cf. W, 485). "Go in peace" is a familiar Jewish form of expressing a farewell. Other NT examples are in Mark 5:34; Luke 7:50; and 8:48.

2:16c θερμαίνεσθε: This structural marker is a second person plural present middle imperative of θερμαίνω that conveys the idea of warming oneself and may be rendered as "warm" (BDAG, s.v. "θερμαίνω," p. 454). **Syntactically**, it too introduces a dependent direct object clause that modifies "someone says" (ϵἴπῃ . . . τις). Once again, we placed the entire clause under τις and in parentheses to visualize its relationship with the previous clause because it is the reported speech of "someone" (τις) who says (ϵἴπῃ). **Semantically**, the imperative present tense verb conveys a general command that may or may not have taken place (W, 722). In this case, the command in the middle voice conveys the idea of keeping yourself warm or "keep warm" (NRSV NIV NET). Because the verb may be parsed as a passive, the passive rendering "be warmed" is also possible (KJV ASV NASB ESV CNT; cf. Adam, 51). In either case, the heartless response described is the same.

χορτάζεσθε: This Greek word is a second person plural present middle imperative of χορτάζω that conveys the idea of being full with food and may be rendered "feed" or "fill" (BDAG, s.v. "χορτάζω" 1b, p. 1087). **Syntactically**, it is connected to the previous imperative with καί and is thereby part of the second verb of the dependent direct object that modifies "someone says" (ϵἴπῃ . . . τις). **Semantically**, the imperative present tense verb conveys a general command that may or may not have taken place (W, 722). In this case, the command in the middle voice conveys the idea of keep yourself filled or "keep filled" (NRSV NIV NET) or more pointedly "eat your fill" (NRSV; cf. NLT). Because the verb may be parsed as a passive, the passive rendering "be filled" is also possible (KJV ASV NASB ESV CNT; cf. Adam, 51). As in the previous clause, the heartless response described is the same in either case.

2:16d δέ: This Greek word has an additive relation with a suggested contrast that may be rendered "and yet" or "at the same time" (BDAG, s.v. "δέ" 3, p. 213). **Syntactically**, it introduces a dependent conjunctive clause. **Semantically**, it is a marker connecting a series of closely related hypotheticals with information expressed in the next verb. While some translations render δέ as "but" (NIV NET NLT), we consider the conjunction as a simultaneous contrast or "and yet" (ASV NASB1995 NRSV CNT; Adam, 51).

μὴ δῶτε: This negated (μή) Greek word is a second person plural aorist active subjunctive of δίδωμι that conveys the idea of generosity and may be rendered as "give" or "donate" (BDAG, s.v. "δίδωμι" 1, p. 242). **Syntactically**, it is the main verb of this dependent clause. It is in the subjunctive mood because ἐάν takes its verb in the subjunctive (W, 469–70; cf. Adam, 51). The entire clause is placed above the verb [ἐστιν] in the apodosis to visualize its grammatical dependence. **Semantically**, the negated (μή) aorist tense is constative in that it describes a hypothetical example as a whole (W, 557–58), namely, withholding assistance for those living in a state of poverty. The shift to a plural verb is easily overlooked but not a problem. The broadening of the reference is intended to apply this problem to the whole community which James is addressing.

2:16e [ἐστιν]: This structural marker is a third person singular present active indicative from the verb εἰμί meaning "is" (BDAG, s.v. "εἰμί" 2a, p. 283). **Syntactically**, the bracketed [ἐστιν] is an ellipsis and the main verb of the independent asyndeton clause. It introduces the apodosis for the complex ἐάν clause of 2:15a–16b. The subject of the verb is "the benefit" (τὸ ὄφελος), and the interrogative pronoun "what" (τί) is the predicate adjective (W, 40–46). Τί appears for the second time in the book and introduces a rhetorical question with no expressed verb, as was the case in 2:14a, and will appear again later in 3:13a; 4:12d; and 5:13a, 13c, and 14a. **Semantically**, it is an equative verb that reveals a question equivalent to the American idiom: "What's the use" (Adam, 49) or "What is the benefit" (cf. KJV ASV NRSV). However, most render the clause: "What good is it" (NIV NET; cf. Irons, 536) or "What good is that" (ESV; cf. NASB CNT).

Semantical Nugget: How does the concluding question τί τὸ ὄφελος deliver James's message? The repetition of the rhetorical question from 2:14 provides an inclusio for this first section. James believes his original question in 2:14 has now been answered by his illustration. It also adds a powerful rhetorical punch by reminding the reader of the serious lack of faith displayed by an outwardly pious but heartless "faith." This second-class conditional sentence in 2:16 inverts the apodosis from the earlier conditional sentence by ending with the repeated powerful question, "what is the benefit?" The noun, ὄφελος, that is often translated as "good" may also be rendered "benefit" or "increase" (BDAG, s.v. "ὄφελος," p. 743). This heightens the rhetorical power of James's response. It is appropriate as a counterbalance to quote Paul's effective semantic parallel: "And if I bestow all my goods to feed the poor, and if I give my body to be burned, but have not love, it profits me nothing" (οὐδὲν ὠφελοῦμαι, 1 Cor. 13:3). James may also be alluding to the teaching of Jesus in the parable of the sheep and the goats (Matt. 25:31–46).

2:17a οὕτως καί: These structural markers are conjunctions. The first is a conjunction that may be rendered as "thus," "so," or "in this manner" (BDAG, s.v. "οὕτως" 1b, p. 742). The second is a conjunction often rendered "also" or "likewise" (BDAG, s.v. "καί" 2a, p. 495). **Syntactically**, they introduce an independent conjunctive clause. While οὕτως is identified as an adverbial comparative conjunction that connects ideas, or in this case, examples together (W, 675, 761–62), καί is an adjectival conjunction that is rendered "also" (NET) or "even" (KJV ASV NASB1995). **Semantically**, they draw a consequential conclusion to James's four previous parallel clauses and may be rendered "so also" (ESV NET) or "in the same way" (NIV).

ἐστιν: This Greek word is a third person singular present active indicative from the verb εἰμί that means "is" (BDAG, s.v. "εἰμί" 2a, p. 283). **Syntactically**, it is the main verb of this independent conjunctive clause. It is the inverted apodosis of a third-class conditional clause. The predicate adjective is νεκρά, describing πίστις. **Semantically**, the verb is stative and is fronted before the protasis for emphasis. It adds to the already mentioned doubt over the nature of this sort of faith ("what is the benefit?") by openly declaring that such a faith (ἡ πίστις) is actually "dead."

2:17b ἐάν: This structural marker is a conjunction meaning "if" (BDAG, s.v. "ἐάν" 1cγ, p. 268). **Syntactically**, it introduces a rather complicated dependent conjunctive clause. The entire clause functions adverbially and is placed below the verb ἐστιν in the apodosis to visualize its dependence. **Semantically**, it introduces a third-class conditional clause that introduces a hypothetical situation for the sake of the discussion (W, 696–99; Adam, 52): "if a brother or sister [is] poorly clothed" (ἐὰν ἀδελφὸς ἢ ἀδελφὴ [ἐστιν] γυμνοὶ ὑπάρχωσιν). Once again, the hypothetical situation is not necessarily describing a scene that James has witnessed or heard that it has taken place in their assemblies. The scene that is portrayed in their "synagogue" *may* have taken place, but it is not necessarily a scene that actually *has* taken place.

μὴ ἔχῃ: This negated (μή) Greek word is a third person singular present active subjunctive of ἔχω that conveys the idea of possessing something and may be rendered as "have" or "own" (BDAG, s.v. "ἔχω" 1aα, p. 420). **Syntactically**, it is the main verb of a dependent conjunctive clause and the protasis for the third-class conditional ἐάν clause. The verb is in the subjunctive mood because ἐάν takes its verb in the subjunctive (W, 469–70). **Semantically**, the negated (μή) present tense is again customary and describes a person who has a pattern of doing [performing] no good deeds (W, 521–22). This concluding verse of the section is an effective aphorism that rounds off the argument and will be repeated in various ways over the next few verses.

> **Lexical Nugget:** How is this kind of faith "dead" (νεκρά)? Some commentators have equated this faith only with a weaker form of saving faith that needs to be awakened from its dormancy. Of the 128 occurrences of νεκρός in the NT, it is difficult to find any meaning other than to be literally "without life." The analogical argument in 2:26 ("as the body without the spirit is dead") also argues that the word as used by James means "without life," or in this case, "without spiritual life." In 2:20, James will make the same statement but replace νεκρά with ἀργή ("worthless" or "useless").

FAITH ASSERTIONS IN GOD ARE UNIVERSAL AND MEANINGLESS (JAMES 2:18–19)

CLAUSAL OUTLINE FOR JAMES 2:18–19

2:18a Ἀλλ' **ἐρεῖ** τις, (Σὺ πίστιν **ἔχεις**, κἀγὼ ἔργα **ἔχω**).
2:18a But someone **will say**, ("**You have** faith, but **I have** deeds").

2:18b **δεῖξόν** μοι τὴν πίστιν σου χωρὶς τῶν ἔργων,
2:18b **Prove** to me your faith apart from your deeds,

2:18c κἀγώ σοι **δείξω** ἐκ τῶν ἔργων μου τὴν πίστιν.
2:18c and **I will prove** to you my faith by my deeds.

2:19a σὺ **πιστεύεις** (ὅτι εἷς **ἐστιν** ὁ θεός),
2:19a **Do you believe** (that God is one)?

2:19b καλῶς **ποιεῖς**·
2:19b **You are doing** well;

²:¹⁹ᶜκαὶ τὰ δαιμόνια **πιστεύουσιν** [(ὅτι εἷς ἐστιν ὁ θεός)]
²:¹⁹ᶜ the demons even **believe** [(*that* God is one)]

²:¹⁹ᵈ καὶ **φρίσσουσιν**.
²:¹⁹ᵈ and **they shudder**.

SYNTAX EXPLAINED FOR JAMES 2:18–19

²:¹⁸ᵃ Ἀλλ': This structural marker is a conjunction that indicates a transition to something different or as a contrast to highlight the other side of an issue and may be rendered "but" or "yet" (BDAG, s.v. "ἀλλά" 2, p. 45). **Syntactically**, it introduces an independent conjunctive clause. **Semantically**, it is a rather strong adversative conjunction and often rendered as "but" (NASB NRSV ESV NIV NET). However, it has also been rendered as "now" (NLT). Nevertheless, its use in this verse signals a disarming opinion that strongly differs from the point that James has made in 2:17—namely, a faith that is alone and without deeds is not a valid faith at all; it is dead (cf. Adam, 52). James employs this conjunction only four other times and always in an adversarial way (1:25c; 26b; 3:15c; 4:11e). Combined with the indefinite pronoun τις, the expression introduces a hypothetical debate partner often referred to as the *interlocutor* (Irons, 513).

ἐρεῖ: This Greek word is a third person singular future active indicative of λέγω that conveys the idea of expressing oneself orally or in writing to someone and may be rendered "say" or "tell" (BDAG, s.v. "λέγω" 1bγ, p. 588). **Syntactically**, it is the main verb of this independent conjunctive clause. It introduces the dialogue that will commence between James and his debate partner. The subject of ἐρεῖ is the indefinite pronoun "someone" (BDAG, s.v. "τις" 1aα, p. 1008), which is an imaginary debate partner created for the sake of this hypothetical situation (cf. Adam, 52–53). **Semantically**, the future tense is a gnomic future, though rare; James is describing an act of speaking that may be true of any time (W, 571). James combined the present form of this verb (λέγῃ) with τις in 2:14 when he introduced this topic. Thus, the voice of this hypothetical debater has been heard in 2:14 and also in 2:16 through his apparently casual response to a real need: "Keep yourself warmed and filled." Now James allows that person to have a voice in the debate that ensues in 2:18–19.

ἔχεις: This Greek word is a second person plural present active indicative of ἔχω that means "have" and is understood here as to experience or "have" an inner emotion (BDAG, s.v. "ἔχω" 7aβ, p. 421) or to be in some state or condition (BDAG, s.v. "ἔχω" 10b, p. 422). **Syntactically**, it is the main verb in a dependent direct object with σύ as its subject. The verb ἔχω has already been used with πίστιν in 2:1a, 14b, and 17a. We have chosen to place the entire clause in parentheses to visualize its relationship as the reported speech of "someone" (τις) who "will say" (ἐρεῖ). **Semantically**, the present tense conveys a current state about faith. The personal pronouns σὺ and κἀγὼ expressed with the verb ἔχω serve to intensify the thrust and parry of the debate. The use of these pronouns continues throughout 2:18 and 19, with the σύ sometimes referring clearly to James (here) and sometimes to the interlocutor (2:19). The second person exchange is also evident in the vocative ὦ ἄνθρωπε κενέ in 2:20 and the βλέπεις of 2:22a.

> **Interpretive Nugget:** The difficult interpretive question is, When does the voice of the imaginary debater cease? Is it after the first clause ("You have faith") or does it continue with the next clause ("and I have deeds")? Or does it extend through the rest of the verse? And when does the voice of James reenter the exchange? Consider the suggestion that σὺ πίστιν ἔχεις ("do you have faith?") is a question standing by itself, expressing the interlocutor's doubts about the author's own faith, just as the author had done in referring to deedless faith as "dead." James then responds, "I also have deeds. Show me your faith without deeds and I will show you my faith by my deeds." This fits the context very well, and also solves the problem of the unlikely response by the interlocutor in his continued response following the disputed clause. It is also more satisfying than the other forced interpretations. In this approach, the doubled κἀγώ initiating the second and fourth clauses both serve as part of James's response, and they add a rhetorical intensity to James's reply. While some have objected to the use of κἀγώ to begin a sentence, this takes place a number of times in Greek literature. This reconstruction of the dialogue resolves the problem of who is saying what in the interchange. Although few commentators and no English translations have adopted it as a solution, this approach is worthy of serious consideration (cf. Varner[2], 108–9).

κἀγώ: This Greek word is a crasis that joins two Greek words into one: καί and ἐγω (BDAG, s.v. "κἀγώ," p. 487). **Syntactically**, it introduces the second verb in a dependent clause and the direct object with an embedded "I" as its subject. The entire clause is placed in parentheses to visualize its relationship as the reported speech of "someone" (τις) who "will say" (ἐρεῖ). **Semantically**, while it may serve as the subject of ἔχω, it also serves as a connector for two statements: faith and deeds. While some translations indicate κἀγώ as only the subject of ἔχω: "You have faith; I have deeds" (NIV NLT), others draw attention to the connecting component of κἀγώ and insert "and": "You have faith and I have deeds" (KJV NASB NRSV ESV NET CNT; Adam, 48). We, however, follow BDAG's insert of "but" (BDAG, s.v. "κἀγώ" 2, p. 487).

ἔχω: This Greek word is a first person present active indicative of ἔχω that means "have" and is understood here as to experience or "have" an inner emotion (BDAG, s.v. "ἔχω" 7aβ, p. 421). **Syntactically**, it is the main verb in the dependent direct object with an embedded "I" as its subject. The entire clause is placed in parentheses to visualize its relationship as the reported speech of "someone" (τις) who "will say" (ἐρεῖ). **Semantically**, the present tense conveys a current statement about deeds. The statement is the response of James to the imaginary debater.

2:18b δεῖξόν: This structural marker is a second person singular aorist active imperative of δείκνυμι that conveys the idea of proving or making clear something by evidence or reasoning and may be rendered "explain" or "prove" (BDAG, s.v. "δείκνυμι" 2, p. 215). **Syntactically**, it is the main verb of this independent asyndeton clause. **Semantically**, the aorist imperative is a specific command concerning proof of faith. The aorist tense is an ingressive aorist in that it reflects a sense of urgency to begin a certain action (W, 719), which translations generally render as "show" (KJV ASV NASB NRSV NIV ESV NET CNT NLT). Yet, we favor the rendering of "prove" in keeping with BDAG. This verb conveys an idea of offering as "proof" or as an example that makes clear one's faith. It also appears again in the imperative in James 3:13: "he should show (δειξάτω) by his good behavior his deeds in the gentleness of wisdom."

2:18c κἀγώ: This structural marker is a crasis that joins two Greek words into one: καί and ἐγω (BDAG, s.v. "κἀγώ," p. 487). **Syntactically**, it introduces an independent conjunctive clause and provides an emphasis for an embedded subject "I will show." **Semantically**, while serving as the embedded subject of δείξω, it also serves as a connector for two statements of proof for one's faith. While some translations indicate κἀγώ as only the subject of δείξω: "Show to me . . .; I will show . . ." (NLT), others draw attention to the connecting component of κἀγώ and insert "and": "Show to me . . ., and I will show . . ." (BDAG, s.v. "κἀγώ" 1, p. 487; cf. KJV NASB NRSV ESV NIV NET CNT; Adam, 48).

δείξω: This Greek word is a first person singular future active indicative of δείκνυμι that conveys the idea of proving or making clear something by evidence or reasoning and may be rendered "explain" or "prove" (BDAG, s.v. "δείκνυμι" 2, p. 215). **Syntactically**, it is the main verb of this independent conjunctive clause in verse 18. **Semantically**, the future tense is a predictive future about action that will occur (W, 568), which translations generally render as "I will show" (KJV ASV NASB NRSV NIV ESV NET CNT NLT). Yet, we favor the rendering of δείξω as "I will prove" that is in keeping with BDAG.

Syntactical Nugget: How does James utilize a chiasm in this verse? This clause completes a chiasm from the previous clause. If we slightly rearrange the second verb, it is more evident:

A δεῖξόν μοι τὴν πίστιν σου
  B χωρὶς τῶν ἔργων,
  B´ ἐκ τῶν ἔργων μου
A´ κἀγώ σοι δείξω . . . τὴν πίστιν.

The contrast with the previous clause by the use of different prepositions, **χωρὶς** τῶν ἔργων and **ἐκ** τῶν ἔργων, is important to note. One is a faith *without* deeds and the other is a faith demonstrated *by* deeds. The entire set of expressions is almost a paraphrase of another statement by the brother of James in Matthew 7:16 and 20: "By their fruits (ἀπὸ τῶν καρπῶν αὐτῶν), you shall know them." The challenge of interpreting the passage is heightened by its rapid-fire style of nine primary clauses, which again is illustrative of the diatribal style. The shorthand way in which the debate is described, combined with the lack of quotation marks in the original, actually contributes to the problem of how to sort out the speakers and when they begin and switch (Varner[2], 109).

2:19a πιστεύεις: This structural marker is a second person singular present active indicative of πιστεύω that conveys the idea of considering something to be true and worthy of a person's trust and may be rendered as "believe" (BDAG, s.v. "πιστεύω" 1aβ, p. 816). **Syntactically**, it is the main verb of this independent conjunctive clause with σὺ as the subject. **Semantically**, the present tense conveys a current action or state about a person's faith. As the debate continues, the question implies an assumption that a person's "faith alone" is enough without any accompanying actions.

ὅτι: This structural marker is a conjunction meaning "that" (BDAG, s.v. "ὅτι" 1c, p. 731). **Syntactically**, it introduces a substantival dependent conjunctive clause: "*that* God is one" (ὅτι εἷς ἐστιν ὁ θεός). The entire ὅτι clause functions as the direct object of the verb: "you believe" (πιστεύεις). It is placed in parentheses in order to visualize its contribution to the independent clause. **Semantically**, it is indirect discourse: "that" (cf. KJV ASV NASB NRSV NIV ESV NET). The entire ὅτι clause provides the content of the negated verb about what is believed (W, 456; Adam, 54). Yet, the specifics of belief are found in the next verb.

ἐστιν: This Greek word is a third person singular present active indicative of εἰμί that conveys the idea of being in close connection with something and may be rendered "is" (BDAG, s.v. "εἰμί" 2a, p. 284). **Syntactically**, it is the main verb in a dependent conjunctive clause that serves as the direct object of πιστεύεις. The subject is ὁ θεός and εἷς is the predicate adjective (W, 42–44; Adam, 55). **Semantically**, the present tense conveys a current statement about God's existence. The expression is an adaptation of the famous *Shema* of Deuteronomy 6:4.

2:19b ποιεῖς: This structural marker is a second person singular present active indicative of ποιέω that conveys the idea of carrying out an obligation of a moral or social nature and may be rendered "do," "keep," "carry out," "practice," or "commit" (BDAG, s.v. "ποιέω" 3a, p. 840). **Syntactically**, it is the main verb in this independent asyndeton clause with the adverb καλῶς that indicates accordance to a standard, namely, the Shema (BDAG, s.v. "καλῶς" 4, p. 505). **Semantically**, the present tense is a customary present (W, 521–22) that conveys a pattern of behavior: "you do well" (KJV ASV NASB NRSV ESV NET CNT), "good for you" (NLT) or simply "good" (NIV). In order to capture the continuous nature of the present, we render the verb as "you *are doing* well."

> **Figure of Speech:** Is "you do well" an irony? While it is possible to take this indicative pronouncement as a favorable one, it may be purely ironic. Perhaps the best approach is to view the statement itself as favorable, since the belief is true, but what follows introduces the irony (Davids, 125–26). This expression is "a biting comment" (Blomberg et al., 135). The irony conveyed by James's response to this supposed creedal confession echoes his earlier response in 2:8 to one who believes the law of loving his neighbor. Together these responses embody Jesus's summation of the law—namely, our love to God and our love to others (Matt. 22:37–39).

2:19c πιστεύουσιν: This structural marker is a third person plural present active indicative of πιστεύω that "considers something to be true and therefore worthy of one's trust" and may be rendered "believe" (BDAG, s.v. "πιστεύω" 1aβ, p. 816). **Syntactically**, it is the main verb of this independent asyndeton clause with δαιμόνια as its subject. The content of belief or the means of belief is the assumed clause: "that God is one" (ὅτι εἷς ἐστιν ὁ θεός) mentioned in the previous clause. Some translations insert "that" (NIV NET) or "this" (NLT). **Semantically**, the present tense is a customary present (W, 521–22) that conveys a habitual belief: "believe" (KJV ASV NASB NRSV NIV ESV NET NLT CNT). The meaning of the verb does not convey saving faith but simply an affirmation of truth about God's existence that even demons can display.

2:19d καί: This structural marker is a conjunction meaning "and" (BDAG, s.v. "καί" 1bζ, p. 494). **Syntactically**, it introduces an independent conjunctive clause.

Semantically, it introduces a result that comes from the preceding clause. It is a coordinating conjunction rendered as "and" (KJV ASV NASB NRSV NIV ESV NET NLT CNT) linking two independent clauses together.

φρίσσουσιν: This Greek word is a third person plural present active indicative of φρίσσω that speaks of a reaction to something or someone who causes fear and may be rendered "shudder" or "tremble" (BDAG, s.v. "φρίσσω," p. 1065). **Syntactically**, it is the main verb of this independent conjunctive clause with the understood "they" as its subject, referring back to δαιμόνια. **Semantically**, the present tense is a customary present (W, 521–22) that conveys a habitual fear: "they tremble" (KJV NET NLT) or "they shudder" (ASV NASB NRSV NIV ESV CNT).

> **Lexical Nugget:** What is the specific meaning of φρίσσουσιν? How do demons "shudder" (BDAG, s.v. "φρίσσω," p. 1065)? That all created things shudder before God the Creator is a very Jewish teaching (Josephus, *War* 5.378). The NT witnesses to the monotheism of demons (Acts 16:17; 19:15) and their fear of Christ whom they recognize (Mark 1:23–24; 5:7). There is a sarcasm contained in this statement. The bare knowledge of a theological truth that even demons affirm has no benefit for those demons. There is also a type of faith that arises out of craven fear but leads only to "shuddering," not to peace (2 Tim. 1:7a: "God has not given us the spirit of fear"). Possible links with the oral and written tradition of Jesus again should not be overlooked. Jesus's use of the same material in what has been called "royal law" of Matthew 22:37–39 provides the meaning and application that James adapts and employs.

ACTION VINDICATES REAL FAITH (JAMES 2:20–26)

CLAUSAL OUTLINE FOR JAMES 2:20–26

2:20 **θέλεις** δὲ **γνῶναι**, ὦ ἄνθρωπε κενέ, (<u>ὅτι</u> ἡ πίστις χωρὶς τῶν ἔργων ἀργή **ἐστιν**);
2:20 But **do you want** **to understand**, O vain person, (<u>that</u> faith without deeds **is** useless)?

2:21a Ἀβραὰμ ὁ πατὴρ ἡμῶν οὐκ ἐξ ἔργων **ἐδικαιώθη**
2:21a **Was** not Abraham our father **vindicated** by deeds
|
2:21b **ἀνενέγκας** Ἰσαὰκ τὸν υἱὸν αὐτοῦ ἐπὶ τὸ θυσιαστήριον;
2:21b *when* **he offered up** his son Isaac on the altar?

²:²²ᵃ **βλέπεις** (ὅτι ἡ πίστις **συνήργει** τοῖς ἔργοις αὐτοῦ
²:²²ᵃ <u>**You see**</u> (<u>that</u> faith **was working together** with his deeds,

> |
>
> ²:²²ᵇ <u>καὶ [ὅτι]</u> ἐκ τῶν ἔργων ἡ πίστις **ἐτελειώθη**).
> ²:²²ᵇ <u>and</u> [<u>*that*</u>] faith **was completed** by *means of* his deeds).

²:²³ᵃ <u>καὶ</u> **ἐπληρώθη** ἡ γραφὴ
²:²³ᵃ <u>In this way</u>, the Scripture **was fulfilled**

> |
>
> ²:²³ᵇ ἡ **λέγουσα**, Ἐπίστευσεν δὲ Ἀβραὰμ τῷ θεῷ,
> ²:²³ᵇ that **says**, "<u>Now</u> Abraham **believed** God

>> |
>>
>> ²:²³ᶜ <u>καὶ</u> **ἐλογίσθη** αὐτῷ εἰς δικαιοσύνην
>> ²:²³ᶜ <u>and</u> **it was counted** to him as righteousness"

>> |
>>
>> ²:²³ᵈ <u>καὶ</u> φίλος θεοῦ **ἐκλήθη**.
>> ²:²³ᵈ <u>and</u> **he was called** "friend of God."

²:²⁴ **ὁρᾶτε** (ὅτι ἐξ ἔργων **δικαιοῦται** ἄνθρωπος καὶ οὐκ ἐκ πίστεως μόνον).
²:²⁴ <u>**You see**</u> (<u>that</u> a person **is being vindicated** *regularly* by *means of* deeds and not by *means of* faith alone).

²:²⁵ᵃ ὁμοίως <u>δὲ</u> καὶ Ῥαὰβ ἡ πόρνη οὐκ ἐξ ἔργων **ἐδικαιώθη**
²:²⁵ᵃ <u>And</u> in the same way, **was** not also Rahab the prostitute **vindicated** by *means of* deeds

>> ²:²⁵ᵇ **ὑποδεξαμένη** τοὺς ἀγγέλους
>> ²:²⁵ᵇ *when* **she welcomed** the scouts

>> |
>>
>> ²:²⁵ᶜ <u>καὶ</u> ἑτέρᾳ ὁδῷ **ἐκβαλοῦσα**:
>> ²:²⁵ᶜ *and when* **she sent them out** by another way?

>> ²:²⁶ᵃ<u>ὥσπερ γὰρ</u> τὸ σῶμα χωρὶς πνεύματος νεκρόν **ἐστιν**,
>> ²:²⁶ᵃ <u>*You see*</u> just as the body apart from the spirit **is** dead,

²:²⁶ᵇ <u>οὕτως καὶ</u> ἡ πίστις χωρὶς ἔργων νεκρά **ἐστιν**.
²:²⁶ᵇ <u>so also</u> the faith that is not accompanied by deeds **is** dead.

Syntax Explained for James 2:20–26

2:20 δέ: This structural marker is a conjunction meaning "but" (BDAG, s.v. "δέ" 4a, p. 213). **Syntactically**, it introduces an independent conjunctive clause. **Semantically**, it is a marker of contrast that connects a series of closely related statements about faith. It is rendered "but" (KJV ASV NASB NET CNT), though some translations leave it untranslated (NRSV NIV ESV NLT). Yet, it continues the diatribal style of interrogation so characteristic of James.

θέλεις: This Greek word is a second person singular present active indicative of θέλω that conveys the idea of having desires for something and may be rendered as "wish to have," "desire," or "want" (BDAG, s.v. "θέλω" 1, p. 448). **Syntactically**, it is the main verb of this independent conjunctive clause where the subject "you" refers to the later vocative ἄνθρωπε κενέ. **Semantically**, the present tense is a customary present that conveys a pattern of behavior (W, 521–22), namely, desiring something that is defined with the next verbal.

γνῶναι: This Greek word is an aorist active infinitive of γινώσκω that conveys the idea of grasping the significance or meaning of something and may be rendered "understand" or "comprehend" (BDAG, s.v. "γινώσκω" 3, p. 200). **Syntactically**, it is part of the main verb of this independent conjunctive clause. **Semantically**, it is a complementary (supplemental) infinitive following θέλεις (W, 598–99; Adam, 55). The aorist tense is an ingressive aorist indicating the beginning of an action (W, 558–59), in this case, a desire to know. A passive translation for the active infinitive ("want to be shown") is justified for rhetorical reasons. The use of this sort of question in the Greek diatribe genre can be seen as well in the NT. Compare the use of οὐκ οἴδατε in 4:4a (also Rom. 6:16; 11:2; 1 Cor. 3:16; 5:6; 6:2–3, 9, 15, 16, 19; 9:13, 24). That faith can attempt to exist without its appropriate accompanying actions is so inconceivable to James that he addresses his opponent with a noun and adjective (ἄνθρωπε κε- νέ—"vain person") that is roughly equivalent to the modern term "blockhead" for even supposing that they can somehow be separated.

> **Lexical Nugget:** What does κενέ mean? This adjective in the vocative case appears in the LXX as meaning "empty" in a literal sense (Exod. 23:15; Deut. 16:16). This literal sense of "empty" appears in the NT in the "Parable of the Wicked Husbandmen" (Mark 12:3). The metaphorical sense of "empty" can describe a "vain" message (Deut. 32:47). This sense of "vain" appears in a warning against "vain" or "empty" preaching (1 Cor. 15:14). When rarely applied to people, the word in the LXX suggests deficiency in understanding as well as moral perversity (Judg. 9:4; 11:3). It is this sense that prepares us for its use here in James. The person is a head without a brain who is incapable of wisdom and understanding and thereby a vain person.

ὅτι: This structural marker is a conjunction meaning "that" (BDAG, s.v. "ὅτι" 1c, p. 731). **Syntactically**, it introduces a substantival dependent conjunctive clause: "*that* faith without deeds is useless." The entire ὅτι clause functions as the direct object of the verb: "do you want to understand" (θέλεις . . . γνῶναι). The clause is placed in parentheses to visualize its contribution to the independent clause. **Semantically**, it introduces indirect discourse because it appears after a verb of perception (W, 456–57) and is rendered: "that" (cf. KJV ASV NASB NRSV NIV ESV NET). The entire ὅτι clause provides the content of understanding. Yet, the specifics of that understanding are found in the next verb.

ἐστιν: This Greek word is a third person singular present active indicative of εἰμί that conveys the idea of being in close connection with and may be rendered as "is" "be" (BDAG, s.v. "εἰμί" 2a, p. 283). **Syntactically**, it is the main verb of this dependent conjunctive clause. The subject is "faith" (ἡ πίστις) and "useless" (ἀργή) is the predicate adjective (W, 40–44). **Semantically**, it equates "faith" (ἡ πίστις) with "useless" (ἀργή) and simply rendered as "is" (KJV ASV NASB NRSV NIV ESV NET NLT CNT). James equates "faith that has no deeds" with "uselessness."

> **Lexical and Text-Critical Nugget:** Why does James switch his adjective to ἀργή in James 2:20? This adjective is not the νεκρά that was used in 2:17. Some later Byzantine scribes attempted to bring this verse into harmony with the wording of 2:17 and 2:26 by using νεκρά here. Surprisingly, however, they are also joined by Sinaiticus and Alexandrinus, while P[74] has the unique reading κενὴ under the influence of the vocative κενέ earlier in the verse. The use of ἀργή is supported by B C* 322 323 945 1739 and the ancient versions, but may also involve a subtle play on words (τῶν ἔργων ἀργή [α + εργη]) (cf. Metzger[1], 610; Metzger[2], 681). There is another reason for the word ἀργή, which relates to the semantics of this word in light of the author's overall rhetorical strategy. The adjective ἀργή is most often translated by "idle" or "useless" (BDAG, s.v. "ἀργός," p. 128). In 2 Peter 1:8, ἀργή is parallel to the adjective, ἄκαρπος ("unfruitful"). The next individual mentioned by James in this passage is Abraham (2:21–24). Who, therefore, could better serve as the exemplar who, although he once was "unfruitful" and "barren," eventually produced an unexpected heir, Isaac, and then assumes a role in this text which teaches that a faith that is accompanied by the right deeds is not "barren"?

2:21a ἐδικαιώθη: This structural marker is a third person singular aorist passive indicative of δικαιόω that conveys the idea of rendering a favorable verdict and may be rendered "vindicate" (BDAG, s.v. "δικαιόω" 2a, p. 249). **Syntactically**, it is the main verb in a primary interrogative clause with Ἀβραὰμ as its subject.

The rhetorical question asked with the negative οὐκ anticipates a positive answer. The question "Wasn't Abraham justified by deeds" expects a "yes, he was" answer. **Semantically**, the aorist tense is a constative aorist in that it describes an event as a whole (W, 557–58). In this case, James merely provides a summary statement about Abraham, namely, that Abraham's deeds vindicated him (cf. Adam, 56). Naturally, translations render ἐξ ἔργων ἐδικαιώθη as "justified by works" (KJV ASV NASB NRSV ESV NET CNT), "considered righteous for what he did" (NIV), or "shown to be right with God" (NLT).

> **Structural Nugget:** What is the significance of the parallel structuring of Abraham and Rahab? The parallel way in which James structures the actions of Abraham and Rahab can be seen in the following comparison of the two main interrogative sentences.
>
> 2:21a Ἀβραὰμ ὁ πατὴρ ἡμῶν οὐκ ἐξ ἔργων ἐδικαιώθη
>
> 2:25a Ῥαὰβ ἡ πόρνη οὐκ ἐξ ἔργων ἐδικαιώθη
>
> In each sentence a rhetorical question that expects a positive answer is asked along with the subject's name (Abraham, Rahab).[3] This is then followed by a one-word description (father, prostitute), along with the adjunct "by deeds" that concludes each initial primary clause. A question asked with the negative οὐκ anticipates a positive response. In other words, the intended response to this question is: "Yes, Abraham was justified by his deeds." James asserts that Abraham did works and that these works were used as the basis for God's ultimate pronouncement over Abraham's life. Abraham had faith and this faith was basic to his acceptance by God (2:22–23). James stresses that the life which has been accepted by God must show the fruit of that relationship by exhibiting good deeds. Paul concentrates on what precedes and enables these deeds. For Paul, one gets *into* God's favor only by faith while James insists that God expects good deeds from those who *are in*.

2:21b ἀνενέγκας: This structural marker is a nominative singular masculine aorist active participle of ἀναφέρω that conveys the act of offering a sacrifice and

---

3. In his concluding chapter, "Four Exemplars—A Unity of Purpose?" (pp. 192–204), Foster restates the threefold common thread that links together Abraham and Rahab as well as two other exemplars about whom James appeals (Job and Elijah). First, they have a whole-hearted commitment to God (pp. 193–95). Second, they are presented as outsiders (pp. 195–96). Finally, they face their tests alone (pp. 196–97). Ultimately, "all four exemplars overcame their faith tests, showed their wisdom and single-minded commitment to God, cared for those in need, spoke God's word or the right words about God and proved themselves to be true doers of the implanted word" (p. 197) and thereby friends of God (p. 204). R. J. Foster, *The Significance of Exemplars for the Interpretation of the Letter of James*, WUNT (Tübingen, Germany: Mohr Siebeck, 2014).

may be rendered as "offer up" (BDAG, s.v. "ἀναφέρω" 3, p. 75). **Syntactically**, it introduces a dependent participial clause that functions adverbially modifying ἐδικαιώθη. The entire clause is placed under ἐδικαιώθη to visualize its dependence on ἐδικαιώθη. **Semantically**, the participle is temporal, conveying antecedent action, "after he did" (W, 623–26; cf. Adam, 56) and is commonly rendered "when he offered" (KJV NASB NRSV ESV NIV NET NLT CNT). The aorist tense functions as a constative aorist, viewing the action as a whole (W, 557–58). Thus, Abraham was vindicated after he offered Isaac as a sacrifice. James employs the same language as Genesis 22:2, 13 for the crucial action in 22:9. Hebrews 11:17–19 declares it was πίστει ("by faith") that Abraham, when he was tested (πειραζόμενος), brought forth Isaac and offered his only son. This is consistent with James's approach.

> **Theological Nugget:** What does it mean that Abraham was vindicated by deeds? The question asked with the negative οὐκ anticipates a positive response (Porter, 278–79). The intended response to this question is: "yes, Abraham was justified by his deeds." There is an apparent conflict with Paul on this issue. For Paul, justification is a sovereign, judicial act in which God, apart from any human "work," declares the sinner to be innocent before him (Rom. 4:5). Some commentators think that James uses the verb ἐδικαιώθη in a demonstrative sense, meaning that Abraham was justified in the sense that he demonstrated his righteous status by performing those good deeds. But the question is not "How can righteousness be demonstrated?" but "What kind of faith secures righteousness?" James is also using the verb in a declarative sense, as Paul also does (Rom. 3:21–26; Gal. 2:15–21). While James uses "justify" and "justification" to refer to God's ultimate declaration of a person's righteousness, Paul uses it to refer to the initial securing of that righteousness by faith. The use of δικαιόω in this eschatological sense is its meaning also in the teaching of Jesus. "By your words you will be justified, and by your words you will be condemned" (Matt. 12:37). James's frequent allusions to Jesus's teaching accentuate this reference. James asserts that Abraham did works and that these works were used as the basis for God's ultimate pronouncement over Abraham's life. Abraham had faith and this faith was basic to his acceptance by God (James 2:22–23). James stresses that the life of the one who has been accepted by God must show the result of that relationship by doing good works. Paul concentrates on what precedes these works. He wants to make clear that one "gets into" God's kingdom only by faith, while James insists that God requires works from those who *are already* in the kingdom.

2:22a βλέπεις: This structural marker is a second person singular present active indicative of βλέπω that conveys a developing awareness of something and may be rendered as "perceive" or "feel" (BDAG, s.v. "βλέπω" 7b, p.

179). **Syntactically**, it is the main verb of this independent clause with the understood "you" of the debate opponent as the subject. **Semantically**, the present tense conveys an ongoing state of a developing awareness (W, 521–22). The declaration points out to the opponent what is obvious from a reading of the account in Genesis.

ὅτι: This structural marker is a conjunction meaning "that" (BDAG, s.v. "ὅτι" 1c, p. 731). **Syntactically**, it introduces a dependent conjunctive clause: "*that* faith was working together with his deeds" (ὅτι ἡ πίστις συνήργει τοῖς ἔργοις αὐτοῦ). The entire ὅτι clause functions as the direct object of the verb "you see" (βλέπεις) and is placed in parentheses to visualize its contribution to the independent clause. **Semantically**, it is an indirect discourse because it appears after a verb of perception (W, 456–57) and is rendered "that" (cf. NASB NRSV NIV ESV NET CNT). The entire ὅτι clause provides the content of understanding. Yet, the specifics of that understanding are found in the next verb.

συνήργει: This Greek verb is a third person singular imperfect active indicative of συνεργέω that conveys the idea of engaging in a cooperative manner and may be rendered as "work together with," "assist," or "help" (BDAG, s.v. "συνεργέω," p. 969). **Syntactically**, it is the main verb in the dependent conjunctive ὅτι clause, which is the direct object of βλέπεις. **Semantically**, the imperfect tense is a progressive imperfect that describes an action that is in progress (W, 543–44) and is rendered as "was working together" (NET; cf. NIV NLT) or "was active along with" (NRSV ESV; cf. KJV ASV CNT). Faith is working together "with deeds" (τοῖς ἔργοις).

> **Semantical Nugget:** How does faith work together with deeds? First, ἡ πίστις συνήργει τοῖς ἔργοις αὐτοῦ and ἐκ τῶν ἔργων ἡ πίστις ἐτελειώθη have two semantically related words (συν**ήργει** τοῖς **ἔργοις** αὐτοῦ). Second, they describe the inseparable nature of the two issues, faith and deeds. The imperfect verb συνήργει conveys the idea that Abraham's faith and actions "were working together." James did not mean to say that Abraham had only deeds and not faith. It is his faith and his deeds that together mark Abraham, as he had earlier argued in 2:18. The imperfective aspect of the verb describes that process as taking place throughout Abraham's journey from the time he initially believed God in Genesis 15:6 (2:23) until the consummation of the "sacrifice of Isaac in Genesis 22. The aorist passive verb, ἐτελειώθη ("was completed"), declares that his faith was completed by his accompanying deed(s). His faith was in a sense incomplete until it was perfected or completed by deeds, another example of James's emphasis on wholeness and perfection.

2:22b καὶ [ὅτι]: This Greek word is a conjunction meaning "and" (BDAG, s.v. "καί" 1b, p. 494) and appears with an elliptical ὅτι (see discussion about the ὅτι above; 2:22a). **Syntactically**, it introduces a second dependent conjunctive ὅτι clause: "*and* [*that*] faith was completed by means of his actions" (καὶ [ὅτι] ἐκ τῶν ἔργων ἡ πίστις ἐτελειώθη). The entire καὶ [ὅτι] clause is placed in parentheses along with the ὅτι clause above in order to visualize its contribution to the independent βλέπεις clause. **Semantically**, it is a coordinating conjunction: "and" (NET ESV NASB NRSV etc.) that presents the second part of the direct object for the verb: "you see" (βλέπεις).

ἐτελειώθη: This Greek word is a third person singular aorist passive indicative of τελειόω that conveys the idea of overcoming or supplanting an imperfect state of things and may be rendered as "complete," or "perfected" (BDAG, s.v. "τελειόω" 2eβ, p. 996). **Syntactically**, it is the main verb in this dependent conjunctive clause, which is also a direct object of βλέπεις. **Semantically**, the aorist tense is a constative aorist that describes an event as a whole (W, 557–58), namely, the completion of Abraham's faith. The passive mood declares that Abraham's faith was completed "*by means of*" (ἐκ; cf. BDAG, s.v. "ἐκ" 3f, p. 297) Abraham's accompanying deeds (Adam, 57). In other words, his faith was in a sense incomplete until it was "perfected" (KJV ASV NASB NET) or "completed" (NRSV NIV ESV NLT CNT) by deeds.

> **Theological Nugget:** What is the significance of faith being completed by means of one's deeds? This is yet another example of James's emphasis throughout his book on wholeness and perfection. James sees faith and deeds as bound together in a unity. It is not that Abraham's faith had to wait for completion during the period from Genesis 15 to 22. It was completed in the sense of supplemented. If, when the test came, the faith had not been matched by works, then it would have been proved to be an incomplete faith. The offering of Isaac crowned his faith.

2:23a καί: This structural marker is a conjunction that may be rendered "therefore," "thus," or "in this way" (BDAG, s.v. "καί" 1bζ, p. 495). **Syntactically**, it introduces an independent conjunctive clause. **Semantically**, it appears to be somewhat inferential to verse 22 in that it provides a concluding thought about Abraham's example in Scripture (W, 673). Although many translations appear to emphasize a coordinate connection between verses 22 and 23 by translating καί as "and" (KJV ASV NASB NIV ESV NET CNT), others view καί as inferential: "thus" (NRSV; Adam, 49) or "and so" (NLT). We provided an inferential force with our rendering as "in this way."

ἐπληρώθη: This Greek word is a third person singular aorist passive indicative of πληρόω that conveys the idea of bringing something to a designated end and may be rendered "fulfill" (BDAG, s.v. "πληρόω" 4a, p. 828). **Syntactically**, it is the main verb of this dependent conjunctive clause with ἡ γραφή as its subject.[4] **Semantically**, the aorist tense is a constative aorist that describes an event as a whole (W, 557–58), namely, the fulfillment of Scripture.

> **Theological and Lexical Nugget:** How was an indicative statement, not a prophecy, "fulfilled"? The word ἐπληρώθη is a different verb than the one in 2:22b (ἐτελειώθη). James does not say that Abraham's *faith* was fulfilled (as in 2:22b), but that the *Scripture* statement was fulfilled. The English word *fulfill* often connotes the idea of a prediction and its divine fulfillment, but the quotation from Genesis 15:6 is a past tense indicative statement, not a future prophetic prediction. The verb πληρόω here means more like "give its true or full meaning," as it also does in Matthew 5:17 and Galatians 5:14 (BDAG, s.v. "πληρόω" 4, p. 828). Paul's use of Genesis 15:6 differs in that he associates the belief in the verse with the circumcisions among Abraham's male household in Genesis 17. His point is that Abraham believed and was declared to be in the right before he underwent the "work" of circumcision. In Paul's argument, this makes perfect sense (Rom. 4:9–12), especially for uncircumcised Gentiles who had believed the gospel. Yet, James's use of the same text also makes sense when we recognize that Abraham's "works" in James were not Jewish national badges, as they appear to be in Romans and Galatians. Deeds in James are obedient acts of love and mercy, which are the necessary accompaniment of a true saving faith. This is a classic example of how NT writers can handle an OT text in different but not contradictory ways.

2:23b ἡ λέγουσα: This articular (ἡ) structural marker is a nominative plural feminine present active participle of λέγω that conveys expressions orally or in written form, in this case in quotations from Scripture, and may be rendered as "utter in words," "say," or "tell" (BDAG, s.v. "λέγω" 1bζ, p. 588). **Syntactically**, it introduces a dependent participial clause that functions adjectivally modifying γραφή. This dependent clause has several independent clauses due to its quotation of an OT passage from Genesis. **Semantically**, the present tense is an iterative present that conveys a retelling time and again (W, 520–21) the recorded events of Abraham (cf. Gen. 15:6). Although the verb λέγω is often used for God's speaking through an OT Scripture (cf. 2:11a and 4:6b), here and in 4:5a the verb is used specifically for ἡ γραφὴ speaking.

---

4.   Abraham is the first significant exemplar in James. And while James underscores what Scripture says about Abraham, there are references to Abraham throughout Jewish tradition, a tradition James follows. Foster (pp. 59–103) provides a detailed examination of those sources and reveals the patriarch's faith works as earning merit and was the basis for God's declaration of righteousness. Abraham's faith was unwavering.

δέ: This structural marker is a conjunction meaning "now" (BDAG, s.v. "δέ" 2, p. 213). **Syntactically**, it introduces a dependent conjunctive clause that functions as the direct object of λέγουσα. It appears in the post-positive position in this OT quotation from Genesis. **Semantically**, it may be considered as a transitional conjunction "now" (NET) that James chose to use rather than the LXX use of καί to describe the further development within the Genesis narrative (cf. Adam, 57). Others, however, render δέ as "and," which is in keeping with the LXX (ASV NASB). Despite these two grammatical understandings, many leave δέ untranslated (cf. KJV NRSV NIV ESV NLT CNT).

ἐπίστευσεν: This Greek word is a third person singular aorist active indicative of πιστεύω that conveys the idea of considering something "to be true and therefore worthy of one's trust" and may be rendered as "believe" (BDAG, s.v. "πιστεύω" 1b, p. 817a). **Syntactically**, it is the main verb of this dependent conjunctive clause within the OT quotation from Genesis with Ἀβραάμ as the subject. **Semantically**, the aorist tense is a constative aorist that describes an event as a whole (W, 557–58), namely, the belief of Abraham. This is the scriptural evidence for Abraham's faith. Paul cites the same text (Gen. 15:6) in Romans 4:3 and Galatians 3:6 but utilizes it in a different way than James.

2:23c καί: This structural marker is a conjunction meaning "and" (BDAG, s.v. "καί" 1b, p. 494). **Syntactically**, it introduces a dependent conjunctive clause. **Semantically**, it is a coordinating conjunction rendered "and" (NET ESV NASB NRSV etc.) that links two clauses together about active and completed faith.

ἐλογίσθη: This Greek word is a third person singular aorist passive indicative of λογίζομαι that conveys the idea of determining by a mathematical process and may be rendered "reckon" or "calculate" (BDAG, s.v. "λογίζομαι" 1a, p. 597). **Syntactically**, it is the main verb of this dependent conjunctive clause within the OT quotation from Genesis with "belief" as the verb's embedded subject. **Semantically**, the aorist tense is a constative aorist that describes an event as a whole (W, 557–58), namely, how Abraham's belief as a whole was calculated. The passive verb has no expressed subject and reproduces the LXX of Genesis 15:6 (ἐλογίσθη αὐτῷ) which renders the Hebrew יַחְשְׁבֶהָ לּוֹ. The Greek verb bears a mathematical sense of "calculate" and is used that way in Acts 19:27.

2:23d καί: This structural marker is a conjunction meaning "and" (BDAG, s.v. "καί" 1b, p. 494). **Syntactically**, it introduces a dependent conjunctive clause. **Semantically**, it is another coordinating conjunction that links two clauses together that is rendered "and" (KJV ASV NASB NRSV ESV NET etc.). This clause adds further information about Abraham.

ἐκλήθη: This Greek word is a third person singular aorist passive indicative of καλέω that conveys the idea of identifying someone by name or by an attribute and may be rendered "call," "call by name," or "name" (BDAG, s.v. "καλέω" 1b, p. 502). **Syntactically**, it is the main verb of this dependent conjunctive clause within the OT quotation from Genesis with the name of Ἀβραάμ assumed in the verb as the subject. **Semantically**, the aorist tense is a constative aorist that describes an event as a whole (W, 557–58). The passive verb indicates that someone else gave this title of "friend of God" to the patriarch, namely, God. Thus, this final clause of the Genesis passage quoted by James describes an event as a whole where God declared Abraham as a friend.

> **Semantical Nugget:** What is the significance of the use of the name "φί- λος θεοῦ"? Abraham was referred to twice by a similar name in canonical literature. The words in both the Hebrew texts and in their LXX translations convey the idea of a "loved one." Furthermore, the LXX Greek word is not the noun φίλος; it is the verb ἀγαπάω (אֹהֲבִי and ὃν ἠγάπησα in Isa. 41:8; אֹהַבְךָ and τῷ ἠγαπημένῳ in 2 Chron. 20:7). By using this title James is not directly referring to either the Isaiah or the Chronicles references, but rather to the noncanonical Jewish literary tradition. In Hellenistic Jewish literature, there are a number of occasions when Abraham was referenced as God's friend by the same Greek noun, φίλος, or its equivalent in other languages.

2:24 ὁρᾶτε: This structural marker is a second person plural present active indicative of ὁράω that conveys the idea of being mentally or spiritually perceptive and may be rendered "perceive" (BDAG, "ὁράω" 4a, p. 720). **Syntactically**, it is the main verb of this independent asyndeton clause with the understood "you" of the debate opponent as the subject. **Semantically**, the present tense conveys a current pattern of behavior. James drops the dialogue with his debate partner since the address is no longer "you [sing.] see," but rather "you [pl.] see," which in turn serves as a concluding statement. The addressees are again the readers and rendered "you see" (KJV ASV NASB NRSV NIV ESV NET NLT CNT). The shift to another verb for "see" is probably due to his focus being shifted from his opponent in debate now to his readers.

ὅτι: This structural marker is a conjunction meaning "that" (BDAG, s.v. "ὅτι" 1c, p. 731). **Syntactically**, it introduces a dependent conjunctive clause: "*that* a person is justified by deeds and not by faith only" (ὅτι ἐξ ἔργων δικαιοῦται ἄνθρωπος καὶ οὐκ ἐκ πίστεως μόνον). The entire ὅτι clause functions as the direct object of the verb "you see" (ὁρᾶτε). It is placed in parentheses in order to visualize its contribution to the independent clause. **Semantically**, it is an indirect discourse because it appears after a verb of perception (W, 456–57) and is rendered "that" (KJV ASV NASB NRSV NIV ESV NET NLT CNT). The entire ὅτι clause provides the content of understanding. Yet, the specifics of that understanding are found in the next verb.

δικαιοῦται: This Greek word is a third person singular present passive indicative of δικαιόω that conveys the idea of rendering a favorable verdict and may be rendered "vindicate" (BDAG, s.v. "δικαιόω" 2a, p. 249). **Syntactically**, it is the main verb in a dependent substantival ὅτι clause that is the direct object of ὁρᾶτε. The noun ἄνθρωπος is its subject. **Semantically**, the present tense conveys an ongoing state (W, 521–22) and is rendered "is justified" (KJV ASV NASB NRSV ESV NET CNT), "we are shown to be right with God" (NLT), or as we render δικαιοῦται, "is being vindicated regularly." The passive mood declares that someone's faith is completed *"by means of"* (ἐκ; cf. BDAG, s.v. "ἐκ" 3f, p. 297) that person's accompanying deeds and not only *by means of* faith (Adam, 58) as it was the case for Abraham in verse 22b.

> **Lexical Nugget:** Why does James use the word ἄνθρωπος? For the second of three times in this section (see the rhetorical questions in 2:21 and 25), James declares that a "person" (ἄνθρωπος) is justified by works (ἐξ ἔργων). The choice of the generic noun for "person" may be due to the fact that he is about to introduce a "matriarch" as the second of his two prime exemplars. Yet, ἄνθρωπος is commonly employed as a general neutral expression that refers to people or humanity in general (Bateman[2], 146–48).

> **Theological Nugget:** What is the theological significance of the word μόνον? The use of this adverb corresponds exactly to the way it was used in 1:22a, where the subject was the contrast between "hearers only" and "doers of the Word." Here, the contrast is between "faith only" and "doing the faith." The μόνον is equivalent to the ἐστιν καθ' ἑαυτήν in 2:17a. While some see a clear contradiction with the Pauline statements in Romans and Galatians, Paul never uses μόνον in this way in Romans 3–4 and Galatians 2–4. Thus far James has contended vigorously for the inseparability of faith and deeds. The function of μόνον is clear. A confession of faith is necessary, but such faith in and of itself will not do, because faith must produce deeds. Jesus had taught this (cf. Matt. 7:15–21), and it would certainly have earned Paul's approval as well (1 Cor. 13:2; 2 Cor. 9:8; Gal. 5:6, 6:4). The idea that faith alone saves has been misunderstood by many. James is firmly opposing throughout his book any notion of a "works = salvation." A truly biblical faith is never alone; it is always accompanied by love and hope (1 Cor. 13:13) as well as by the other Christian virtues

(2 Peter 1:5–8). Paul would also oppose a bifurcation between faith and works (Gal. 5:6; Eph. 2:8–10). When he is not condemning a salvation that seeks to be based on the "works of the law," he uses "works" for deeds of love and kindness more than any other NT writer (see, e.g., Rom. 2:6, 7; 13:3; 1 Cor. 3:13, 14; 15:58; 2 Cor. 9:8; Gal. 6:4). A cliché captures the sense well. "A person is saved by faith alone, but not by a faith that is alone."

2:25a ὁμοίως δὲ καί: These are three structural markers. The Greek adverb ὁμοίως is underscored with the two conjunctions δὲ καί. The adverb conveys something being similar in some respect to what precedes and may be rendered "likewise," "so," or "in the same way" (BDAG, s.v. "ὁμοίως," p. 708). **Syntactically**, these words introduce an independent conjunctive clause that continues the discussion of James's diatribal style of interrogation about Abraham in verse 21. **Semantically**, they are "a compound expression that stacks up the adverb ὁμοίως" (Adam, 59) intended to connect the rhetorical question about the faith of Abraham with the rhetorical question about the faith of another person in the past. They are rendered "in the same way" (NASB NIV CNT), "and in the same way" (ESV; cf. ASV), "and similarly" (NET; Zerwick et al., 696), or simply "likewise" (KJV NRSV).

ἐδικαιώθη: This Greek word is a third person singular aorist passive indicative of δικαιόω that conveys the idea of rendering a favorable verdict and may be rendered "vindicate" (BDAG, s.v. "δικαιόω" 2a, p. 249). **Syntactically**, it is the main verb in a primary interrogative clause with Ῥαάβ as its subject. The rhetorical question asked with the negative οὐκ anticipates a positive answer. The question "Wasn't Rahab justified by deeds" expects a "Yes, she was" answer. **Semantically**, the aorist tense is a constative aorist in that it describes an event as a whole (W, 557–58). In this case, James merely provides a summary statement about Rahab's deeds vindicating her similar to the one about Abraham's deeds vindicating him in verse 21 (cf. Adam, 59). Naturally, translations render ἐξ ἔργων ἐδικαιώθη as "justified by works" (KJV ASV NASB NRSV ESV NET CNT), "considered righteous for what she did" (NIV), or "shown to be right with God" (NLT).

Lexical Nugget: What is the meaning of πόρνη? James resists the attempts by later Jewish writers to blunt the nature of Rahab's profession as a "harlot" (πόρνη). Attempting to present the stories of Israel in their best light to his Greek readers, Josephus referred to her as an "innkeeper" (*Ant.* 5.8). He does not call her a πόρνη and refers to her house as a καταγώγιον, or an "inn" (Montanari, s.v. καταγώγιον, 1048.A). The Greek word in the LXX and the Hebrew word it translates (זוֹנָה), however, are both quite clear about the nature of her profession. Hearers and readers of James's letter would have been aware of her confession of faith, which was clearly recorded in Joshua 2:9–11. That she was an evident "believer" is shown by the fact that she became a heroine in Jewish religious history. Later rabbinic tradition mentions that she married Joshua and became an ancestress of Jeremiah and Ezekiel (*b. Meg.* 14b, 15a). Matthew's genealogy records that this Jericho prostitute's husband was "Salmon" and that she was an ancestress of Jesus (Matt. 1:5).

2:25b ὑποδεξαμένη: This structural marker is a nominative singular feminine aorist middle participle of ὑποδέχομαι that conveys the idea of extending hospitality and may be rendered "receive," "welcome," or "entertain as a guest" (BDAG, s.v. "ὑποδέχομαι," p. 1037). **Syntactically**, it introduces a dependent participial clause that functions adverbially modifying ἐδικαιώθη. It is placed under ἐδικαιώθη to visualize its dependence on the verb. **Semantically**, it is a temporal participle drawing attention to when Rahab offered hospitality to the spies (W, 623–27). While it is possible that the feminine participle is causal (W, 631–32), it is best to treat it simply as temporal: "when she received" (KJV NASB ESV CNT), "when she welcomed" (NRSV NET), or "when she hid" (NLT). The aorist participle functions as a constative aorist, viewing Rahab's historical event as a whole (W, 557–58). This prostitute, who had come to faith in the God of Israel, welcomed "the scouts" and then sent them out another way.

Lexical Nugget: Why does James use the noun τοὺς ἀγγέλους for the spies? James does not employ the LXX verb in Joshua (κατασκοπέω) nor the noun that is used in Hebrews 11:31 (κατάσκοπος). James consciously chose this word in reflection on Abraham's earlier hospitality to the ἀγγελοι (Gen. 19:1). As Abraham showed acts of kindness to those ἀγγελοι that came to him, so Rahab showed the same actions to the ἀγγελοι who came to her. In both cases, those who came to Abraham and Rahab were scouts. Those who came to Abraham were angelic scouts for God while those who came to Rahab were human scouts for Joshua (cf. BDAG, s.v. "ἀγγελος" 1a and 2a, p. 8).

2:25c ἐκβαλοῦσα: This structural marker is a nominative singular feminine aorist active participle of ἐκβάλλω that conveys the idea of causing, without force, the removal of someone from a position and may be rendered "send out/ away," "release," or "bring out" (BDAG, s.v. "ἐκβάλλω" 2, p. 299). **Syntactically**, it introduces a second dependent participial clause that functions adverbially modifying ἐδικαιώθη. It too is placed under ἐδικαιώθη to visualize its dependence on ἐδικαιώθη. **Semantically**, it is a temporal participle drawing attention to when Rahab sent spies on their way (W, 623–27). Unlike most translations who render the participle as "and sent" (KJV ASV NASB NRSV NIV ESV NET), we identify the temporal force of the participle in our rendering "and when she sent" to accentuate the two specific deeds. The participle draws attention to Rahab's *advice* to escape the pursuers.[5] The aorist tense functions as a constative aorist that views Rahab's historical event as a whole (W, 557–58). Unlike Joshua who says nothing about Rahab's faith (Bateman et al.[1], 317–18), James emphasizes that no matter what she said, she acted out her faith by sending out the scouts "by another way" (ἑτέρᾳ ὁδῷ).

Historical Nugget: What do we know about Jericho and Rahab? Concerning Jericho, the text in Joshua mentions a "mountain" (Josh. 2:16), which was probably the large hill directly west of Jericho. The deeds of Rahab exemplify the "mercy" that triumphs over judgment (2:13) and effectively pull together these two sections (2:1–13 and 14–26). Furthermore, her two deeds also parallel and contrast with the condemned actions of the heartless interlocutor in 2:16: "be warmed" and "go your way." Concerning Rahab, Bateman notes in his commentary on Hebrews that Joshua says little about Rahab's faith, nor does Jewish literature (Josephus, *Ant.* 5.1–30 §§5–30). Yet, Rahab, though at first a pagan Canaanite, was a "Jewish ancestor" in that she was eventually accepted into the Israelite community (Josh. 6:25; cf. Butler, 1983, 71) as a proselyte (*Mekilta* on Exodus), and perhaps even presented with her own land (Josephus, *Ant.* 5.1.8 §30). Furthermore, Josephus (*Ant.* 5.1.2 §8) never referred to Rahab as a "prostitute," but rather she is described here and in Hebrews 11:31 as a person who "engaged in sexual relations for hire" (BDAG, s.v. "πόρνη" 1, p. 854). Unlike other prostitutes of her day, she was not a cultic prostitute. In Joshua, the spies she hid were referred to as "clients" (NET), and in Josephus she's presented as a person who owns an "inn" (καταγωγίῳ) whereby strangers visiting Jericho could take up lodging (*Ant.* 5.1.2 §8). (cf. Bateman et al.[1], 317).

2:26a γάρ: This structural marker is a conjunction meaning "for" or "you see" (BDAG, s.v. "γάρ" 2, p. 189). **Syntactically**, it introduces a dependent conjunctive clause of comparison (cf. BDAG, s.v. "ὥσπερ" a, p. 1106). **Semantically**, it serves as a continuation of James's argument that clarifies his perspective about faith (cf. Adam, 59). It is typically rendered as "for" (KJV ASV NASB NRSV ESV NET CNT) even though some do not translate γάρ (NIV NLT).

ἐστιν: This Greek word is a third person singular present active indicative of εἰμί and as it appears in this explanation shows how something is to be understood and may be rendered "is" (BDAG, s.v. "εἰμί" 2c, p. 284). **Syntactically**, it is

---

5. Rahab is the second significant exemplar in James. Rahab did something Abraham did not do: she entrusted her life and left her life in God's hands (Foster, 127). And like Abraham, Jewish tradition speaks of Rahab and serves as a basis for Foster's (pp. 104–127) conclusion that "faith and works are not merely co-workers: they have no independent life of their own because they are both essential for the community's eschatological salvation."

the main verb for this dependent conjunctive comparative clause (γάρ ὥσπερ) with τὸ σῶμα as subject and νεκρόν as the predicate adjective (W, 42–56). **Semantically**, the present tense conveys a regular reality about a body without a spirit: it is dead.

> **Lexical Nugget:** What is meant by πνεύματος? As a body is not alive without its animating or life-giving principle, so no faith is alive or useful that does not necessarily entail works. The noun πνεῦμα without a definite article signifies "spirit" in the sense of the life principle that animates the body (BDAG, s.v. "πνεῦμα" 2, p. 832), a theme found in OT writers (Judges 15:19; Ps. 30:6; Ezek. 37:10), and also reflected in other NT passages (Luke 8:55; 23:46; 1 Cor. 7:34).

2:26b οὕτως καί: These structural markers are conjunctions. The first, οὕτως, is a conjunction that may be rendered as "thus," "so," or "in this manner" (BDAG, s.v. "οὕτως" 1b, p. 742). The second Greek word is a conjunction often rendered "also" or "likewise" (BDAG, s.v. "καί" 2a, p. 495). **Syntactically**, they introduce an independent conjunctive clause. While οὕτως is identified as an adverbial comparative conjunction that connects ideas or, in this case, examples together (W, 675, 761–62), καί is an adverbial adjective that is rendered "also" (ESV NET) or "even" (KJV ASV NASB). **Semantically**, they are the second part of James's comparative statement of manner (W, 675, 761–62) and are the apodosis of the comparative clause (cf. BDAG, s.v. "ὥσπερ" a, p. 1106). Most translations render οὕτως καί as "so also" (NASB ESV NET NLT) or "so" (KJV NRSV CNT).

ἐστιν: This Greek word is a third person singular present active indicative of εἰμί, and as it appears in James's explanation, shows how something is to be understood and may be rendered "is" (BDAG, s.v. "εἰμί" 2c, p. 284). **Syntactically**, it is the main verb for this independent conjunctive comparative clause with ἡ πίστις as subject and νεκρόν as the predicate adjective (W, 42–56). **Semantically**, the present tense conveys a regular reality about faith without deeds: it is dead.

> **Structural Nugget:** What is significant about the way James ends this paragraph? The paragraph ends in the way that James often rounds off an argument—with an aphorism conveyed in the structure of a simile. As a body is not alive without its animating or life-giving principle, so no faith is alive or useful that does not necessarily entail works. Here James returns to the main point and the exact wording he used in 2:17. Although he had shifted from the adjective νεκρά to the adjective ἀργή in 2:20, his wording moves back to νεκρά here. The article ἡ before πίστις again serves an anaphoric function in pointing back to the dead and barren

faith mentioned in 2:17 and 2:20. Both the similarities and the differences between the three verses can be visualized in this abbreviated sentence flow layout:

2:17 ἡ πίστις, ἐὰν μὴ ἔχῃ ἔργα, νεκρά ἐστιν καθ᾽ ἑαυτήν.
2:20 ἡ πίστις χωρὶς τῶν ἔργων ἀργή ἐστιν.
2:26 ἡ πίστις χωρὶς ἔργων νεκρά ἐστιν.

Theological Nugget: What is the best summary conclusion about James and Paul on faith and works? Too often James has been read only as a foil to Pauline theology. James is not anti-Pauline, but maybe should be viewed as ante-Pauline, since he writes prior to Galatians and Romans. But also James and Paul use the same words but in different senses. It is helpful to see the differences between the two by looking at the views of their opponents. Paul is opposing those who desire to make "works of the law" an essential component in what makes a person right with God, in addition to the role of faith. James opposes the advocates of a faith-only position that does not require deeds. James and Paul are not opponents facing each other with swords drawn. They are standing with their backs to each other, each drawing swords as they face a different opponent. Finally, Paul's focus is on the "deeds of the law," while James's focus is on "deeds of love and kindness." Paul also emphasizes a believing person's entrance into justification by faith, while James emphasizes what a valid faith looks like. According to Paul, NT faith is never alone since it is always accompanied by hope and love (1 Cor. 13:13). In one of the two books where Paul teaches justification by faith "alone," he offers the balanced statement, "For in Christ Jesus neither circumcision nor uncircumcision counts for anything, but only faith (πίστις) working (ἐνεργουμένη) through love" (Gal. 5:6). James would heartily agree.

JAMES 3:1-12

Big Greek Idea: Within admonitions about the great responsibility that comes with being a teacher in the church are expressed concerns about controlled speech and a realization that speech has great power and destructive potential.

Structural Overview: While speech ethics runs throughout James (1:19, 2:1–4; 4:11, 13; 5:12), this section underscores the destructive effects of the tongue (vv. 1–12; cf. Varner[2], 115–40) or more specifically the effects of our speech (Baker et al., 80–89). James opens this section with an admonition about teaching in which he points out the great responsibility taken on by anyone who teaches in the church and that this requires an ability to control their speech (vv. 1–2). He then develops his admonition with a positive example about the size of the tongue in relation to the rest of the body and yet, so powerful and unmistable in our speech (vv. 3–5). James closes with a negative example about the destructive potential of the tongue apparent in our speech (vv. 6–12). To accentuate his point about the tongue, James employs several analogies. They come from nature (vv. 3, 5, 7, 11–12), Jewish literature (vv. 1, 5, 6, 9), and Jesus sayings (vv. 10, 11, 12).

Outline:[1]

> The Responsibility of Church Teachers Involves Controlled
> > Speech (3:1–2).
> Speech Has Great Power (3:3–5).
> Speech Has Destructive Potential (3:6–12).

THE RESPONSIBILITY OF CHURCH TEACHERS INVOLVES CONTROLLED SPEECH (JAMES 3:1-2)

CLAUSAL OUTLINE FOR JAMES 3:1-2

3:1a Μὴ πολλοὶ διδάσκαλοι **γίνεσθε**, ἀδελφοί μου,
3:1a <u>Not</u> many of you **should become** teachers, my brothers *and sisters*,

|

> > 3:1b **εἰδότες** (<u>ὅτι</u> μεῖζον κρίμα **λημψόμεθα**).
> > 3:1b *because* **you know** (<u>that</u> **we** *who teach* **will receive** a stricter judgment).

3:2a πολλὰ γὰρ **πταίομεν** ἅπαντες.
3:2a *You see,* **we** *repeatedly* **stumble** in many ways.

---

1. A suggested sermon entitled "Tongue in Check" may be preached in four points: "Beware the Controlling Tongue (3:1–5)," "Beware the Consuming Tongue (3:6)," "Beware of the Contrary Tongue" (3:7–8), and "Beware the Condemning Tongue (3:9–12)" (see Baker et al., 89–96).

3:2b εἴ τις ἐν λόγῳ οὐ **πταίει**,
3:2b If anyone **does** not **stumble** in what he says,

|

3:2c οὗτος [ἐστιν] τέλειος ἀνήρ,
3:2c this one [is] a perfect man,

|

3:2d **δυνατὸς χαλιναγωγῆσαι** καὶ ὅλον τὸ σῶμα.
3:2d **who is able** also **to bridle** his whole body.

Syntax Explained for James 3:1–2

3:1a Μὴ . . . γίνεσθε: This negated (μή) structural marker is a second person plural present middle imperative of γίνομαι that conceptually indicates an entry into a new condition and may be rendered "become" (BDAG, s.v. "γίνομαι" 5a, p. 198). **Syntactically**, it is the main verb in the independent asyndeton clause. Since "many" (πολλοί) is more definite than "teachers" (διδάσκαλοι), it is the subject and "teachers" (διδάσκαλοι) is the predicate nominative (W, 42–46). **Semantically**, the imperative with μή is an imperative of a prohibition (W, 487–88; cf. BDF, §433). The present tense is a customary present that conveys a regular practice, namely, "*becoming*" a teacher (W, 521–22). Together, the present tense imperative with μή describes the cessation of activity in progress (W, 724–25). In other words, stop continuing to seek a teaching position. It could be simply translated "*should become* teachers" (NRSV ESV NET NLT; cf. NIV) or "*let not* many *become* teachers" (NASB CNT).

Syntactical and Style Nugget: What is the significance of μή used in an imperative in James? The combination of the negated particle μή with an imperative appears in only seven of the nearly sixty imperative expressions in the book. The other actions that are discouraged in this way are those of being deceived (1:16), showing partiality (2:1), boasting and lying (3:14), slandering (4:11), complaining (5:9), and swearing an oath (5:12). The present imperative should not be overread to assume that James is commanding the cessation of a practice that is taking place. The present imperative can express that idea, but the context must bear that out, and it is difficult to clearly determine if that is the case here. It expresses a general command that is always appropriate. The present imperative of γίνομαι conveys a dynamic action of "becoming" teachers, rather than a more stative idea that would be conveyed if he had used the imperative of the verb εἰμί, as he did with the present imperatives ἔστω/ἤτω in 1:19 and 5:12.

Lexical Nugget: What is a διδάσκαλος? The cognate verb διδάσκω appears in the NT ninety-seven times, while the substantive διδάσκαλος appears fifty-nine times. In the Gospels the noun used with the article designates Jesus absolutely as "The Teacher" (Matt. 23:8; Mark 14:14; John 13:13), and this title corresponds to the Hebrew/Aramaic term *rabbi*, which was common in Judaism. In John 1:38, the address to Jesus as *rabbi* is translated διδάσκαλε (cf. John 20:16). Nicodemus used this term for Jesus in John 3:2, and Jesus also used it of Nicodemus in 3:10. Teachers were prominent in the Jewish-Christian assemblies (Acts 13:1; Heb. 5:12) and were ranked just below apostles and prophets by Paul (1 Cor. 12:28; Eph. 4:11). In Acts 13:1 five prophets and teachers are mentioned. Teachers in Jewish and Christian contexts were highly esteemed and revered (Matt. 13:52), and Paul affirmed that one role of the "overseer" was teaching (1 Tim. 3:1–2). Since διδάσκαλοι were one of the *charismata* (Rom. 12:7; Eph. 4:11), few could rightly exercise this gift.

3:1b εἰδότες: This Greek word is a nominative plural masculine perfect active participle of οἶδα that conveys the idea of having information and is often rendered "know" (BDAG, s.v. "οἶδα" 1e, p. 693). **Syntactically**, it introduces a dependent participial clause that is functioning adverbially modifying γίνεσθε. **Semantically**, the perfect tense is a "perfect with a present force" (W, 579–80) and is interpreted as a causal participle (W, 631–32; Adam, 60). James uses the causal participle elsewhere only in 1:3, where he also appeals to information that his readers should already know: ". . . because you know [γινώσκοντες] that the testing of your faith produces endurance." A fine distinction in "knowing" between the verbs γινώσκω and οἶδα does not seem to be linguistically justified.

ὅτι: This structural marker is a conjunction translated here as "that" (BDAG, s.v. "ὅτι" 1c, p. 732). **Syntactically**, it introduces a dependent conjunctive clause. The entire clause functions as the direct object of the causal participle: "because you know" (εἰδότες). The clause is placed in parentheses in the structural outline in order to visualize the clause's contribution to the independent clause. **Semantically**, it introduces an indirect quotation and is translated "that" (KJV ASV NASB NRSV NIV ESV NET etc.; W, 454–55; Adam, 60). It provides the content of what his readers know, namely, that a stricter judgment exists for teachers.

λημψόμεθα: This Greek word is a first person plural future middle indicative of λαμβάνω that conveys the idea of receiving something and is often rendered "receive," "get," or "obtain" (BDAG, s.v. "λαμβάνω" 10a, p. 584). **Syntactically**, it is the main verb of the dependent conjunctive ὅτι clause, which is the direct object clause of "because you know" (W, 454–55). **Semantically**, the future tense is a predictive future indicating something that will occur in the future (W, 568–69). Few should become teachers because "we *who teach* will be judged" (NRSV ESV NLT CNT) or "we will be judged" (ASV NET).

Semantical Nugget: What does the verb λημψόμεθα tell us about James? James switches here to the first person plural "we." This usage becomes a characteristic in this overall section, appearing three times in 3:2–3 and twice in 3:9. Efforts to explain this by the editorial or literary "we" neglect seeing that this first person plural is our author expressing a self-designation. In other words, James considers himself also as a "teacher." Apart from 1:1 this is the only passage where we learn something about the author himself. Note particularly the verbal similarity with the following saying of Jesus: οὗτοι λήμψονται περισσότερον κρίμα (Mark 12:40 and Luke 20:47). If James is referencing the teaching of Jesus, it also provides an explanation why James can appeal to both his knowledge and that of his hearers/readers ("because *we* know"). They are expected to be familiar with the teachings of the Master.

3:2a γάρ: This structural marker is a conjunction meaning "for" or "you see" (BDAG, s.v. "γάρ" 2, p. 189). **Syntactically**, it introduces an independent conjunctive clause. **Semantically**, it clarifies James's argument about his perspective on faith (cf. Adam, 59). It is typically rendered as "for" (KJV ASV NASB NRSV ESV NET CNT) or "indeed" (NLT) even though some do not translate γάρ (NIV). We emphasize James's clarification with the rendering "you see."

πταίομεν: This Greek word is a first person plural present active indicative of πταίω that conveys the idea of losing one's footing and is often rendered "stumble" or "trip" (BDAG, s.v. "πταίω" 1, p. 894). **Syntactically**, it is the main verb of this independent conjunctive clause. **Semantically**, the present tense is an iterative present indicating time and time again or repeated action (W, 520–21). This clause asserts an additional supporting reason for the warning in the opening imperative command of 3:1. James often utilizes a similar pattern to develop his argument. First, he will issue an imperative command. Then he will set forth an example of how that command can be broken. Then he will support his point by a further argument, and he finally concludes with an apothegm, or wise saying, that rounds off and seals his argument. In this paragraph, he issues a command (3:1), then provides a reason (3:2), then offers extended support by analogies echoing Scripture (3:3–11), and finally concludes with a wise saying (3:12).

3:2b εἰ: This structural marker is a conjunction meaning "if" (BDAG, s.v. "εἰ" 1aβ, p. 277). **Syntactically**, it introduces a dependent conjunctive clause: "*if* anyone (does not) stumble in what he says" (εἴ τις ἐν λόγῳ οὐ πταίει). The entire clause modifies the bracketed elliptical [ἐστιν] and appears above [ἐστιν] to visualize its dependence on the subsequent clause. **Semantically**, "if" (εἰ) introduces a first-class conditional clause, which usually assumes the reality of the condition and the protasis of the clause (W, 686–94; Adam, 61). In this case, here James's assumption is clarified with the clause's verb, πταίει.

πταίει: This Greek word is a third person singular present active indicative of πταίω that conveys the idea of losing one's footing and is often rendered "stumble" or "trip" (BDAG, s.v. "πταίω" 1, p. 894). **Syntactically**, it is the main verb of this dependent conjunctive clause. **Semantically**, the present tense is an iterative present indicating time and time again or repeated action (W, 520–21). The protasis repeats the verb πταίει from the previous independent clause (3:2a). James clearly desires for believers to bridle their tongues, though presumably he does not expect them to do it perfectly or without relapse. James has not yet, used the word "tongue," nor will he do so until 3:5a. While there is a small transition in thought from 3:1, λόγος is probably chosen because of this word's appropriate application to teachers.

> **Lexical Nugget:** What is a τέλειος ἀνήρ? James employs ἀνήρ on six occasions (1:8, 12, 20, 23; 2:2; 3:2) and uses ἄνθρωπος seven times (1:7, 19; 2:20, 24; 3:8, 9; 5:17). "St. James commonly uses ἀνήρ with some characteristic word, as μακάριος 1:12, κατανοῶν 1:23, χρυσοδακτύλιος 2:2, τέλειος 3:2, keeping ἄνθρωπος for more general expressions, ἐκεῖνος, πᾶς, οὐδείς, etc. This agrees fairly with the use in the LXX and Gospels: in the other epistles ἀνήρ is almost exclusively used in opposition to γυνή" (Mayor, 42). This affirmation in 3:2c also recalls the important word τέλειος in 1:4a, where it embodies the goal of becoming a mature believer.

3:2c [ἐστιν]: This structural marker is a third person singular present active indicative from the verb εἰμί that conveys something that is in close connection with something else and is often rendered "is" (BDAG, s.v. "εἰμί" 2a, p. 283). **Syntactically**, the bracketed [ἐστιν] is an ellipsis and is the main verb of the independent asyndeton clause that is the apodosis for the εἰ clause. While the subject of the verb is the more definite demonstrative pronoun "this one" (οὗτος), the other nominative, "man" (ἀνήρ), is the predicate nominative (W, 40–46). **Semantically**, the verb is equative in that it reveals the close connection of "he" or "such a person" (οὗτος; cf. Adam, 61) with a "perfect man" (τέλειος ἀργή). The elliptical verb is simply rendered as "is" (KJV ASV NASB NRSV NIV ESV NET NLT CNT).

3:2d δυνατός: This structural marker is a nominative singular masculine adjective that conveys the idea of being capable or competent and may be rendered "able" (BDAG, s.v. "δυνατός" 1ba, p. 264). **Syntactically**, it is an adjectival phrase that modifies "man" (ἀνήρ). **Semantically**, it functions appositionally.

χαλιναγωγῆσαι: This Greek word is an aorist active infinitive of χαλιναγωγέω that conveys the idea of holding something in check and is often rendered as "bridle" or "hold in check" (BDAG, s.v. "χαλιναγωγέω," p. 1076). **Syntactically**, it is part of the main verb of this dependent adjectival clause that functions appositionally. **Semantically**, it is a complementary (supplemental) infinitive following the adjective δυνατός (W, 606–7; Adam, 62). The combination of δυνατὸς and χαλιναγωγῆσαι is often rendered in translations as "able to bridle" (KJV ASV NASB1995 ESV CNT), "able to keep" (NRSV NIV), or "able to control" (NET). The aorist tense is a constative aorist describing an event as a whole (W, 557–58). In this case, it speaks of being a perfect or complete person.

> **Lexical Nugget:** How does James use the vivid verb χαλιναγωγῆσαι? The complementary aorist infinitive "to bridle" (χαλιναγωγῆσαι) was previously used in 1:26b and cataphorically by anticipating the literal use of the noun χαλινοὺς in 3:3a. James's comment prepares the reader for his colorful analogies in the following verses. The infinitive χαλιναγωγῆσαι ("to bridle") immediately leads to an equestrian analogy in 3:3a with clear references to horses and their "bridles" (χαλινοὺς). Furthermore, the expression ὅλον τὸ σῶμα is repeated in 3:3c and 3:6c. James sees one's tongue or speech as crucial because of the potential harm or good it can also do to the "body."

SPEECH HAS GREAT POWER (JAMES 3:3–5)

CLAUSAL OUTLINE FOR JAMES 3:3–5

3:3a **ἴδε** τῶν ἵππων τοὺς χαλινοὺς εἰς τὰ στόματα **βάλλομεν**
3:3a **Consider** *that* **we put** bridles into the mouths of horses

> 3:3b **εἰς τὸ πείθεσθαι**
> αὐτοὺς ἡμῖν,
> 3:3b **so that** they **obey** us,

3:3c <u>καὶ</u> ὅλον τὸ σῶμα αὐτῶν **μετάγομεν**.
3:3c <u>and</u> **we guide** their whole bodies.

3:4a **ἰδοὺ** καὶ τὰ πλοῖα.
3:4a **Consider** also ships!

> 3:4b τηλικαῦτα **ὄντα**
> 3:4b *Although* **they are** so large
>
> 3:4c <u>καὶ</u> ὑπὸ ἀνέμων σκληρῶν **ἐλαυνόμενα**
> 3:4c <u>and</u> *though* **they are driven** by strong winds,

3:4d **μετάγεται** ὑπὸ ἐλαχίστου πηδαλίου
3:4d **they are guided** by a very small rudder

> 3:4e <u>ὅπου</u> ἡ ὁρμὴ τοῦ εὐθύνοντος **βούλεται**.
> 3:4e <u>wherever</u> the will of the pilot **directs**.

^{3:5a} <u>οὕτως καὶ</u> ἡ γλῶσσα μικρὸν μέλος **ἐστὶν**,
^{3:5a} <u>So also</u>, the tongue **is** a small member,

^{3:5b} <u>καὶ</u> μεγάλα **αὐχεῖ**.
^{3:5b} <u>yet</u>, **it** *repeatedly* **boasts** of great *things*.

^{3:5c} **Ἰδοὺ** ἡλίκον πῦρ
^{3:5c} **Consider** a small fire,

^{3:5d} ἡλίκην ὕλην **ἀνάπτει**.
^{3:5d} **it sets ablaze** a great forest!

Syntax Explained for James 3:3–5

^{3:3a} ἴδε: This structural marker is a second person singular aorist active imperative of ὁράω that conveys the idea of pointing out something to which the speaker wishes to draw attention and is often rendered "look!" or "see!" (BDAG, s.v. "ἴδε" 1, p. 468). **Syntactically**, it is the main verb of this independent asyndeton clause calling attention to bridles for horses (BDF, §467). The textual choice of ἴδε over εἰ δέ (see the Text-Critical Nugget below) alters the verse from being a conditional clause to becoming two independent clauses. **Semantically**, it is a discourse marker. The aorist imperative of command conveys a specific command whereby the expected action is viewed as a whole (W, 485–86; 719–18). In this case, it is viewing the idea of bridling a horse as a whole. As we shall see, the discourse markers ἴδε and ἰδου call attention to the three examples from natural life—the horse/bridle, the ship/rudder, and the fire/forest—and also effectively combine to make a powerful rhetorical argument for the unexpected power of the tongue, both for good and for evil. Therefore, James expects to draw attention to something and this marker may be rendered "look!," "behold" (KJV), or "consider."

Text-Critical Nugget: Why is the textual reading ἴδε and not **εἰ** δέ as evident in NA²⁸ and UBS⁵? While there is a good deal of external evidence that supports **εἰ** δέ (A B K; cf. Metzger¹, 611; Adam, 62; Irons, 537), ἴδε is supported by Codex Sinaiticus and is followed by many later manuscripts. "The editor must therefore choose the reading that . . . is most appropriate in the context" (Metzger¹, 611; Metzger², 681–82). Based upon internal evidence, therefore, it seems the ἴδε reading is best for the following reasons. (1) In every other case in which the conditional εἰ δέ appears in James, the δέ clearly expresses an idea that is adversative to what he has just stated (1:5a; 2:9a, 11b; 3:14a; 4:11d). Such an adversative idea is *not* the case if there is a conditional sentence beginning 3:3. (2) If 3:3 is a conditional sentence, the καί that initiates the proposed apodosis seems to be out of place. Although

English translators have recognized this by rendering it as "also," it is not the normal role of an apodosis in a conditional sentence to add new information to the protasis, but rather to show the result of fulfilling the hypothetical condition in the protasis. (3) Because James uses the aorist middle imperative of ὁράω (ἰδού) to call attention to the ship/rudder in 3:4a and to the fire/forest in 3:5c, the parallelism is more evident if he uses the aorist active imperative of ὁράω (ἴδε) in 3:3a. (4) If someone objects that it would be inconsistent to utilize both ἴδε and ἰδού in such a close context, it should be noted that the following passages have these two different imperative forms utilized together in quite close context: Matthew 25:6, 20, 22, 25; Mark 3:32, 34; John 16:29, 32; and Galatians 1:20; 5:2 (Varner[2], 125–26).

βάλλομεν: This Greek word is a first person plural present active indicative of βάλλω that conveys the idea of putting or placing something in a location and is often rendered "put," "place," or "lay" (BDAG, s.v. "βάλλω" 3b, p. 163). **Syntactically**, it is the main verb of this independent asyndeton clause with the general "we" as its subject. **Semantically**, the present tense is an iterative present that conveys the idea of time and time again (W, 520–21). In this case, horses are bridled. Although the verb often contains the stronger sense of "throw" (e.g., Mark 4:26), sometimes as here it simply has a meaning of "put," as is the case with Peter putting his sword in his sheath (John 18:11; cf. Adam, 63).

3:3b πείθεσθαι: This structural marker is a present passive infinitive of πείθω that conveys the idea of being won over and is often rendered "obey" or "follow" (BDAG, s.v. "πείθω" 3b, p. 792). **Syntactically**, it is the main verb of this dependent infinitival clause that functions adverbially modifying βάλλομεν and is introduced by εἰς τό. The accusative subject (αὐτούς) of the infinitive is specified, namely, the horses. The entire clause is placed under βάλλομεν to visualize the dependency on the previous clause, indicating why bridles are placed into horses' mouths. **Semantically**, the infinitive introduced by εἰς τό indicates purpose or intention (W, 611; Adam, 63; Zerwick et al., 696). Thus, it may be rendered "that" (KJV ASV CNT), "so that" (NASB ESV), or "in order that" (BDAG, s.v. "εἰς" 4f, p. 290). Yet, this purpose clause could be translated passively, "in order that they may be persuaded by us." The present tense is a customary present indicating continuous action, namely, that the horse always obeys the rider. The illustration also suggests a rhetorical question. If we do this with such strong animals as horses, a mere touch of the rein turning them around, should we not do this with ourselves, who are much more than horses? It is not the bridle/bit that ultimately controls the horse, it is the rider who controls the horse.

3:3c καί: This structural marker is a conjunction meaning "and" (BDAG, s.v. "καί" 1b, p. 494). **Syntactically**, it introduces an independent conjunctive clause. **Semantically**, it is a coordinating conjunction that links two clauses together and is rendered "and" (KJV), even though other translations render καί as an adverbial, often rendered "as well" (NASB ESV NET cf. ASV; Adam, 63) or just do not translate the conjunction (NRSV NIV NET CNT). Our rendering indicates that James is adding further information about the significance of the bridling of a horse.

μετάγομεν: This Greek word is a first person plural present active indicative of μετάγω that conveys the idea of directing or leading to another place and is often rendered as "guide" (BDAG, s.v. "μετάγω" 1, p. 638). **Syntactically**, it is the main verb of this independent conjunctive clause with the general "we" as its subject. **Semantically**, the present tense is an iterative present that conveys the idea of time and time again (W, 520–21). In this case, horses are guided. The verb appears in the NT only here and in verse 4d concerning the guiding of horses and ships.

3:4a ἰδού: This structural marker is a second person singular aorist middle imperative of ὁράω that conveys a closer consideration and contemplation of something and is often rendered "consider," "look," or "remember" (BDAG, s.v. "ὁράω" 1c, p. 468). **Syntactically**, it is the main verb of this independent asyndeton clause calling attention to ships. **Semantically**, while it is often used as a prompter of attention and rendered "look" (NASB NRSV ESV NET CNT; cf. Adam, 63) or "behold" (KJV), we render it as "consider" and thereby call closer consideration of its object, a ship. Similar to the idea of "consider" is "take for example" (NIV).

> **Lexical Nugget:** What is meant by the adjective τηλικαῦτα? This word is used elsewhere only in 2 Corinthians 1:10; Hebrews 2:3; and Revelation 16:18, where the meaning is "great" in relation to importance, whereas here it is "great" in relation to size (BDAG, s.v. "τηλικαῦτος," pp. 1001–2). While James obviously had not seen our modern mammoth ships, the one on which Paul travelled to Malta did carry 276 people (Acts 27:37). The emphasis here and throughout the passage is the influence of the smaller on the larger.

3:4b ὄντα: This structural marker is a nominative plural neuter present active participle of εἰμί that conveys the idea of being in close connection with and may be rendered as "is" or "to be" (BDAG, s.v. "εἰμί" 2a, p. 283). **Syntactically**, it is the main verb of this dependent participial clause that functions adverbially modifying μετάγεται. The entire clause is placed above μετάγεται to visualize its dependence on μετάγεται. **Semantically**, the participle has concessive force that implies the action of the main verb it modifies, namely, "guide" (μετάγεται), and is true despite the action of ὄντα (W, 634–35; cf. Adam, 63; Irons, 537). It is typically rendered "though" (KJV ASV NASB NRSV ESV NET) or "although" (NIV).

$^{3:4c}$ καί: This structural marker is a conjunction meaning "and" (BDAG, s.v. "καί" 1b, p. 494). **Syntactically**, it introduces an independent conjunctive clause. **Semantically**, it is a coordinating conjunction that links two clauses together and is rendered "and" (KJV ASV NASB ESV NIV NET).

ἐλαυνόμενα: This Greek word is a nominative plural neuter present passive participle of ἐλαύνω that conveys the idea of propelling along by the wind and is often rendered "drive" (BDAG, s.v. "ἐλαύνω," p. 314). **Syntactically**, it is the main verb of this dependent conjunctive clause that is functioning adverbially modifying μετάγεται. The entire clause is placed above μετάγεται to visualize its dependence on μετάγεται. **Semantically**, the participle has concessive force that implies the action of the main verb it modifies, namely that "ships are "guided" (μετάγεται) in spite of the action of ἐλαυνόμενα (W, 634–35; Adam, 63; Irons, 537). While translations do not indicate the concessive force of the participle, we do with "though they are driven."

$^{3:4d}$ μετάγεται: This structural marker is a third person singular present middle/ passive indicative of μετάγω that conveys the idea of directing or leading to another place and is often rendered as "guide" (BDAG, s.v. "μετάγω" 1, p. 638). **Syntactically**, it is the main verb of an independent asyndeton clause with the general "they" as its subject. It speaks of the ships (πλοῖα) mentioned in verse 3. **Semantically**, the present tense is an iterative present that conveys the idea of time and time again (W, 520–21). In this case, ships are time and again guided. The agent of the passive verb is the word "rudder" (πηδαλίου), which is used elsewhere in the NT only in the one sea voyage account (Acts 27:40). It is the "impulse," "inclination," or "desire" (BDAG, s.v. "ὁρμή," p. 724) of the helmsman that is the ultimate factor in the guiding of the ship. The word ὁρμή only occurs here and in Acts 14:5 (of a "rush" or "onset" of the people).

$^{3:4e}$ ὅπου: This structural marker is a relative adverb denoting a place reached by being in motion and may be rendered "there" or "where" (BDAG, s.v. "ὅπου" 1bα, p. 717). **Syntactically**, it introduces a dependent relative clause that functions as an adverbial clause modifying μετάγεται. The entire clause is placed under μετάγεται to visualize the clause's dependence on μετάγεται. **Semantically**, it indicates location (W, 664) and is thereby rendered "wherever" (NASB NRSV NIV ESV NET CNT).

> **Grammatical Nugget:** What is the significance of τοῦ εὐθύνοντος? This genitive participle is a substantival participle meaning "the one who guides" or "the one who keeps something on course" (BDAG, s.v. "εὐθύνω," p. 406). In this case, it is the pilot who time and again is inclined to guide a ship (Adam, 63). Whereas the ship is steered by the rudder, the rudder is controlled by the pilot. This move in both examples from the "object

of control" to the one who "steers" that control is consistent with James's recognition elsewhere that the forces that drive our actions are our inner hearts and motives (1:14, 15; 2:2; 18; 3:13–17; 4:1, 2). Our deeds are simply the outward expressions that emerge from within. In other words, our tongues are controlled by our hearts.

βούλεται: This Greek word is a third person singular present middle indicative of βούλομαι that conveys the idea of planning a course of action and is often rendered "intend," "plan," or "will" (BDAG, s.v. "βούλομαι" 2aζ, p. 182). **Syntactically**, this is the main verb of the substantival participle τοῦ εὐθύνοντος in a dependent clause with "the will" (ἡ ὁρμή) as its subject. **Semantically**, the present tense is an iterative present that conveys the idea of time and time again (W, 520–21). In this case, ships time and again are directed by a pilot (cf. NRSV ESV NET CNT). It expresses the decisive will of the pilot, not just a "wish." It is where "the pilot chooses to go" (NLT).

3:5a οὕτως καί: These structural markers are conjunctions. The first, οὕτως, is a conjunction that may be rendered as "thus," "so," or "in this manner" (BDAG, s.v. "οὕτως" 1b, p. 742). The second Greek word is a conjunction often rendered "also" or "likewise" (BDAG, s.v. "καί" 2a, p. 495). **Syntactically**, they introduce an independent conjunctive clause. While οὕτως is identified as an adverbial comparative conjunction that connects ideas or in this case links examples together (W, 675, 761–62), καί is an adjectival conjunction that is frequently rendered "also" (NASB NRSV ESV CNT), "too" (NET), or "even" (KJV). This Greek combination launches a new train of thought, so we follow the traditional versification and view 3:5b as the concluding member of the ἴδε-ἰδοὺ-ἰδοὺ trilogy in 3:3–5. **Semantically**, οὕτως is a comparative of manner (W, 675, 761–62) that "directs attention to the resolution of the preceding comparisons" (Adam, 64). It is most frequently rendered "so" (KJV ASV NASB NRSV ESV CNT). Yet, some translations provide a less literal rendering for οὕτως καί: "In the same way" (NLT).

ἐστίν: This structural marker is a third person singular present active indicative of εἰμί that conveys the idea of being in close connection with and may be rendered as "is" or "be" (BDAG, s.v. "εἰμί" 2a, p. 283). **Syntactically**, it is the main verb of this independent asyndeton clause. Its subject is "the tongue" (ἡ γλῶσσα) and "a small member" (μικρὸν μέλος) is the predicate nominative (W, 40–44). **Semantically**, the verb is equative in that it reveals the close connection of "the tongue" (ἡ γλῶσσα) with "a small member" (μικρὸν μέλος) of a person's body and simply rendered as "is" (KJV ASV NASB NRSV NIV ESV NET NLT CNT).

3:5b καί: This structural marker is a conjunction connecting negative and affirmative clauses together that may be rendered "but" or perhaps "yet" (BDAG, s.v.

"καί" 1bε, p. 494). **Syntactically**, it introduces an independent conjunctive clause. **Semantically**, it is an adversative coordinating conjunction rendered "yet" (NRSV ESV NET), "but" (NIV), or "and yet" (NASB CNT).

αὐχεῖ: This Greek verb is a third person singular present active indicative of αὐχέω that conveys the idea of boasting of great things and often is rendered "boasting" or "being prideful" (BDAG, s.v. "αὐχέω," p. 154). **Syntactically**, it is the main verb of this independent conjunctive clause with ἡ γλῶσσα as its subject. **Semantically**, the present tense is an iterative present that conveys the idea of time and again (W, 520–21). In this case, the tongue boasts time and time again. Most translations translate this as "boasts" (NASB NRSV NIV ESV CNT), and it may also be rendered "*repeatedly* boasts." And yet, to render the verb as "makes grand speeches" (NLT) captures the sense of the verb's action.

> **Lexical Nugget:** How should the tongue be interpreted here? The verb αὐχεῖ is unattested in the LXX or elsewhere in the NT, but similar usages of the verb can be found in Josephus who describes Ethiopians who boasted of their great achievements (*Ant.* 2.16.4 §380) and Carthaginians who boasted of the great Hannibal (*War* 2.10.2 §252). While it is possible that boasting with the tongue is not being denounced because the tongue's claims are correct, it is better to see his description of the tongue as negative, since James's use of the analogies in this passage indicate that all of them are destructive for the community. The following passages describe the negative use of the tongue: 3:14–16; 4:1–6. This boasting, therefore, is a description of the arrogant speech that engenders strife, not peace (Davids, 140).

3:5c ἰδού: This structural marker is a second person singular aorist middle imperative of ὁράω that conveys a closer consideration and contemplation of something and is often rendered "consider," "look," or "remember" (BDAG, s.v. "ὁράω" 1c, p. 468). **Syntactically**, it is the main verb of this independent asyndeton clause calling attention to the tongue. Most English translations view its appearance as the beginning of a new paragraph (NASB NRSV ESV CNT). **Semantically**, it is often used as a prompter of attention and is rendered "look" (NET; cf. Adam, 63), "see" (NASB CNT), "behold" (KJV ASV), and "consider" (NIV). It is calling for closer consideration of its object, namely, a small fire.

> **Lexical Nugget:** How does the range of meaning of ἡλίκον / ἡλίκην affect this passage? The doubled adjectives ἡλίκον / ἡλίκην, differing only in gender, are used to describe an initially *small* fire that can eventually consume a *huge* forest. This apparently contradictory usage is resolved by recognizing that this word simply expresses alarm at the size of something

("such a," "what a," "how!"; BDAG, s.v. "ἡλίκος," p. 436). It is a word that comments on the relative size of something, whether big or small. The wordplay in 3:5 would then be in the close combination of the modifier ἡλίκην and the noun ὕλην.

3:5d ἀνάπτει: This structural marker is a third person singular present active indicative of ἀνάπτω that conveys the idea of a fire being kindled and is often rendered "kindle" (BDAG, s.v. "ἀνάπτω," p. 71). **Syntactically**, it is the main verb of this independent asyndeton clause with πῦρ as its subject. **Semantically**, the present tense is an iterative present that conveys the idea of time and time again (W, 520–21). Time and time again small fires grow and spread throughout forests. This final clause of 3:5 completes the triad of attention-getters (see ἴδε in 3:3a and ἰδοὺ in 3:4a). With the prefix ἀν- the verb appears only here and in an eschatological Jesus *logion* (Luke 12:49). The common theme connecting the three analogies is the great effect that a small component wields within a larger system, but particular emphases vary within the three. The emphasis with the bridle and horse analogy is the small size and the great impact. The emphasis of a small rudder on a large ship also stresses guidance. The small flame and large forest emphasize great destructiveness.

SPEECH HAS DESTRUCTIVE POTENTIAL (JAMES 3:6–12)

CLAUSAL OUTLINE FOR JAMES 3:6–12

3:6a καὶ ἡ γλῶσσα πῦρ [ἐστιν].
3:6a And the tongue [*is*] a fire.

3:6b ὁ κόσμος τῆς ἀδικίας ἡ γλῶσσα **καθίσταται** ἐν τοῖς μέλεσιν ἡμῶν
3:6b The tongue **has been made** the sum total of iniquity among our members,

3:6c ἡ **σπιλοῦσα** ὅλον τὸ σῶμα
3:6c **staining** the whole body,

3:6d καὶ **φλογίζουσα** τὸν τροχὸν τῆς γενέσεως
3:6d and **setting on fire** the entire course of life,

3:6e καὶ **φλογιζομένη** ὑπὸ τῆς γεέννης.
3:6e and **set on fire** by hell.

3:7a πᾶσα γὰρ φύσις θηρίων τε καὶ πετεινῶν, ἑρπετῶν τε καὶ ἐναλίων **δαμάζεται**
3:7a Now every kind of beasts and birds, of reptiles and of sea creatures **is tamed**

³:⁷ᵇ **καὶ** [πᾶσα φύσις θηρίων τε καὶ πετεινῶν, ἑρπετῶν τε καὶ ἐναλίων]
δεδάμασται τῇ φύσει τῇ ἀνθρωπίνῃ,

³:⁷ᵇ **and** [*every kind of beasts and birds, of reptiles and of sea creatures*] **has been tamed** by mankind,

³:⁸ᵃ τὴν δὲ γλῶσσαν οὐδεὶς **δαμάσαι δύναται** ἀνθρώπων,

³:⁸ᵃ but no one **is able to tame** the tongue.

³:⁸ᵇ ἀκατάστατον κακόν [*ἐστιν*], μεστὴ ἰοῦ θανατηφόρου.

³:⁸ᵇ [*It is*] a restless evil, full of deadly poison.

³:⁹ᵃ ἐν αὐτῇ **εὐλογοῦμεν** τὸν κύριον καὶ πατέρα

³:⁹ᵃ With it, **we** *repeatedly* **bless** our Lord and Father,

³:⁹ᵇ **καὶ** ἐν αὐτῇ **καταρώμεθα** τοὺς ἀνθρώπους

³:⁹ᵇ and with it, **we** *repeatedly* **curse** people
|
³:⁹ᶜ τοὺς καθ' ὁμοίωσιν θεοῦ **γεγονότας**·
³:⁹ᶜ **who are made** in the likeness of God.

³:¹⁰ᵃ ἐκ τοῦ αὐτοῦ στόματος **ἐξέρχεται** εὐλογία καὶ κατάρα.

³:¹⁰ᵃ **Does** blessing and cursing **come** from the same mouth?

³:¹⁰ᵇ οὐ **χρή**, ἀδελφοί μου, ταῦτα οὕτως **γίνεσθαι**.

³:¹⁰ᵇ My brothers *and sisters*, these things **ought** not **to be** so.

³:¹¹ μήτι ἡ πηγὴ ἐκ τῆς αὐτῆς ὀπῆς **βρύει** τὸ γλυκὺ καὶ τὸ πικρόν;

³:¹¹ Does a spring pour forth from the same opening both fresh and bitter [*water*]?

³:¹²ᵃ μὴ **δύναται**, ἀδελφοί μου, συκῆ ἐλαίας **ποιῆσαι** ἢ ἄμπελος σῦκα;

³:¹²ᵃ **Is it possible**, my brothers *and sisters*, for a fig tree to produce olives, or a grapevine figs?

³:¹²ᵇ οὔτε [*δύναται*] ἁλυκὸν γλυκὺ **ποιῆσαι** ὕδωρ.

³:¹²ᵇ Neither [*is it possible for*] a salt [*pond*] **to produce** fresh water.

SYNTAX EXPLAINED FOR JAMES 3:6–12

³:⁶ᵃ καί: This structural marker is a conjunction meaning "and" (BDAG, s.v. "καί" 1b, p. 494). **Syntactically**, it introduces an independent conjunctive clause. **Semantically**, it is a coordinating conjunction that links together two clauses describing aspects about the tongue. It is often rendered "and" (NET ESV NASB NRSV etc.) and presents another description of

the tongue. A boastful tongue is linked with James's likening the tongue with fire.

[ἐστιν]: This Greek word is a third person singular present active indicative from the verb εἰμί that conveys something that is in close connection with something else and is often rendered "is" (BDAG, s.v. "εἰμί" 2a, p. 283). **Syntactically**, the bracketed [ἐστιν] is an ellipsis that serves as the main verb of the independent conjunctive clause. While the subject of the verb is the more definite "the tongue" (ἡ γλῶσσα), the other nominative, "fire" (πῦρ), is the predicate nominative (W, 40–46; con. Irons, 537). **Semantically**, the elliptical [ἐστιν] is equative in that it reveals the close connection of "the tongue" (Adam, 61) with a "fire" (πῦρ). It is simply rendered as "is" (KJV ASV NASB NRSV NIV ESV NET NLT CNT). James picks up the catchword πῦρ from the last clause of 3:5, applies the metaphor in this verbless clause, and then describes the awful power of that metaphor in the rest of the verse.

3:6b καθίσταται: This structural marker is a third person singular present passive indicative of καθίστημι that conveys the idea of causing someone to experience something and may be rendered "make" or "cause" (BDAG, s.v. "καθίστημι" 3, p. 492). **Syntactically**, it is the main verb in this independent asyndeton clause with ἡ γλῶσσα as subject. **Semantically**, the present tense is a customary present of an event that occurs regularly (W, 521–22). In this case, it refers to the tongue as having been made "the sum total of iniquity" (BDAG, s.v. "κόσμος" 8, p. 563) over the other parts of a person's body. Thus, the word "world" is a figure of speech for "iniquity" within one's members or might be rendered "the world of wickedness" (Zerwick et al., 696). There is no elucidation for this expression gained from anywhere but in Jewish sources and was self-evident to Jews as well as to Christians, namely, the evil world. 1 John 5:19 says, ". . . the whole world is in the power of the evil one" (ὁ κόσμος ὅλος ἐν τῷ πορηρῷ κεῖται).

3:6c ἡ σπιλοῦσα: This structural marker is a nominative singular feminine present active participle of σπιλόω and is often rendered "stain" or "defile" (BDAG, s.v. "σπιλόω," p. 938). **Syntactically**, this is the main verb of a dependent participial clause that functions as an adjective modifying γλῶσσα. **Semantically**, the present tense is an iterative present that conveys the idea of time and time again (W, 520–21). Time and time again, the tongue stains a person (W, 521–22).

3:6d καί: This structural marker is a conjunction meaning "and" (BDAG, s.v. "καί" 1b, p. 494). **Syntactically**, καί introduces an independent conjunctive clause. **Semantically**, it is a coordinating conjunction that links two clauses together, is rendered "and" (KJV ASV NASB NET etc.), and it adds further information about the tongue, more specifically as affecting the course of life for an individual.

φλογίζουσα: This Greek word is a nominative singular feminine present active participle of φλογίζω that is often rendered "set on fire" (BDAG, s.v. "φλογίζω," p. 1060). **Syntactically**, it is the main verb of this dependent conjunctive clause. It too is functioning as an adjective modifying γλῶσσα. **Semantically**, the present tense is an iterative present that conveys the idea of time and time again (W, 520–21). Time and time again the tongue is like the setting of a fire symbolic for the destruction of a person's life.

> **Semantical Nugget:** Does James reflect Stoic Greek thought in the expression τὸν τροχὸν τῆς γενέσεως? Explanations of the expression ("the entire course of life") often delve into Stoic philosophy (BDAG, s.v. "τροχός" pp. 1017–18). The expressions here, however, are rooted not in the writings of Stoic philosophers but in both canonical and Second Temple Period Jewish literature (Ps. 32:9; Prov. 10:19; Eccl. 5:1; Sir 14:1, 20:1–8; 1 En. 48.7). See also some similar fiery expressions in Luke 16:9, 11; 18:6. The expression describes the whole circle of inner passions (hence the translation: *the entire course of life*). The wheel's being set on fire means that wrong use of the tongue engenders jealousy, and faction, and vile deeds throughout the whole of one's life (cf. 3:16). In fact, the three vivid participles modifying γλῶσσα describe the destructive power of the tongue.

3:6e καί: This structural marker is a conjunction meaning "and" (BDAG, s.v. "καί" 1b, p. 494). **Syntactically**, it introduces an independent conjunctive clause. **Semantically**, it is another coordinating conjunction that links two clauses together is rendered "and" (KJV ASV NASB NRSV ESV NET etc.), and adds further information about the tongue, more specifically its destructiveness as having roots in hell.

φλογιζομένη: This Greek word is a nominative singular feminine present passive participle of φλογίζω that is often rendered "set on fire" (BDAG, s.v. "φλογίζω," p. 1060). **Syntactically**, it is the main verb of this dependent conjunctive clause. It too is functioning as an adjective modifying γλῶσσα. **Semantically**, the present tense is an iterative present that conveys the idea of time and time again (W, 520–21). Time and time again the tongue is like an ongoing fire symbolic of a destruction that originates in Gehenna, a term used for referring to hell (Matt. 5:22; cf. Bauckham, 130; Zerwick et al., 697).

3:7a γάρ: This structural marker is a conjunction meaning "for," "you see," or "now" (BDAG, s.v. "γάρ" 2, p. 189). **Syntactically**, it introduces an independent conjunctive clause of clarification that serves to initiate a new issue. **Semantically**, it is a transitional conjunction of clarification. It initiates a new issue, and we render it as "now." Nevertheless, it is typically rendered as "for" (KJV ASV NASB NRSV ESV NET CNT) or not rendered at all (NIV NLT).

δαμάζεται: This Greek word is a third person singular present passive indicative of δαμάζω that is often rendered "subdue" or "tame" (BDAG, s.v. "δαμάζω" a, p. 211). **Syntactically**, it is the main verb of this independent conjunctive clause with πᾶσα . . . φύσις as its subject (Adam, 67). **Semantically**, the present tense is an iterative present that conveys the idea of time and time again (W, 520–21; con. Irons, 538). Time and time again animals are tamed.

3:7b καί: This structural marker is a conjunction meaning "and" (BDAG, s.v. "καί" 1b, p. 494). **Syntactically**, it introduces an independent conjunctive clause. **Semantically**, it is a coordinating conjunction that links two clauses together about the taming of animals and is rendered "and" (KJV ASV NASB NRSV ESV NIV NET CNT).

δεδάμασται: This Greek word is a third person singular perfect passive indicative of δαμάζω that is often rendered "subdue" or "tame" (BDAG, s.v. "δαμάζω" a, p. 211). **Syntactically**, it is the main verb for this independent conjunctive clause with an elliptical [πᾶσα . . . φύσις] as its subject (Adam, 67). **Semantically**, the perfect tense is an intensive perfect that emphasizes the present situation of a past action (W, 574–76), namely, that animals were tamed in the past and yet, remain tamed in the present "by humans," the agents who do the taming (BDF, §191.3; Zerwick, §59).

> **Semantical Nugget:** How does James express the taming of animals by humans? This comparison of the taming of animals with the wildness of the tongue is picked up by the *Shepherd of Hermas*, who often adapts the language and thought of James. He writes that "the evil desire . . . you shall bridle and direct it as you wish. For the evil desire is wild and only tamed with difficulty" (*Hermas* 44.2), and later argues that since God has subjected all his creation to man, so that he is its master, so man ought to be able to master God's commandments (*Hermas* 47.2).

3:8a δέ: This structural marker is a conjunction meaning "but" (BDAG, s.v. "δέ" 4a, p. 213). **Syntactically**, it introduces an independent conjunctive clause. **Semantically**, it continues James's discussion about the tongue, but as a marker of contrast and thereby is rendered as "but" (KJV ASV NASB NIV ESV NET CNT NLT). James contrasts the unruly nature of the tongue with an adversative clause (δέ) that fronts the direct object τὴν γλῶσσαν for emphasis.

δαμάσαι: This Greek word is an aorist active infinitive of δαμάζω and is often rendered "subdue" or "tame" (BDAG, s.v. "δαμάζω" b, p. 211). **Syntactically**, it is part of the main verb for this dependent conjunctive clause. **Semantically**, it is a complementary (supplemental) infinitive that is preceding δύναται (W, 598–99; Adam, 67). The aorist is constative in that it describes an event as a whole (W, 557–58). The tongue is difficult to subdue.

δύναται: This Greek word is a third person singular present middle/passive indicative of δύναμαι that conveys the idea of possessing capability and may be rendered "can" or "is able, be capable" (BDAG, s.v. "δύναμαι" aβ, p. 262). **Syntactically**, it is the main verb of this independent conjunctive clause with οὐδείς as its subject. It is a verb that requires a complement, which is provided by the preceding δαμάσαι. **Semantically**, the present tense is a customary present (W, 521–22). So, even if a person can tame wild beasts on a regular basis, the same individual (οὐδείς . . . ἀνθρώπων) may not be able to control his tongue. The language here, as in verse 2a, is hyperbolic: to strive to do what is impossible. James's use of hyperbole and paradox is not pessimistic. The rhetorical language graphically challenges his readers to the difficult task of managing this small member.

3:8b [ἐστιν]: This structural marker is a third person singular present active indicative from the verb εἰμί that conveys something that is in close connection with something else and is often rendered "is" (BDAG, s.v. "εἰμί" 2a, p. 283). **Syntactically**, the bracketed [ἐστιν] is an ellipsis that serves as the main verb of this independent asyndeton clause (BDF, §137.3). The subject "it" is assumed in the verb and the nominative "restless" (ἀκατάστατον) is the predicate (W, 40–46). **Semantically**, the elliptical [ἐστιν] is equative in that it reveals the close connection of "it", which is a reference to the tongue, with "restless" (ἀκατάστατον). It is simply rendered as "is" (KJV ASV NASB NIV ESV NET NLT CNT).

Text-Critical Nugget: What is the correct reading, ἀκατάστατον or ἀκατάσχετον? The first reading ἀκατάστατον describes the tongue as "a restless evil" and is supported by ℵ A B P 1739, as well as the ancient versions. This is the reading followed by all modern English versions, and is the reading adopted by the NA and TH texts. The variant ἀκατάσχετον describes the tongues as "an uncontrollable evil" and is supported by some later majuscules and Byzantine manuscripts. The adopted reading, ἀκατάστατον, describes the tongue as "a pest that will not keep still" (NJB). The later variant, ἀκατάσχετον, probably reflects the work of scribes attempting to make this statement fit with the preceding one, which speaks of how impossible it is for men to tame the tongue.

> **Lexical Nugget:** How does James employ the verbal root of ἀκατάστα-
> τον throughout his book? What James describes as "unruly" or "rest-
> less" here in a vivid metaphor, he will assign as a characteristic of the
> wisdom that is *not* from above in 3:16b (ἀκατάστατον here and ἀκα-
> τάστασία there; cf. BDAG, s.v. "ἀκατάστατος," p. 35). It is evil behav-
> ior that is marked by "instability" and is the chief characteristic of the
> individual who is so strongly exhorted in this book: the "double-minded"
> person (1:8).

3:9a εὐλογοῦμεν: This structural marker is a first person plural present active
indicative of εὐλογέω that conveys the idea of saying something commen-
datory and may be rendered "speak well of," "praise," or "extol" (BDAG, s.v.
"εὐλογέω" 1, p. 408). **Syntactically**, it is the main verb of this independent
asyndeton clause with the general "we" as its subject. James continues his
identification with his readers by using a first-person plural verb εὐλογοῦμεν. **Semantically**, the present tense is an iterative present that conveys the
idea of time and time again (W, 520–21). Time and time again the tongue is
used to bless "our Lord and Father" (τὸν κύριον καὶ πατέρα), which is an
example of the Granville Sharp Rule (W, 274). The action expressed in the
component parts of the Greek verb εὐλογέω is to "say good" or "praise."

> **Semantical Nugget:** How do biblical and Jewish tradition use the ex-
> pression "to bless God"? Religious Jews often add the words "blessed
> is he" after the name of God. See Mark 14:61 where ὁ εὐλογητός (the
> Blessed One) is used in reference to God. While readers may be more
> accustomed to the verb "praise," the practice of "blessing" God is prom-
> inent in both the OT (Gen. 9:26; Exod. 18:10; Ruth 2:20; 1 Sam. 25:32;
> 2 Sam. 6:21; 1 Kings 1:48; 1 Chron. 29:10; Pss. 40:14; 68:19–20) as well
> as in the NT (Luke 1:68; 2:28; Rom. 1:25; Eph. 1:3; 1 Peter 1:3). The ac-
> tion expressed in the component parts of the Greek verb εὐλογέω is to
> "say good" or "pronounce well of" (BDAG, s.v. "εὐλογέω" 1, p. 408). It
> can be used of both God's blessing people and vice-versa. God blesses
> people by conferring good on them. People bless God by praising the
> good that is in him.

3:9b καί: This structural marker is a conjunction meaning "and" (BDAG, s.v. "καί"
1b, p. 494). **Syntactically**, it introduces an independent conjunctive clause.
Semantically, it is another coordinating conjunction that links two clauses
together and is rendered "and" (KJV ASV NASB NRSV ESV NET etc.) and
thereby adds further information about the tongue that blesses God: more
specifically, it also curses people.

καταρώμεθα: This Greek word is a first person plural present middle indicative of καταράομαι that is often rendered "to curse" or "execrate" (BDAG, s.v. "καταράομαι," p. 525). **Syntactically**, it is the main verb of an independent conjunctive clause with the general "we" as its subject. **Semantically**, the present tense is an iterative present that conveys the idea of time and time again (W, 520–21). Time and time again the tongue is used to curse people.

> **Lexical Nugget:** What is the true sense of καταράομαι? This unbecoming behavior of the tongue is not slander nor backbiting nor lying, but personal abuse, such as results from loss of temper in a heated controversy (Rom. 12:13). The verb καταράομαι is found frequently in the LXX (Gen. 12:3; 27:29; Lev. 24:15; Num. 22:6; Deut. 21:23; Ps. 36:22), illustrating its divergent use. For instance, a parallel passage exists in the *Testament of Benjamin* 6.5 where it says, "the good mind does not have two tongues, one of blessing and one of cursing" (ἡ ἀγαθὴ διάνοια οὐκ ἔχει δύο γλώσσας εὐλογίας καὶ κατάρας).

3:9c τοὺς ... γεγονότας: This articular (τούς) structural marker is an accusative plural masculine perfect active participle of γίνομαι that conveys the idea of coming into existence and may be rendered "be made," "be created," or "be manufactured" (BDAG, s.v. "γίνομαι" 2, p. 197). **Syntactically**, it introduces a dependent participial clause that functions as an attributive participle modifying τοὺς ἀνθρώπους. **Semantically**, the perfect tense is an intensive perfect that emphasizes the present situation of a past action (W, 574–76), namely, that people were made in God's likeness in the past and currently remain in that likeness, which is typically rendered "we are made" (KJV NRSV ESV NET). Yet, some translations emphasize an extensive force of the perfect and rendered it as "have been made" (NASB NIV NLT CNT) and thereby give emphasis to the past act of being created in God's likeness.

> **Theological Nugget:** What is the theological emphasis here about being made in the likeness of God? James adapts Genesis 1:26, where the LXX reads κατ᾽ εἰκόνα ἡμετέραν καὶ κατ᾽ ὁμοίωσιν. The Hebrew דְּמוּת (LXX ὁμοίωσις) is synonymous with צֶלֶם (LXX εἰκών). Just as a murderous attack on a man is an attack on God (Gen. 9:6), so cursing one's fellow man amounts to cursing God. Although ὁμοίωσις appears often in the LXX, this verse is its only occurrence in the NT. That the "image" relates to the human's spiritual similarity to God is illustrated by the Pauline statement using εἰκών in Colossians 3:10: "Put on the new man who is being renewed in knowledge after the image of its creator" (κατ᾽ εἰκόνα τοῦ κτίσαντος).

³:¹⁰ᵃ ἐξέρχεται: This structural marker is a third person singular present middle indicative of ἐξέρχομαι that is often rendered "go out," "come out," "go away," or "retire" (BDAG, s.v. "ἐξέρχομαι" 1bγ, p. 348). **Syntactically**, it is the main verb of this independent asyndeton clause with its subject the two nouns εὐλογία καὶ κατάρα. **Semantically**, the present tense is an iterative present that conveys the idea of time and time again (W, 520–21). People regularly praise God and curse people. The verb recalls the ἐξέρχεσθαι of Matthew 15:19, where Jesus taught that what comes out of a person is what defiles that person (Matt. 15:11, 20). Like his brother, James understands that a people's speech is an outward barometer of their inner spirituality (Matt. 12:33–37). Paul exhorts the same thing and adds the positive alternative (Eph. 4:29).

> **Grammatical Nugget:** Why does the Greek sentence extend from verse 9–10a? The Letter of James is known for simple sentences with few subordinate clauses and the use of asyndeton (lack of conjunctions). The long sentence in 1:25 is probably the closest that James ever comes to what is called a classical "periodic sentence" (see the comments on 1:25). In 3:9–10 James uses a compound clause plus a subordinate clause, completed in 3:10 with what in English would probably follow a semicolon at the end of verse 9. While this is not too complex for the reader to piece together, it is the exception in James to include this many clauses in one sentence. This pales in comparison with the large number of complex sentences utilized by the author of the Letter to the Hebrews. Even this longer sentence in 3:9–10 is mild when compared also to many passages in Paul and Peter. The usual clipped style of James may not please an Attic rhetorician, but it is that very forceful, direct style that has endeared James to so many readers.

³:¹⁰ᵇ οὐ χρή: This negated (οὐ) structural marker is a third person present active indicative of the impersonal verb χρή that conveys that which should happen and is often rendered "it is necessary" or "it ought" (BDAG, s.v. "χρή," p. 1089). **Syntactically**, it is the main verb in an independent asyndeton clause with "these" (ταῦτα) as the subject. **Semantically**, the present tense conveys a general command. While this is the only use of this impersonal verb (from χράω) in the NT, it is similar to "it is appropriate" (πρέπει; Robertson[2], VI, 44–45) and "we ought" (ὀφείλομεν), each of which conveys the idea to be under obligation to meet certain social and moral expectations (see 3 John 8; Bateman et al.[1], 392–93). Here, οὐ χρή is typically rendered as "ought not" (KJV ASV NASB1995 NRSV ESV CNT) or "should not" (NIV NET). One could paraphrase it as: "This is not right" (NLT). James continues his exposure of the "double-minded" person, and here "double-mindedness" (1:8) is revealed as also being "double-tongued."

γίνεσθαι: This Greek verb is the present middle infinitive of γίνομαι that conveys the idea of coming into or possessing certain characteristics and often rendered "be," "prove to be," or "turn out to be" (BDAG, s.v. "γίνομαι" 7, p. 199). **Syntactically**, the infinitive is functioning adverbially as part of the main verb of the independent clause, namely, χρή. **Semantically**, it is a complementary (supplemental) infinitive that is preceding δύναται (W, 598–99; Adam, 69). The present tense is a customary present that underscores something that ought to occur regularly or in this case "ought not to be" (οὐ χρή . . . γίνεσθαι) as a pattern of behavior (W, 521–22).

3:11 βρύει: This structural marker is a third person singular present active indicative of βρύω that is often rendered "pour forth" (BDAG, s.v. "βρύω," p. 184). **Syntactically**, it is the main verb of this independent asyndeton clause. It is an interrogative clause with "a spring" (ἡ πηγή) as its subject. The assumed answer to this rhetorical question is "no" (Zerwick et al., 697). **Semantically**, the present tense is a customary present (W, 521–22) that underscores something that does not occur regularly, namely, that a spring does not produce two types of water at the same time.

> **Grammatical Nugget:** What is the significance of the particle μήτι? The negative particle μήτι introduces a clause that signals a question that expects an emphatically negative answer (BDAG, s.v. "μήτι," p. 649; Adam, 69). It prepares the way for additional rhetorical questions. Because contrary actions from springs of water do not happen in nature, similar happenings in human life with the tongue must be regarded as monstrosities. The point is that the same spring does not emit sweet water one minute and then bitter water the next minute. Its water may be good or bad, but it is consistent in producing the same kind of water. The tragedy of a divided tongue is its tendency to bless God with one opening of the mouth, and yet, to curse men with the next opening!

> **Semantical Nugget:** Does James use a nature allusion with the words τὸ γλυκὺ καὶ τὸ πικρόν? With these figures, James is probably alluding to the Dead Sea, which was (and is) exceedingly bitter and had both salt and fresh springs on its shores, but not a spring that produced both! He will return to this illustration in 3:12b. Other examples of bitter waters are Marah (Exod. 15:23), "the water that causes the curse" (Num. 5:18–27), as well as Revelation 8:11. The reflections here in James of Judean nature scenes continue in 3:12. These comparisons also reflect a writer who must have been familiar with Judean geography.

3:12a μὴ δύναται: This negated (μή) structural marker is a third person singular present middle indicative of δύναμαι that conveys the idea of possessing capability and may be rendered "can" or "am able, be capable" (BDAG, s.v. "δύναμαι" aβ, p. 262). **Syntactically**, it is the main verb of this independent asyndeton clause. It is an interrogative clause with "fig tree" (συκῆ ἐλαίας) as its subject. It is a verb that requires a complement, which is provided later by the infinitive ποιῆσαι. **Semantically**, the present tense is a customary present indicating continual action (W, 521–22). The negative μή attends a question that again not only expects a negative answer, but is almost absurd in its query (BDAG, s.v. "μή" 3, p. 646). No fruit tree of one kind produces a different kind of fruit!

ποιῆσαι: This Greek word is an aorist active infinitive of ποιέω that conveys undertaking or doing something that brings about the natural process of growth and is often rendered "send out," "produce," "bear," or "yield" (BDAG, s.v. "ποιέω" 2g, p. 839). **Syntactically**, it is part of the main verb of this independent asyndeton clause, namely, δύναται, that is rendered as "to produce" (Irons, 538). **Semantically**, it is a complementary (supplemental) infinitive that is preceding δύναται (W, 598–99; Adam, 69). The aorist tense is a constative aorist that discusses events about a fig tree as a whole (W, 557–58) as well as about olive trees and grapevines. These are some of the most abundant "staple" fruits in the land of Israel and were considered as part of the "seven varieties" of agricultural products in the promised land (Deut. 8:8). The absurdity of the question asked is so patent that it does not need further comment. The point is that such inconsistent speech is also absurd.

3:12b οὔτε [δύναται]: This negated (οὔτε) structural marker is a third person singular present middle indicative of δύναμαι that conveys the idea of possessing capability and may be rendered "can," or "am able," or "be capable" (BDAG, s.v. "δύναμαι" αβ, p. 262). **Syntactically**, the bracketed [δύναται] is an ellipsis with the negative correlative "neither" (BDF, §445.1). It serves as a portion of the main verb of the independent clause, namely, ποιῆσαι.

ποιῆσαι: This Greek word is an aorist active infinitive of ποιέω that conveys an undertaking or doing something that brings about the natural process of growth and is often rendered "send out," "produce," "bear," or "yield" (BDAG, s.v. "ποιέω" 2g, p. 839). **Syntactically**, it is the second of two infinitives complementary to the indicative verb that is presented in brackets [δύναται] as an ellipsis and is rendered as "to produce" (Adam, 70; Irons, 538). **Semantically**, the aorist is a constative aorist that discusses events about a salt pond as a whole (W, 557–58).

> **Lexical Nugget:** How does the infinitive ποιῆσαι relate to the agricultural imagery? This verb usually translated "make" or "do" may appear to be unusual, but the word is used for trees "bearing" fruit in the LXX of Genesis 1:11 and in Matthew 3:10. It is impossible for the evil tongue to "make" itself good. We should also recognize again the echoes of various Jesus *logia* in these graphic word pictures (see esp. Matt. 7:16 and Luke 6:44).

JAMES 3:13–4:10

Big Greek Idea: Divine wisdom is identifiable in people who are not vile but pure, who are not hostile but peaceable, and who are not proud but humble.

Structural Overview: James shifts from his theme of teaching (3:1–12) to a new theme, wisdom. Yet, his theme of wisdom is linked with living lives of virtue (3:13–18), peace (4:1–4), and humility (4:5–10).[1] He introduces these acts with three rhetorical questions (3:13; 4:1; 4:5). James opens with an overarching theme of wisdom whereby he contrasts the world's concept of wisdom as vile with that of God's wisdom which is pure (3:13–18). He then moves his discussion of wisdom to that of relationships whereby he describes conflicts between discontented and, hostile people and those who are content and live peaceably with God (4:1–4). James concludes with divine wisdom as evident in the lives of people who are humble and not proud (4:5–10).

Outline:[2]
> Divine Wisdom Is Identifiable in People Who Live Virtuously (3:13–18).
> Divine Wisdom Is Identifiable in People Who Live Peaceably (4:1–4).
> Divine Wisdom Is Identifiable in People Who Live Humbly (4:5–10).

DIVINE WISDOM IS IDENTIFIABLE IN PEOPLE WHO LIVE VIRTUOUSLY (JAMES 3: 13–18)

CLAUSAL OUTLINE FOR JAMES 3:14–18

3:13a Τίς [ἐστιν] σοφὸς καὶ ἐπιστήμων ἐν ὑμῖν;
3:13a Who [is] wise and understanding among you?

3:13b **δειξάτω** ἐκ τῆς καλῆς ἀναστροφῆς τὰ ἔργα αὐτοῦ ἐν πραΰτητι σοφίας.
3:13b **He should prove it** by good conduct in actions with the gentleness of wisdom.

---

1. "Functionally, 3:13–18," according to Taylor, "gathers key concepts raised in 1:2–3:12 and anticipates the next major movement in the discourse. Contextually, the passage reveals grounding in Jewish concepts of wisdom, emphasizing the practical obedience of a life marked by the possession of wisdom as a gift of God." M. Taylor, *A Text-Linguistic Investigation into the Discourse Structure of James* (London: T&T Clark, 2006), 116.
2. A suggested sermon entitled "Take the High Road" may be preached in three points: "Respond to Worldly Understanding with Godly Wisdom (3:13–18)," "Respond to Worldly Ambitions with Godly Motives (4:1–3)," and "Respond to Worldly Associations with Godly Relationships (4:4–10)" (see Baker et al., 108–17).

3:14a εἰ δὲ ζῆλον πικρὸν **ἔχετε** καὶ ἐριθείαν ἐν τῇ καρδίᾳ ὑμῶν,
3:14a But if **you have** bitter jealousy and selfish ambition in your hearts,

|

3:14b μὴ **κατακαυχᾶσθε**
3:14b stop **boasting**

3:14c καὶ [*μὴ*] **ψεύδεσθε** κατὰ τῆς ἀληθείας.
3:14c and [*stop*] **lying** against the truth.

3:15a οὐκ **ἔστιν** αὕτη ἡ σοφία ἄνωθεν
3:15a This **is** not the wisdom . . . from above,

|

3:15b **κατερχομένη**
3:15b **that comes down**

3:15c ἀλλ' [*ἔστιν*] ἐπίγειος, ψυχική, δαιμονιώδης.
3:15c but [*it is*] earthly, unspiritual, demonic.

3:16a ὅπου γὰρ ζῆλος καὶ ἐριθεία [*ἔστιν*],
3:16a You see, where jealousy and selfish ambition [*exist*],

|

3:16b ἐκεῖ [*ἔστιν*] ἀκαταστασία καὶ πᾶν φαῦλον πρᾶγμα
3:16b there [*is*] disorder and every vile practice.

3:17a ἡ δὲ ἄνωθεν σοφία πρῶτον μὲν ἀγνή **ἔστιν**,
3:17a But the wisdom that comes from above **is** first pure,

3:17b ἔπειτα [*ἔστιν*] εἰρηνική, ἐπιεικής, εὐπειθής, μεστὴ ἐλέους καὶ καρπῶν ἀγαθῶν, ἀδιάκριτος, ἀνυπόκριτος
3:17b then [*is*] peaceable, gentle, open to reason, full of mercy and good fruits, impartial, sincere.

3:18a καρπὸς δὲ δικαιοσύνης ἐν εἰρήνη **σπείρεται**
3:18a And a harvest of righteousness **is sown** in peace

|

3:18b **τοῖς ποιοῦσιν** εἰρήνην.
3:18b *by* **those who work** for peace.

SYNTAX EXPLAINED FOR JAMES 3:13–18

3:13a [*ἔστιν*]: This structural marker is a third person singular present active indicative from the verb εἰμί that conveys something that is in close connection with something else, and is often rendered "is" (BDAG, s.v. "εἰμί" 2a, p. 283).

Syntactically, the bracketed [ἐστιν] is an ellipsis that serves as the main verb of this independent asyndeton clause. The subject is "who" (τίς), and "understanding" (ἐπιστήμων) is the predicate adjective (W, 40–44). **Semantically**, the elliptical [ἐστιν] is equative in that it reveals a close connection of any person "who" (τίς) has "understanding" (ἐπιστήμων). It is simply rendered as "is" (KJV ASV NASB NRSV NIV ESV NET CNT). It is part of a rhetorical question introduced with the interrogative pronoun "who" (τίς; BDF, §298.4) that is addressed to those "among you" (ἐν ὑμῖν)—the first of six occurrences of this expression, all in the latter half of the book (cf. 4:1a; 5:13a, 14a, 19a).

> **Semantical Nugget:** What is the OT background of the words σοφὸς καὶ ἐπιστήμων? This combination of words does not appear elsewhere in the NT, but the collocation would be familiar to those who honored the wise men of Israel who produced the LXX. Moses issued the following command: "Assign for yourselves men, wise and discerning [σοφοὺς καὶ ἐπιστήμονας] and prudent [σοφούς] for your tribes, and I will appoint them as your leaders" (Deut. 1:13). The response of the people was to do just that, and wise and understanding men were so appointed (Deut. 1:15). In Deuteronomy 4:6, Israel was told that if they kept the statutes, they would be a "wise and understanding [σοφὸς καὶ ἐπιστήμων] people"—the exact pair of wisdom words found in James 3:13. Daniel, at both an early age and in his older years, was referred to by the same two coupled adjectives (Dan. 1:4; 5:11).

3:13b δειξάτω: This structural marker is a third person singular present active imperative of δείκνυμι that conveys the idea of proving or making clear by evidence or reasoning and may be rendered as "explain" or "prove" (BDAG, s.v. "δείκνυμι" 2, p. 214). **Syntactically**, it is the main verb of this independent asyndeton clause with the subject being the one who is the σοφὸς καὶ ἐπιστήμων person from the previous question in 3:13a. **Semantically**, the third person imperative is that of expectation, "he should show" (NET) or just "show" (NRSV), even though δειξάτω is frequently rendered "let him show" (KJV ASV NASB NIV ESV CNT; cf. Adam, 71). Although the latter rendering is typically perceived as a permissive force (W, 485–86), the imperatival force conveys that if there is a true understanding of God's ways, the person is expected to "prove it" (NLT). The aorist is a constative aorist that views action as a whole (W, 557–58). The expectation echoes the message that the one aspiring to be wise must demonstrate it by attractive (καλῆς) behavior displayed through his works of faith (cf. 2:18) and through his gentleness (3:13b).

> **Lexical Nugget:** What is meant by πραΰτητι? Plato (*Symp.* 197) and Aristotle (*Eth. Nic.* 1125) used it to describe a calm disposition. Philo (*Mos.* 1,

328) used the word about Moses to describe his calmness. It is attributed to Moses (Num. 12:3), as well as to David (Ps. 132:1), to the godly person (Ps. 37:11), and to the coming Messiah (Zech. 9:9). The noun is also often associated with the "fear" of the Lord in wisdom literature (Prov. 15:33; 22:4). James is talking about the same wisdom that comes down from God and about those who humble themselves to receive it. The example of Jesus defines the word for the rest of its use in the NT. Jesus presented himself as meek and lowly of heart (πραΰς εἰμι καὶ ταπεινὸς τῇ καρ-δίᾳ)—a trait in the literature that is to be characteristic of teachers. The following definition seems balanced: "the quality of not being overly impressed by a sense of one's self-importance, *gentleness, humility, courtesy, considerateness, meekness*" (BDAG, s.v. "πραΰς," p. 861). It is the lowly attitude of heart that is full of gentleness and mildness toward others, the opposite of arrogant self-assertion. James us this term to denote the attitude with which the implanted Word is to be received (1:21), which also implies being "teachable."

3:14a δέ: This structural marker is a conjunction meaning "but" (BDAG, s.v. "δέ" 4a, p. 213). **Syntactically**, it introduces a dependent conjunctive clause and appears in a post-positive position that links segments of thoughts together. **Semantically**, it is rendered as a contrastive "but" (KJV ASV NASB NRSV NIV ESV NET NLT) that provides a contrast to people who exhibit good conduct and meekness.

εἰ: This Greek word is a conjunction meaning "if" (BDAG, s.v. "εἰ" 1aβ, p. 277). **Syntactically**, it too introduces a dependent conjunctive clause: "but *if* you have bitter jealousy and selfish ambition in your hearts" (εἰ δέ ζῆλον πικρὸν ἔχετε καὶ ἐριθείαν ἐν τῇ καρδίᾳ ὑμῶν). The entire clause functions adverbially modifying "boasting" and appears above the verb κατακαυ-χᾶσθε to visualize its dependence on the subsequent clause. **Semantically**, "if" (εἰ) introduces a first-class conditional clause and is the protasis of the conditional sentence (W, 682–89). James is assuming that his readers have bitter jealousy and selfish ambition for the sake of his argument (W, 690–94; Adam, 72). The protasis extends through σοφίας and assumes the reality of the various conditions.

ἔχετε: This Greek verb is a second person plural present active indicative of ἔχω that means "have" and is understood here as to experience or "have" an inner emotion (BDAG, s.v. "ἔχω" 7aβ, p. 421). **Syntactically**, it is the main verb of this dependent conjunctive clause of the first-class εἰ conditional clause with "you" as its subject. The indicative mood assumes the reality of the condition for the sake of his argument (W, 450–51). **Semantically**, the present tense is an iterative present indicating action that happens time and time again (W, 520–21). James assumes for the sake of his argument believers who time and again "have" or act out their bitter jealousy and selfish ambition.

3:14b μὴ κατακαυχᾶσθε: This negated (μή) structural marker is a second person plural present middle imperative of κατακαυχάομαι that conveys the idea of boasting at the expense of another and is often rendered "boast against" or "exult over" (BDAG, s.v. "κατακαυχάομαι" 1, p. 517). **Syntactically**, it is the main verb of this independent asyndeton clause and the first of two commands about speech in the apodosis of the first-class conditional εἰ clause. **Semantically**, the imperative with μή is an imperative of a prohibition (W, 487–88; Adam, 72). The present tense is a customary present that conveys a regular practice, namely, "*becoming*" boastful or arrogant (W, 521–22). Together, the present tense imperative with μή describes the cessation of activity in progress (W, 487, 724–25). In other words, stop continuing your arrogance or boasting. Most often it is translated simply as "do not boast" (NIV ESV NET CNT; cf. NRSV) or "do not be arrogant" (NASB).

> **Theological Nugget**: What is the significance of this second use of "boasting" (κατακαυχάομαι)? This verb κατακαυχᾶσθε was used previously in 2:13 with a genitive to denote the triumph of one principle (mercy) over another (judgment). So it does also in the only other passage where it occurs in NT: Romans 11:18 (μὴ κατακαυχῶ τῶν κλάδων). This warning against boasting connected to wisdom indicates that James may have in mind the warning from Jeremiah 9:23–24: "Let not the wise man boast in his wisdom . . . but let him who boasts boast about this: that he understands and knows Me."

3:14c καί: This structural marker is a conjunction meaning "and" (BDAG, s.v. "καί" 1b, p. 494). **Syntactically**, it introduces an independent conjunctive clause. **Semantically**, it is a coordinating conjunction often rendered "and" (NET ESV NASB NRSV etc.) that underscores another form of misconduct, namely, lying.

[μὴ] ψεύδεσθε: This Greek word is a second person plural present middle imperative of ψεύδομαι that conveys the idea of telling falsehoods and is rendered "lie" (BDAG, s.v. "ψεύδομαι" 1, p. 1096). **Syntactically**, it is the main verb of this independent conjunctive clause and the second of two commands about speech in the apodosis of the first-class conditional εἰ clause. **Semantically**, this second person imperative with an assumed μή is also an imperative of a prohibition (W, 487–88; Adam, 72). The present tense is a customary present that conveys a regular practice, namely, "*becoming*" liars (W, 521–22). Together, the present tense imperative with μή describes the cessation of activity in progress (W, 487, 724–25). In other words, stop the continuation of your lies. Contrary to the KJV and ASV that carry over an assumed μή in their rendering of ψεύδεσθε ("lie not"), most translations assume the idea of stopping bad behavior and render ψεύδεσθε simply as "tell lies" (NET; cf. NASB NLT), "deny" (NIV), or "be false" (NRSV ESV CNT). We, however, tend to reflect a KJV and ASV rendering with "[*stop*] lying."

> **Theological Nugget:** What is the significance of James's concern about lying (ψεύδομαι)? Lying is not taken lightly in the NT. There is a similar expression in 1 John 1:6: "we lie and we are not practicing the truth" (ψευδόμεθα καὶ οὐ ποιοῦμεν τὴν ἀλήθειαν). John presents a hypothetical example of someone who says one thing yet, practices another (Bateman et al.[1], 76, 82). The reference to lying against the truth reflects the tendency to personalize what we view as abstract concepts. Consider the parallel idea in Acts 5:3, where Ananias's deed of "lying against the Holy Spirit" means something like "falsifying the Holy Spirit" or "counterfeiting the life guided by the Spirit." Therefore, "lying against the truth" means living in a manner contrary to the "Word of Truth" (1:18) that was planted in them and which they were to receive "with meekness" (1:21).

3:15a οὐκ ἔστιν: This negated (οὐκ) structural marker is a third person singular present active indicative of εἰμί that conveys something that is in close connection with something else and is often rendered "is" (BDAG, s.v. "εἰμί" 2a, p. 283). **Syntactically**, it is the main verb of an independent asyndeton clause. The more definite nominative "this" (αὕτη) is the subject, and "wisdom" (ἡ σοφία) is the predicate nominative (W, 40–44; Adam, 72). **Semantically**, the negated ἔστιν functions as an equative verb. It negates a close connection with "this" (αὕτη). This pronoun is a demonstrative pronoun that functions anaphorically by referring back to jealousy and selfish ambition as something that is "not" (οὐκ) to be equated with "wisdom" (ἡ σοφία). The negated verb is typically rendered as "is not" (ASV NASB NIV ESV NLT CNT; cf. NLT) or "does not" (NRSV NIV NET). Whereas James encourages his readers to pray for wisdom in chapter 1, here he provides a true definition for what wisdom is not.

> **Grammatical Nugget:** What is the significance of James's use of a negated ἔστιν? It is notable that the negated being verb (οὐκ ἔστιν) should come first in the sentence. Of the ninety-eight occurrences of οὐκ ἔστιν in the NT, only nine times does it initiate a sentence. Four of those are in synoptic sayings of Jesus (Matt. 10:24/Luke 6:40 and Matt. 28:6/Luke 24:6) and two of them are in OT quotations (Rom. 3:11, 18). Such a rare choice must be for a reason, and it relates to another grammatical question in the verse—whether the participle κατερχομένη is part of a periphrastic construction (functioning like the indicative expression οὐ κατέρχεται) or if

it expresses a new idea about wisdom. The placement of οὐκ ἔστιν—five words distant from the participle—makes it unlikely that it is periphrastic (con. Adam, 72). Rather, James affirms that "this is not the wisdom that comes down from above." While "worldly wisdom" may be a valid implication of his language, James is careful not to apply the word σοφία in any way to the vices he is about to describe.

3:15b κατερχομένη: This structural marker is a nominative singular feminine present middle participle of κατέρχομαι that conveys the idea of moving "in a direction considered the opposite of up" and is often rendered as "come down" (BDAG, s.v. "κατέρχομαι" 1, p. 531). **Syntactically**, it introduces a dependent participial clause that functions as an attributive participle modifying σοφία (W, 617–18). **Semantically**, the present tense is a customary present in that wisdom continually comes down from God "above" (W, 521–22).

> **Lexical Nugget:** What is the meaning of ἄνωθεν? The NIV rendering "from heaven" is functionally equivalent to the Greek ἄνωθεν, which is literally rendered as "from above" (BDAG, s.v. "ἄνωθεν" 1, p. 92). James uses this word in 1:17a to identify the direction from which all good gifts come. This is God's realm and thereby it identifies the source of wisdom (see John 3:31). God delights in granting his children what they request—especially wisdom (see 1:5). The wisdom that James commends does not come to the believer through intellectual effort or study, but as the wisdom literature has clearly taught, it is God's gift (Prov. 2:6).

3:15c ἀλλ': This structural marker is a conjunction meaning "but" (BDAG s.v. "ἀλλά" 2, p. 45). **Syntactically**, it introduces an independent conjunctive clause with an assumed or elliptical verb in brackets [ἐστιν] but it is an evident carryover from the preceding clause. **Semantically**, the conjunction functions to introduce a contrast that provides the other kind of wisdom, the wisdom that is not from God. It is actually functioning as a corrective conjunction (Adam, 73).

[ἐστιν]: This Greek word is a third person singular present active indicative from the verb εἰμί that conveys something that is in close connection with something else and often is rendered "is" (BDAG, s.v. "εἰμί" 2a, p. 283). **Syntactically**, the bracketed [ἐστιν] is an ellipsis that serves as the main verb of this independent conjunctive clause. The subject of the verb is "it" as the assumed subject in [ἐστιν] with three predicate adjectives ἐπίγειος, ψυχική, δαιμονιώδης (W, 40–46). **Semantically**, the elliptical [ἐστιν] is equative in that it shows that wisdom from selfish ambition and jealousy has a close connection with things that are earthly (ἐπίγειος), unspiritual (ψυχική), or demonic (δαιμονιώδης). It is simply rendered as "is" (KJV ASV NASB NRSV NIV ESV NET NLT CNT).

3:16a γάρ: This structural marker is a conjunction meaning "for" or "you see" (BDAG, s.v. "γάρ" 2, p. 189). **Syntactically**, it introduces a dependent conjunctive clause of continuation. **Semantically**, it clarifies James's argument about wisdom (cf. Adam, 73). It is typically rendered as "for" (KJV ASV NASB NRSV NIV ESV NET NLT CNT), but "you see" provides a clearer understanding of James's use as evident in BDAG.

[ἐστιν]: This Greek word is a third person singular present active indicative from the verb εἰμί that means "be" and "exist" (BDAG, s.v. "εἰμί" 1, p. 282). **Syntactically**, the bracketed [ἐστιν] is an ellipsis that serves as the main verb of this independent conjunctive clause. The subject of the verb is "jealousy and selfish ambition" (ζῆλος καὶ ἐριθεία). **Semantically**, the verb underscores the existence of jealousy and selfish ambition and is simply rendered as "exists" (NASB ESV CNT) or "there is" (NRSV NET NLT; cf. KJV ASV).

3:16b [ἐστιν]: This structural marker is a third person singular present active indicative from the verb εἰμί that conveys something that is in close connection with something else and is often rendered "is" (BDAG, s.v. "εἰμί" 2a, p. 283). **Syntactically**, the bracketed [ἐστιν] is an ellipsis that serves as the main verb of this independent asyndeton clause. The subject of the verb is "there," with "disorder" (ἀκαταστασία) as the predicate nominative (W, 40–46; con. Adam, 73). An adverb introduces the clause and is rendered "there" in reference to a place (BDAG, s.v. "ἐκεῖ" 2, p. 301). **Semantically**, the elliptical [ἐστιν] is equative in that it reveals the close connection of "jealousy and selfish ambition" (ζῆλος καὶ ἐριθεία) with "disorder" (ἀκαταστασία). It is simply rendered as "is" (KJV ASV NASB NRSV NIV ESV NET NLT CNT).

> **Lexical Nugget:** What is the significance of James's use of adjectival descriptors? James listed the vices by means of adjectives, but here he uses nouns to describe the *results* of those vices—jealousy, selfish ambition, and disorder. When this type of attitude is displayed "there" (ἐκεῖ) is where "disorder" against an established authority is found (BDAG, s.v. "ἀκατάστατος" 2, p. 35). In 1:8, James calls the double-minded person "unstable" (ἀκατάστατος) and in 3:8, he describes the tongue as a "restless [ἀκατάστατον] evil." Whatever be the immediate cause, the result of this is "anarchy," which is heightened with the inclusion of "every vile practice" (πᾶν φαῦλον πρᾶγμα). While "disorder" (ἀκατάστατος) has inherited the concept of instability from its related adjective (1:8), this noun focuses more on the results of instability and restlessness.

3:17a δέ: This structural marker is a conjunction meaning "but" (BDAG, s.v. "δέ" 4a, p. 213). **Syntactically**, it introduces an independent conjunctive clause and appears in a post-positive position. **Semantically**, the Greek particle links segments of thoughts together. It is rendered as a contrast: "but" (KJV ASV NASB NRSV NIV ESV NET NLT). It is a marker that moves to provide a contrast to jealousy and selfish ambition that results in disorder.

ἐστιν: This Greek word is a third person singular present active indicative of εἰμί that conveys something that is in close connection with something else and is often rendered "is" (BDAG, s.v. "εἰμί" 2a, p. 283). **Syntactically**, it is the main verb of an independent conjunctive clause with the more definite nominative "wisdom" (ἡ . . . σοφία) as the subject and "pure" (ἀγνή) the predicate adjective (W, 40–46; Adam, 74). **Semantically**, the verb is equative in that it reveals the close connection of divine "wisdom" (ἡ . . . σοφία) with "pure" (ἀγνή). It is simply rendered as "is" (KJV ASV NASB NRSV NIV ESV NET NLT CNT). This positive note balances the negative one in 3:15: οὐκ ἔστιν αὕτη ἡ σοφία ἄνωθεν.

> **Grammatical Nugget:** How should μέν be understood and thereby rendered? Because of the μέν, we should not automatically expect a corresponding δέ in verse 18 (con. BDF, §447.2). It is typical, however, for anacoluthon in enumerations, where the μέν is found alone continued in some manner that is irregular in form and thereby rendered "in the first place" (πρῶτον μέν; cf. BDAG, s.v. "μέν" 2c, p. 630). This also appears in Romans 1:8; 3:2; 1 Corinthians 11:18. So, translations typically render it simply as "first" (KJV ASV NASB NRSV NIV ESV NET CNT).

3:17b [ἐστιν]: This structural marker is a third person singular present active indicative from the verb εἰμί that conveys something that is in close connection with something else and is often rendered "is" (BDAG, s.v. "εἰμί" 2a, p. 283). **Syntactically**, the bracketed [ἐστιν] is an ellipsis that serves as the main verb of the independent asyndeton clause. The subject of the verb is "it" (referring back to "wisdom") as the assumed subject in [ἐστιν] has three predicate adjectives ἐπίγειος, ψυχική, and δαιμονιώδης (W, 40–46; Adam, 74). An adverb introduces the clause and is rendered "then" in reference to being next in position of James's enumeration of items (BDAG, s.v. "ἔπειτα" 2, p. 361). **Semantically**, the elliptical [ἐστιν] reveals the close connection between selfish ambition and jealousy, which are earthly (ἐπίγειος), unspiritual (ψυχική), and demonic (δαιμονιώδης). It is simply rendered as "is" (KJV ASV NASB NRSV NIV ESV NET NLT CNT).

> **Grammatical Nugget:** How does James use alliteration to convey his message in this verse? Six consecutive words beginning with epsilon

appear in rapid sequence: ἡ δὲ ἄνωθεν σοφία πρῶτον μὲν ἁγνή ἐστιν, ἔπειτα εἰρηνική, ἐπιεικής, εὐπειθής, μεστὴ ἐλέους. Furthermore, the third, fourth, and fifth words rhyme by ending with a similar sound: -ή, -ής, -ής. This is followed by three words that are initiated by an alpha: καὶ καρπῶν ἀγαθῶν, ἀδιάκριτος, ἀνυπόκριτος. This intentional alliteration contrasts aurally in a graphic manner with the preceding vice list, which has no such alliteration. The contrast of the sounds conveys an oral message about the difference between the behavioral disharmony that comes from below and the harmonious order of the behavior that descends from above. This rhetorical impact of their collective sounds, to the ancient auditor, also conveyed a meaning. This impact is muted in our silent reading culture but was magnified in the public reading and hearing of the Scriptures in ancient times.

3:18a δέ: This structural marker is a conjunction meaning "and" (BDAG, s.v. "δέ" 1, p. 213). **Syntactically**, it introduces an independent conjunctive clause and appears in the post-positive position. **Semantically**, it is a marker that connects a series of statements and typically is rendered as "and" (KJV ASV NRSV ESV NET NLT).

σπείρεται: This Greek word is a third person singular present passive indicative of σπείρω that conveys the idea of sowing seed, whether literal or metaphorical, and may be rendered as "sow seed" (BDAG, s.v. "σπείρω" 1bγ, p. 936). **Syntactically**, it is the main verb in the independent conjunctive clause with καρπὸς as its subject. **Semantically**, the present tense is a customary present and conveys action that continually happens (W, 521–22). Seeds are sown on a regular basis. This final verse rounds off the points that James has made in 3:13–17 and also is thematically connected to 4:1–10. Righteousness and peace are "fruits" often associated in the OT (Pss. 71:7 [LXX]; 85:10; Isa. 32:17). The "fruit of righteousness" (καρπὸς δικαιοσύνης) is a phrase familiar in the LXX, though usually without an exact equivalent in the Hebrew text (Prov. 3:9, 11:30; Amos 6:12).

3:18b τοῖς ποιοῦσιν: This articular (τοῖς) structural marker is a dative plural masculine present active participle of ποιέω that conveys the idea of undertaking to do something that brings about an event or condition and is often rendered as "bring about," "make," or "establish" (BDAG, s.v. "ποιέω" 2c, p. 839). **Syntactically**, it introduces a dependent participial clause. It is an adverbial clause that modifies the verb "is sown" (σπείρεται) with "peace" (εἰρήνην) functioning as the object of the preposition. **Semantically**, the dative case is probably a dative of agency (W, 163–66; Adam, 75; BDF, §191.4; Zerwick, §59). It is typically rendered "by those who make" (NASB ESV CNT). The present tense is a customary present and conveys action that continually happens (W, 521–22). The emphasis is on the regular conditions that bring about peace. The appropriate intertextual echo undoubtedly reflects the famous *logion* of Jesus: "Blessed are the peacemakers, for they shall be called sons of God" (Matt. 5:9).

> **Grammatical Nugget:** Are the references to "wisdom" allusions to the Holy Spirit? Apart from the disputed reference to τὸ πνεῦμα in 4:5b, James has no explicit reference to the Holy Spirit. Some have suggested that "wisdom" effectively functions as the Holy Spirit does in other NT writings. A comparison of the characteristics of the wisdom "from above" in 3:17–18 with the Pauline "fruit of the spirit" in Galatians 5:22–23 illustrates clearly this possible identity of wisdom with the Spirit. Other references where James uses language about the gift of wisdom (1:5–8) are paralleled by references to the gift of the Spirit in Paul (Rom. 8:9–11, 14–15; 1 Cor. 1:18–31; Eph. 1:17; Col. 1:28). Not only are there fruits of wisdom (3:13–18), but wisdom is also a moral force to help overcome testing and temptation (1:5–8)—ministries all related to the Spirit elsewhere.

DIVINE WISDOM IS IDENTIFIABLE IN PEOPLE WHO LIVE PEACEABLY (JAMES 4:1–4)

CLAUSAL OUTLINE FOR JAMES 4:1–4

4:1a Πόθεν [*ποιεῖτε*] πόλεμοι
4:1a What [*causes*] quarrels

4:1b καὶ πόθεν [*ποιεῖτε*] μάχαι ἐν ὑμῖν;
4:1b and what [*causes*] fights among you?

4:1c οὐκ ἐντεῦθεν [*ἐστιν*], ἐκ τῶν ἡδονῶν
4:1c [*Is it*] not from your passions

4:1d ὑμῶν **τῶν στρατευομένων** ἐν τοῖς μέλεσιν ὑμῶν;
4:1d **that are at war** in your members?

4:2a **ἐπιθυμεῖτε**
4:2a **You desire**

4:2b καὶ οὐκ **ἔχετε**
4:2b and **you do** not **own**

4:2c [*καὶ*] **φονεύετε**.
4:2c [*and so*] **you murder**.

4:2d καὶ **ζηλοῦτε**
4:2d Likewise, **you covet**

4:2e καὶ οὐ **δύνασθε ἐπιτυχεῖν**
4:2e and **are** not **able to obtain** *things*

4:2f [*καὶ*] **μάχεσθε**
4:2f [*and so*] **you fight**

4:2g καὶ **πολεμεῖτε**.
4:2g and **quarrel**.

4:2h οὐκ **ἔχετε**
4:2h **You do** not **own**
      |
        4:2i διὰ τὸ μὴ **αἰτεῖσθαι** ὑμᾶς,
        4:2i because you **do** not **ask**.

4:3a **αἰτεῖτε**,
4:3a **You ask**,

4:3b καὶ οὐ λαμβάνετε
4:3b and yet **you do** not **receive**
      |
        4:3c διότι κακῶς **αἰτεῖσθε**,
        4:3c because **you ask** wrongly,
            |
              4:3d **ἵνα** ἐν ταῖς ἡδοναῖς ὑμῶν **δαπανήσητε**.
              4:3d so that **you might spend it** on your pleasures.

4:4a μοιχαλίδες, οὐκ **οἴδατε** (ὅτι ἡ φιλία τοῦ κόσμου ἔχθρα τοῦ θεοῦ **ἐστιν**);
4:4a Adulteresses, **do you** not **know** (that friendship with the world **means** enmity with God)?

4:4b (ὃς ἐὰν οὖν **βουληθῇ** φίλος **εἶναι** τοῦ κόσμου) ἐχθρὸς τοῦ θεοῦ **καθίσταται**.
4:4b Therefore, (whoever **decides to be** the world's friend) **makes himself** God's enemy.

SYNTAX EXPLAINED FOR JAMES 4:1–4

4:1a [ποιεῖτε]: This structural marker is a second person plural present active indicative of ποιέω that conveys the idea of doing something that brings about an event or a condition and may be rendered "do," "cause," or "bring about" (BDAG, s.v. "ποιέω" 2h, p. 840). **Syntactically**, the bracketed [ποιεῖτε] is an ellipsis and serves as the main verb of this independent asyndeton clause with "quarrels" (πόλεμοι) as its subject. **Semantically**, the present tense is an iterative present indicating action that occurs time and time again (W, 520–21). In this case, James asks from what source are quarrels repeatedly triggered. Most translations insert "causes" in this verbless clause (NIV ESV CNT).

> **Lexical Nugget:** What is meant by πόλεμοι and μάχαι? These words contrast with εἰρήνην, the last word of James 3:18b. The first, πόλεμος, pictures a continual campaign or "war." The second, μάχαι, describes the separate conflicts or battles in that war (Trench, 32). It may not be that helpful to finely distinguish between the two words, since James's purpose in using the words is to be as comprehensive as possible in his condemnation. In other words, James covers the whole problem by using both words. The reference in this context is obviously to personal and not national "conflicts." The first word (πόλεμοι) is used elsewhere only of military conflicts (1 Cor. 14:8; and of apocalyptic war in Rev. 9:7; 12:7; 16:14; 20:8). The latter word (μάχαι) is clearly used for personal strife elsewhere in the NT (2 Cor. 7:5; 2 Tim. 2:23–24; Titus 3:9).

4:1b καί: This structural marker is a conjunction meaning "and" (BDAG, s.v. "καί" 1b, p. 494). **Syntactically**, it introduces an independent conjunctive clause. **Semantically**, it is a coordinating conjunction often rendered "and" (NET ESV NASB NRSV etc.) that underscores James's discussion of passions with the next verb.

[ποιεῖτε]: This Greek word is a second person plural present active indicative of ποιέω that conveys the idea of doing something that brings about an event or a condition and may be rendered "do," "cause," or "bring about" (BDAG, s.v. "ποιέω" 2h, p. 840). **Syntactically**, the bracketed [ποιεῖτε] is an ellipsis and serves as the main verb of this independent conjunctive clause with "fights" (μάχαι) as its subject. **Semantically**, the present tense is an iterative present indicating action that occurs time and time again (W, 520–21). In this case, James asks from what source are fights repeatedly triggered.

4:1c [ἐστιν]: This structural marker is a third person singular present active indicative from the verb εἰμί that conveys something that is in close connection with something else and is often rendered "is" (BDAG, s.v. "εἰμί" 2a, p. 283). **Syntactically**, the bracketed [ἐστιν] is an ellipsis that serves as the main verb of this independent asyndeton clause. It is an interrogative clause expecting a negative answer (Adam, 76). The subject of the verb is "it" as the assumed subject in [ἐστιν], and the prepositional phrase "from your passions" (ἐκ τῶν ἡδονῶν) is the predicate (W, 47–48). **Semantically**, the elliptical [ἐστιν] reveals the close connection between "conflicts and quarrels" (= assumed "it" here) of verses 1a and 1b, which is, namely, personal passions (BDAG, s.v. "ἐντεῦθεν" 2, p. 339). It is simply rendered as "is" (KJV ASV NASB NRSV ESV CNT).

4:1d τῶν στρατευομένων. This articular (τῶν) structural marker is a genitive plural feminine present middle participle of στρατεύω that conveys the idea of engaging in a conflict and is often rendered as "wage battle" or "fight" (BDAG, s.v. "στρατεύω" 2, p. 947). **Syntactically**, it introduces a dependent participial clause that functions attributively modifying ἡδονῶν. **Semantically**, the present tense is an iterative present indicating action that occurs time and time again (W, 520–21). Personal desires or passions that cause conflict and quarrels are time and time again "at war" (στρατεύω) within every person (μέλεσιν). This comparison with "waging war" is an effective use of personification.

> **Lexical Nugget:** What is meant by ἡδονῶν? James places the source of these outward conflicts of 4:1c in our inward "desires" or "passions" (ἡδονῶν). He repeats the expression ἡδονῶν ὑμῶν in 4:3c where it describes the selfish desires that are satisfied by things one acquires. This repetition emphasizes those desires as the theme and the real problem being addressed in this passage. This important word, ἡδονή, usually means "pleasure," but it can also carry the sense of a "desire for pleasure" (Xenophon, *Mem.* 1, 2, 23; 4 Macc 5:23). "The fact that James follows immediately with *epithymein* suggests that this is also the meaning here (compare Luke 8:14; Titus 3:3; 2 Pet. 2:13)" (Johnson, 276).

4:2a ἐπιθυμεῖτε: This structural marker is a second person plural present active indicative of ἐπιθυμέω that conveys the idea of having strong desires to secure something and may be rendered "desire" or "long for" (BDAG, s.v. "ἐπιθυμέω" 1, p. 371). **Syntactically**, it is the main verb of this independent asyndeton clause (BDF, §494). The subject of the verb is the "you" assumed in ἐπιθυμεῖτε. **Semantically**, the present tense is an iterative present indicating action that occurs time and time again (W, 520–21). James speaks of his readers having desires or longings for things time and time again.

> **Literary Nugget:** What is the literary significance of James's alternating between negative and positive statements? James's abrupt style continues in 4:2–3 with a series of short, second person plural statements, which alternate between the negative (ἐπιθυμεῖτε, φονεύετε, ζηλοῦτε, μάχεσθε, πολεμεῖτε, οὐ λαμβάνετε) and the positive. It is also possible to detect a

chiastic structure to them. If the secondary clauses are removed, the primary clauses can be structured as follows:

A ἐπιθυμεῖτε,   καὶ οὐκ ἔχετε·
   B φονεύετε καὶ ζηλοῦτε   οὐ δύνασθε ἐπιτυχεῖν·
   B´ μάχεσθε καὶ πολεμεῖτε   οὐκ ἔχετε
A´ αἰτεῖτε   καὶ οὐ λαμβάνετε,

The A clause parallels the A´ clause, and the B and B´ compound clauses also are parallel, structurally as well as semantically. The addition of the secondary clauses in lines B´ and A´ completes the charge by explaining both the causes (4:2) and the result (4:3) of requests that are driven by selfish desires.

4:2b καί: This structural marker is a conjunction meaning "and" (BDAG, s.v. "καί" 1b, p. 494). **Syntactically**, it introduces an independent conjunctive clause. **Semantically**, καί is a coordinating conjunction often rendered "and" (NET ESV NASB NRSV etc.) that underscores James's discussion of desires with the next verb.

οὐκ ἔχετε: This negated (οὐκ) Greek word is a second person plural present active indicative of ἔχω that conveys the idea of possessing and may be rendered "have" or "own" (BDAG, s.v. "ἔχω" 1a, p. 420). **Syntactically**, it is the main verb of this independent conjunctive clause. The subject is the assumed "you" in ἔχετε. **Semantically**, the present tense is an iterative present indicating action that occurs time and time again (W, 520–21). James speaks of his readers "having" things time and time again. The verb's sense involves not just "not having" but "possessing" or "owning."

4:2c [καί]: This structural marker is a conjunction meaning "and then" or "and so" (BDAG, s.v. "καί" 1bζ, p. 495). **Syntactically**, the bracketed [καί] is an ellipsis that introduces an independent conjunctive clause. **Semantically**, it is a coordinating conjunction of result that comes from unfulfilled desires often rendered as "so" (ESV NASB NRSV CNT) or "and so." The result of unfulfilled desires is clarified with the next verb. The syntax concerning the ellipsis of καί is difficult.

φονεύετε: This Greek word is a second person plural present active indicative of φονεύω that conveys the idea of murdering another and may be rendered "murder" or "kill" (BDAG, s.v. "φονεύω," p. 1063). **Syntactically**, it is the main verb of this independent conjunctive clause. The subject of the verb is the "you" assumed in φονεύετε. **Semantically**, the present tense is an iterative present indicating action that occurs time and time again (W, 520–21). James speaks of his readers "murdering" people time and time again.

Figure of Speech Nugget: What does James really mean concerning "murder" in verse 2? The sense is probably metaphorical murder as was taught by Jesus (Matt. 5:21–22). Any attempt to see actual murder here ignores all the rhetorical language being utilized, including the use of the phrase "within you" (Davids, 156). This type of language no more literally refers to murder than does the exclamation "adulteresses" (4:4a). When the rhetorical language is recognized, we must conclude that these expressions are hyperbolic and overstated for effect. The Pauline admonition is also appropriate here: "But if you bite and devour one another, watch out that you are not consumed by one another" (Gal. 5:15).

4:2d καί: This structural marker is a conjunction meaning "also" or "likewise" (BDAG, s.v. "καί" 2a, p. 495). **Syntactically**, it introduces an independent conjunctive clause. **Semantically**, it functions as an additive conjunction that is often rendered "also" or "likewise." James is adding to the list of things that are included in the "passions" of verse 1. While some may render καί as "and" (KJV ASV NRSV NET CNT), most translations tend not to translate καί (NASB1995 ESV NLT). The syntax concerning the appearance of καί here in verse 2 is difficult.

ζηλοῦτε: This Greek word is a second person plural present active indicative of ἔχω that conveys any intense negative feelings over another person's achievements or success and may be rendered as "be filled with jealousy" or to "be filled with envy" toward another person (BDAG, s.v. "ἔχω" 2, p. 420). **Syntactically**, it is the main verb of this independent conjunctive clause. **Semantically**, the present tense is an iterative present indicating action that occurs time and time again (W, 520–21). James speaks of the intense negative feelings that emerge regularly among believers. Envy and murder are often found in the Septuagint tradition (Wis 2:24: "through the devil's envy death entered the world"). Christian writings make the same connection (Matt. 27:18; Mark 15:10; Acts 5:17; 7:9; 13:45; 17:5).

4:2e καί: This structural marker is a conjunction meaning "and" (BDAG, s.v. "καί" 1b, p. 494). **Syntactically**, it introduces an independent conjunctive clause. **Semantically**, it is a coordinating conjunction often rendered "and" (NET ESV NASB NRSV etc.) that adds to James's observation about coveting with the next verb.

δύνασθε: This Greek word is a second person plural present middle indicative of δύναμαι that conveys the idea of possessing capability and may be rendered "can" or "am able, be capable" (BDAG, s.v. "δύναμαι" αβ, p. 262). **Syntactically**, it is the main verb of this independent conjunctive clause. The subject is the "you" assumed in δύνασθε. **Semantically**, the present tense is a customary present indicating continual action (W, 521–22).

ἐπιτυχεῖν: This Greek word is an aorist active infinitive of ἐπιτυγχάνω that conveys the idea of successfully achieving or gaining what a person seeks and is often rendered "obtain," "attain to," or "reach" (BDAG, s.v. "ἐπιτυγχάνω," p. 385). **Syntactically**, it is part of the main verb δύνασθε of this independent conjunctive clause. **Semantically**, it is a complementary infinitive. The aorist tense is a constative aorist that discusses events about coveting as a whole (W, 557–58). The verb is used with the genitive τῆς ἐπαγγελίας in Hebrews 6:15 and 11:33; with the accusative τοῦτο twice in Romans 11:7; and with the object supplied from the previous clause here.

4:2f [καί]: This structural marker is a conjunction meaning "and then" or "and so" (BDAG, s.v. "καί" 1bζ, p. 495). **Syntactically**, the bracketed [καί] is an ellipsis that introduces an independent conjunctive clause. **Semantically**, the elliptical [καί] is a coordinating conjunction of result that comes from unfulfilled desires and is often rendered as "so" (ESV NASB NRSV CNT) or "and so." The result of unfulfilled desires is clarified in the next verb. The syntax concerning the ellipsis of καί here is difficult.

μάχεσθε: This Greek word is a second person plural present middle indicative of μάχομαι that conveys the idea of engaging in heated disputes without weapons and is often rendered as "fight," "quarrel," or "dispute" (BDAG, s.v. "μάχομαι" 2, p. 622). **Syntactically**, it is the main verb of this independent conjunctive clause. The subject is the "you" assumed in μάχεσθε. **Semantically**, the present tense is an iterative present indicating action that occurs time and time again (W, 520–21). James speaks of the intense negative fighting or quarreling that emerges regularly among his audience.

4:2g καί: This structural marker is a conjunction meaning "and" (BDAG, s.v. "καί" 1b, p. 494). **Syntactically**, it introduces an independent conjunctive clause. **Semantically**, καί is a coordinating conjunction often rendered "and" (NET ESV NASB NRSV etc.) that adds to James's observation about fighting with the next verb.

πολεμεῖτε: This Greek word is a second person plural present active indicative of πολεμέω that conveys the idea of opposition and may be rendered as "be hostile," typically used in military imagery (BDAG, s.v. "πολεμέω" 2, p. 844). **Syntactically**, it is the main verb of this independent conjunctive clause with the subject "you" assumed in πολεμεῖτε. **Semantically**, the present tense is an iterative present indicating action that occurs time and time again (W, 520–21). James speaks of his readers committing intense offenses regularly among themselves. In its five other occurrences, the verb means "to make war" in the apocalyptic language of Revelation 2:16; 12:7; 13:4; 17:14; and 19:1. Because of its pairing with μάχεσθε here, its meaning is "to wrangle" or "to quarrel."

4:2h οὐκ ἔχετε. This structural marker is a second person plural present active indicative of ἔχω that conveys the idea of possessing and may be rendered "have" or "own" (BDAG, s.v. "ἔχω" 1a, p. 420). The subject of the verb is the "you" assumed in ἔχετε. **Syntactically**, it is the main verb of this independent asyndeton clause. **Semantically**, the present tense is an iterative present indicating time and time again (W, 520–21). James speaks of his readers "not having" things time and time again. The verb's sense involves not just "having" but "possessing" or "owning."

4:2i διὰ τὸ μὴ αἰτεῖσθαι: This negated (μή) articular (τό) structural marker is a present middle infinitive of αἰτέω that conveys the idea of asking with an expected answer and is often rendered "ask," "ask for," or "demand" (BDAG, s.v. "αἰτέω," p. 30). **Syntactically**, it is the main verb of this dependent infinitival clause that modifies ἔχετε. It is placed under the ἔχετε to visualize the clause's dependence. **Semantically**, the infinitive introduced with διὰ τό is causal (W, 596–97, 662; Adam, 77; Irons, 539). The present tense is an iterative present indicating action that occurs time and time again (W, 520–21). James speaks of his readers not asking God for help with their needs on a regular basis.

> **Theological Nugget:** What message is conveyed through the infinitive clause διὰ τὸ μὴ αἰτεῖσθαι ὑμᾶς? James is addressing people who are choosing pleasure as their goal. They cut themselves off from the source of good things (1:17). They find that their prayers aiming at their own pleasures and not his service are thereby unacceptable. So, people do ask but they do not "have"? There are again possible echoes of Jesus's teaching like that in Matthew 6:31–33. The verb αἰτέω ("ask") here is also an echo of James 1:5b. If people do not live according to the "wisdom from above," it is not likely that they will turn to God with their requests.

4:3a αἰτεῖτε: This structural marker is a second person plural present active indicative of αἰτέω that conveys the idea of asking with an expected answer and is often rendered "ask," "ask for," or "demand" (BDAG, s.v. "αἰτέω," p. 30). **Syntactically**, it is the main verb of this independent asyndeton clause. The subject of the verb is the "you" assumed in αἰτεῖτε. **Semantically**, the present tense is an iterative present indicating action that occurs time and time again (W, 520–21), namely, asking for something time and again or on a need basis (1:6a).

4:3b καί: This structural marker is a conjunction connecting a fact considered surprising or unexpected or noteworthy, and may be rendered "and yet," "and in spite of that," or "nevertheless" (BDAG, s.v. "καί" 1bη, p. 495). **Syntactically**, it introduces an independent conjunctive clause. **Semantically**, it is an adversative coordinating conjunction rendered "and yet." Nevertheless, many translations render καί as "and" (KJV ASV NASB NRSV ESV NET CNT). Some, however, do not render καί at all (NIV NLT).

οὐ λαμβάνετε: This negated (οὐ) Greek word is a second person plural present active indicative of λαμβάνω that conveys the idea of being a receiver and may be rendered "receive," "get," or "obtain" (BDAG, s.v. "λαμβάνω" 10, p. 584). **Syntactically**, it is the main verb of this independent conjunctive clause. The subject of the verb is the "you" assumed in λαμβάνετε. **Semantically**, the present tense is an iterative present indicating action that occurs time and time again (W, 520–21), namely, a person's "not" (οὐ) getting something regardless of how many times it is requested.

4:3c διότι: This structural marker is a conjunction that makes a connection between two statements and may be rendered "because" (BDAG, s.v. "διότι" 1, p. 251). **Syntactically**, it introduces a dependent conjunctive clause and functions adverbially modifying λαμβάνετε. It is placed under λαμβάνετε to visualize the clause's dependence. **Semantically**, it is causal: "because" (Zerwick et al., 698). The structure of the verse makes it clear that this causal clause (KJV NASB NRSV NIV ESV NET etc.) explains the reason for something expressed with the next verb.

αἰτεῖσθε: This Greek word is a second person plural present middle indicative of αἰτέω that conveys the idea of asking with an expected answer and is often rendered "ask," "ask for," or "demand" (BDAG, s.v. "αἰτέω," p. 30). **Syntactically**, it is the main verb of this dependent clause introduced by διότι. The subject of the verb is the "you" assumed in αἰτεῖσθε. **Semantically**, the present tense is an iterative present indicating action that occurs time and time again (W, 520–21), namely, the request is time and time again being asked wrongly and is evident in the next dependent clause.

> **Theological Nugget:** What exactly is James saying here about prayer? There are some who fail to ask and then others who ask wrongly. Those who sometimes fail to ask God at other times ask him in the wrong spirit. Note that the verse does not say that God does not hear, but that we *do not receive*. The problem is on our end of the communication act. The switch to the active αἰτεῖτε probably does specify another use of the Jesus *logion* mentioned in Matthew 7:7–10. James is balancing Jesus's prayer promise by stressing that asking should be accompanied by right motives, not with the goal of simply spending the answer to satisfy one's own pleasures. In James 1:6–8, prayer is not successful if it is the prayer of a doubter. In 2:16, the "prayer" fails because it is not accompanied by appropriate action. Here in 4:2–3, prayer is unanswered because it is made for the wrong purpose.

4:3d ἵνα: This structural marker is a conjunction that makes a connection between two statements and may be rendered "so that" or "that" (BDAG, s.v. "ἵνα" 3, p. 477). **Syntactically**, it introduces a dependent conjunctive clause with δαπανήσητε as its main verb. It is placed under αἰτεῖσθε to visualize the clause's adverbial dependence. **Semantically**, it is a purpose-result (W, 473–74) and is rendered "so that" (NASB CNT) or "that" (KJV ASV NIV). Although purpose is possible (NRSV; Adam, 77), we prefer purpose-result in that ἵνα is used for the result that follows according to the purpose of the next verb.

δαπανήσητε: This Greek word is a second person plural aorist active subjunctive of δαπανάω that conveys the idea of using up or paying out and may be rendered "spend" or "spend freely" (BDAG, s.v. "δαπανάω" 1, p. 212). **Syntactically**, it is the main verb of this dependent conjunctive clause. It is in the subjunctive mood because ἵνα only takes its verb in the subjunctive (W, 471; Adam, 78). **Semantically**, the aorist tense is a constative aorist that describes an event as a whole. The verb can also imply a historical form of extravagance (see Luke 15:14, of the prodigal). James condemns those who ask for resources to enable them to obtain the objects of their desire and craving.

4:4a ουκ οἴδατε: This negated (ουκ) structural marker is a second person plural perfect active indicative of οἶδα that conveys the idea of having information about something and is often rendered "know" (BDAG, s.v. "οἶδα" 1e, p. 693). **Syntactically**, it is the main verb of this independent asyndeton clause. It is an interrogative rhetorical question asked with ουκ and thereby expects a positive answer (W, 418; Adam, 78). The subject of the verb is the "you" assumed in αἰτεῖσθε. **Semantically**, the perfect is a perfect with present force (W, 579–80). Thus, the result of knowing is knowing. This question lays out the binary opposition between friendship with God and friendship with the world and is a diatribal rebuke for not acting upon a recognized store of shared knowledge (see also Rom. 6:16; 11:2; 1 Cor. 3:16; 5:6; 6:2; 9:13).

Text-Critical and Lexical Nugget: What is the variant reading for μοιχαλίδες? Byzantine copyists must have understood the word μοιχαλίδες ("adulteresses") only in its literal sense and were puzzled why only women were mentioned, so they added a reference to men as well (μοιχοὶ καί). The shorter reading, however, is strongly supported by both Alexandrian and Western witnesses (ℵ* A B it vg). In scriptural imagery, μοιχαλίς ("adulteress") is used figuratively of Israel as the unfaithful spouse of Yahweh (Ps. 73:27; Isa. 54:5; Jer. 3:20; Ezek. 16 and 23; Hos. 9:1), and this is also the case in the NT (Matt. 12:39; 16:4; Mark 8:38; cf. BDAG, s.v. "μοιχαλίς" b, p. 656).

Grammatical Nugget: What is meant by the construction ἡ φιλία τοῦ κόσμου? The construction is an example of the objective genitive, as is also the case later in the verse (ἡ φιλία τοῦ κόσμου; ἔχθρα τοῦ θεοῦ). "The genitive substantive functions semantically as the direct object of the verbal idea implicit in the head noun" (W, 116). There is no better commentary on this than 1 John 2:15–17: "Do not love the world or the things in the world. If anyone loves the world, the love of the Father is not in him. For all that is in the world—the desires of the flesh and the desires of the eyes and pride in possessions—is not from the Father but is from the world. And the world is passing away along with its desires, but whoever does the will of God abides forever" (cf. Bateman et al.[2], 124–27).

ὅτι: This structural marker is a conjunction meaning "that" (BDAG, s.v. "ὅτι" 1c, p. 731). **Syntactically**, it introduces a substantival dependent conjunctive clause: "*that* friendship with the world means enmity with God" (ὅτι ἡ φιλία τοῦ κόσμου ἔχθρα τοῦ θεοῦ ἐστιν). The entire clause functions as the direct object of the verb "know" (οἴδατε). It is placed in parentheses in order to visualize its contribution to the independent clause. **Semantically**, it is an indirect discourse: "that" (cf. KJV NASB ESV NIV NET; W, 454–56). The entire ὅτι clause provides the content of the negated verb of mental perception: "do you not know" (οὐκ οἴδατε; W, 456). Yet, the specifics are found in the next verb.

ἐστιν: This Greek verb is a third person singular present active indicative of εἰμί that conveys something in an explanation and may be rendered as "means" (BDAG, s.v. "εἰμί" 2cα, p. 283). **Syntactically**, it is the main verb of this dependent conjunctive clause. The more definite nominative, "friendship" (ἡ φιλία), is the subject, and "enemy" (ἔχθρα) is the predicate nominative (W, 40–46; Adam, 78). **Semantically**, it is equative and reveals the close connection between divine "friendship" (ἡ φιλία) with "enemy" (ἔχθρα). While many translations render ἐστιν as "is" (KJV ASV NASB NRSV ESV CNT), in an explanation it is better understood as "means" (NET). The genitive τοῦ θεοῦ is objective, receiving the verbal action implied in ἔχθρα. The entire expression is the semantic counterpoint to ἡ φιλία τοῦ κόσμου.

4:4b οὖν: This structural marker is a conjunction that may be rendered "therefore" (BDAG, s.v. "οὖν" 1a, p. 736). **Syntactically**, it introduces an independent conjunctive clause with an embedded relative clause: "whoever, *therefore*, wants to be a friend of the world" (ὃς ἐὰν οὖν βουληθῇ φίλος εἶναι τοῦ κόσμου). It is in a post-positive position. **Semantically**, it is an inferential conjunction that introduces the result or deduction from what was said previously: "therefore" (KJV NASB NRSV ESV CNT), though some leave it as unrendered (NIV NET NLT). James is drawing a deduction, conclusion, or summary about adulteresses in 4:4a.

ὃς ἐάν: This structural marker (ὃς) introduces a masculine singular nominative of the relative pronoun ὃς that is combined with the particle ἐάν indicating a possibility that may be rendered "who," "the one who," or "whoever" (BDAG, s.v. "ὅς" 1bα, p. 725; s.v. "ἐάν" 3, p. 268; cf. Zerwick et al., 698; Irons, 539). **Syntactically**, these two words introduce an embedded subject. The dependent relative clause is placed in parentheses to visualize its substantival contribution to the independent conjunctive οὖν clause. While ὅς functions as the subject of the relative clause, the entire relative clause functions as the subject of "makes himself" (καθίσταται) and is placed in parentheses to visualize its relationship to the main verb καθίσταται ("makes himself") in the sentence.

βουληθῇ: This Greek word is a third person singular aorist passive subjunctive of βούλομαι that conceptually conveys the idea of desiring to have or experience something with an implication of planning accordingly and may be rendered "wish," "want," "desire" (BDAG, s.v. "βούλομαι" 2, p. 182). **Syntactically**, it is the main verb in this substantival relative clause. The relative pronoun ὅς is its subject. The verb βουληθῇ is in the subjunctive mood because ἐάν takes its verb in the subjunctive (W, 663). **Semantically**, the aorist tense is a constative aorist that describes an event as a whole (W, 557–58), namely, wanting something. The verb βούλομαι is a θῇ middle verb that cannot be translated with a passive sense. This verb should be read in light of its previous use concerning God's decision to birth us (1:18) and the decision of the ship's pilot (3:4). It is stronger than the "wish" expressed by a word like θέλω (2:20). This is a settled "desire" of a person who has decided to be friendly with the world. James completes his attack in 4:4b with a "therefore" plus two more rhetorical questions in 4:5.

εἶναι: This Greek word is a present active infinitive of εἰμί that conveys the idea of having something to do with something and is rendered "to be" (BDAG, s.v. "εἰμί" 10 & 11, p. 285). **Syntactically**, the infinitive is part of the main verb "wish" (βουληθῇ) in the substantival relative clause. **Semantically**, it functions as a complementary infinitive to βουληθῇ (W, 598–99). The present tense functions as a customary present that describes a person who regularly wants to experience something (W, 521–22), in this case, the world.

καθίσταται: This Greek word is a third person singular present middle indicative of καθίστημι/καθιστάνω that conveys the idea of causing someone to experience something and may be rendered "make" or "cause" (BDAG, s.v. "καθίστημι/καθιστάνω" 3, p. 492) and suggests that the middle/passive should be translated here as "be made" or "becomes." **Syntactically**, it is the main verb of this independent conjunctive clause with the previous relative clause functioning as its subject. **Semantically**, the present tense is a customary present that describes action that happens on a regular basis (W, 521–22). Those who directly engage with this world order become God's enemies rather than his friends. This verb takes a complement that is in the nominative case (ἐχθρός). This could be called the nominative of appellation, which is treated as a proper name. Earlier, Abraham was given the name "friend of God" (2:23). Now the friend of the world is given the title "enemy of God." James 4:4 is one of the central verses of the entire letter since it captures the main thrust of the letter's argument.

Divine Wisdom Is Identifiable in People Who Live Humbly (James 4:5–10)

Clausal Outline for James 4:5–10

4:5a ἢ **δοκεῖτε** (ὅτι κενῶς ἡ γραφὴ **λέγει**),
4:5a **Do you think** (that the Scripture **speaks** to no purpose)?

4:5b Πρὸς φθόνον **ἐπιποθεῖ** τὸ πνεῦμα
4:5b **Does** the spirit . . . **long enviously**?

> 4:5c ὃ **κατῴκισεν** ἐν ἡμῖν;
> 4:5c whom *God* **has caused** to dwell in us

4:6a μείζονα δὲ **δίδωσιν** χάριν;
4:6a But *God* **gives** more grace.

4:6b διὸ **λέγει**,
4:6b Therefore **it says**,

> 4:6c ('Ο θεὸς ὑπερηφάνοις **ἀντιτάσσεται**,
> 4:6c ("God **opposes** proud people,

> 4:6d ταπεινοῖς δὲ **δίδωσιν χάριν**).
> 4:6d but **gives** grace to humble ones").

4:7a **ὑποτάγητε** οὖν τῷ θεῷ,
4:7a Therefore, **submit yourselves** to God,

4:7b **ἀντίστητε** δὲ τῷ διαβόλῳ,
4:7b but **resist** the devil,

4:7c καὶ **φεύξεται** ἀφ' ὑμῶν
4:7c and **he will flee** from you.

4:8a **ἐγγίσατε** τῷ θεῷ
4:8a **Draw near** to God

^{4:8b} καὶ **ἐγγιεῖ** ὑμῖν.
^{4:8b} and **he will draw near** to you.

^{4:8c} **καθαρίσατε** χεῖρας, ἁμαρτωλοί,
^{4:8c} **Cleanse** your hands, you sinners,

^{4:8d} καὶ **ἁγνίσατε** καρδίας, δίψυχοι.
^{4:8d} and **purify** your hearts, you double-minded.

^{4:9a} **ταλαιπωρήσατε**
^{4:9a} **Grieve**

^{4:9b} καὶ **πενθήσατε**
^{4:9b} and **mourn**

^{4:9c} καὶ **κλαύσατε**.
^{4:9c} and **weep**.

^{4:9d} ὁ γέλως ὑμῶν εἰς πένθος **μετατραπήτω** καὶ ἡ χαρὰ εἰς κατήφειαν.
^{4:9d} Your laughter **must be turned** to mourning and your joy to gloom.

^{4:10a} **ταπεινώθητε** ἐνώπιον τοῦ κυρίου
^{4:10a} **Humble yourselves** before the Lord,

^{4:10b} καὶ **ὑψώσει** ὑμᾶς.
^{4:10b} and **he will exalt** you.

SYNTAX EXPLAINED FOR JAMES 4:5–10

^{4:5a} δοκεῖτε: This structural marker is a second person plural present active indicative of δοκέω that conveys the idea of considering something as probable and may be rendered as "think," "believe," "suppose," or "consider" (BDAG, s.v. "δοκέω" 1d, p. 254). **Syntactically**, it is the main verb of this independent asyndeton clause and is interrogative. This rhetorical question is not meant to search for an answer but to function as a more powerful statement. **Semantically**, the present tense is a customary present that describes thinking that happens on a regular basis (W, 521–22) and is typically rendered as "think" (KJV ASV NASB NIV NET NLT CNT) or "suppose" (NRSV ESV). This is the second of three rhetorical questions in 4:4–5. The expression ἢ δοκεῖτε is also used to question a false opinion in Matthew 26:53, and elsewhere the verb introduces a false opinion in Mark 6:49; Luke 12:51; 24:37; 1 Corinthians 3:18; 8:2; 10:12; 14:37. James has already used δοκέω in this manner about false opinion in 1:26.

ὅτι: This structural marker is a conjunction meaning "that" (BDAG, s.v. "ὅτι" 1c, p. 731). **Syntactically**, it introduces a substantival dependent conjunctive clause: "*that* the Scripture speaks to no purpose" (ὅτι κενῶς ἡ γραφὴ λέγει). The entire ὅτι clause functions as the direct object of the verb "speaks" (δοκεῖτε). The clause is placed in parentheses in order to visualize its contribution to the independent clause. **Semantically**, it is an indirect discourse: "that" (cf. ASV NASB NRSV NIV NET CNT; W, 454–56). The entire ὅτι clause provides the content of what was spoken in Scripture. Yet, the specifics are found in the next verb.

λέγει: This Greek word is a third person singular present active indicative of λέγω that conveys quotations in Scripture and may be rendered as "says" or "speaks" (BDAG, s.v. "λέγω" 1bη, p. 589). **Syntactically**, it is the main verb of this dependent conjunctive clause. It is the direct object of the verb δοκεῖτε with "Scripture" (γραφή) as its subject (W, 454–56). **Semantically**, the present tense is an iterative present. The verb expresses the dynamic nature of the Scripture "speaking" over and over again and is used this way elsewhere in James 2:23b; and 4:6b, as well in numerous other NT examples. It is typically rendered "says" (NRSV ESV NIV NET) or "speaks" (ASV NASB1995 CNT).

4:5b ἐπιποθεῖ: This structural marker is a third person singular present active indicative of ἐπιποθέω that conveys the idea of having strong desires for something with an implication of a need and may be rendered "long for" or "desire" (BDAG, s.v. "ἐπιποθέω," p. 377). **Syntactically**, it is the main verb of this independent interrogative clause with "spirit" (πνεῦμα) as its subject. **Semantically**, the present tense is a customary present that describes a longing that happens on a regular basis (W, 521–22). This entire sentence should be taken as a rhetorical question with the intent that no Scripture says these things (cf. KJV ASV NASB NRSV NIV ESV NET).

> **Grammatical Nugget:** What is the correct reading and understanding of ἐπιποθεῖ in James 4:5? The so-called quotation from "Scripture" is best viewed as a question about the human spirit's longing toward envy. "Does the spirit that he has caused to dwell in us long enviously?"[3] Thus, the unmentioned "God" or the "Spirit" is not the subject of the verb ἐπιποθεῖ, a verb that never takes God or the divine Spirit as its subject anywhere else in Scripture. It is important to note that the only other reference to "the spirit" in James is to the human spirit (2:26). The adjunct phrase πρὸς φθόνον functions adverbially ("jealously" or "enviously"). Finally, if we remove from our thinking that this is a citation from Scripture, canonical or not,

---

3.   This view was presented in an article by Sophie Laws, "Does Scripture Speak in Vain? A Reconsideration of James iv.5," *NTS* 20 (1973–74): 210–15.

and read it as a question that expects a negative answer, the answer to the question would be as follows: "No, the spirit which God has caused to dwell in us (κατῴκισεν) does not long enviously." In other words, God did not create man this way, i.e., with a spirit that longs enviously. This is because God is the source of only good (1:13–18).

4:5c ὅ: This structural marker is a nominative singular neuter from the relative pronoun ὅς that may be rendered "who," "the one who," or "whoever" (BDAG, s.v. "ὅς" 1a, p. 725). **Syntactically**, it introduces a dependent relative clause. While it functions as the direct object of κατῴκισεν within the clause (Adam, 80), the entire relative clause modifies "the spirit" (τὸ πνεῦμα) and is placed immediately under "spirit" (πνεῦμα) to visualize the relative clause's dependence. The relative pronoun ὅ is rendered "that" (KJV NRSV ESV NIV NET) or "which" (ASV NASB1995 CNT).

κατῴκισεν: This Greek word is a third person singular aorist active indicative of κατοικίζω that is often rendered "cause to dwell," "establish," or "settle" (BDAG, s.v. "κατοικίζω," p. 535). **Syntactically**, it is the main verb of this dependent relative clause that modifies "spirit" (πνεῦμα). The assumed agent is God (cf. NET). **Semantically**, the aorist tense is a constative aorist that describes the event of God's spirit living in us as a whole (W, 557–58). As it was the case in 4:5a, this rhetorical question is not meant to search for an answer but to function as a more powerful statement. That statement would be, "The Scripture does not speak to no purpose!" From the wider perspective of the book as a whole (i.e., the discourse), an additional rhetorical question like this fits better with the thrust of the diatribal style that James is using.

4:6a δέ: This structural marker is a conjunction meaning "but" (BDAG, s.v. "δέ" 4a, p. 213). **Syntactically**, it introduces an independent conjunctive clause and appears in a post-positive position. **Semantically**, it is used to link segments of thoughts together and functions as a contrast: "but" (KJV ASV NRSV NIV ESV NET CNT), though some may render δέ as "and" (NLT). It is a marker that moves to provide a contrast between jealousy and grace.

δίδωσιν: This Greek word is a third person singular present active indicative of δίδωμι that relates to an activity of God and may be rendered "extend" or "offer" (BDAG, s.v. "δίδωμι" 17b, p. 243). **Syntactically**, it is the main verb of this independent conjunctive clause that foreshadows the forthcoming quotation in the clauses that follow. **Semantically**, the present tense is gnomic present that conveys God's grace as a timeless truth about God (W, 523–24). James is doing away with any justification for the human conduct he is condemning and states that God offers not only an alternative to prideful self-seeking but also the grace to enable humble people to choose him as their friend.

^{4:6b} διό: This structural marker is a conjunction often rendered "therefore" or "for this reason" (BDAG, s.v. "διό," p. 250). **Syntactically**, it introduces an independent conjunctive clause. **Semantically**, it is inferential drawing a conclusion about God's grace (Adam, 81) and is rendered "therefore" (NASB NRSV ESV NET CNT; cf. KJV ASV; Zerwick et al., 698) or "that's why" (NIV).

λέγει: This Greek word is a third person singular present active indicative of λέγω that conveys an expression that was written and is often rendered as "utter in words," "say," "tell," or "give expression to" (BDAG, s.v. "λέγω" 1aβ, p. 588). **Syntactically**, it is the main verb of this independent conjunctive clause. **Semantically**, the present tense is an instantaneous present that conveys God having spoken at a specific point in the moment (W, 117–18), in this case in a quotation from Proverbs 3:34. This is another example of James's use of a dynamic verb that conveys the living way that God and Scripture communicate (see 2:11a, 23b).

^{4:6c} ἀντιτάσσεται: This structural marker is a third person singular present middle indicative of ἀντιτάσσω that conveys opposition and may be rendered as "oppose" or "resist" (BDAG, s.v. "ἀντιτάσσω," p. 90). **Syntactically**, it is the first main verb within the scriptural citation from Proverbs 3:34. Yet, it serves as a direct object to λέγει. Due to space, it is placed under λέγει in parentheses to show its relationship to λέγει. **Semantically**, it is a direct discourse to λέγει.

> **Grammatical Nugget:** How does James use the OT quotation to contrast the ὑπερηφάνοις and the ταπεινοῖς? The quotation from the LXX of Proverbs 3:34 expands what he has affirmed and prepares the reader for what follows in 4:7–10. The first group, ὑπερηφάνοις ("proud ones"), is in the dative case and functions as the direct object of the verb "opposes" (ἀντιτάσσεται). The second group, ταπεινοῖς ("humble ones"), is the more common dative of indirect object. The lack of definite articles before each of the substantives (like the LXX but different from the MT) denotes not "the proud" and "the humble" as classes of people, but "proud" and "humble" as a characteristic of anyone who can be one but become the other, which the following call to humility in 4:7–10 makes clear.

^{4:6d} δίδωσιν: This structural marker is a third person singular present active indicative of δίδωμι that relates to an activity of God and may be rendered "extend" or "offer" (BDAG, s.v. "δίδωμι" 17b, p. 243). **Syntactically**, it is the second main verb within the scriptural citation from Proverbs 3:34. Yet, it serves as a direct object to λέγει. Due to space, it is placed under λέγει in parentheses to show its relationship to λέγει. **Semantically**, it too is a direct discourse to λέγει. The present tense of δίδωσιν is a gnomic present that conveys God's support of the humble as a timeless truth about God (W, 523–24).

4:7a οὖν: This structural marker is a conjunction that may be rendered "therefore" (BDAG, s.v. "οὖν" 1a, p. 736). **Syntactically**, it introduces an independent conjunctive clause. It is in the post-positive position: "*Therefore*, submit yourselves to God" (ὑποτάγητε οὖν τῷ θεῷ). **Semantically**, it is an inferential conjunction that introduces the result or deduction from what was said previously: "therefore" (KJV ASV NASB NRSV ESV CNT), though some leave it unrendered (NET NLT). James is drawing a deduction, conclusion, or summary about what Scripture says concerning being humble in 4:5–6.

ὑποτάγητε: This Greek verb is a second person plural aorist passive imperative of ὑποτάσσω that conveys the idea of being submissive and may be rendered as "subject oneself," "be subjected," or "be subordinated" (BDAG, s.v. "ὑποτάσσω" 1bβ, p. 1042). **Syntactically**, it is the main verb of this independent conjunctive clause and the first of ten imperatives in 4:7–10. **Semantically**, this aorist imperative depicts a command as a whole (W, 485–86) about submitting to God. The verb is regularly used of submission to human authority in the NT (Luke 2:51; Rom. 13:1; Eph. 5:22; Titus 2:9; 1 Peter 2:13), but only here and in Hebrews 12:9 is it used of submission to God (Bateman et al.[1], 332). This exhortation is addressed to the ὑπερηφάνοις (the proud) in the previous verse. Because God opposes (ἀντιτάσσω) them, they are to submit (ὑποτάσσω) to him.

4:7b δέ: This structural marker is a conjunction meaning "but" (BDAG, s.v. "δέ" 4a, p. 213). **Syntactically**, it introduces an independent conjunctive clause and appears in a post-positive position. **Semantically**, it serves as a contrast: "but" (ASV NET CNT), though some translations do not translate δέ (KJV NASB1995 NRSV NIV ESV NLT). It is a marker that moves to provide a contrast about people who submit to God but resist the devil.

ἀντίστητε: This Greek word is a second person plural aorist active imperative of ἀνθίστημι that conveys the idea of being in opposition to someone or set oneself against another and may be rendered "oppose" (BDAG, s.v. "ἀνθίστημι" 1a, p. 80). **Syntactically**, it is the main verb of an independent conjunctive clause and is the second of the imperative clauses in 4:7–10. **Semantically**, this aorist imperative depicts a command as a whole (W, 485–86) about opposing Satan.

4:7c καί: This structural marker is a conjunction meaning "and" (BDAG, s.v. "καί" 1b, p. 494). **Syntactically**, it introduces an independent conjunctive clause. **Semantically**, it is a coordinating conjunction often rendered "and" (NET ESV NASB NRSV etc.). It adds to James's expectation about resisting the devil.

φεύξεται: This Greek word is a third person singular future middle indicative of φεύγω that conveys the idea of seeking safety in flight and may be rendered "flee" (BDAG, s.v. "φεύγω" 1, 1052). **Syntactically**, it is the main verb of this independent conjunctive clause. The subject of the verb is "he" and is assumed in the verb φεύξεται. **Semantically**, the future tense is a predictive future (W, 568). James says when resistance to Satan takes place then he will flee. It will happen.

> **Theological Nugget:** How do we resist the devil so that he flees? The clearest parallel is the command to resist the devil in 1 Peter 5:9, where the quotation of Proverbs 3:34 also precedes the command (see also Eph. 6:11–17). James affirms that Satan is not omnipotent, but human beings can resist him and when they do, he will then flee in the face of such resistance (see also 1 Peter 5:8–9). James 4:7 is the only place in the Bible where Satan is said to flee if he is resisted. James suggests that the ultimate source of personal evil is supernatural—that is, the devil (so also Matt. 4:1–11; Luke 22:31; John 13:2, 27). The best example of resisting Satan is that of Jesus during his temptation in the wilderness. It was not inner strength that led to the departure of Satan, but dependence on a Word from God (Eph. 6:18).

4:8a ἐγγίσατε: This structural marker is a second person plural aorist active imperative of ἐγγίζω that conveys the idea of moving closer to a transcendent being (figuratively speaking) and may be rendered "draw near," "come near," or "approach" (BDAG, s.v. "ἐγγίζω" 1aα, p. 270). **Syntactically**, it is the main verb of this independent asyndeton clause. It is the third imperative clause in 4:7–10. **Semantically**, this aorist imperative depicts a command as a whole (W, 485–86) about approaching God. This verb, appearing forty-two times in the NT, recalls OT imagery by which Israel's relationship with God is expressed in terms of a literal "approaching." At Mount Sinai, the people were told not to "approach" God (Exod. 19:21), whereas the priests and Moses could "approach" the mountain (Exod. 19:22; 24:2). In Hebrews 7:19, it is used figuratively about a person's relational nearness with God due to the better hope established in Jesus (Bateman et al.[1], 219–20). Here, James exhorts believers to develop a relational nearness with God.

4:8b καί: This structural marker is a conjunction meaning "and" (BDAG, s.v. "καί" 1b, p. 494). **Syntactically**, it introduces an independent conjunctive clause. **Semantically**, it is a coordinating conjunction often rendered "and" (NET ESV NASB NRSV etc.) that adds to James's expectation about drawing near to God.

ἐγγιεῖ: This Greek verb is a third person singular future active indicative of ἐγγίζω that conveys the idea of moving closer to a transcendent being (figuratively speaking) and may be rendered "draw near," "come near," or "approach" (BDAG, s.v. "ἐγγίζω" 1aα, p. 270). **Syntactically**, it is the main verb of this independent conjunctive clause. The subject of the verb is "he" and is assumed in the verb ἐγγιεῖ. **Semantically**, the future tense is a predictive future (W, 568). James says when one attempts to draw near in a relationship with God, it will happen. It is a promise of God's reciprocal response, a divine action regarded as exceptional when Israel's God approached his people: "What great nation is there to whom their god approaches (ἐγγίζων) as the Lord our God does for all those who call upon him?" (Deut. 4:7; also Hos. 12:7). In the NT, however, only the heavily Jewish James and Hebrews 7:19 contain this specific linguistic way of describing "approaching God" (Bateman et al.[1], 219–20).

4:8c καθαρίσατε: This structural marker is a second person plural aorist active imperative of καθαρίζω that conveys the idea of purifying through some sort of ritual cleansing and may be rendered "make clean" or "declare clean" (BDAG, s.v. "καθαρίζω" 3bα, p. 488). **Syntactically**, it is the main verb of this independent asyndeton clause. It is the fourth imperative clause in 4:7–10. **Semantically**, it is an aorist imperative that depicts a command as a whole (W, 485–86) about being made clean.

> **Theological Nugget:** How does James describe the relationship between hands and hearts? These verses echo Psalm 24:3–4: "Those who have clean hands and pure hearts. . ." The heart is the seat of both one's affections and decisions (Gen. 6:5; Deut. 8:2). The "pure heart" is the symbol for one who is in a right relationship with God (Ps. 50:1–12; see also Matt. 5:8). This balance between the outward "hands" and the inward "hearts" echoes another familiar note in James. The problems with mankind, as well as their solutions, lie deep within the inner person, not simply in reforming their outward behavior.

4:8d καί: This structural marker is a conjunction meaning "and" (BDAG, s.v. "καί" 1b, p. 494). **Syntactically**, it introduces an independent conjunctive clause. **Semantically**, it is a coordinating conjunction often rendered "and" (NET ESV NASB NRSV etc.) that adds to James's expectation about being made clean.

ἁγνίσατε: This Greek word is a second person plural aorist active imperative of ἁγνίζω that conveys the idea of causing a person to become morally pure and may be rendered "purify" (BDAG, s.v. "ἁγνίζω" 2, p. 12). **Syntactically**, it is the main verb of an independent conjunctive clause. It is the fifth of the imperative clauses in 4:7–10. **Semantically**, it is an aorist imperative that depicts a command as a whole (W, 485–86). It adds to James's expectation about being made morally pure.

> **Theological Nugget:** What is the significance of the last two imperatives: "make clean" and "purify"? The last two imperatives are addressed to the ones who need the cleansing and purifying—namely, the sinners and double-minded. The economic use of words, with no personal pronouns and

asyndeton (no conjunctions), heightens the intensity and provides balance amid the flurry of the other imperatives. With each of these verbs James uses Jewish language associated with OT cultic purity (Exod. 19:10; 30:17–21; Num. 8:21; 19:12; 31:23). From ritual washing, which was familiar to NT readers (Mark 7:3), there emerged a figurative use of this language, seen in such OT texts as Isaiah 1:16; Job 17:9; and 22:30. The combination of both verbs in the LXX of Isaiah 66:17 (ἁγνιζόμενοι καὶ καθαριζόμε-νοι) provides James with an additional OT context that deals, as he does here, with moral purification. The "pure heart" is the symbol for one who is in a right relationship with God (Ps. 50:1–12; see also Matt. 5:8). This balance between the outward "hands" and the inward "hearts" is another clear indication that both the moral problems and their solutions lie deep within the inner person, not simply in reforming their outward behavior.

4:9a ταλαιπωρήσατε: This structural marker is a second person plural aorist active imperative of ταλαιπωρέω that conveys the idea of expressing distress and may be rendered "be miserable," "feel miserable," or "lament" (BDAG, s.v. "ταλαι-πωρέω," p. 988). **Syntactically**, it is the main verb of an independent asyndeton clause. It is the sixth of the imperative clauses in 4:7–10. This imperative is intransitive (no direct objects needed) because it is obvious who is addressed. **Semantically**, this aorist imperative depicts a command as a whole (W, 485–86) about lamenting, though an ingressive aorist of conduct about to occur is possible ("*become* wretched"; BDF, §337). This verb, often associated with hardship and harsh labor, is a NT *hapax* that in the LXX often described Israel's response to catastrophes (Jer. 4:13, 20; 9:18; 10:20; 12:12; Hos. 10:2; Joel 1:10; Mic. 2:4; Zech. 11:2–3). It is rendered as "grieve" (NIV NET), "lament" (NRSV), "be wretched" (ESV), "be miserable" (NASB CNT), or "be afflicted" (KJV ASV).

4:9b καί: This structural marker is a conjunction meaning "and" (BDAG, s.v. "καί" 1b, p. 494). **Syntactically**, it introduces an independent conjunctive clause. **Semantically**, it is a coordinating conjunction often rendered "and" (NET ESV NASB NRSV). It adds to James's expectation about lamenting or feeling miserable.

πενθήσατε: This Greek word is a second person plural aorist active imperative of πενθέω that conveys the idea of experiencing sadness as the result of some condition or circumstance and may be rendered "be sad," "grieve," or "mourn" (BDAG, s.v. "πενθέω" 1, p. 795). **Syntactically**, it is the main verb of this independent conjunctive clause and the seventh imperative in 4:7–10. This imperative is intransitive (no direct objects needed) because it is obvious who is addressed. **Semantically**, this aorist imperative depicts a command as a whole (W, 485–86) about mourning. This verb appears in the prophets for punishment on Israel for apostasy from the covenant with Yahweh (e.g., Isa. 24:4; Jer. 4:28; Ezek. 7:27; Joel 1:9–10; Amos 1:2). It is also used in the NT for general mourning (Mark 16:10; Luke 6:25;

2 Cor. 12:21) and is typically rendered "mourn" (KJV ASV NASB NRSV NIV ESV NET CNT). The most striking NT parallel is Matthew 5:4, "Blessed are those who mourn (οἱ πενθοῦντες), for they shall be comforted."

4:9c καί: This structural marker is a conjunction meaning "and" (BDAG, s.v. "καί" 1b, p. 494). **Syntactically**, it introduces an independent conjunctive clause. **Semantically**, it is a coordinating conjunction often rendered "and" (NET ESV NASB NRSV etc.). It adds to James's expectation about grieving and mourning.

κλαύσατε: This Greek word is a second person plural aorist active imperative of κλαίω that may be rendered "weep" or "cry" (BDAG, s.v. "κλαίω" 1, p. 545). **Syntactically**, it is the main verb of this independent conjunctive clause and is the eighth imperative clause in 4:7–10. This imperative is intransitive (no direct objects needed) because it is obvious who is addressed. **Semantically**, this aorist imperative depicts a command as a whole (W, 485–86) about weeping. This verb in the LXX describes Israel's sorrow at the punishment from Yahweh (Isa. 22:4; Jer. 8:12; Lam. 1:1; Hos. 12:5; Joel 1:5; 2:17). It is a common verb in the NT for crying, but its combination with the previous verb (πενθέω) to describe the repentance of David (2 Sam. 19:1) illustrates the intensity and vividness of James's commands. Translations typically render the imperative here as "weep" (KJV ASV NASB NRSV ESV NET CNT).

4:9d μετατραπήτω: This structural marker is a third person singular aorist passive imperative of μετατρέπω that conveys the idea of turning around and may be rendered "be turned" (BDAG, s.v. "μετατρέπω," p. 642). **Syntactically**, it is the main verb of this independent asyndeton clause and is the ninth imperative clause in 4:7–10. James shifts to a third person imperative for the subject γέλως, but this does not lessen the imperatival force of the verb. The verb is not expressed in the second clause which has χαρά as its subject (Adam, 82). **Semantically**, this aorist imperative depicts a command as a whole (W, 485–86) about turning around, in this case, turning laughter into grief.

> **Lexical Nugget:** What is the meaning of κατήφειαν? This noun is another *hapax legomenon* in the NT and does not appear in the LXX. James's desire is to express the need for the "laughter" and "joy" of sinners to be transformed into outward actions that manifest inner repentance, "mourning," and "gloom" (BDAG, s.v. "κατήφεια," p. 533). "It describes the condition of one with eyes cast down (κατ-) like the publican in Luke 18:13" (Mayor, 142). This is once more illustrative of James's love for the language of reversal (see James 1:9–11; 2:5). James is not suggesting that the righteous should go about in a state of morbid depression over their sins. If such people turn to God, they discover that those activities and objects that previously gave them joy are evidence of the distance that separated them from God.

4:10a ταπεινώθητε: This structural marker is a second person plural aorist passive imperative of ταπεινόω that conveys the idea of causing to be or becoming humble and is rendered "be humble" (BDAG, s.v. "ταπεινόω" 3, p. 990). **Syntactically**, it is the main verb of this independent asyndeton clause and is the tenth imperative clause in 4:7–10. **Semantically**, this aorist tense imperative depicts a command as a whole (W, 485–86) about humility and is rendered "humble" (KJV ASV NASB NRSV NIV ESV NET NLT CNT). This verse serves with 4:7 as an inclusio to the entire paragraph. We are to submit to God (4:7a) and to be humbled before God (4:10). James thus picks up the promise in 4:6b to the "humble" (ταπεινοῖς) receiving divine grace by exhorting us in 4:10a to "be humbled" (ταπεινώθητε) before the Lord.

4:10b καί: This structural marker is a conjunction meaning "and" (BDAG, s.v. "καί" 1b, p. 494). **Syntactically**, it introduces an independent conjunctive clause. **Semantically**, it is a coordinating conjunction often rendered "and" (NET ESV NASB NRSV etc.) that adds to James's expectation to be humble.

ὑψώσει: This Greek word is a third person singular future active indicative of ὑψόω that conveys the idea of causing an enhancement in honor, fame, and position and may be rendered "exalt" (BDAG, s.v. "ὑψόω" 2, p. 1046). **Syntactically**, it is the main verb of an independent conjunctive clause. The subject of the verb is "he" and is assumed in the verb ἐγγιεῖ. **Semantically**, the future tense is a predictive future (W, 568). James says when a person humbles him or herself, God will exalt that person. It will happen. This verb indicates that our self-humbling will lead to God's lifting us up.

> **Theological Nugget:** How does humbling lead to exaltation? While self-humbling leads to God's exaltation, the reverse follows if people exalt themselves. This is expressed in Job 5:11: "He who makes the humble ones exalted (τὸν ποιοῦντα ταπεινοὺς εἰς ὕψος)." We can also hear echoes of such Jesus-sayings as Luke 6:25 (laughter turned to weeping) and 14:11 (the humbled being exalted). Note Peter's same quotation from Proverbs 3:34 in 1 Peter 5:5, which is also followed by the exhortation: "Humble yourselves therefore, under God's mighty hand, that he may lift you up in due time."

James 4:11–5:6

Big Greek Idea: Forewarnings are extended to self-important people who slander others as self-appointed judges, to overconfident business people who devise and boast about their futures, and to self-sufficient rich people whose confidence is their wealth and their misuse of it.

Structural Overview: Admittedly, the connection of 4:11–12 is difficult to discern (Davids, 168). All the same, James 4:11–5:6 exhorts and warns three groups of people: slanderers, business people, and rich people. In so doing, James revisits themes tackled earlier in his letter: speech (1:17–27; 3:1–12) and wealth (James 1:9–11; 2:1–7, 14–17), but with a different perspective. He opens with an exhortation to people who slander others and warns them of their self-importance and self-appointments as arbiters over others (4:11–12). James then shifts his exhortations to business people and warns them of their over-confidence in organizing and boasting of their futures (4:13–17). He closes with exhortations to rich people and warns them of their sense of self-suffiency and improper usage of their wealth (5:1–6).

Outline:[1]

Slanderers Are Warned about Self-Importance (4:11–12).
Business people Are Warned about Over-confidence (4:13–17).
Rich People Are Warned about Self-Sufficiency (5:1–6).

SLANDERERS ARE WARNED ABOUT SELF-IMPORTANCE (JAMES 4:11–12)

CLAUSAL OUTLINE FOR JAMES 4:11–12

4:11a <u>Μὴ</u> **καταλαλεῖτε** ἀλλήλων, ἀδελφοί.
4:11a **Do not slander** each other, brothers *and sisters.*

4:11b (ὁ **καταλαλῶν** ἀδελφοῦ **ἢ κρίνων** τὸν ἀδελφὸν αὐτοῦ) **καταλαλεῖ** νόμου
4:11b (**The one who slanders** a brother or **condemns** his brother), **slanders** the law

4:11c καὶ [[(*ὁ καταλαλῶν ἀδελφοῦ ἢ κρίνων τὸν ἀδελφὸν αὐτοῦ*)] **κρίνει** νόμου·
4:11c and [[(*the one who slanders a brother or condemns his brother*)], **condemns** the law.

---

1. A suggested sermon entitled "A New Perspective" has been offered for these verses (see Baker et al., 127–36). Three points might be "A Godly Perspective on Finding Fault" (4:11–12), "A Godly Perspective on the Future" (4:13–17), and "A Godly Perspective on Finances: Be Careful What You Love" (5:1–6).

^{4:11d} **εἰ** δὲ νόμον **κρίνεις**,
^{4:11d} But **if you condemn** the law,

|

^{4:11e} <u>οὐκ **εἶ**</u> ποιητὴς νόμου ἀλλὰ κριτής.
^{4:11e} **you are** <u>not</u> a doer of the law but a judge.

^{4:12a} εἷς **ἐστιν** ὁ νομοθέτης καὶ κριτὴς
^{4:12a} The lawgiver and judge **is** one

      |

      ^{4:12b} <u>ὁ **δυνάμενος** σῶσαι</u>
      ^{4:12b} **who is able to save**

      |

      ^{4:12c} <u>καὶ</u> [*δυνάμενος*] **ἀπολέσαι**
      ^{4:12c} <u>and</u> [*who is able*] **to destroy**.

^{4:12d} σὺ <u>δὲ</u> τίς **εἶ**
^{4:12d} <u>But</u> who **are** you

    └─────┐

      ^{4:12e} <u>ὁ κρίνων</u> τὸν πλησίον;
      ^{4:12e} <u>who condemns</u> *your* neighbor?

Syntax Explained for James 4:11–12

^{4:11a} Μὴ καταλαλεῖτε: This negated (μή) structural marker is a second person plural present active imperative of καταλαλέω that conveys the idea of speaking degradingly of someone or speaking evil of another and may be rendered "defame" or "slander" (BDAG, s.v. "καταλαλέω," p. 519). **Syntactically**, it is the main verb in this independent asyndeton clause. **Semantically**, the negated (μή) present imperative conveys a general precept, but it does not make a "comment about whether the action is ongoing or not" (W, 485–87; 724–25; Zerwick, 246). Thus, it should not be assumed that with the present prohibition James is commanding something to cease (W, 487).

> **Grammatical Nugget:** What is the significance of μὴ καταλαλεῖτε? This sort of negated present imperative appears nine times elsewhere in James (1:7, 16, 22; 2:1; 3:1, 14 [2]; 5:9, 12). Some grammarians and commentators have taught that a negated present imperative commands the ceasing of an action that is already in progress. While this *could* be the case, such a kind of action (*aktionsart*) should be determined only from a close examination of the context in which the command is found. A better approach to this subject is in recognizing that the present tense of the imperative mood is intended to convey a general rather than a more specific prohibition. In the case of 4:11, therefore, it is the *practice* of slander that is

forbidden. Further reflection on the specific use of imperatives by James reveals that when he employs an aorist imperative, it is always accompanied by an adjunct expression that indicates the time of the command, or its reason, or its result (1:2; 21; 4:7–10; 5:1, 7, 8, 10). When James employs a present imperative, the command is more general and the specifics of time or result or reasons will follow only in subsequent comments about that command (2:1, 12; 4:11; 5:9, 12). Furthermore, the general nature of this letter as an "encyclical" also suggests that this is a general rather than a specific exhortation.

4:11b ὁ καταλαλῶν . . . κρίνων: These two Greek words are nominative singular masculine present active participles of καταλαλέω and κρίνω respectively. Whereas καταλαλῶν conveys the idea of speaking degradingly of someone or speaking evil of another and may be rendered "defame" or "slander" (BDAG, s.v. "καταλαλέω," p. 519), κρίνων conveys the idea of passing unfavorable judgment upon someone and may be rendered as "judge," "criticize," or "condemn" (BDAG, s.v. "κρίνω" 2b, p. 567). **Syntactically**, they make up the dependent participial clause that serves as the subject of the verb "slander" (καταλαλεῖ). The entire participial clause is placed in parentheses to visualize their contribution to the independent clause. **Semantically**, the present tense is an iterative present indicating action that occurs time and time again (W, 520–21). James speaks of his readers speaking evil and judging one another on a regular basis.

καταλαλεῖ: This structural marker is a third person singular present active indicative of καταλαλέω that conveys the idea of speaking degradingly of someone or speaking evil of another and may be rendered "defame" or "slander" (BDAG, s.v. "καταλαλέω," p. 519). **Syntactically**, it is the main verb of this independent asyndeton clause with καταλαλῶν and κρίνων as its subject. **Semantically**, the present tense is an iterative present indicating action that occurs time and time again (W, 520–21). James warns his readers against defaming people on a regular basis.

Lexical Nugget: What does "defame" (καταλαλέω) mean? Classical writers use the verb in the sense of "speak against" or "to accuse someone" with a suggestion of the false or exaggerated sense of "calumniate" (Polybius, *Hist.* 3, 90, 6). In the LXX (nine times) it bears the emphasis of hostility toward whoever is denoted by the prefixed preposition κατα-, whether against God (Num. 21:5, 7; Hos. 7:13; Mal. 3:13), his servant Moses (Num. 12:8), or frequently one's neighbor (Pss. 49:20; 100:5; Prov. 20:13). The verb appears three times in 4:11, and in light of the LXX and Hellenistic usage, is best rendered as "to slander" rather than by the more generic translation, "speak against" (NET NASB). This latter translation reflects an overly mechanical transference of the verb's component parts (κατα and λαλέω). The rendering "speak evil" in other translations like the AV, ESV, and NRSV is better, but only translations like the NIV and the NJB convey accurately the semantics of the word by their "do not slander." A person may actually speak against someone else or even criticize them and still speak the truth and not engage in slander. The sin that is being condemned in 4:11b, however, is the kind of speech that is both inaccurate and also damaging to someone's character and reputation ("bearing false witness"). The usage of the cognate noun elsewhere in the NT (2 Cor. 12:20; 1 Peter 2:1) further supports the rendering of the verb here as "to slander."

4:11c [(ὁ καταλαλῶν . . . κρίνων)]: These two articular (ὁ) Greek words are nominative singular masculine present active participles of καταλαλέω and κρίνω respectively. Whereas καταλαλῶν conveys the idea of speaking degradingly of someone or speaking evil of another and may be rendered "defame" or "slander" (BDAG, s.v. "καταλαλέω," p. 519), κρίνων conveys the idea of passing unfavorable judgment upon someone and may be rendered as "judge," "criticize," or "condemn" (BDAG, s.v. "κρίνω" 2b, p. 567). **Syntactically**, the bracketed [(ὁ καταλαλῶν . . . κρίνων)] is an ellipsis that introduces this dependent participial clause. It serves as the subject of the verb "condemns" (κρίνει). The entire participial clause is in parentheses to visualize its contribution to the independent clause. **Semantically**, the present tense is an iterative present indicating action that occurs time and time again (W, 520–21). James speaks of his readers speaking evil and judging one another on a regular basis.

κρίνει: This structural marker is a third person singular present active indicative of κρίνω that conveys the idea of passing unfavorable judgment upon someone and may be rendered as "judge," "criticize," or "condemn" (BDAG, s.v. "κρίνω" 2b, p. 567). **Syntactically**, it is the main verb of this independent asyndeton clause with [(καταλαλῶν and κρίνων)] as its subject. **Semantically**, the present tense is an iterative present indicating action that occurs time and time again (W, 520–21). James speaks of his readers who condemn or slander the law on a regular basis. The person who deliberately breaks a law and does not repent slanders that law and also disrespects that law, since it is the essence of a law to require obedience, and he who refuses obedience, in effect, says it ought not to be a law. Thus, the one who slanders a brother, in effect, also slanders the law.

Lexical Nugget: What does κρίνω mean? The verb and its cognate noun κριτής often share the same semantic field of καταλαλέω. These words appear six times in 4:11–12, and the word group includes the idea of "condemn." This meaning fits here and also is demanded by the use of the verb in 5:9b and the noun in 5:12c. In both these appearances, the context indicates that it is an eschatological condemnation that is implied. Because the English verb "to judge" can also result in a judgment of "innocent," I suggest that the word "condemn" more accurately conveys the meaning of the action described here that always results in the judgment of "guilty." It is the attitude of always condemning a brother that is forbidden. "The Christian community also needed the unity which slander destroyed, so among Christians it also comes up frequently in vice lists (Rom. 1:30; 2 Cor. 12:20; 1 Peter 2:1; 2 Peter 2:12; 3:16)" (Davids, 169).

4:11d δέ: This structural marker is a conjunction meaning "but" (BDAG, s.v. "δέ" 4a, p. 213). **Syntactically**, it introduces a dependent conjunctive clause and appears in the post-positive position. **Semantically**, it serves as a contrast: "but" (KJV ASV NASB NRSV ESV NET NLT CNT), though some versions do not translate δέ (NIV). It is a marker that provides a contrast to people who condemn the law with those who are condemned by the law.

εἰ: This Greek word is a conjunction meaning "if" (BDAG, s.v. "εἰ" 1aβ, p. 277). **Syntactically**, it introduces a dependent conjunctive clause. The entire clause is a dependent adverbial modifying "is" (εἰ): "but *if* you condemn the law" (εἰ δὲ νόμον κρίνεις). **Semantically**, "if" (εἰ) introduces a first-class conditional clause and is the protasis of the conditional sentence (W, 682–89). James is assuming that his readers are condemning the law (W, 690–94; Adam, 84).

κρίνεις: This Greek word is a second person singular present active indicative of κρίνω that conveys the idea of passing unfavorable judgment upon someone and may be rendered as "judge," "criticize," or "condemn" (BDAG, s.v. "κρίνω" 2b, p. 567). **Syntactically**, it is the main verb of this dependent conjunctive clause. The clause is the protasis in a first-class conditional sentence. **Semantically**, the present tense is an iterative present indicating action that occurs time and time again (W, 520–21). James speaks of his readers who condemn or slander the law on a regular basis. The idea of "judging" here is not the action of "rendering an opinion." The more specific practice within the semantic field—namely, "condemning"—is the action that is forbidden by this passage. The irony involved is biting. We who should stand condemned by the law actually end up condemning the law when we utter slanderous speech!

4:11e οὐκ εἰ: This negated (οὐκ) structural marker is a second person singular present active indicative of εἰμί that conveys the idea of being in close connection with something and may be rendered as "is" (BDAG, s.v. "εἰμί" 2b,

p. 282). **Syntactically**, it is the main verb of this independent asyndeton of a first-class conditional sentence. **Semantically**, it is the main verb of an independent conjunctive clause with the "you" within εἰ as its subject and "doer" (ποιητής) the predicate nominative (W, 40–46; Adam, 84). The verb is equative in that it describes a person as a doer. Yet, here, this conditional sentence declares that the person who condemns both his brother and the law becomes "no longer" (οὐκ) a "doer" (ποιητής) of the law but rather becomes a judge (κριτής) of the law. This hypothetical "judge" performs the ironic role of condemning the very law that he is supposed to uphold!

4:12a ἐστιν: This structural marker is a third person singular present active indicative of εἰμί that conveys the idea of being in close connection with something and may be rendered as "is" (BDAG, s.v. "εἰμί" 2b, p. 282). **Syntactically**, it is the main verb of this independent asyndeton clause with "lawgiver and judge" (ὁ νομοθέτης καὶ κριτής) as its subject and "one" (εἷς) as its predicate nominative (W, 40–46; Adam, 85). **Semantically**, the verb is equative in that it reveals the oneness of the "lawgiver and judge" (ὁ νομοθέτης καὶ κριτής). While many translations render ἐστιν as "is" (KJV ASV NASB NRSV NIV ESV NET NLT CNT).

4:12b ὁ δυνάμενος: This structural marker is a nominative singular masculine present middle participle of δύναμαι that conveys the idea of possessing capability and may be rendered "can," "am able," or "be capable" (BDAG, s.v. "δύναμαι" aα, p. 262). **Syntactically**, it introduces a dependent participial clause. It is an attributive participle that modifies "lawgiver and judge" (νομοθέτης καὶ κριτής). It is placed under νομοθέτης to visualize the clause's dependence (BDF, §412.4). **Semantically**, the present tense is a customary present that conveys continuous habitual action (W, 521–22) about God's ability that is further described with the next verb.

σῶσαι: This Greek word is an aorist active infinitive of σώζω that conveys the idea of saving or preserving from eternal destruction and may be rendered "save" (BDAG, s.v. "σώζω" 2aα, p. 982). **Syntactically**, it is part of the substantival participle ὁ δυνάμενος in the dependent participial clause. **Semantically**, it is a complementary infinitive that completes ὁ δυνάμενος (W, 598–99). The aorist is a constative aorist that discusses events about an eternal salvation as a whole (W, 557–58). Throughout the OT God is able to save (σῶσαι) his people (Deut. 33:29; Judges 2:16; 3:9; 6:14; 1 Sam. 4:3; Ps. 3:8; Isa. 19:20; 33:2; Jer. 15:20; 26:27; Zech. 9:16). The point of this construction is that there is only one who can "save."

4:12c καί: This structural marker is a conjunction meaning "and" (BDAG, s.v. "καὶ" 1b, p. 494). **Syntactically**, it introduces a dependent conjunctive clause. **Semantically**, it is a coordinating conjunction often rendered "and" (NET ESV NASB NRSV etc.) that adds to James's description of God's capabilities.

[ὁ δυνάμενος]: This Greek word is a nominative singular masculine present middle participle of δύναμαι that conveys the idea of possessing capability and may be rendered "can" or "am able, be capable" (BDAG, s.v. "δύναμαι" aα, p. 262). **Syntactically**, the bracketed [ὁ δυνάμενος] is an elliptical participle of this dependent conjunctive clause. It is in apposition to the previous "lawgiver and judge" (νομοθέτης καὶ κριτής). It is placed under νομοθέτης to visualize the clause's dependence. **Semantically**, the present tense is a customary present that conveys continuous habitual action (W, 521–22) about God's ability that is further described with the next verb.

ἀπολέσαι: This Greek word is an aorist active infinitive of ἀπόλλυμι that may be rendered "ruin" or "destroy" (BDAG, 116a). **Syntactically**, it is part of the elliptical substantival participle [ὁ δυνάμενος] of this dependent conjunctive clause that is in apposition to "lawgiver and judge" (νομοθέτης καὶ κριτής). **Semantically**, it is a complementary infinitive. The aorist is a constative aorist that discusses events about an eternal destruction as a whole (W, 557–58). Throughout the OT God is able to destroy (ἀπολέσαι) his people (Exod. 19:24; Lev. 17:10; Num. 14:12; Deut. 2:12, 21; Josh. 24:10; Pss. 5:7; 9:6; Isa. 1:25; Jer. 25:10; 26:8; Ezek. 25:7, 16). The point of this infinitive is that there is only one who can "destroy." There can be only one judge of divine law who in this way carries out the sanctions of his own divine law.

> **Syntactical Nugget:** What is the significance of the Greek word order concerning "the one who is able" (ὁ δυνάμενος) and "the one who judges" (ὁ κρίνων)? These substantival participles (ὁ δυνάμενος and ὁ κρίνων) further define the subjects that are expressed earlier in each sentence. In any translation of the first sentence, it is important to maintain the order of the Greek words, in which the numerical adjective εἷς precedes the copula ἐστιν. A translation like "there is one lawgiver and judge" (KJV NASB NIV ESV NET etc.) misses the significance of the order. The rendering "the lawgiver and judge is one" is better. By respecting the word order, the oneness of the lawgiver and judge is brought to a prominent position in 4:12a. It also reflects the structure of Deuteronomy 6:4, the Torah statement which this verse echoes: "Hear O, Israel, the Lord our God, the Lord is one." The LXX rendering of the Shema also locates the numerical adjective before the verb (κύριος εἷς ἐστιν). Therefore, this order would be readily recognizable to a Jewish reader/hearer.

4:12d δέ: This structural marker is a conjunction meaning "but" (BDAG, s.v. "δέ" 4a, p. 213). **Syntactically**, it introduces an independent conjunctive clause and appears in the post-positive position. **Semantically**, it serves as a contrast: "but" (ASV NASB NIV ESV CNT), though some do not translate δέ as "but" (KJV NET NLT; cf. Irons, 539). It is a marker that provides a contrast between judgers of the law.

εἶ: This Greek word is a second person singular present active indicative of εἰμί that conveys the idea of being in close connection with something and may be rendered as "is" (BDAG, s.v. "εἰμί" 2b, p. 282). **Syntactically**, it is the main verb in an independent conjunctive clause. It is an interrogative clause with τίς as its subject and "you" (σύ) as the predicate nominative (W, 40–46; Adam, 85). **Semantically**, the verb is equative in that it advances the diatribal challenge that pulses throughout this passage. The switch from condemning the brother or sister in 4:11b to the condemning of the "neighbor" (πλησίον) at the end of 4:12e is another echo of the love command delivered in Leviticus 19:18. This allusion also evokes the surrounding context of Leviticus 19:11–18 in which the "neighbor" (πλησίον) is mentioned no fewer than six times. James's desire, however, is to filter his use of Leviticus 19 through the very same love command cited by Jesus in Matthew 22:39.

4:12e ὁ κρίνων: This structural marker is a nominative singular masculine present active participle of κρίνω that conveys the idea of passing an unfavorable judgment upon someone and may be rendered "criticize," "find fault with," or "condemn" (BDAG, s.v. "κρίνω" 2b, p. 567). **Syntactically**, it introduces a dependent participial clause that modifies σύ in the preceding clause. The entire clause is placed under "you" (σύ) to visualize its dependence on the subsequent clause (BDF, §412.4). Yet, it is possible to view the clause as modifying "who" (τίς). **Semantically**, the present tense is a customary present that conveys continuous habitual action (W, 521–22) about judging.

> **Historical Nugget:** What is the "law" to which James refers? This is another example of James's references to the law/Torah function in a similar way. When he refers to the law, different descriptors convey careful nuances about that specific law (law of liberty, royal law, etc.). This "law" is the one delivered through Moses, but it is also the same law as it was expounded and applied by Jesus. When this unity is recognized, these references to slandering and condemning a brother are another allusion to the Jesus-saying found in Matthew 7:1–2: "Do not condemn (κρίνετε), that you be not condemned (κριθῆτε). For with the condemnation you condemn you will be condemned (κρίματι κρίνετε κριθήσεσθε), and with the measure you use it will be measured to you."

Business people Are Warned about Over-confidence
(James 4:13–17)

Clausal Outline for James 4:13–17

4:13a Ἄγε νῦν οἱ λέγοντες, Σήμερον ἢ αὔριον **πορευσόμεθα** εἰς τήνδε τὴν πόλιν

4:13a <u>Now</u> **listen**, you who say, "Today or tomorrow **we will go** into such and such a city

> 4:13b καὶ **ποιήσομεν** ἐκεῖ ἐνιαυτὸν
> 4:13b and **will spend** a year there

> 4:13c καὶ **ἐμπορευσόμεθα**
> 4:13c and **will trade**

> 4:13d καὶ **κερδήσομεν**,
> 4:13d and **will make a profit**."

4:14a οἵτινες [ἐστιν]
4:14a <u>Whoever</u> [*you are*]

4:14b οὐκ **ἐπίστασθε** τὸ τῆς αὔριον
4:14b **you do** not **know** what will happen tomorrow.

4:14c ποία [ἐστιν] ἡ ζωὴ ὑμῶν
4:14c <u>What</u> [*is*] your life?

4:14d ἀτμὶς γάρ **ἐστε**
4:14d *Your lives* **are** *like smoky vapor,*

> 4:14e ἡ πρὸς ὀλίγον **φαινομένη**
> 4:14e *namely, that your life* **appears** *for a little while*

> 4:14f ἔπειτα καὶ **ἀφανιζομένη**.
> 4:14f and then *your life* **vanishes**.

4:15a ἀντὶ τοῦ **λέγειν** ὑμᾶς, ἐὰν ὁ κύριος **θελήσῃ**
4:15a <u>Instead</u> of *your saying*, you **say**, ("If the Lord **wills**

4:15b καὶ **ζήσομεν** καὶ **ποιήσομεν** τοῦτο ἢ ἐκεῖνο.
4:15b **we will** both **live and accomplish this** or that.")

^{4:16a} νῦν δὲ **καυχᾶσθε** ἐν ταῖς ἀλαζονείαις ὑμῶν·
^{4:16a} <u>As it is</u>, **you boast** so arrogantly.

^{4:16b} πᾶσα καύχησις τοιαύτη πονηρά **ἐστιν**.
^{4:16b} All such arrogant boasting **is** evil.

> ^{4:17a} **εἰδότι** οὖν καλὸν **ποιεῖν**
> ^{4:17a} Therefore, **whoever knows to do** the right *thing*
>
> |
>
> ^{4:17b} καὶ μὴ **ποιοῦντι** [καλόν],
> ^{4:17b} and **does** not **do** [*the right thing*],
>
> |

^{4:17c} ἁμαρτία αὐτῷ **ἐστιν**.
^{4:17c} it **is** sin to him.

SYNTAX EXPLAINED FOR JAMES 4:13–17

^{4:13a} Ἄγε νῦν: The first Greek word is a second person singular present active imperative of ἄγω that may be rendered "come" (BDAG, s.v. "ἄγε," p. 9). **Syntactically**, it is the main verb of this dependent conjunctive clause introduced with the temporal adverbial conjunction νῦν by a "parenthetic nominative" (οἱ λέγοντες; W, 53–54). It is an anomaly in that it is followed by a plural anacoluthon: "today or tomorrow we will go . . ." (Σήμερον ἢ αὔριον πορευσόμεθα . . .). **Semantically**, the present tense imperative is a general command that has more of a rhetorical function. It is an interjection or orienter that derives its meaning from whatever verb that follows. Therefore, a translation like "Come now" does not communicate the urgency of the expression (cf. ASV NASB NRSV ESV NET; Zerwick et al., 699). The NIV captures the rhetoric nicely, "Now listen, you who say . . ." or as the NLT renders it "Look here, you who say . . ."

> **Syntactical Nugget:** What is the meaning of the expression ἄγε νῦν? The expression ἄγε νῦν is found in Greek literature and is effectively used by the diatribal moralists (e.g., Epictetus, *Diatrib.* 3.24.40). While this exact expression here and in 5:1a does not appear elsewhere in the LXX, a similar use of the imperative verb alone can be seen in the B manuscript of Judges 19:6 (ἄγε δή) and also in Isaiah 43:6 (ἄγε καί). While ἄγε is certainly an imperative, it is frozen grammatically as a particle that derives its meaning by whatever verb that follows, as is the case with the imperative κλαύσατε following it in 5:1a. Yet, no such verb appears in the reported speech of 4:13a. This anacoluthon is only the first of the grammatical anomalies in this passage. After this "attention getter" or "orienter" that opens 4:13, James follows up with a challenging question in 4:14c.

πορευσόμεθα: This Greek word is a first person plural future middle indicative of πορεύω that conveys the idea of moving over an area with a point of departure and may be rendered as "go," "proceed," or "travel" (BDAG, s.v. "πορεύω" 1, p. 853). **Syntactically**, it is the main verb of a dependent conjunctive clause that is functioning as the direct object of "you who say" (οἱ λέγοντες). The subject is the "we" assumed in the verb. It is the first of four verbs in the quoted speech of an imagined business person or merchant James addresses. **Semantically**, it is the future tense and is a predictive future that indicates that something will happen (W, 568). It lays out a future agenda of an imaginary business person that appears to express a smug sense of implied certainty concerning travel plans.

4:13b καί: This structural marker is a conjunction meaning "and" (BDAG, s.v. "καί" 1b, p. 494). **Syntactically**, it introduces a dependent conjunctive clause. **Semantically**, it is a coordinating conjunction often rendered "and" (NET ESV NASB NRSV etc.) that adds to James's description of an imagined business person's business plans.

ποιήσομεν: This Greek word is a first person plural future active indicative of ποιέω that conveys doing something to another person and may be rendered as "stay" or with an accusative "spend" (BDAG, s.v. "ποιέω" 4c, p. 841). **Syntactically**, it is the main verb of a dependent conjunctive clause that is functioning as part of the direct object for "you who say" (οἱ λέγοντες). The subject is the "we" assumed in the verb. It is the second of four verbs in the quoted speech of an imagined business person James addresses and another part of the direct object. **Semantically**, it is the future tense and is a predictive future that indicates that something will happen (W, 568). It lays out a future agenda of an imaginary merchant that appears to express a confident sense of implied certainty about time spent in a given place. The verb carries more the sense of "spend" (ASV NASB NRSV NIV ESV NET CNT) or "stay" (NLT) rather than its usual meaning of "make."

4:13c καί: This structural marker is a conjunction meaning "and" (BDAG, s.v. "καί" 1b, p. 494). **Syntactically**, it introduces a dependent conjunctive clause. **Semantically**, it is a coordinating conjunction often rendered "and" (NET ESV NASB etc.) that adds to James's description of an imagined business person's business plans.

ἐμπορευσόμεθα: This verb is the first person plural future middle indicative of ἐμπορεύομαι that conveys the idea of carrying on an activity of buying and selling and may be rendered "be in business" or "carry on business" (BDAG, s.v. "ἐμπορεύομαι" 1, p. 324). **Syntactically**, it is the main verb of a dependent conjunctive clause that is functioning as part of the direct object for "you who say" (οἱ λέγοντες). The subject is the "we" assumed in the verb. It is the third of four verbs in the quoted speech of the imagined business person that James addresses. **Semantically**, it is the future tense and is a predictive future that indicates that something will happen (W, 568). It lays out a future agenda of an imaginary merchant that appears to express an overly confident sense of implied certainty about "trading" (ASV ESV), "doing business" (ASV NASB NRSV NIV NET NLT CNT), or "buying and selling" (KJV). Ultimately, it is a presupposition about engaging in commerce.

4:13d καί: This structural marker is a conjunction meaning "and" (BDAG, s.v. "καί" 1b, p. 494). **Syntactically**, it introduces a dependent conjunctive clause. **Semantically**, it is a coordinating conjunction often rendered "and" (NET ESV NASB NRSV etc.) that adds to James's description of an imagined business person's economic plans.

κερδήσομεν: This Greek word is a first person plural future active indicative of κερδαίνω that conveys the idea of acquiring something by effort or investment and may be rendered as "gain" (BDAG, s.v. "κερδαίνω" 1a, p. 541). **Syntactically**, it is the main verb of a dependent conjunctive clause that is functioning as part of the direct object for "you who say" (οἱ λέγοντες). The subject is the "we" assumed in the verb. It is the fourth of four verbs in the quoted speech of an imagined business person James addresses. **Semantically**, it is the future tense and is a predictive future that indicates that something will happen (W, 568). It lays out a future agenda of an imaginary merchant that appears to express an almost arrogant sense of implied certainty about financial "gains," (KJV ASV) "profits" (NASB NET NLT CNT), or "making money" (NRSV NIV).

> **Semantical Nugget:** What is the significance in the context of the verbs πορευσόμεθα, ποιήσομεν, ἐμπορευσόμεθα, and κερδήσομεν? The future tenses convey a confidence that is ill conceived. This confident merchant works on the assumption that he can accomplish what he intends, and he does not expect death or any other obstacle to stop him. He has the time and places all set and he does not think at all about how God might regard his plans. It is not that these "merchants" are engaged in a sinful or "secular" occupation. "It is not their occupation, but their attitude, that has become secular" (Blomberg et al., 207). James knows that even believing business people are not immune to this temptation to presumption. The problem is the same one described in the parable of the rich fool in Luke 12:16–21, which may very well supply the background for this warning.

4:14a οἵτινες: This structural marker is a nominative plural masculine indefinite relative pronoun that conveys any person and may be rendered as "whoever" or "everyone" (BDAG, s.v. "ὅστις" 1, p. 730). **Syntactically**, it introduces a dependent relative clause where οἵτινες serves as the subject of an elliptical verb "[ἐστιν]" that modifies "you know" (ἐπίστασθε) in the subsequent independent clause. While most render οἵτινες as "you" (KJV ASV NASB NRSV NIV ESV NET NLT CNT), we prefer "whoever" (BDAG, s.v. "ὅστις" 1, p. 730; cf. Irons, 539).

[ἐστιν]: This Greek word is a third person singular present active indicative of εἰμί that conveys the idea of being in close connection with something and may be rendered as "is" (BDAG, s.v. "εἰμί" 2b, p. 282). **Syntactically**, the bracketed elliptical verb is the main verb of the dependent relative clause with "whoever" (ὁ νομοθέτης καὶ κριτής) as its subject (cf. Adam, 86). The indefinite pronoun usually takes its verb in the third person. Thus, the appearance of [ἐστιν] in the brackets, though we translate it as "you are."

4:14b οὐκ ἐπίστασθε: This negated (οὐκ) structural marker is a second person plural present middle indicative of ἐπίσταμαι that conveys acquiring information about something and may be rendered as "know" or "be acquainted with" (BDAG, s.v. "ἐπίσταμαι" 2, p. 380). **Syntactically**, it is the main verb of an independent asyndeton clause with "you" assumed in ἐπίστασθε as its subject (con. Adam, 86). The negation (οὐκ) identifies what you do *not* know. **Semantically**, the present tense is a customary present that underscores action that regularly occurs (W, 521–22). In this case, no one regularly knows what the future holds the next day (cf. BDF, §266.3).

> **Syntactical Nugget:** How are the complex series of clauses to be rendered in 4:14? The anacoluthon is actually a single sentence that consists of three clauses: a relative clause (οἵτινες οὐκ ἐπίστασθε τὸ τῆς αὔριον), then a question (ποία ἡ ζωὴ ὑμῶν), and finally a causal statement of why their boastful planning is wrong (ἀτμὶς γάρ ἐστε . . . ἀφανιζομένη). Compounding the syntactical problem is the fact that the critical Greek texts punctuate 4:14a as an initial declarative clause, ending just before the ἀτμὶς. Thus, it is translated this way by some versions as: "You do not know what your life will be tomorrow" (NASB NLT). This creates some grammatical problems because the required punctuation takes the interrogative pronoun as the object or complement of the verb even though it is in the nominative case (ἡ ζωή). In its thirty-four other NT occurrences, ποῖος almost always is either the subject of an interrogative clause or serves as an adjunct within such a clause. Matthew 24:42 is the only verse where ποῖος is in the nominative case as a complement to an indicative verb. Its function here, therefore, is most probably as the initial inquiry in a question that follows the first clause (NRSV NIV ESV NET). Yet, we have rendered οἵτινες,

> the relative pronoun, as introducing a dependent relative clause with an elliptical verb [ἐστιν] that modifies ἐπίστασθε.

4:14c [ἐστιν]: This structural marker is a third person singular present active indicative from the verb εἰμί that conveys the significance of something and often rendered "is" (BDAG, s.v. "εἰμί" 2cα, p. 284). **Syntactically**, the bracketed [ἐστιν] is an ellipsis that serves as the main verb of the independent asyndeton clause that has an interrogative force (BDF, §459.4; Adam, 87). While the subject of the verb is "life" (ἡ ζωὴ), the interrogative pronoun "what" (ποία) is the predicate (W, 47–48; BDAG, s.v. "ποία" 1aβ, p. 843; BDF, §298.2). **Semantically**, the elliptical [ἐστιν] is inquiring the significance of life. Most translations provide a translation of the elliptical [ἐστιν] as "is" (KJV ASV NRSV NIV ESV NET CNT) or as though the ellipsis is a future form of εἰμί: "will be" (NASB NLT).

4:14d γάρ: This structural marker is a conjunction and is left untranslated in English (BDAG, s.v. "γάρ" 1f, p. 189). **Syntactically**, it introduces an independent conjunctive clause of continuation. **Semantically**, it serves as a marker, but it is left untranslated (NASB NIV NLT). Nevertheless, some translations render γάρ as "for" (ASV NRSV ESV NET CNT) as though a marker of reason.

ἐστε: This Greek word is a second person plural present active indicative of εἰμί that conveys the idea of having a close connection with something and is often rendered "is" (BDAG, s.v. "εἰμί" 2cα, p. 284). **Syntactically**, it is the main verb of an independent conjunctive clause with an understood "you" (pl) as its subject and "smoky vapor" (ἀτμίς) as a predicate nominative (W, 47–48; BDAG, s.v. "ἀτμίς," p. 149). **Semantically**, the present tense is a gnomic present (W, 523) that conveys a timeless truth and equates a person's life with something that is short lived. It is something about life that happens.

4:14e φαινομένη: This structural marker is a nominative singular feminine present middle participle of φαίνω that conveys the idea of becoming visible and may be rendered "appear" (BDAG, s.v. "φαίνω" 2a, p. 1047). **Syntactically**, it is a dependent participial clause that modifies ἀτμίς. The entire clause is placed under ἀτμίς to visualize the association between ἀτμίς and the φαινομένη clause. **Semantically**, the present tense is a gnomic present that describes a timeless truth about "fog" or "vapor" (ὀλίγον), namely, that fog happens (W, 523–24) and is typically rendered as "appear" (NASB NRSV NIV ESV NET CNT; cf. KJV ASV).

4:14f καί: This structural marker is a conjunction meaning "and" (BDAG, s.v. "καί" 1b, p. 494). **Syntactically**, it introduces a dependent conjunctive clause. **Semantically**, it is a coordinating conjunction often rendered "and" (NET ESV NASB NRSV etc.) that adds to James's description of an imagined merchant's business plans.

ἀφανιζομένη: This Greek word is a nominative singular feminine present middle participle of ἀφανίζω that conveys the idea of causing something to disappear and may be rendered "destroyed," "perish," or "disappear" (BDAG, s.v. "ἀφανίζω" 1b, p. 154). **Syntactically**, it is the main verb of a dependent conjunctive clause. The entire clause is placed under ἀτμίς to visualize the association between ἀτμίς and the φαινομένη clause. **Semantically**, the present tense is a gnomic present that describes a timeless truth about fog or vapor (ὀλίγον), namely, that it disappears (W, 523–24).

> **Syntactical Nugget:** How should the syntax be understood in James 4:13–14? The complexity of the clauses, the use of anacoluthon, and the abrupt style that begs for additional conjunctions for smooth transitions all combine to offer a serious challenge to anyone seeking to unpack the structure and meaning of these verses. Is it possible that the apparent disorder and lack of precision in the syntax of 4:13–14 are also intended to convey the resulting disorder that characterizes a life that is lived without God in its plans? Therefore, even the language James uses to communicate this message seems to be uncertain and in disorder. On the other hand, the contrast evident by the simple and straightforward syntax in 4:15 may also be intended to convey the simplicity and order of a life that is lived in conscious awareness of God's will. Recognizing the original orality of these texts will help us to better appreciate their rhetorical thrust! There are intertextual echoes with an echo from Proverbs 27:1: "Don't boast [καυχῶ] about tomorrow [αὔριον], for you do not know [γινώσκεις] what the next day may bring forth." Hosea 13:3 says that idolaters "shall be like the morning mist, or like the dew that goes away early."

4:15a ἀντί τοῦ λέγειν: This articular (τοῦ) structural marker (λέγειν) is a present active infinitive of λέγω that conveys the idea of expressing oneself in a specific way and may be rendered "say" (BDAG, s.v. "λέγω" 2d, p. 589). **Syntactically**, it is a dependent infinitival clause that introduces an independent clause. The infinitive is both articular (τοῦ) and governed by a preposition (ἀντί; cf. W, 593). While there are many examples of articular infinitives with prepositions in the NT, this is the only example with this preposition. As a result, the rendering of the entire clause is difficult. **Semantically**, the present tense is an iterative present indicating action that occurs time and time again (W, 520–21). James is directing his readers about how to approach their planning on a regular basis. It conveys something to the contrary with the genitive (W, 364). So, the meaning here is clear: "just the opposite should be said." While typically rendered "instead you ought" (KJV NASB NRSV NIV ESV NET NLT CNT), we offer the alternative rendering in BDAG: "instead of your saying" (Zerwick et al., 699; Adam, 87), which stands in stark contrast to what the hypothetical business person has said in verses 13–14.

> **Grammatical Nugget:** What is the meaning of the rare construction ἀντὶ τοῦ λέγειν ὑμᾶς? The fronted articular infinitive construction conveys the rebuke often rendered: "Instead, you ought to say." The preposition ἀντί is one of the rarer prepositions, appearing only here in James and elsewhere in the NT only twenty-one times. This is the only time it appears with an articular infinitive. While the use of the preposition ἀντί with an articular infinitive appears often in classical orators, there is only one appearance in the LXX, Psalm 108:4: ἀντὶ τοῦ ἀγαπᾶν με ἐνδιέβαλλόν με ("Instead of my love, they slander me"). The clause conveys "just the opposite should be said." Indeed, this is the type of "anti-language" so typical of the counterintuitive contrast between earthly and heavenly behavior (3:13–18) that James impresses on every passage in his book.

ἐάν: This structural marker is a conjunction meaning "if" (BDAG, s.v. "ἐάν" 1cγ, p. 268). **Syntactically**, it introduces a dependent conjunctive clause that functions as the direct object identifying what should not be said (τοῦ λέγειν). Second, the ἐάν clause, "If the Lord wills" (ἐὰν ὁ κύριος θελήσῃ), is placed in parentheses to visualize its dependence within the dependent infinitival clause. **Semantically**, it is a third-class conditional clause that introduces a hypothetical situation for the sake of the discussion (W, 696–99; Adam, 88). So, the hypothetical situation is not necessarily describing a scene that he has witnessed or heard that has taken place in their assemblies. The scene that is portrayed in their "synagogue" *may* have taken place, but it is not necessarily a scene that actually *has* taken place.

θελήσῃ: This Greek word is a third person singular aorist active subjunctive of θέλω that conveys having something in mind for oneself and may be rendered "will," "wish," "want," or "be ready" (BDAG, s.v. "θέλω" 2, p. 448). **Syntactically**, it is the main verb in the dependent conjunctive clause that is functioning as the protasis of a third-class conditional ἐάν clause that is the reported speech of those addressed. **Semantically**, the aorist tense is a constative aorist that describes an event as a whole (W, 557–58). It describes an event of a person living life and dependent on and trusting God one day at time.

4:15b καὶ . . . καί: This Greek combination of the καὶ . . . καί conjunctions may be rendered "both . . . and" or "not only . . . but also" (BDAG, s.v. "καί" 1f, p. 495). **Syntactically**, καὶ . . . καί are markers for two independent clauses (cf. BDF, §442.7). **Semantically**, the conjunctions are rendered "and also" (NASB) or just "and" (KJV NIV NET CNT). We render the combination as "both . . . and" (cf. BDAG, s.v. "καί" 1f, p. 495; Adam, 88).

> **Theological Nugget:** What is the significance of the saying "if the Lord wills" in 4:15? The "quotation" that follows contrasts with the pattern of the overly confident speech in 4:13. The uncertainty conveyed by this conditional clause contrasts vividly with the boastful planning previously announced. James urges these merchants to add a key clause to their planning: "If it is the Lord's will." The attitude that it expresses is widespread among NT characters and authors. Most familiar is its inclusion in the "Lord's Prayer" (Matt. 6:10), but see also Matthew 26:42; Acts 21:14; Romans 15:32; 1 Peter 3:17. Paul frequently verbalized his own submission to the Lord's will in his plans for missionary labors (Acts 18:21; Rom. 1:10; 1 Cor. 4:19; 16:7). Even more significant for James is that Jesus himself expressed this same submission to the Father's will at the great crisis in Gethsemane (Luke 22:42).

ζήσομεν: This structural marker is a first person plural future active indicative of ζάω that conveys the idea of being alive physically and often rendered as "live" (BDAG, s.v. "ζάω" 1aδ, p. 424). **Syntactically**, it is the first main verb of this independent asyndeton clause that also serves as the apodosis of the third-class conditional ἐάν clause. **Semantically**, the future tense is a predictive future (W, 568). James says that people will make plans for their lives. It will happen.

ποιήσομεν: This structural marker is a first person plural future active indicative of ποιέω that conveys the idea of undertaking or doing something that brings about an accomplishment and may be rendered "do," "accomplish," or "make" (BDAG, s.v. "ποιέω" 2a, p. 839). **Syntactically**, it is the second main verb of this independent asyndeton clause that serves as the apodosis of the third-class conditional ἐάν clause. **Semantically**, the future tense is a predictive future that indicates that something will happen (W, 568). It lays out a future agenda for an individual. The four future indicative verbs in 4:13 are balanced with the two future indicative verbs here in verse 15. The difference is that the last two indicatives are based on God's will and not human arrogance.

4:16a νῦν δέ: These structural markers are a conjunctive combination that conveys the idea of a contrast to the real state of affairs and may be rendered "as it is" (BDAG, s.v. "νῦν" 2a, p. 681). **Semantically**, it introduces an independent conjunctive clause. **Syntactically**, it is inferential to further illustrate the arrogance depicted in the preceding verses regarding the presumptuous planners. James 4:15 informs the readers what they should do to avoid the presumption so condemned in 4:13–14—i.e., to include God's plan in their plans. Then 4:16 returns to the original problem with the additional charge that the attitude he is condemning is not just one that is a poor choice.

καυχᾶσθε: This Greek word is a second person plural present middle indicative of καυχάομαι that conveys taking pride in something and may be rendered "boast" (BDAG, s.v. "καυχάομαι" 1, p. 537). **Syntactically**, it is the main verb of this independent conjunctive clause. Its subject "you" is assumed in the verb. **Semantically**, the present tense is a customary present that underscores action that regularly occurs (W, 521–22). In this case, it speaks of a person who boasts on a regular basis. It is a pattern of behavior. It is actually an example of "evil and arrogant boasting." Since the semantic field of the verb καυχάομαι can include "boasting" in a positive sense (Rom. 5:2, 3, 11), James adds a qualifying phrase (ἐν ταῖς ἀλαζονείαις ὑμῶν) that should be understood adverbially: "for how can you boast *in* your arrogant boastings?"

> **Lexical Nugget:** What is the meaning of the word group καυχᾶσθε / καύχησις? Since the semantic field of the verb καυχάομαι can include "boasting" in a positive sense (Rom. 5:2, 3, 11), James adds a qualifying phrase (ἐν ταῖς ἀλαζονείαις ὑμῶν) understood adverbially: "for how can you boast *in* your arrogant boastings?" By the word "arrogantly" the plans expressed in 4:13 are meant. The expression does not denote the subject of "glorying" (like ἐν τῷ ὕψει 1:9a), but the manner in which glorying was shown.

4:16b ἐστιν: This structural marker is a third person singular present active indicative of εἰμί that conveys the idea of being in close connection with something and may be rendered as "is" (BDAG, s.v. "εἰμί" 2b, p. 282). **Syntactically**, it is the main verb of the independent asyndeton clause with "boasting" (καύχησις) as its subject and "evil" (πονηρά) as its predicate adjective (W, 40–46; Adam, 88). **Semantically**, the verb is equative in that it warns that boasting "is" evil. The copulative ἐστιν ends the sentence, something he has also done in 2:20, 26 and again in 4:17, each of which are also climactic statements. Translations render ἐστιν as "is" (KJV ASV NASB NRSV NIV ESV NET NLT CNT).

4:17a οὖν: This structural marker is a conjunction meaning "therefore" (BDAG, s.v. "οὖν" 1a, p. 736). **Syntactically**, it introduces a dependent conjunctive clause. It is in the post-positive position: "*Therefore*, whoever knows the right thing to do" (εἰδότι οὖν καλὸν ποιεῖν). **Semantically**, it is an inferential conjunction that introduces the result or deduction for what was said previously: "therefore" (KJV ASV NASB CNT), though some render it as "so" (NET ESV) or as "then" (NRSV NIV). Regardless of its rendering, James is drawing a conclusion or summary about what Scripture says about life in 4:14–16. The οὖν in 4:17 is the third of its five appearances (see also 4:4b, 7a; 5:7a, 16a) and provides a transition to the effective proverb.

εἰδότι: This Greek word is a dative singular masculine perfect active participle of οἶδα that conveys the idea of understanding how and may be rendered as "can" or "be able" (BDAG, s.v. "οἶδα" 3, p. 694). **Syntactically**, it is the main verb of this dependent participial clause that modifies αὐτῷ in 4:17c. **Semantically**, it functions as a dative of reference that directs attention to any person (W, 144–45; Adam, 88; Irons, 540). The perfect is a perfect with present force (W, 579–80; cf. Zerwick et al., 699). Thus, the result of knowing is knowing. James concludes his paragraph with another proverbial saying.

ποιεῖν: This Greek word is a present active infinitive of ποιέω that conveys the idea of doing something that brings about an event or a condition and may be rendered "do," "cause," or "bring about" (BDAG, s.v. "ποιέω" 2e, p. 840). **Syntactically**, it is part of the main verb "know" (εἰδότι) in the dependent participial clause. **Semantically**, it functions as a complementary infinitive to εἰδότι (W, 598–99). The present tense functions as a customary present that describes a person who regularly knows what is right to do (W, 521–22), in this case, making correct ethical decisions.

4:17b καί: This structural marker is a conjunction meaning "and" (BDAG, s.v. "καί" 1b, p. 494). **Syntactically**, it introduces an independent conjunctive clause. **Semantically**, it is a coordinating conjunction often rendered "and" (NET ESV NASB NRSV etc.) that adds to James's description of living ethically.

μὴ ποιοῦντι: This negated (μή) Greek word is a dative singular masculine present active participle of ποιέω that conveys the idea of doing something that brings about an event or a condition and may be rendered "do," "cause," or "bring about" (BDAG, s.v. "ποιέω" 2e, p. 840). **Syntactically**, it is the main verbal of this dependent conjunctive clause that modifies αὐτῷ in the next clause. **Semantically**, it functions as a dative of reference that directs attention to any person (W, 144–45; Adam, 88). The present tense is customary or iterative. The expression "doing good" (with forms of καλός and ἀγαθός) is mentioned elsewhere about the Lord Jesus (Acts 10:38) and among his followers (Luke 6:27; Rom. 7:21; Heb. 13:6; 1 Peter 3:11).

4:17c ἐστιν: This structural marker is a third person singular present active indicative of εἰμί that conveys the idea of being in close connection with something and may be rendered as "is" (BDAG, s.v. "εἰμί" 2b, p. 282). **Syntactically**, it is the main verb of the independent asyndeton clause. The subject "it" is assumed in ἐστιν (ἐστιν), and "sin" (ἁμαρτία) is its predicate nominative

(W, 40–46; Adam, 89). **Semantically**, the verb is equative in that it reveals the oneness of "it" (intentional wrongdoing) with "sin" (ἁμαρτία). The copulative ἐστιν ends the sentence, something James has also done in 2:20, 26a and b, and 4:16b, each of which are also climactic statements. Translations render ἐστιν as "is" (KJV ASV NASB NIV ESV NET NLT CNT).

> **Theological Nugget:** What is the OT/Jewish background that informs the meaning of this verse? The sentiment here reflects the Jewish search for hidden guilt, in which every sin of omission is important. This sentiment can be seen in the NLT rendering of the prayer in Psalm 19:12: "How can I know all the sins lurking in my heart? Cleanse me from these hidden faults." When Job examines himself for sins, he expressly mentions sins of omission (Job 31:16–18), while Zophar indicates the possibility of secret guilt (Job 11:6).

RICH PEOPLE ARE WARNED ABOUT SELF-SUFFICIENCY (JAMES 5:1–6)

CLAUSAL OUTLINE FOR JAMES 5:1–6

5:1a Ἄγε νῦν οἱ πλούσιοι, **κλαύσατε**
5:1a Now **listen**, you who are rich, **burst into weeping**

|
5:1b **ὀλολύζοντες** ἐπὶ ταῖς ταλαιπωρίαις ὑμῶν
5:1b _by_ **howling with grief** because of your miseries

|
5:1c ταῖς **ἐπερχομέναις**.
5:1c **that are coming**.

5:2a ὁ πλοῦτος ὑμῶν **σέσηπεν**
5:2a Your wealth **is rotten**,

5:2b καὶ τὰ ἱμάτια ὑμῶν σητόβρωτα **γέγονεν**,
5:2b and your clothes **are** moth-eaten.

5:3a ὁ χρυσὸς ὑμῶν καὶ ὁ ἄργυρος **κατίωται**
5:3a Your gold and silver **are corroded**,

5:3b καὶ ὁ ἰὸς αὐτῶν εἰς μαρτύριον ὑμῖν **ἔσται**
5:3b and the corrosion **will be** evidence against you

5:3c καὶ [ὁ ἰὸς] **φάγεται** τὰς σάρκας ὑμῶν ὡς πῦρ.
5:3c and [_the corrosion_] **will eat** your flesh like fire.

5:3d **ἐθησαυρίσατε** ἐν ἐσχάταις ἡμέραις.
5:3d It is in the last days that **you have hoarded wealth**.

5:4a **ἰδοὺ** ὁ μισθὸς τῶν ἐργατῶν . . . ἀφ᾿ ὑμῶν **κράζει**,
5:4a **Consider** *how* the wage of the laborers . . . **cries out** against you,

       |
      5:4b τῶν **ἀμησάντων** τὰς χώρας ὑμῶν
      5:4b from **those who mowed** your fields

   |
  5:4c ὁ **ἀπεστερημένος**
  5:4c which **you have stolen**

5:4d κ̲α̲ὶ̲ αἱ βοαὶ τῶν θερισάντων εἰς τὰ ὦτα κυρίου Σαβαὼθ **εἰσεληλύθασιν**.
5:4d a̲n̲d̲ the cries of the harvesters **have reached** the ears of the Lord of *Sabaoth*.

5:5a **ἐτρυφήσατε** ἐπὶ τῆς γῆς
5:5a **You have lived for pleasure** on earth

5:5b κ̲α̲ὶ̲ **ἐσπαταλήσατε**,
5:5b a̲n̲d̲ **you have lived in luxury**.

5:5c **ἐθρέψατε** τὰς καρδίας ὑμῶν ἐν ἡμέρᾳ σφαγῆς_
5:5c **You have fattened** your hearts for the day of slaughter,

5:6a **κατεδικάσατε**,
5:6a **you have condemned**,

5:6b [κ̲α̲ὶ̲] **ἐφονεύσατε** τὸν δίκαιον·
5:6b [*a̲n̲d̲*] **you have murdered** the righteous person.,

5:6c ο̲ὐ̲κ̲ **ἀντιτάσσεται** ὑμῖν.
5:6c **Does he (God) not oppose** you?

SYNTAX EXPLAINED FOR JAMES 5:1–6

5:1a Ἄγε νῦν: The first Greek word is a second person singular present active imperative of ἄγω that may be rendered "come" (BDAG, s.v. "ἄγε," p. 9). **Syntactically**, it is the main verb of an independent conjunctive clause with the
temporal adverbial conjunction νῦν that introduces this paragraph (see Lex-
ical/Syntactical Nugget 4:13a). As was the case in 4:13a, ἄγε νῦν occurs with
a "parenthetic nominative" (οἱ πλούσιοι; W, 53–54). It is an anomaly in that it
is followed by an anacoluthon: "weep . . ." (κλαύσατε . . .). **Semantically**, the
present tense imperative is a general command that has a rhetorical function. It

is more an interjection or orienter than a simple verb that derives its meaning from whatever verb that follows. Therefore, a translation like "Come now" does not communicate the urgency of the expression (cf. ASV NASB NRSV ESV NET; Zerwick et al., 700). The NIV captures the rhetoric nicely, "Now listen, you rich people . . ." or as the NLT renders it "Look here, you rich people . . .".

> **Lexical Nugget:** Who are "the rich" (οἱ πλούσιοι)? The rich were addressed earlier (1:10–11; 2:6; and 4:13–16 by implication). The intense rhetoric of invective in this passage permits the rich being addressed as a class, even as the prophets addressed the rich in ancient Israel (e.g., Amos 4:1–3; 6:1–7). The nominative of address, accompanied by the article, indicates that the rich are apostrophized as an ungodly social caste (BDAG, s.v. "πλούσι- ος" 1, p. 831), similar to what Paul does with "the rich" in 1 Timothy 6:17 (τοῖς πλουσίοις).

κλαύσατε: This Greek word is a second person plural aorist active imperative of κλαίω that conveys the idea of lamenting and may be rendered "weep" or "cry" (BDAG, s.v. "κλαίω" 1, p. 545). **Syntactically**, it is the main verb of this independent clause. The subject is "the rich" (οἱ πλούσιοι) who are being addressed. **Semantically**, this aorist imperative depicts a command as a whole (W, 485–86) about weeping over forthcoming miseries. While most translations link "weep" with "cry out" as though a second imperative were joined by "and" (KJV ASV NASB NRSV NIV ESV NET NLT CNT; cf. Adam, 90), we view the following participle differently.

5:1b ὀλολύζοντες: This structural marker is a nominative plural masculine present active participle of ὀλολύζω that conveys the idea of verbally crying out loudly and may be rendered "cry out" (BDAG, s.v. "ὀλολύζω," p. 704). **Syntactically**, it is the main verb of this dependent participial clause that functions adverbially modifying the ones commanded in the preceding imperative verb "weep" (κλαύσατε). It is placed immediately under κλαύσατε to visualize its relationship. **Semantically**, it is a participle of manner describing the crying: "*by* howling with grief" (W, 627–28). The present tense is an iterative present indicating action that occurs time and time again, stressing the repeated crying out that is commanded in the imperative (W, 520–21). The idea conveyed by the vivid combination of imperative and participle is: "burst into weeping [aorist active of κλαίω as in 4:9c], by howling with grief." The participle is onomatopoetic and in the NT only appears here.

> **Lexical Nugget:** How is "crying out" (ὀλολύζω) to be understood in the LXX? The LXX uses the verb exclusively as laments for disasters visited on the people by the Lord for their apostasy (Isa. 10:10; 13:6; 14:31; 15:2–3; 16:7; 23:1, 6, 14; Hos. 7:14; Amos 8:3; Zech. 11:2). A NT verb that can be

compared to this *hapax legomenon* is ἀλαλαζω. "They came to the house of the synagogue official; and he saw a commotion, and people loudly weeping and wailing (ἀλαλάζοντας)" (Mark 5:38). The action expressed is like that of the Latin verb *ululare* (*ululantes* in the Vulgate), from which we derive the English word *ululate*.

5:1c ταῖς ἐπερχομέναις: This articular (ταῖς) structural marker is a dative plural feminine present middle participle of ἐπέρχομαι that conveys the idea of an event that may happen in the course of time and may be rendered as "come (on)" or "approach" (BDAG, s.v. "ἐπέρχομαι" 2bα, p. 361). **Syntactically**, it is the main verb of this dependent participial clause that functions adverbially modifying "miseries" (ταῖς ταλαιπωρίαις). It is placed immediately under ταλαιπωρίαις to visualize its grammatical relationship. **Semantically**, the present tense is a futuristic present (W, 535–37) stressing the process of the coming judgment. The vivid attributive participle places the judgment in an eschatological context.

> **Lexical Nugget:** How is "miseries" (ταλαιπωρίαις) to be understood in the LXX? The apocalyptic writings have a good deal to say about the "miseries" (ταλαιπωρίαις) "that are coming" (ταῖς ἐπερχομέναις) upon them (Dan. 12:1; Joel 2:10–14; Zech. 14:12–15). The Gospels connect them also with the Day of the Lord (Mark 13:14–27; Luke 21:9–19). In 5:3 the context is clearly eschatological (5:3d: ἐν ἐσχάταις ἡμέραις) and is heightened in its vividness by its present tense and imperfective aspect. The verb was used of judgment "coming upon" sinners in the Day of the Lord and is mentioned in Luke 21:26 and Acts 13:40.

5:2a σέσηπεν: This structural marker is a third person singular perfect active indicative of σήπω that conveys the idea of a rich person's treasures and may be rendered as "decay" or "rot" (BDAG, s.v. "σήπω," p. 922). **Syntactically**, it is the main verb of the independent asyndeton clause. The subject is "the wealth" (ὁ πλοῦτος) of the rich. **Semantically**, the perfect tense is an intensive perfect that emphasizes the result of the present state produced by a past action and rendered as "are corrupted" (KJV ASV) or "is rotten" (W, 576–77). Yet, others render σέσηπεν as an extensive perfect that emphasizes the completed action of the past (W, 577–78) and translate it "have rotted" (NASB NRSV ESV NET CNT).

> **Lexical Nugget:** How has "is rotten" (σέσηπεν) been understood in other literature? The verb σήπω is a NT *hapax legomenon* but is used by LXX translators in Psalm 37:6; Job 19:20; 33:21; and Sirach 14:19. The vividness of the present tense verbs in 5:1 is now amplified by a series of perfect verbs that follow in 5:2–3. These verbs raise to a higher level of prominence the

condemnation that James is delivering. The following six primary clauses in verses 2–3 are anchored by three perfect verbs (σέσηπεν, γέγονεν,
κατίωται), each of which conveys the current state of the rich people's
possessions. Their hoarded wealth decays in a state of rottenness. Their
fine clothes are useless because they are in a moth-eaten condition. Their
precious money lies in a state of corrosion. The perfect tense/aspect serves
to create a vivid sense of the imminence of the miseries. A greater prominence is also delivered through these perfects by the deliberate use of prophetic diction.

5:2b καί: This structural marker is a conjunction meaning "and" (BDAG, s.v. "καί"
1b, p. 494). **Syntactically**, it introduces an independent conjunctive clause.
Semantically, it is a coordinating conjunction often rendered "and" (NET
ESV NASB NRSV etc.) that adds to James's description about the wealthy.

γέγονεν: This Greek word is a third person singular perfect active indicative
of γίνομαι that conveys the idea of experiencing a change in nature with an
ultimately new condition and may be rendered "become" (BDAG, s.v. "γίνομαι" 5a, p. 198). **Syntactically**, it is the main verb of this independent conjunctive clause. The subject is "the garments" (τὰ ἱμάτια) of the rich. **Semantically**, the perfect tense is an intensive perfect that emphasizes the result of
the present state produced by a past action (W, 576–77) and is rendered "are
moth-eaten" (KJV ASV NRSV ESV NLT CNT). Yet, others render γέγονεν
as an extensive perfect that emphasizes the completed action of the past (W,
577–78) and translate it as "have become moth-eaten" (cf. NASB NET).

> **Lexical Nugget:** What is the meaning of σητόβρωτα in James 5:2? The
> word σητόβρωτα is a "late and rare compound from σης ("moth") and
> βρωτος. It is a verbal adjective of βιβρώσκω ("to eat"; BDAG, s.v. "σητό-
> βρωτος," p. 922). While this is a NT *hapax legomenon*, the destruction of
> clothes by moths echoes OT passages like Isaiah 51:8: "For the moth will
> devour them like a garment, and the worm will eat them like wool," and Job
> 13:28: "Man wears out like something rotten, like a moth-eaten garment."
> The closest parallel, however, is again found in the words of Jesus promot-
> ing the value of a "treasure in heaven" that is resistant to moths, rust, and
> thieves (Matt. 6:19–20; Luke 12:33). The tendency of wealth to offer false
> security is also targeted in other NT passages like Matthew 13:22; Mark
> 4:19; Luke 8:14; 12:21; and 1 Timothy 6:9. It is the fragility of wealth that
> is exposed.

5:3a κατίωται: This structural marker is a third person singular perfect passive indicative of κατιόω that conveys the idea of becoming tarnished and may be
rendered "rusted" or "corroded" (BDAG, s.v. "κατιόω," p. 534). **Syntactically**, it

is the main verb of the independent asyndeton clause. The subject is the "gold" and "silver" (ὁ χρυσὸς and ὁ ἄργυρος) of the rich. **Semantically**, the perfect tense is an intensive perfect that emphasizes the result of the present state produced by a past action (W, 576–77) and rendered "are corroded" (ASV NIV NLT; KJV). Yet, others translate κατίωται as an extensive perfect that emphasizes the completed action of the past (W, 577–78) and render it "have rusted" (NASB NRSV NET CNT; cf. ESV).

> **Lexical Nugget:** How can "corrosion" apply to gold, which does not actually rust? This figure is found also in the Epistle of Jeremiah 11–12, which says of silver, golden, and wooden gods that they "cannot save themselves from rust and corrosion" (similar idea in Sir 29:10). Louw and Nida explain: "Pure gold is not affected significantly by oxidation, but much of the gold of the ancient world was not pure, and therefore oxidation and resulting tarnish did take place. If there is no satisfactory term to indicate the deterioration in gold and silver resulting in extreme tarnish, it may be possible to translate James 5:3 as 'your gold and silver will be ruined and this will serve as a witness against you' (LN, 27). Nevertheless, the apparent conflict has continued to intrigue commentators. "The word 'rust' (ἰός) also proves intriguing, because it can mean both rust and poison or venom (as in 3:8). In some ways the latter definition fits best with the flesh-eating fire of the second half of the verse" (Blomberg et al., 221). Jesus also warned the rich in similar words (Matt. 6:20, after mention of the "moth"!) that their treasures (undoubtedly of "gold and silver") would rust.

5:3b καί: This structural marker is a conjunction meaning "and" (BDAG, s.v. "καί" 1b, p. 494). **Syntactically**, it introduces an independent conjunctive clause. **Semantically**, it is a coordinating conjunction often rendered "and" (NET ESV NASB NRSV etc.) that adds to James's description about the wealthy.

ἔσται: This Greek word is a third person singular future middle indicative of εἰμί that conveys the idea of something taking place as a phenomenon or event and may be rendered "take place," "become," "occur," or "be" (BDAG, s.v. "εἰμί" 6, p. 285). **Syntactically**, it is the main verb of an independent conjunctive clause with "the corrosion" (ὁ ἰός) as its subject and "evidence" (εἰς μαρτύριον) as the predicate nominative (BDF, §145). **Semantically**, the future tense is a predictive future that speaks of something that will take place (W, 568–69; Adam, 91; Irons, 540). It will happen. The corrosion of precious metals is personified as someone giving testimony or "will be" against them (KJV ASV NASB1995 NRSV ESV NET CNT; cf. NIV). The idea echoes a common idiom as in Jesus's instruction to the cleansed leper in Matthew 8:4: "Go, show yourself to the priest and offer the gift Moses commanded, as a testimony (εἰς μαρτύριον) to them."

⁵:³ᶜ καί: This structural marker is a conjunction meaning "and" (BDAG, s.v. "καί" 1b, p. 494). **Syntactically**, it introduces an independent conjunctive clause. **Semantically**, it is a coordinating conjunction often rendered "and" (ESV NASB NRSV etc.) that adds to James's description about the wealthy.

φάγεται: This Greek word is a third person singular future middle indicative of ἐσθίω that conveys the idea of doing away with something and may be rendered "devour" or "consume" (BDAG, s.v. "ἐσθίω" 2, p. 396). **Syntactically**, it is the main verb of an independent conjunctive clause with the elliptical noun "the corrosion" [ὁ ἰός] as its subject (con. Adam, 91). **Semantically**, the future tense is a predictive future that speaks of something that will take place (W, 568–69). It will happen. The corrosion of precious metals is personified as someone giving testimony or "will consume" them (KJV ASV NASB NRSV ESV NET CNT; cf. NIV). A rich person's money will actually turn back against them and will eat their flesh like fire. This may be referred to as an eschatological reversal.

> **Theological Nugget:** What is the eschatological reversal evident in James 5:3? Eschatological reversal is best conveyed in English by switching the order of the components. The sense would be: "Although you have amassed all this wealth (and have not adequately shared it as the following passage states), what you have hoarded so selfishly for the future will all be lost because 'it is in the last days that you *have* hoarded it'!" Here the theme of an eschatological reversal (alluded to briefly in 1:11–12) is elevated to the prominent context of this entire paragraph. The gruesome comment that the corrosion will also consume their flesh with fire is a mixing of metaphors intended to portray the horror of the eschatological fire reserved for the selfish rich. The reference in James 5:3 prepares a reader for the following condemnation charged against the fraudulent employers who have deprived their day-laborers of their pay (5:4). They will face, not a present day for feasting, but a future day for slaughter (5:5), because God himself resists their selfish actions (5:6). The reference to fire recalls 3:5–6 where fire was not only destructive, but its source was hell. This language emerges from a strong OT tradition that connects God's judgment with fire (Isa. 30:27, 30; Jer. 5:14; Ezek. 15:7; Amos 1:12, 14), and there is a similar use of "fire" by Jesus (Matt. 13:42; Mark 9:47–48).

⁵:³ᵈ ἐθησαυρίσατε: This structural marker is a second person plural aorist active indicative of θησαυρίζω that conveys the idea of keeping some material thing safe by storing it someplace and may be rendered "lay up" or "store" (BDAG, s.v. "θησαυρίζω" 1, p. 456). **Syntactically**, it is the main verb of the independent asyndeton clause. The subject is the "you" assumed in the verb (ἐθησαυρίσατε), which of course continues James's discussion about the rich. **Semantically**, the aorist tense is a consummative aorist that stresses

the cessation of an act. It implies that an act was brought to a conclusion (W, 559–60). Thus, "you *have* hoarded treasure" (NET; cf. NIV NLT), "you *have* laid up treasure" (ASV NRSV ESV CNT), "you *have* stored up your treasure" (NASB; cf. KJV).

5:4a ἰδού: This structural marker is a second person singular aorist middle imperative of ὁράω that conveys a closer consideration and contemplation of something and is often rendered "consider," "look," or "remember" (BDAG, s.v. "ὁράω" 1c, p. 468). **Syntactically**, it introduces an independent asyndeton clause calling attention to the defrauding of a worker's wage by an employer. **Semantically**, it is often used as prompter of attention and rendered "look" (NIV NET CNT; cf. Adam, 92), "behold" (KJV ASV NASB ESV CNT), or "listen" (NRSV). Here we render it as "consider *how*," thereby calling closer consideration of its object, worker, defrauded of their wages (cf. 3:4).

> **Semantical Nugget:** What is the function of ἰδού? This word is not defined simply by its parsing but is an "orienter" that draws attention to a following example of a principle just stated or alerts the reader to look at the subject in more of its details (BDAG, s.v. "ἰδού" 1c, p. 468). In 3:4–5, the word points to examples in life of small things that have inordinately large effects. In 5:7b, it calls attention to the farmer, who is an example of patience. In 5:9c, it calls attention to the divine judge, who is an example of correct judging. In 5:11a–b, it points to Job, who is an example of endurance. Here in 5:4a, it calls attention to the defrauding of wages by employers, an example of the selfishness of some rich people.

κράζει: This Greek word is a third person singular present active indicative of κράζω that conveys the idea of communicating something with a loud voice and may be rendered "call" or "cry out" (BDAG, s.v. "κράζω" 2bβ, p. 564). **Syntactically**, it is the main verb of the independent asyndeton clause with "the wage" (ὁ μισθός) as its subject. Thus, the noun "the wage" (ὁ μισθός) is personified with speech capabilities. **Semantically**, the present tense is an iterative present that depicts action that occurs time and time again (W, 520–21). It is vividly portraying "the wage" "crying out" on a regular basis. This action recalls the figure of Abel's blood personified and described as crying out to God (Gen. 4:10), and later when Abel's faith is personified and described as crying out (Heb. 11:4; cf. Bateman et al., 303–4).

5:4b τῶν ἀμησάντων: This articular (τῶν) structural marker is a genitive plural masculine aorist active participle of ἀμάω that may be rendered "mow fields" (BDAG, s.v. "ἀμάω," p. 52). **Syntactically**, it is the main verb of this dependent participial clause that functions adverbially modifying "the laborers" (τῶν ἐρ-γατῶν). It appears under τῶν ἐργατῶν to visualize the clause's dependence.

Semantically, the aorist tense is a constative aorist that discusses events about the worker as a whole, namely, he mows fields (W, 557–58).

> **Syntactical Nugget:** How is the complex syntax for 5:4 to be understood? The Greek syntax in the first clause of 5:4 can appear to be a bit complex, so translators have struggled to express the thought clearly while not straying too far from its formal structure and word order. The attributive participle clause ὁ ἀπεστερημένος clearly references the wage (μισθός) since both are singular and in the nominative case. The intervening attributive participle clause "those who mowed your fields" (τῶν ἀμησάντων τὰς χώρας ὑμῶν) provides a challenge for rendering a faithful but smooth translation, because the predicate is at the end of the sentence and the subject is at its beginning. For purposes of clarity, it is advisable to avoid using the passive voice and express the ideas by two coordinate clauses: "You have defrauded the workers who mow your fields and their missing wages are crying out against you to the Lord of *Sabaoth*."

5:4c ὁ ἀπεστερημένος This articular (ὁ) structural marker is a nominative singular masculine perfect passive participle of ἀποστερέω that conveys the idea of causing another to suffer monetary loss by way of illicit means and may be rendered as "stolen" or "held back" (BDAG, s.v. "ἀποστερέω" 1, p. 121). **Syntactically,** it is the main verb of this dependent participial clause that functions adverbially modifying "the wage" (ὁ μισθός). Although this participial clause is separated by another attributive clause, it is placed under ὁ μισθός to visualize its relationship to the independent asyndeton clause. **Semantically,** the perfect tense is an extensive perfect that emphasized the completed action of the past (W, 577–78) and is rendered "you *have* held back" (NET; Zerwick et al., 700), "you *have* cheated of their pay" (NLT), or as we have rendered it "you *have* stolen." Yet, it is possible to interpret the perfect tense as an intensive perfect that emphasizes the result of the present state produced by a past action and rendered as "you kept back" (KJV ASV NRSV ESV CNT) or "you failed to pay" (NIV).

> **Text-Critical Nugget:** What is the variant reading for ἀπεστερημένος in James 5:4? The reading ἀπεστερημένος is supported by the manuscripts A B² Ψ 33, the Majority Text, and the Tyndale House GNT. The variant ἀπεστερημένος is thought to be an Alexandrian refinement by the editors of NA²⁸ but has strong textual support from ℵ and B*. The difference in meaning between the two readings is not all that significant, nor does it necessarily affect the meaning of 5:4. It is possible that the earliest reading is ἀπεστερημένος but was later emended to match Malachi 3:5, to which James alludes. "A majority of the Committee preferred to read ἀπεστερημένος, but the minority preferred the

rare word ἀπυστερημένος, which copyists emended to a more familiar word" (Metzger², 685; cf. Metzger¹, 614).

5:4d καί: This structural marker is a conjunction meaning "and" (BDAG, s.v. "καί" 1b, p. 494). **Syntactically**, it introduces an independent conjunctive clause. **Semantically**, it is a coordinating conjunction often rendered "and" (NET ESV NASB NRSV etc.) that adds to James's description about the defrauding of an employee.

εἰσεληλύθασιν: This Greek word is a third person plural perfect active indicative of εἰσέρχομαι that conveys the idea of initiating an event and may be rendered "reach" or "come" (BDAG, s.v. "εἰσέρχομαι" 3, p. 294). **Syntactically**, it is the main verb of this independent conjunctive clause with "the cries" (αἱ βοαί) as its subject. **Semantically**, the perfect tense is an extensive perfect that emphasizes the completed action of the past cries of an employee (W, 577–78) and is rendered "have reached" (NASB NRSV NIV ESV NET NLT CNT). The verb describes how the cries of day laborers who have been defrauded of their promised daily wage (cf. the scene in Matt. 20:1–16). They "have entered into the ears of the Lord of *Sabaoth*" (εἰς τὰ ὦτα κυρίου σαβαωθ εἰσεληλύθασιν). The anthropomorphism about God's ears is apparent and telling. . . . God hears our cries.

Quotation Nugget: What is the significance of the Isaiah quotation in James 5:4? This is another OT allusion, even a quotation, and it is indicated that way by the italicized form of those words in NA²⁸ and by the footnote in UBS⁵. The quotation is from either Isaiah 5:9 or 22:14 (in the LXX) and becomes obvious when we realize that these two verses are the only other places where the figurative expression, "the ears of the Lord of Hosts," is utilized before James employs it. The citation is even more obvious when we recognize that the context of Isaiah 5:9 is about the oppression of the poor and the context of Isaiah 22:14 describes the extravagant lives of the rich, both of which are echoed in the language of James in the context of 5:1–6. In a similar scene of suffering, "the cries" (αἱ βοαί) of the defrauded Israelites in Egypt ascended to God (Exod. 2:23).

5:5a ἐτρυφήσατε: This structural marker is a second person plural aorist active indicative of τρυφάω that conveys the idea of leading a life of self-indulgence and may be rendered as "live for pleasure" or "carouse" (BDAG, s.v. "τρυφάω," p. 1018). **Syntactically**, it is the main verb of this independent asyndeton clause with "you" assumed in ἐτρυφήσατε as the subject. James's focus remains on the rich person. **Semantically**, the aorist tense is a consummative aorist that stresses the cessation of an act whereby it implies that an act was already in progress and the aorist brings the action to a conclusion (W, 559–60).

Thus, the rich "*have* lived for pleasure" (KJV NASB NRSV NIV ESV NET CNT) or "*have* lived in luxury" (Zerwick et al., 700).

⁵:⁵ᵇ καί: This structural marker is a conjunction meaning "and" (BDAG, s.v. "καί" 1b, p. 494). **Syntactically**, it introduces an independent conjunctive clause. **Semantically**, it is a coordinating conjunction often rendered "and" (NET ESV NASB NRSV etc.) that adds to James's description about living for pleasure.

ἐσπαταλήσατε: This Greek word is a second person plural aorist active indicative of σπαταλάω that conveys the idea of indulging oneself in things beyond property and may be rendered as "live luxuriously" (BDAG, s.v. "σπαταλάω," p. 936). **Syntactically**, it is the main verb of this independent asyndeton clause with "you" assumed in ἐσπαταλήσατε as the subject. James's focus remains on the rich person. **Semantically**, the aorist tense is a consummative aorist that stresses the cessation of an act whereby it implies that an act was already in progress and the aorist brings the action to a conclusion (W, 559–60). Thus, the rich "*have* lived in luxury."

⁵:⁵ᶜ ἐθρέψατε: This structural marker is a second person plural aorist active indicative of τρέφω that conveys the idea of caring for by providing food or nourishment and may be rendered "feed," "nourish," or "fatten" (BDAG, s.v. "τρέφω" 1, p. 1015). **Syntactically**, it is the main verb of an independent asyndeton clause with "you" assumed in ἐθρέψατε as the subject. James's concern again remains the rich person. **Semantically**, the aorist tense is a consummative aorist that stresses the cessation of an act whereby it implies that an act was already in progress and that the aorist brings the action to a conclusion (W, 559–60). Thus, it is rendered "you *have* fattened your hearts" (NASB NRSV ESV NET CNT), "you *have* fattened yourselves" (NIV NLT), or "you *have* nourished hearts" (KJV ASV). The description "day of slaughter" (ἡμέρα σφαγῆς; genitive of description) affects our choice of "fatten" for the translation of ἐθρέψατε. It also recalls the prophetic denunciation (as it does throughout this entire passage) of a passage like Isaiah 22:12–13. The expression thus balances "in the last days" in 5:3d. The wealthy landowners, like well-fed oxen, were unconsciously fattening themselves for their slaughter.

Grammatical Nugget: How does the repetitive use of the aorist tense in James 5:5–6 affect James's message? The five consecutive clauses, each anchored by an aorist indicative verb, deliver in rapid-fire style the accusations against the rich defrauders. They have engaged in gross self-enrichment, which James conveys by the colorful alliteration of the aorist verbs (ἐτρυφήσατε, ἐσπαταλήσατε, ἐθρέψατε). They led prodigal lives at the same time they inflicted such terrible hardships on their poor employees. The aorist tenses convey that idea from the perspective of the future judgment. While the cries of their victims ascended to *heaven*, the rich were living in luxury on *earth*, oblivious of the wrath to come. The aorist tense of these five verbs conveys a consummative idea, pointing toward the conclusion of what they have done. The verbs stands alone, with no modifiers like prepositional phrases, but they further indicate the voluptuous lives that these oppressors had led.

5:6a κατεδικάσατε: This structural marker is a second person plural aorist active indicative of καταδικάζω that conveys the idea of pronouncing someone guilty of something and may be rendered as "condemn" (BDAG, s.v. "καταδικάζω," p. 516). **Syntactically**, it is the main verb of this independent asyndeton clause with "you" assumed in κατεδικάσατε as the subject. James's concern again remains the rich person. **Semantically**, the aorist tense is a consummative aorist that stresses the cessation of an act whereby it implies that an act was already in progress and the aorist brings the action to a conclusion (W, 559–60). Thus, it is rendered "you *have* condemned" (KJV ASV NASB NRSV NIV ESV NET NLT CNT).

Historical Nugget: What is the significance of James's appeal to the rich who condemn the poor? The actions listed here of the rich and greedy landowners include judicial acts of condemnation (κατεδικάσατε) and even murder (ἐφονεύσατε). The verb καταδικάζω is often found in a forensic context, as a sentence of condemnation given against someone for committing a crime (Job 34:29; Josephus, *Ant.* 7.271; Matt. 12:37; Acts 25:15). The judicial nature of 5:6 recalls the earlier, vividly described court scene in 2:1–4. In that passage, it was said that the rich drag the poor believers into court and deal with them unjustly (2:6–7). It is a description of the abuse of power by the powerful against the powerless, a theme that runs throughout the OT. The use of this verb appears in the same context in the LXX (Ps. 93:21; Lam. 3:36). See also this action described and condemned in Sirach 34:25–27. Another appearance of this verb in the NT offers an interesting parallel: "If you had known what this means, 'I want mercy and not sacrifice,' you wouldn't have *condemned* [κατεδικάσατε] the innocent" (Matt. 12:7).

5:6b [καί]: This structural marker is a conjunction meaning "and" (BDAG, s.v. "καί" 1b, p. 494). **Syntactically**, it introduces an independent conjunctive clause. **Semantically**, the bracketed [καί] is an ellipsis that serves as a coordinating conjunction rendered as "and," and is often inserted by translations (NASB NRSV ESV NET NLT CNT). It adds to James's description about the ill treatment of the poor.

ἐφονεύσατε: This Greek word is a second person plural aorist active indicative of φονεύω that conveys the idea of eliminating the life of another and may be rendered as "murder" or "kill" (BDAG, s.v. "φονεύω," p. 1063). **Syntactically**, it is the main verb of this independent conjunctive clause with "you" assumed in ἐφονεύσατε as the subject. James's focus again remains on the rich person. **Semantically**, the aorist tense is a consummative aorist that stresses the cessation of an act whereby it implies that an act was already in progress and the aorist brings the action to a conclusion (W, 559–60). Thus, it is rendered "you *have* murdered" (Zerwick et al., 700).

> **Lexical and Figurative Nugget:** Are "the righteous" (τὸν δίκαιον) and the "murderer" (ἐφονεύσατε) literal in James 5:6? A lot of evidence can be assembled for the idea that this substantive serving as the direct object of the predicate ἐφονεύσατε actually refers to the Righteous One—namely, the Messiah. This was a title applied to Jesus by early sermonizers as Peter (Acts 3:14), Stephen (Acts 7:52), and Paul (Acts 22:14). Linguistic roots for this messianic title can also be found in such OT texts as Isaiah 3:10 and 53:11. It is also possible that the substantive adjective is a collective term for the righteous poor, who are the subjects of the oppression described in the context. Thus, the murder accusation may be hyperbolic in its rhetoric. Rhetorical "murder" may be the charge. We cannot, however, reject outright the idea that this should be taken in a very literal sense. If laborers who depend on receiving their pay at the end of the day (Matt. 20:1–16) are thus defrauded, the loss of their promised daily bread may actually lead to the deaths of family members. These heartless employers, therefore, are directly to blame for their sufferings and possible deaths (Moo, 2000, 219).

5:6c οὐκ ἀντιτάσσεται: This negated (οὐκ) structural marker is a third person singular present middle indicative of ἀντιτάσσω that conveys the idea of resisting another person and may be rendered "oppose" or "resist" (BDAG, s.v. "ἀντιτάσσω," p. 90). **Syntactically**, it is the main verb of this independent asyndeton clause with God as the subject of an interrogative question expecting a positive answer (Varner[2], 349–51). **Semantically**, the present tense is a gnomic present that describes an action that generally happens or a timeless fact about God (W, 523–24), namely, God does resist the rich from the mistreatment of the poor.

> **Quotation Nugget:** Does the Proverbs quotation in James 4:6 affect identifying the subject of the interrogative question of James 5:6? One of the keys to determining the subject of James 5:6 is the sudden switch in tense from the series of aorist verbs to this single present verb, ἀντιτάσσεται, and the appearance of that same form of the verb in 4:6: ὁ θεὸς ὑπερηφάνοις

ἀντιτάσσεται. Thus 5:6c then becomes a question, with God the one who is doing the opposing: "Does he [God] not oppose you?" The simple argument is that ἀντιτάσσεται has appeared earlier in this exact tense form in 4:6, where it is part of a quotation from LXX Proverbs 3:34: "God opposes [ἀντιτάσσεται] the proud but gives grace to the humble." James 5:6c, therefore, concludes the subsequent commentary by James on that quotation. This approach best explains the present tense of ἀντιτάσσεται and the lack of a specific subject. This proposal also helps to explain the lack of a conjunction that would connect the clause to what precedes. For example, some have suggested that the sense of the verse is: "You murdered the righteous one, *but* he does not oppose you." The asyndeton, however, supports the idea that someone other than "the righteous one" who was just mentioned is the actual subject of ἀντιτάσσεται (Varner[2], 176).

James 5:7–20

Big Greek Idea: Ingredients for living life well involve following several simple expectations: be patient, be positive, be honest, and be a person of prayer.

Structural Overview: James opens with a string of exhortations about patience (vv. 7–8), grumbling (v. 9), integrity (v. 12), and prayer (vv. 13, 16). He opens with three distinct expectations about living life with patience like a farmer, followed closely by expectation of enduring life's difficulties without grumbling like the prophets and Job, followed by an expectation to be honest with one another to prevent judgment (vv. 7–12). James transitions to a new theme about prayer, beginning with the expectation to pray in the midst of any suffering, followed by an expectation to call elders to pray when ill, followed by an expectation to confess and pray about wrongdoing, and closes with an expectation to pray for those who may be drifting away from God (vv. 13–20).

Outline:

Live Life with Patience, with Positivity, and with Integrity (5:7–12).
Live Life by Praying if Suffering, if Ill, if Drifting from God (5:13–20).

LIVE LIFE WITH PATIENCE, WITH POSITIVITY, AND WITH INTEGRITY (JAMES 5:7–12)[1]

CLAUSAL OUTLINE FOR JAMES 5:7–12

5:7a **Μακροθυμήσατε** <u>οὖν</u>, ἀδελφοί, ἕως τῆς παρουσίας τοῦ κυρίου.
5:7a <u>Therefore</u>, **be patient,** brothers *and sisters,* until the coming of the Lord.

5:7b **ἰδοὺ** ὁ γεωργὸς **ἐκδέχεται** τὸν τίμιον καρπὸν τῆς γῆς
5:7b **Consider** *how* the farmer **waits** for the precious fruit of the earth

        |
        5:7c **μακροθυμῶν** ἐπ᾽ αὐτῷ,
        5:7c *by* **being patient** about it,

        |
        5:7d <u>ἕως</u> **λάβῃ** πρόϊμον καὶ ὄψιμον
        5:7d <u>*until*</u> **it receives** the early and the late rains.

5:8a **μακροθυμήσατε** καὶ ὑμεῖς,
5:8a You, also, **be patient,**

---

1. A suggested sermon entitled "Rich in Virtues" has been offered for these verses (see Baker et al., 148–154). Four points might be "Be Patient" (5:7–8), "Be Positive" (5:9), "Be Persistent" (5:10–11), and "Be Prudent" (5:12).

5:8b **στηρίξατε** τὰς καρδίας ὑμῶν,
5:8b **establish** your hearts,

|
5:8c <u>ὅτι</u> ἡ παρουσία τοῦ κυρίου **ἤγγικεν**.
5:8c <u>because</u> the coming of the Lord **is at hand**.

5:9a <u>μὴ</u> **στενάζετε**, ἀδελφοί, κατ' ἀλλήλων,
5:9a **Do** <u>not</u> **grumble** against one another, brothers *and sisters*,

|
5:9b <u>ἵνα μὴ</u> **κριθῆτε**·
5:9b <u>in order that</u> **you may** not **be judged**.

5:9c **ἰδοὺ** ὁ κριτὴς πρὸ τῶν θυρῶν **ἕστηκεν**
5:9c **Consider** *how* the judge at the gates **judges**.

5:10a ὑπόδειγμα **λάβετε**, ἀδελφοί, τῆς κακοπαθείας καὶ τῆς μακροθυμίας
τοὺς προφήτας
5:10a As an example of patient suffering, brothers *and sisters*, **take** the prophets

5:10b οἳ **ἐλάλησαν** ἐν τῷ ὀνόματι κυρίου.
5:10b <u>who</u> **spoke** in the name of the Lord.

5:11a **ἰδοὺ μακαρίζομεν** τοὺς ὑπομείναντας·
5:11a **Consider** *how* *we call* **blessed** those who have endured.

5:11b τὴν ὑπομονὴν Ἰὼβ **ἠκούσατε**
5:11b **You have heard** of the endurance of Job,

5:11c <u>καὶ</u> τὸ τέλος κυρίου **εἴδετε**,
5:11c <u>and</u> **you have seen** the Lord's outcome,

|
5:11d <u>ὅτι</u> πολύσπλαγχνός **ἐστιν** ὁ κύριος καὶ οἰκτίρμων.
5:11d <u>that</u> the Lord **is** compassionate and merciful.

5:12a Πρὸ πάντων <u>δέ</u>, ἀδελφοί μου, <u>μὴ</u> **ὀμνύετε** μήτε τὸν οὐρανὸν μήτε τὴν
γῆν μήτε ἄλλον τινὰ ὅρκον·
5:12a <u>And</u> above all, my brothers *and sisters*, **do** <u>not</u> **swear** an oath, neither by heav-
en nor by earth nor by any other oath.

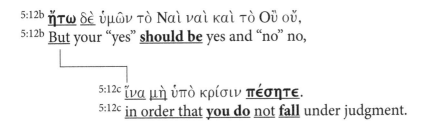

5:12b **ἤτω** δὲ ὑμῶν τὸ Ναὶ ναὶ καὶ τὸ Οὒ οὔ,
5:12b But your "yes" **should be** yes and "no" no,

5:12c ἵνα μὴ ὑπὸ κρίσιν **πέσητε**.
5:12c in order that **you do** not **fall** under judgment.

Syntax Explained for James 5:7–12

5:7a οὖν: This structural marker is a conjunction that may be rendered "therefore" (BDAG, s.v. "οὖν" 1a, p. 736). **Syntactically**, it introduces an independent conjunctive clause: "Be patient, *therefore*, brothers *and sisters*" (μακροθυμή-σατε οὖν, ἀδελφοί), and appears in a post-positive position. **Semantically**, it is an inferential conjunction that introduces the result or deduction from what was said previously: "therefore" (KJV NASB NRSV ESV CNT) or "then" (NIV), though some leave it as unrendered (NET NLT). James is drawing a deduction, conclusion, or summary about the rich mentioned in previous verses and the forthcoming need for the poor to be patient (Adam, 95). Yet, this unit could be seen as a new section (Varner[2], 180).

μακροθυμήσατε: This Greek word is a second person plural aorist active imperative of μακροθυμέω that conveys the idea of remaining tranquil while waiting and may be rendered "have patience" or "wait" (BDAG, s.v. "μακρο-θυμέω" 1, p. 612). **Syntactically**, it is the main verb of this independent conjunctive clause with "you" as the subject embedded in μακροθυμήσατε. The following prepositional phrase "until the coming of the Lord" (ἕως τῆς πα-ρουσίας τοῦ κυρίου) is its complement. **Semantically**, the aorist imperative depicts a command as a whole (W, 485–86; BDF, §337) about a farmer's patience. Thus, "be patient" (Zerwick et al., 700).

> **Lexical Nugget:** What is the significance of the "patience" in James 1:2–12 and 5:7a, 11a? Unlike in 1:2–12 where the emphasis was on the endurance (ὑπομένω/ὑπομονή) of difficult situations, here in 5:7a the emphasis is on patience (μακροθυμέω/μακροθυμία) with other people (the Lord) and is also portrayed in the illustration of Job in James 5:11a. Although rare in secular Greek, the μακροθυμ-cognates are commonly used in the LXX, sometimes with reference to God's attribute of "long-suffering" (Ps. 86:15), and sometimes in passages commending the virtue to people (Prov. 19:11).

5:7b ἰδού: This structural marker is a second person singular aorist middle imperative of ὁράω that conveys a closer consideration or contemplation of something and is often rendered "consider," "look," or "remember" (BDAG, s.v. "ὁράω" 1c, p. 468). **Syntactically**, it introduces an independent asyndeton clause calling attention to the farmer's patience. **Semantically**, it is often used as a prompter of attention and rendered "think" (NET), "consider" (NLT), "behold" (KJV ASV) or "see" (NIV ESV CNT). Still other translations leave it untranslated (NRSV). Here we render it as "consider *how*" and thereby call closer consideration of its object, a farmer's patience (cf. 3:4a; 5:4a).

ἐκδέχεται: This Greek word is a third person singular present middle indicative of ἐκδέχομαι that conveys the idea of remaining in a place while awaiting the arrival of someone and may be rendered "wait" (BDAG, s.v. "ἐκδέχομαι," p. 300). **Syntactically**, it is the main verb in this independent asyndeton clause with "the farmer" (ὁ γεωργός) as the subject and "for the precious fruit" (τὸν τίμιον καρπόν) as its direct object. **Semantically**, the present tense is customary present (W, 521–22). It describes a regular pattern of behavior of the farmer, namely, how the farmer waits: patiently (NASB NRSV NIV ESV NET CNT). The verb elsewhere twice describes Paul waiting for his co-workers (Acts 17:16; 1 Cor. 16:11), believers waiting for one another at communion (1 Cor. 11:33), and Abraham's waiting for the future city (Heb. 11:10; cf. Bateman et al.[1], 308–9).

5:7c μακροθυμῶν: This structural marker is a nominative singular masculine present active participle of μακροθυμέω that conveys the idea of remaining tranquil while waiting and may be rendered as "have patience" or "wait" (BDAG, s.v. "μακροθυμέω" 1, p. 612). **Syntactically**, it is the main verb of this dependent participial clause that functions adverbially modifying the verb "wait" (ἐκδέχεται). It is placed immediately under ἐκδέχεται to visualize its relationship. **Semantically**, it is a participle of manner that expresses how a farmer acts emotionally or what that farmer's attitude is (W, 627–28) and is rendered "*by* being patient." The present tense is customary present (W, 521–22). It describes a regular pattern of behavior for the farmer, he waits: "the farmer waits" (NASB NRSV NIV ESV NET CNT). Between the fronted imperatives μακροθυμήσατε in 5:7a and 5:8a, James sets forth an illustration of that patience: the farmer's patient waiting for the early and late rains in the autumn and spring seasons.

5:7d ἕως λάβῃ: This structural marker, ἕως, is a preposition appearing before a third person singular aorist active subjunctive of λαμβάνω that conveys the idea of being a receiver of something and may be rendered as "receive," "get," or "obtain" (BDAG, s.v. "λαμβάνω" 10b, p. 584). **Syntactically**, it introduces an adverbial clause: "*until* it receives" (ἕως λάβῃ), which modifies "wait" (ἐκδέχεται) and is placed under ἐκδέχεται to visualize its contribution to the independent asyndeton clause. Its subject is the pronoun "it" (αὐτῷ), which refers back to "the earth" (τῆς γῆς), and its direct object is πρόϊμον καὶ ὄψιμον. **Semantically**, it has a temporal force due to the improper preposition "until" (ἕως; W, 362; Adam, 81). The aorist tense is a constative aorist that stresses action as a whole (W, 557–58), namely, the farmer's patience.

> **Backgrounds Nugget:** What is the seasonal distinction of πρόϊμον καὶ ὄψιμον in James 5:7? The farmer patiently waits (μακροθυμῶν) for the early and later rains in the autumn and spring seasons. The "early rain" was the rain of seed time, and the "later rain" was the rain of ripening before harvest. The first rain still falls in Israel about the beginning of November, after the seed is sown. The second rain ends around April, when the grain is ripening, and is thus prepared for the full harvest in the late spring. Without these two rains, the earth would be unfruitful. These "rains" were promised by God in the OT (Deut. 11:14). For these seasonal blessings, the Israelites were not only to wait patiently, but also to pray (see Zech. 10:1). This agricultural analogy is consistent with an eastern Mediterranean provenance for the letter.

5:8a μακροθυμήσατε: This structural marker is a second person plural aorist active imperative of μακροθυμέω that conveys the idea of remaining tranquil while waiting and may be rendered as "have patience" or "wait" (BDAG, s.v. "μακροθυμέω" 1, p. 612). **Syntactically**, it is the main verb of this independent asyndeton clause with the assumed "you" as subject embedded in μακροθυμήσατε. **Semantically**, this aorist imperative depicts the command as a whole (W, 485–86; BDF, §337) about patience of the poor to model that of a farmer.

5:8b στηρίξατε: This structural marker is a second person plural aorist active imperative of στηρίζω that conveys the idea of causing something to be inwardly firm and may be rendered "establish," "confirm," or "strengthen" (BDAG, s.v. "στηρίζω" 2, p. 945). **Syntactically**, it is the main verb of this independent asyndeton clause with "you" as subject embedded in στηρίξατε and with "your hearts" (τὰς καρδίας ὑμῶν) as its direct object. **Semantically**, this aorist imperative depicts a command as a whole (W, 485–86) about patience of the poor to be strong. It is rendered as "establish" (KJV ASV ESV), "strengthen" (NASB NRSV NET), or "take courage" (NLT). James is obviously expressing a contrast with the rich who fatten their hearts for their own future judgment (slaughter) in 5:5c.

5:8c ὅτι: This structural marker is a conjunction translated here as "because" (BDAG, s.v. "ὅτι" 4a, p. 732). **Syntactically**, it introduces a dependent conjunctive clause. The entire ὅτι clause functions adverbially modifying the verb "establish" (στηρίξατε). The clause is placed under στηρίξατε in order to visualize the clause's relationship to the independent asyndeton clause. **Semantically**, it is causal, providing the reason for the poor to establish their hearts (W, 460–61; Adam,

96). While we render the causal relationship with "because" (cf. NIV), others render it with "for" (KJV ASV NASB NRSV ESV NET NLT CNT).

ἤγγικεν: This Greek word is a third person singular perfect active indicative of ἐγγίζω that conveys the idea of drawing near in a temporal sense and may be rendered as "draw near," "come near," or "approach" (BDAG, s.v. "ἐγγίζω" 2, p. 270). **Syntactically**, it is the main verb of a dependent conjunctive clause that states the reason to be patient. Its subject is "the coming" (ἡ παρουσία). **Semantically**, the perfect tense is an intensive perfect that emphasizes the result of the present state produced by a past action (W, 574–76) and rendered as "is near" (NASB NRSV NIV NET NLT CNT) or "is at hand" (ASV ESV). It is part of an eschatological theme that has been evident throughout the passage (5:1, 3, 5, 7) and here continues with another clear reference to the παρουσία.

> **Theological Nugget:** What is the significance of ἡ παρουσία in 5:7a and 5:8c? This Greek word for "coming" or "arrival" quickly became a technical term for Jesus's coming in glory and as judge. The use of ἡ παρουσία elsewhere in the NT refers to the return of Jesus—and that is undoubtedly the use of τοῦ κυρίου here. Therefore, this is the third explicit reference to Jesus in the book (see 1:1; 2:1). The noun is a technical term in other NT documents from the earliest to the latest periods of their composition: Matthew 24:3, 27, 37, 39; 1 Corinthians 15:23; 1 Thessalonians 2:19; 3:13; 4:15; 5:23; 2 Thessalonians 2:1, 8, 9 (contrasted with the coming of the Antichrist); 2 Peter 1:16; 3:4; and 1 John 2:28.

5:9a μὴ στενάζετε: This negated (μή) structural marker is a second person plural present active imperative of στενάζω that conveys the idea of expressing discontent and may be rendered as "complain" or "groan" (BDAG, s.v. "στενάζω" 2, p. 942). **Syntactically**, it is the main verb of this independent asyndeton clause with "you" as the subject assumed in the imperative στενάζετε but with no direct object because it is an intransitive verb. **Semantically**, the imperative with μή is an imperative of a prohibition (W, 487–88; cf. BDF, §427(4)). The present tense is a customary present that conveys a regular practice of complaining (W, 521–22). Together, the present tense imperative with μή describes the cessation of activity in progress (W, 724–25). In other words, stop your continual complaining. It is simply translated "murmur not" (ASV), "do not complain" (NASB), or "do not grumble" (NRSV NIV ESV NET NLT CNT). While the three imperatives in 5:7–8 were positive and commended appropriate behaviors and attitudes to emulate, here the negated imperative is fronted and forbids the negative act of grumbling.

> **Lexical Nugget:** What is the meaning of στενάζετε in James 5:9a? The verb is frequently used in the LXX for the utterance of various kinds of

pain and grief (Exod. 2:23; Jer. 22:23; Lam. 1:11). A farmer may be tempted to grumble when the needed rains are delayed. In the same manner,
the brothers may be tempted to grumble impatiently when the Lord seems
to delay his coming. We ought to cultivate patience, and we ought not to
blame one another for our undeserved distress, for it is part of the inevitable and temporary evil of the present age. So, the negated imperative is
fronted and forbids the negative characteristic of complaining, rather than
the legitimate sense of "groaning" found in Acts 7:34 and Romans 8:26.

5:9b ἵνα: This structural marker is a conjunction meaning "that" or "in order that"
as an objective marker (BDAG, s.v. "ἵνα" 1aα, p. 475). **Syntactically**, it introduces a dependent conjunctive clause that is functioning adverbially modifying "do not grumble" (μὴ στενάζετε): "*in order that* you may not be judged"
(ἵνα μὴ κριθῆτε). **Semantically**, it is considered as purpose: "in order that"
or "that" (ASV; cf. W, 472–73; Adam, 97). The entire clause provides the intention of James's command to stop grumbling, namely, in order that his readers
might not be judged. Admittedly, however, it is difficult to discern the difference from a result clause, "so that" (NASB NRSV ESV NET), and may be
considered a purpose–result (cf. W, 473–74). Some, however, choose not to
translate ἵνα (NIV NLT).

μὴ κριθῆτε: This negated (μή) Greek word is a second person plural aorist passive subjunctive of κρίνω that conveys the idea of engaging in judicial
process presided over by God and may be rendered as "judge" or "condemn"
(BDAG, s.v. "κρίνω" 5bα, p. 568). **Syntactically**, it is the main verb of this
dependent conjunctive clause, a clause that is functioning adverbially with
"you" as its subject assumed in the verb κριθῆτε. The verb is in the subjunctive mood because ἵνα takes its verb in the subjunctive. **Semantically**, the
negated (μή) aorist tense is a constative aorist describing an event as a whole
(W, 557–58) and is typically rendered: "you may not be judged" (NASB NRSV
ESV NET CNT). This may echo a Jesus-saying about judging in Matthew 7:1.
It is also appropriately employed here, especially with the similar use of the
word group κρίνω/κριτὴς in the verse.

5:9c ἰδού: This structural marker is a second person singular aorist middle imperative of ὁράω that conveys a closer consideration or contemplation of
something and is often rendered "consider," "look," or "remember" (BDAG,
s.v. "ὁράω" 1c, p. 468). **Syntactically**, it introduces an independent asyndeton
clause calling attention to judges. **Semantically**, it is often used as a prompter
of attention and rendered "see" (NRSV NET; cf. NLT), or "behold" (KJV ASV
NASB ESV CNT). Still one version leaves it untranslated (NIV). Here we render it as "consider *how*," thereby calling closer consideration of its object, a
judge's judging at the gates of a city (cf. 3:4a; 5:4a, 7b).

ἕστηκεν: This Greek word is a third person singular perfect active indicative of ἵστημι that conveys the idea of being at a place where the emphasis is not so much on standing but rather being there, and may be rendered "standing" or "existing (there)" (BDAG, s.v. "ἵστημι" C2a, p. 483). **Syntactically**, it is the main verb of this independent asyndeton clause with "the judge" (ὁ κριτής) as the subject. **Semantically**, the perfect tense is an intensive perfect that emphasizes the result of the present state produced by a past action (W, 574–76; Adam, 97) and is rendered as "is standing" (NASB NRSV NIV NLT CNT) or "stands" (KJV ASV NET). Yet, we render "is standing" as "judges" because it was at the city gates where judges stood and where they made their judgments.

> **Theological Nugget:** Why does James focus on God's judgment in 5:9b? The statement echoes 5:8a as a positive reason to establish the hearts of the patient sufferers in 5:8c. It underscores the danger believers face if they wrongfully judge and condemn one other. James utilizes a phrase that Jesus himself had used (cf. Matt. 24:33; Mark 13:29). The sense may be as much spatial as it is temporal, for James notes at once that "the judge stands before the gate." Such categories used with reference to God are anthropomorphic.

5:10a λάβετε: This structural marker is a second person plural aorist active imperative of λαμβάνω that conveys the idea of getting hold of something by laying hands on or grasping something and may be rendered "take," "take hold of," or "grasp" (BDAG, s.v. "λαμβάνω" 1, p. 583). **Syntactically**, it is the main verb of this independent asyndeton clause addressing the ἀδελφοί with ὑπόδειγμα as its direct object. **Semantically**, the aorist tense is a constative aorist that describes an event as a whole (W, 557–58), namely, the patient suffering of the prophets.

> **Grammatical Nugget:** How are the prophets as an example of ὑπόδειγμα . . . τοὺς προφήτας in 5:10a to be rendered? These two accusatives are a "double accusative" construction (ὑπόδειγμα . . . τοὺς προφήτας) following the command to "take" (Porter, 89). The two articular nouns τῆς κακοπαθείας καὶ τῆς μακροθυμίας are also an example of a hendiadys (cf. Adam, 97). The initial ὑπόδειγμα is in a prominent position and may be rendered *"As an example of **patient suffering**, brothers and sisters, take the prophets . . ."* By fronting the second accusative, ὑπόδειγμα, the reader's attention is drawn to the two prominent "exemplars"—both the prophets in this verse and Job in 5:11. The LXX text says as much in Jeremiah 20:9 and 44:16. Even the most eminent servants of God had been exposed to suffering and hardship. The noun was used earlier in Jewish literature to call attention to the example of Israel's spiritual heroes (Sir

44:16; 2 Macc 6:28, 31). The prophets are also exemplars *of patient suf-fering* in Matthew 5:12, 37; 23:34; Luke 11:49; Acts 7:52; 1 Thessalonians 2:15; and Hebrews 11:33.

5:10b οἵ: This structural marker is a nominative plural masculine from the relative pronoun ὅ meaning "who" (BDAG, s.v. "ὅ" 1a, p. 725). **Syntactically**, it iden-tifies the clause as a dependent relative clause: "*who* spoke in the name of the Lord" (οἳ ἐλάλησαν ἐν τῷ ὀνόματι κυρίου). Because οἵ agrees in number and gender with τοὺς προφήτας, the entire clause modifies "the prophets" (τοὺς προφήτας). Since οἵ is nominative, it is the subject of "spoke" (ἐλά-λησαν).

ἐλάλησαν: This Greek word is a third person plural aorist active indicative of λαλέω that conveys the idea of uttering words and may be rendered as "speak" (BDAG, s.v. "λαλέω" 2aβ, p. 582). **Syntactically**, it is the main verb in the dependent relative clause introduced by οἵ as its subject, and the object of the verb is the prepositional phrase ἐν τῷ ὀνόματι κυρίου. **Semantically**, the aorist tense is a constative aorist that describes an event as a whole (W, 557–58), namely, the prophets of the past "who spoke" (NASB NRSV NIV ESV NET NLT).

5:11a ἰδού: This structural marker is a second person singular aorist middle imperative of ὁράω that conveys a closer consideration or contempla-tion of something and is often rendered "consider," "look," or "remember" (BDAG, s.v. "ὁράω" 1c, p. 468). **Syntactically**, it introduces an indepen-dent asyndeton clause calling attention to those who are blessed. **Seman-tically**, it is often used as a prompter of attention and rendered "think" (NET), "indeed" (NRSV), or "behold" (KJV ASV ESV). Still other trans-lations leave it untranslated (NASB NLT). Here we render it as "consider *how*" and thereby calling closer consideration of its object, those who are blessed (cf. 3:4a; 5:4a, 7b, 9c).

μακαρίζομεν: This Greek word is a first person plural present active in-dicative of μακαρίζω that conveys considering someone who is happy and may be rendered as "call blessed," "call happy," or "call fortunate" (BDAG, s.v. "μακαρίζω," p. 610). **Syntactically**, it is the main verb in the independent asyndeton clause with an epistolary plural "we" as its subject (W, 397; Adam, 98), by which James identifies with his readers. Its direct object is "those who have endured" (τοὺς ὑπομείναντας). **Semantically**, the present tense is customary present and affirms what is done on a regular basis (W, 521–22) and is rendered "we consider" (ESV), "we regard" (NET), and "we count" (KJV NASB NIV). More pointedly, "we give great honor" (NLT) to people who have suffered (cf. examples in Heb. 11:1–40; Bateman et al., 299–322).

The verb recalls its cognate noun in such passages as Daniel 12:12: μακάριος ὁ ἐμμένων. The beatitude in Matthew 5:11–12 may also be recalled.

5:11b ἠκούσατε: This structural marker is a second person plural aorist active indicative of ἀκούω that conveys the idea of receiving news or information about something and may be rendered as "learn" (BDAG, s.v. "ἀκούω" 3b, p. 38). **Syntactically**, it is the main verb of the independent asyndeton clause with "you" as the subject assumed in the verb ἠκούσατε. James is appealing to his readers' knowledge of the OT. **Semantically**, the aorist tense is a consummative aorist that stresses the cessation of an act whereby it implies that an act was already in progress and the aorist brings the action to a conclusion (W, 559–60). Thus, it is rendered "you *have* heard" (KJV ASV NASB NRSV NIV ESV NET CNT). The verb reminds us that these believing Jewish readers would have often heard about Job.[2] He appeals to their shared knowledge (cf. "you know" in NLT).

> **Semantical Nugget:** How is Job an example of "endurance" (τὴν ὑπομονήν) rather than "patience" (μακροθυμία)? Job was not always *patient* in his dialogues with his friends that are recorded in Job 3–37. Job also was apparently impatient with God on some occasions (Job 9:27–35; 21:4). If a careful distinction is recognized about the "endurance" (τὴν ὑπομονήν) that Job displayed throughout his trials rather than his "patience" (μακροθυμίας), the problem of Job's improper response at times can be better appreciated. Job was not always patient with his so-called friends, but he did begin and end his trial well (Job 1–2; 42). While struggling with the *why* of God's dealings with him, he never cursed God, although he was encouraged to do so by his wife (Job 2:9). He struggled because of his lack of knowledge of the entire situation, but he endured until the final outcome.

5:11c καί: This structural marker is a conjunction meaning "and" (BDAG, s.v. "καί" 1b, p. 494). **Syntactically**, it introduces an independent conjunctive clause. **Semantically**, it is a coordinating conjunction often rendered "and" (NET ESV NASB NRSV etc.) that adds to James's description about the blessed person who endures life's trials.

εἴδετε: This Greek word is a second person plural aorist active indicative of ὁράω that conveys the idea of mental or spiritual perception and may be rendered "to see" or "perceive" (BDAG, s.v. "ὁράω" 4, p. 719). **Syntactically**, it is the main verb of this independent conjunctive clause with "you" as the

---

2.   Job is the third significant exemplar in James. Job, according to Foster (p. 164), may have been chosen here in the midst of condemning the rich because "the patriarch used his wealth to help the poor." Extra-biblical Jewish sources reveal Job's "'steadfast endurance' rather than the more celebrated 'patience'" (Foster, 128–64).

subject assumed in εἴδετε and "the outcome" (τὸ τέλος) as its direct object. **Semantically**, the aorist tense is a consummative aorist that stresses the cessation of an act whereby it implies that an act was already in progress and the aorist brings the action to a conclusion (W, 559–60; Adam, 98; Irons, 540). Thus, it is rendered "you *have* seen" (KJV ASV NASB NRSV NIV ESV NET CNT). It recalls what his readers "saw" in the OT about the outcome of Job.

> **Quotation Nugget:** What is significant about the OT allusion to Job in 5:11? There are evident verbal links with the OT, especially in the LXX. Job states in 6:11: "What is my strength that I should endure [ὑπομέ-νω]?" In 14:14, he declares: "All the days of my service I would endure [ὑπομενῶ], till my renewal should come," and in 14:19 he states: "So you destroy man's endurance [ὑπομονὴν]," using the same noun as in James 5:11b. The English words "endure" and "endurance" better convey Job's experience than "patience." The English word *outcome* is the best meaning of the word τέλος as well, and it is that outcome which he tells his readers "you have seen" by means of their hearing and/or reading the biblical text. This is an experience that James assumes on the part of his own hearers and readers! Rather than "purpose" or "end," the translation of τέλος as "outcome" better focuses on the end-events of Job's trials in Job 42.

5:11d ὅτι: This structural marker is a conjunction translated here as "that" (BDAG, s.v. "ὅτι" 2a, p. 732). **Syntactically**, it introduces a dependent conjunctive clause. The entire clause is explanatory modifying the noun "the outcome" (τὸ τέλος). The clause is placed under τὸ τέλος in the structural outline in order to visualize the clause's relationship to the independent clause. **Semantically**, it is epexegetical, explaining or clarifying the outcome of the events of Job's trial (W, 459–60; Adam, 98). While ὅτι is typically rendered as "that" (KJV NASB NET; or "how that," ASV), some translations render ὅτι as "how" (NRSV ESV NLT CNT).

ἐστιν: This Greek word is a third person singular present active indicative of εἰμί that conveys identity and may be rendered as "is" (BDAG, s.v. "εἰμί" 2a, p. 283). **Syntactically**, it is the main verb of the dependent conjunctive clause that equates its subject ὁ κύριος with its predicate adjectives πολύσπλαγ-χνός and οἰκτίρμων (W, 42–44; Adam, 98). **Semantically**, it functions as an equative verb in that the Lord's identity is united with compassion and mercy. The subject and the predicate are united: "the Lord is compassionate and merciful" (NRSV ESV) or "the Lord is full of compassion and mercy" (NASB NIV NET CNT; cf. NLT).

5:12a δέ: This structural marker with the additive πρὸ πάντων is a conjunction that may be rendered as "and" (BDAG, s.v. "δέ" 2, p. 213). **Syntactically**, it introduces an independent conjunctive clause. It appears in the post-positive position. **Semantically**, it is a conjunction indicating continuation "and" (NET), even though some translations render δέ as a contrast (KJV ASV NASB ESV NLT CNT) and others do not translate δέ (NRSV NIV). Nevertheless, we view δέ as a marker that suggests a continuation of things to consider in verses 7–11, particularly as it concerns the exercising of patience.

> **Grammatical Nugget:** What is the significance of the expression πρὸ πάντων? Some have thought that this expression begins the conclusion to the letter, but such is not the function of the expression either in its other NT occurrence (1 Peter 4:8) nor in its only use in the Apostolic Fathers (Didache 10:4). Polycarp, *Philippians* 5:3, uses the singular expression, πρὸ παντός, not to conclude the letter, but rather to alert young men to be concerned with purity. The preposition is a "marker of precedence in importance or rank," translated as "above all" (BDAG, s.v. "πρό" 3, p. 864; BDF, §213).

μὴ ὀμνύετε: This negated (μή) Greek word is a second person plural present active imperative of ὀμνύω that conveys affirming the veracity of a person's statement by invoking a transcendent entity and may be rendered "swear" or "take an oath" (BDAG, s.v. "ὀμνύω," p. 705). **Syntactically**, it is the main verb of this independent conjunctive clause with its subject as the ἀδελφοί being addressed. There is no direct object, but there is an accusative of oath that follows (W, 204–5). **Semantically**, the imperative with μή is an imperative of a prohibition (W, 487–88; cf. BDF, §427(4)). The present tense is a customary present that conveys a regular practice of swearing (W, 521–22). Together, the present tense imperative with μή describes the cessation of activity in progress (W, 724–25). In other words, stop your swearing on a transcendent entity. It is simply translated "do not swear" (NASB NRSV NIV ESV NET CNT; cf. KJV ASV) or "do not take an oath" (NLT).

> **Historical Nugget:** Why was it important for James to address taking oaths in 5:12a? To swear or to take an oath was a common cultural custom of the ancient Near East and in second temple Judaism. In the Bible, oaths had significant judicial value and were to be taken seriously (Pss. 15:4; 63:11; Eccl. 5:4–5; Matt. 23:16–22). And though some Jewish writers warned against oath taking (Sir 23:9–11; Philo, *Spec. Leg.* 2.1–2), people of the Jewish Essene sect in Judea swore oaths for community initiation purposes (Josephus, *War* 2.139–42). The phrase "observe what comes out of your lips" (Deut. 23:24) was interpreted to mean that every binding oath a person promised with regard to the Law could not

be broken, even if it meant death (4Q270 frag. 9 col 2.16:6–8; cf. Wise et al., 1996, 66). In Psalm 95:11 (LXX 94:11) God took an oath against the exodus generation that drew attention to their stubborn disbelief that led to their rebellion at Kadesh Barnea (Num. 14:1–4, 10), their punishment (vv. 11–12), Moses's intercession and God's forgiveness (vv. 19–20), and God's honoring his oath (vv. 40–45). See Hebrews 3:11 and 6:16 (Bateman et al.[1], 146–47; 203–4). James, however, may be echoing the judgment warning from Jesus found in Matthew 12:36–37: "I tell you, on the day of judgment, people will give account for every careless word they speak, for by your words you will be justified, and by your words you will be condemned."

5:12b δέ: This structural marker is a conjunction that conveys a contrast and may be rendered "but" (BDAG, s.v. "δέ" 4a, p. 213). **Syntactically**, it introduces an independent conjunctive clause and appears in the post-positive position. **Semantically**, it serves as a contrast: "but" (KJV ASV NASB NRSV ESV CNT), though some translations do not translate δέ (NIV NLT). Nevertheless, it is a marker that suggests a contrast between exhortations about swearing oaths.

ἤτω: This Greek word is a third person singular present active imperative of εἰμί that conveys an explanation to show how something should be understood and may be rendered "be" (BDAG, s.v. "εἰμί" 2ca, p. 282). **Syntactically**, it is the main verb of this independent conjunctive clause and literally means "is to be." Its subject is both the articular particles τὸ ναί and τὸ οὔ. Its predicate nominative is ναί and οὔ. The neuter article with interjections such as these is rare (W, 237). **Semantically**, the present imperative embodies a general command, and its imperatival force is not lessened by its being in the third person (W, 486): "your yes is to be" or "*let* your yes *be*" (KJV ASV NRSV ESV NET CNT). It is not a question of uttering a specific formula but rather a question of one's being truthful. The sense of the clause is: "Let your 'yes' be true and your 'no' be true." The problem that James addresses is that rash vows are often broken, thus questioning a person's character and Christian testimony.

Quotation Nugget: Writers on James have suggested as many as twenty-five sayings in James that may refer back to Jesus (Deppe, 238–45). A more conservative estimate is that there are eight firm allusions to Jesus's teachings, as we know them in the Synoptic Gospels.[3]

---

3.   Dean B. Deppe, *The Sayings of Jesus in the Epistle of James* (Chelsea, MI: Bookcrafters, 1989). The chart given here was constructed from data in Deppe and Varner's analysis of the sayings of Jesus in James.

James 1:5	Matt. 7:7//Luke 11:9	ask and you will receive
James 2:5	Luke 6:20b//Matt. 5:3	kingdom belongs to the poor
James 4:2c–3	Matt. 7:7//Luke 11:9	ask and you will receive
James 4:9	Luke 6:21, 25b	those who laugh will mourn
James 4:10	Matt. 23:12//Luke 18:14b	humble will be exalted
James 5:1	Luke 6:24	woe to the rich
James 5:2–3	Matt. 6:19–20// Luke 12:33b	do not store up wealth
James 5:12	Matt. 5:33–37	oaths

Despite the large number of shared expressions and themes, not one of them qualifies as a direct verbal quotation of the *logia* of Jesus as we have them in the Synoptic Gospels (Varner[2], 30–34). The closest example is James's warning about oaths in 5:12 with its striking verbal similarities to Matthew 5:33–37. The use of oral sayings of Jesus also supports an early date for James, before the Synoptic Gospels were written.

5:12c ἵνα: This structural marker is a conjunction meaning "that" or "in order that" as an objective marker (BDAG, s.v. "ἵνα" 1aα, p. 475). **Syntactically**, it introduces a dependent conjunctive clause that is functioning adverbially modifying "should be" (ἤτω): "*in order that* you do not fall under judgment" (ἵνα μὴ ὑπὸ κρίσιν πέσητε). **Semantically**, it is considered as purpose: "in order that" or "that" (KJV ASV; cf. W, 472–73; Adam, 100). The entire clause provides the intention of James's command to stop swearing. Admittedly, however, it is difficult to discern the difference from a result clause, "so that" (NASB NRSV ESV NET NLT), and may be considered as purpose-result (cf. W, 473–74). Some however, choose not to translate ἵνα (NIV).

μὴ . . . πέσητε: This negated (μή) Greek word is a second person plural aorist active subjunctive of πίπτω that conveys the idea of experiencing loss of status or condition and may be rendered as "fall" or "be destroyed" (BDAG, s.v. "πίπτω" 2c, p. 816). **Syntactically**, it is the main verb of this dependent conjunctive clause. It is in the subjunctive because ἵνα takes its verb in the subjunctive mood (W, 471). The entire clause is placed under ἤτω so to visualize its dependence on ἤτω. **Semantically**, the aorist tense with μή is a constative aorist that depicts not falling under divine judgment as a whole (W, 557–58). While most translations link "weep" with "cry out" as though a second imperative is joined by "and" (KJV ASV NASB NRSV NIV ESV NET NLT CNT; cf. Adam, 90), we view the following participle differently. The entire clause provides the intention of James's command to stop swearing, namely, in order that his readers might not be judged. James often connects his negative commands with statements about judgment (see 2:4b, 12–13; 4:11–12; 5:9b).

Live Life by Praying if Suffering, if Ill, if Sinning, if Drifting (James 5:13–20)[4]

Clausal Outline for James 5:13–20

5:13a **Κακοπαθεῖ** τις ἐν ὑμῖν,
5:13a Is anyone among you **suffering**?

5:13b **προσευχέσθω**·
5:13b **Let him pray**.

5:13c **εὐθυμεῖ** τις
5:13c Is anyone **cheerful**?

5:13d **ψαλλέτω**
5:13d **Let him sing praise**.

5:14a **ἀσθενεῖ** τις ἐν ὑμῖν,
5:14a Is anyone among you **sick**?

5:14b **προσκαλεσάσθω** τοὺς πρεσβυτέρους τῆς ἐκκλησίας
5:14b **Let him call** for the elders of the church,

5:14c καὶ **προσευξάσθωσαν** ἐπ᾽ αὐτὸν
5:14c and **they should pray** over him,

     5:14d **ἀλείψαντες** αὐτὸν ἐλαίῳ ἐν τῷ ὀνόματι τοῦ κυρίου.
     5:14d *by* **anointing** him with oil in the name of the Lord.

5:15a καὶ ἡ εὐχὴ τῆς πίστεως **σώσει** τὸν κάμνοντα
5:15a And the prayer of faith **will save** the one who is sick,

5:15b καὶ **ἐγερεῖ** αὐτὸν ὁ κύριος·
5:15b and the Lord **will raise** him **up**.

     5:15c κἂν ἁμαρτίας **ᾖ πεποιηκώς**,
     5:15c And if **he has committed** sins,

5:15d **ἀφεθήσεται** αὐτῷ
5:15d he **will be forgiven**.

---

4. A suggested sermon entitled "It's a Matter of Prayer" has been offered for these verses (see Baker et al., 154–61). Three points might be "When Should One Pray" (5:13–16a), "How Should One Pray" (5:16b–17), and "What Should One Pray" (5:19–20).

5:16a **ἐξομολογεῖσθε** οὖν ἀλλήλοις τὰς ἁμαρτίας
5:16a Therefore, **confess** sins to one another,

5:16b καὶ **εὔχεσθε** ὑπὲρ ἀλλήλων,
5:16b and **pray** for one another
|
    5:16c ὅπως **ἰαθῆτε**.
    5:16c in order that **you may be healed**.

5:16d πολὺ **ἰσχύει** δέησις δικαίου
5:16d The prayer of a righteous person **has power**
|
    5:16e **ἐνεργουμένη**.
    *5:16e when **active**.*

5:17a Ἠλίας ἄνθρωπος **ἦν** ὁμοιοπαθὴς ἡμῖν
5:17a Elijah **was** a human being with a nature like ours,

5:17b καὶ προσευχῇ **προσηύξατο**
5:17b and **he prayed** fervently
|
    5:17c τοῦ μὴ **βρέξαι**
    *5:17c in order that **it might** not **rain**,*

5:17d καὶ οὐκ **ἔβρεξεν** ἐπὶ τῆς γῆς ἐνιαυτοὺς τρεῖς καὶ μῆνας ἕξ
5:17d and for three years and six months **it did** not **rain** on the earth.

5:18a καὶ πάλιν **προσηύξατο**,
5:18a Then **he prayed** again,

5:18b καὶ ὁ οὐρανὸς ὑετὸν **ἔδωκεν**
5:18b and heaven **gave** rain,

5:18c καὶ ἡ γῆ **ἐβλάστησεν** τὸν καρπὸν αὐτῆς.
5:18c and the earth **bore** its fruit.

5:19a Ἀδελφοί μου, <u>ἐάν</u> τις ἐν ὑμῖν **πλανηθῇ** ἀπὸ τῆς ἀληθείας

5:19a My brothers *and sisters*, <u>if</u> anyone among you **is misled** from the truth

|

5:19b <u>καὶ</u> [<u>ἐάν</u>] **ἐπιστρέψῃ** τις αὐτόν,

5:19b <u>and</u> [<u>if</u>] someone **brings him back**,

|

5:20a **γινωσκέτω** (<u>ὅτι</u> **ὁ ἐπιστρέψας** ἁμαρτωλὸν ἐκ πλάνης ὁδοῦ αὐτοῦ **σώσει** ψυχὴν αὐτοῦ ἐκ θανάτου

5:20a **let him know** (<u>that</u> whoever turns a sinner from his straying **will save** his soul from death)

|

     5:20b <u>καὶ</u> [ὁ ἐπιστρέψας ἁμαρτωλὸν ἐκ πλάνης ὁδοῦ αὐτοῦ] **καλύψει** πλῆθος ἁμαρτιῶν).

     5:20b <u>and</u> [whoever turns a sinner from his straying] **will cover** a multitude of sins).

Syntax Explained for James 5:13–20

5:13a κακοπαθεῖ: This structural marker is a third person singular present active indicative of κακοπαθέω that conveys the idea of suffering misfortune and may be rendered "suffer" (BDAG, s.v. "κακοπαθέω" 1, p. 500). **Syntactically**, it is the main verb in an independent asyndeton clause with the indefinite pronoun τις as its subject that introduces a question. **Semantically**, the present tense verb is a customary present that speaks of suffering that occurs regularly and is an ongoing state of the sufferers among "you" (ἐν ὑμῖν) is evident (W, 521–22). The verb refers to experiencing calamity of every sort, not just physical sickness, and is not limited to being the opposite of the following εὐθυμέω ("cheerful"). See also the earlier use of the verb's cognate genitive noun κακοπαθίας ("suffering") in 5:10a.

> **Syntactical Nugget:** How should the three verbs (κακοπαθεῖ, εὐθυμεῖ, ἀσθενεῖ) in the dependent clauses followed by τις in 5:13–14a be rendered? While it is possible to render these three dependent clauses as conditional without a conditional particle and thereby three implicit conditional clauses (W, 687–89), the absence of a conditional particle is not in keeping with James's style. The majority of translations render the three dependent clauses as interrogative: "Is anyone" (KJV ASV NASB NIV ESV NET CNT) or "Are anyone" (NRSV NLT). See Adam, 100. Sentences consisting of a question followed by an answer are characteristic of the diatribe. The mention of prayer introduces the overall topic of the entire paragraph (5:13–18).

5:13b προσευχέσθω: This structural marker is a third person singular present middle imperative of προσεύχομαι that conveys the idea of petitioning a deity and may be rendered "pray" (BDAG, s.v. "προσεύχομαι," p. 879). **Syntactically**, it is the main verb in the independent asyndeton clause with "him" as the subject assumed in προσευχέσθω (BDF, §494). **Semantically**, the present tense imperative is an imperative of command (W, 485–86): "Let him pray" (KJV ASV ESV) or "he should pray" (NRSV NIV NET NLT CNT). The present tense forms of this and the following imperative have been viewed as expressing praying and singing continuously. A better approach is to recognize that the two present commands in 5:13 generally apply in all situations, while in 5:14 the two aorist commands apply specifically to severe illnesses.

5:13c εὐθυμεῖ: This structural marker is a third person singular present active indicative of εὐθυμέω that conveys the idea of being cheerful and may be rendered as "being cheerful" (BDAG, s.v. "εὐθυμέω," p. 406). **Syntactically**, it is the main verb in an independent asyndeton clause with the indefinite pronoun τις as its subject that introduces a question. **Semantically**, the present verb is a customary present that speaks of cheerfulness that occurs regularly as an ongoing state (W, 521–22). The verb can also mean "to take courage" (Acts 27:22, 25, 36). The English translation "be cheerful" (RSV) is accurate but should not be understood simply as describing someone as being in high spirits. It stands here in contrast to κακοπαθέω ("suffer") and ἀσθενέω ("be sick"), so the translation "feeling good" is more appropriate. In the NT, the word group εὐθυμ- is found elsewhere only in Acts 24:10 (εὐθύμως), and Acts 27:22, 25 (εὐθυμέω).

5:13d ψαλλέτω: This structural marker is a third person singular present active imperative of ψάλλω that conveys the idea of singing songs of praise and may be rendered as "sing" or "sing praise" (BDAG, s.v. "ψάλλω," p. 1096). **Syntactically**, it is the main verb in the independent asyndeton clause with "him" as the subject assumed in ψαλλέτω (BDF, §494). **Semantically**, the present tense imperative is an imperative of command (W, 485–86). Thus, "let him sing praises" (KJV ASV NIV ESV CNT) is probably better as "he should sing praises" (NET; cf. NRSV NLT).

> **Grammatical and Lexical Nugget:** What is the meaning of the imperative ψαλλέτω? The third person does not lessen the force of the imperative. Thus, "let him sing a hymn" is probably better as "he should sing a hymn" or "sing praise" (see the verb in Rom. 15:9; 1 Cor. 14:15; Eph. 5:19; and the noun ψαλμός in 1 Cor. 14:26; Eph. 5:19; Col. 3:16). The verb was originally "play the harp" and is therefore used frequently in the OT, especially in Psalms (forty times) where it usually renders the verb זָמַר, "sing to the music of a harp" (Pss. 7:17; 98:4). The use of the word in Hellenistic Greek does not necessarily imply the use of an instrument (BDAG, s.v. "ψάλλω," p. 1096).

^{5:14a} ἀσθενεῖ: This structural marker is a third person singular present active indicative of ἀσθενέω that generally refers to someone who is suffering a debilitating physical illness and may be rendered as "sick" or "ill" (BDAG, s.v. "ἀσθενέω" 1, p. 142). **Syntactically**, it is the main verb in an independent asyndeton clause with the indefinite pronoun τις as its subject that introduces a question. **Semantically**, the present verb is a customary present that speaks of physical illness that occurs regularly among "you" (ἐν ὑμῖν; W, 521–22) and is rendered "is anyone among you ill" (NET) or "is anyone among you sick" (KJV NASB NRSV NIV ESV NLT CNT).

> **Lexical Nugget:** How is ἀσθενεῖ different than the previous κακοπαθεῖ? The verb ἀσθενέω means "is weak," as in a limb (Ps. 109:24) or an organ (Ps. 88:9). The NT also uses it in the sense of moral weakness (Rom. 4:19; 1 Cor. 8:7, 11–12), but the physical sense is most often present (Matt. 10:8; 25:36; Luke 9:2; John 4:46; 5:3; Acts 9:37; Phil. 2:26). Physical weakness because of sickness is clearly the intended meaning here (cf. τὸν κάμνοντα in 5:15). How sick is "sick"? The answer to that question is in the verse itself—sick enough that the patient cannot go to the πρεσβύτεροι of the church but must have them come to his or her house.

^{5:14b} προσκαλεσάσθω: This structural marker is a third person singular aorist middle imperative of προσκαλέω that conveys the idea of calling to notify someone in order to secure someone's presence and may be rendered "call on" or "invite" (BDAG, s.v. "προσκαλέω" 1a, p. 881). **Syntactically**, it is the main verb in the independent clause with "him" as the subject assumed in ψαλλέτω and the direct object is πρεσβυτέρους. **Semantically**, this aorist imperative depicts a command as a whole (W, 485–86) about praying. It is rendered as "let them call" (KJV NIV ASV ESV CNT) or "they should call" (NRSV NET NLT). This is the first of two aorist imperatives that point to specific rather than general commands to be obeyed *within* the believing community, an emphasis that dominates this last section.

> **Lexical Nugget:** What is τῆς ἐκκλησίας? The term refers to a local worshiping community, an *ecclesia* (ἐκκλησία). In the Greek world, the ἐκκλησία referred to a gathered group of people (an "assembly") rather than to the place of meeting (Herodotus, *Hist.* 3.142; Aristotle, *Pol.* 1285A; Josephus, *Ant.* 12.164; *Life* 268). The reference here is not to a building but to the communal gathering of believers. It is also interesting that it is the elders who are to be called—not apostles or someone else thought to have the gift of healing. Previously in James 2:2, the spiritual center of these believing communities is described as a building called a *synagogue*. Here the term that is used refers to a local worshiping community, an *ecclesia* (ἐκκλησία). The reference here is also not to a building but to the communal gathering of believers.

^{5:14c} καί: This structural marker is a conjunction meaning "and" (BDAG, s.v. "καί" 1b, p. 494). **Syntactically**, it introduces an independent conjunctive clause. **Semantically**, it is a coordinating conjunction often rendered "and" (NET ESV NASB NRSV etc.) that adds to James's description about the person who is ill and the expectation to call the elders.

προσευξάσθωσαν: This Greek word is a third person plural aorist middle imperative of προσεύχομαι that conveys the idea of petitioning a deity and may be rendered "pray" (BDAG, s.v. "προσεύχομαι," p. 879). **Syntactically**, it is the main verb in the independent conjunctive clause with "they" as the subject assumed in προσευξάσθωσαν. **Semantically**, this aorist imperative depicts a command as a whole (W, 485–86) about the actions of a person who is ill. It is rendered as "let them pray" (KJV ASV ESV CNT) or "they are to pray" (NASB NET). The elders are commanded to pray "over him" (ἐπ' αὐτὸν). This is the second of two aorist imperatives that point to specific rather than general commands to be obeyed *within* the believing community, an emphasis that dominates this last section.

> **Historical Nugget:** Why were elders to be called when a person was sick in 5:14b? The elders were not summoned because they were especially skilled in medicine. Physicians were available at this period, especially in the cities. If medicinal healing art is present at all in the passage, the case described is probably one in which medicine has already done all that it can. James would undoubtedly approve the advice given in Sirach 38:9: "My son, in your sickness be not negligent, but pray to the Lord, and he will make you whole." The passage continues, "Then give way to the physician, for the Lord has created him. Let him not depart from you, for you have need of him. There is a time when in their hands there is good success" (Sir 38:12, 13). Possibly something similar may have occurred in this situation in James, so that after the physician had done his part, and perhaps with no success, the sick person would summon the elders to offer prayer.

^{5:14d} ἀλείψαντες: This structural marker is a nominative plural masculine aorist active participle of ἀλείφω that conveys the idea of literally anointing a person with a liquid such as oil or perfume and may be rendered as "anoint" (BDAG, s.v. "ἀλείφω" 1, p. 41). **Syntactically**, it introduces a dependent participial clause that is functioning adverbially modifying "they should pray" (προσευξάσθωσαν). The clause describes an action that accompanies the second of the main imperative commands that precedes it. It could be called "concurrent but subordinate action" (Blomberg et al., 243). **Semantically**, the participle expresses the means of their praying: "*by* anointing" (W, 628–29). The aorist tense is a constative aorist, viewing the action as a whole (W,

557–58). The tense may express an antecedent action for the anointing, prior to the praying, but a fine distinction in the timing of the aorist participle, however, is not inherent in the tense, and the action could simply be simultaneous (Davids, 193).

> **Historical Nugget:** Was the application of oil intended to play a sacramental role (cf. Mark 6:13), or did the oil play a medicinal role (cf. Luke 10:34)? The sacramental explanation fails for lack of substantive evidence. The application of oil externally is medically sensible in some cases, but evidence is lacking for the medically internal consumption of oil. Since the OT function of anointing with oil was to "consecrate" someone, the anointing here was probably intended to "consecrate" or "set apart" the sick one for concentrated prayer offered by the community (Varner[1], 190–91). Anointing, therefore, was to remind the sick person that he belongs to God, as the anointed ones in the OT were so viewed, and to remind the community that the sick one is now "set aside" for concentrated prayer.

5:15a καί: This structural marker is a conjunction meaning "and" (BDAG, s.v. "καί" 1b, p. 494). **Syntactically**, it introduces an independent conjunctive clause. **Semantically**, it is a coordinating conjunction often rendered "and" (NET ESV NASB NIV etc.) that adds to James's description about the person who prays.

σώσει: This Greek word is a third person singular future active indicative of σῴζω that conveys the idea of preserving or rescuing a person from physical disease and may be rendered "save," "preserve," or "rescue" (BDAG, s.v. "σῴζω" 1c, p. 982). **Syntactically**, it is the main verb of this independent conjunctive clause with "the prayer" (ἡ εὐχή) as its subject and "the one who is sick" (τὸν κάμνοντα) as the direct object. **Semantically**, the future tense is a predictive future that indicates something that will take place (W, 568). It will happen. The verb does not refer to a person's spiritual salvation, but to the saving of the person from the sickness. In order for prayer to be effective, it must be offered out of a person's faith in trusting God.

> **Semantical Nugget:** What is ἡ εὐχὴ τῆς πίστεως? Prayer must be offered out of a person's faith in trusting God. A cry out of desperation will not prevail. "What James means by 'prayer of faith' is probably revealed in 1:5–6: praying without wavering or doubting. This is not a prayer that believes something *specific* about what God will do, although that is not excluded, but a prayer that is offered out of a basic unconditional trust that God knows what is best and can handle the situation" (Witherington, 544–45).

5:15b καί: This structural marker is a conjunction meaning "and" (BDAG, s.v. "καί" 1b, p. 494). **Syntactically**, it introduces an independent conjunctive clause. **Semantically**, it is a coordinating conjunction often rendered "and" (NET ESV NASB NRSV etc.) that adds to James's description about the person who prays a prayer of trust in God.

ἐγερεῖ: This Greek word is a third person singular future active indicative of ἐγείρω that conveys the idea of restoring someone from an illness and may be rendered "restore to health" (BDAG, s.v. "ἐγείρω" 8, p. 272). **Syntactically**, it is the main verb of this independent conjunctive clause with "the Lord" (ὁ κύριος) as its subject and "him" (αὐτόν) as the direct object. **Semantically**, the future tense is a predictive future that indicates something that will take place (W, 568). It will happen. God will heal the person, the person is cured and raised up from the sickbed.

> **Theological Nugget:** How do we handle the problem that the text of 1 Kings does not clearly state that Elijah prayed? Elijah's language in 1 Kings 17:1 implies a prayer: "As the Lord, the God of Israel, lives, *before whom I stand*, there shall be neither dew nor rain these years, except by my word." Furthermore, the language used to describe the prelude to the long-awaited deluge in 1 Kings 18:42 also implied an accompanying prayer: "And he bowed himself down on the earth and *put his face between his knees*." Furthermore, this is not a reference to the resurrection at the last day but is a prayer of faith for the sick person, made by others who have come to pray over the sick one. In other words, this verse cannot be used to suggest that healing depends on the degree of faith in the ill person, who must also pray for himself.

5:15c κἄν: This Greek word is a crasis from καὶ ἐάν that is rendered "and if" (BDAG, s.v. "κἄν" 1, p. 507). **Syntactically**, it introduces an independent conjunctive clause that is the protasis of the entire sentence. **Semantically**, it functions like a third-class conditional clause that presents an uncertain condition of fulfilment (W, 696–99; Adam, 102).

ᾖ πεποιηκώς: The first of these two Greek words, ᾖ, is the third person singular present active subjunctive of εἰμί that is an auxiliary verb and may be rendered "to be" (BDAG, s.v. "εἰμί" 11, p. 285). The second verb, πεποιηκώς, is a nominative singular masculine perfect active participle of ποιέω that conveys the idea of carrying out something and thus being guilty of a moral obligation that may be rendered "do," "keep," "carry out," or "commit" (BDAG, s.v. "ποιέω" 3c, p. 840). **Syntactically**, together they serve as the main verb of this dependent conjunctive clause, which is in the protasis portion of a third-class dependent clause. **Semantically**, they are a periphrastic construction, which reflects a roundabout way of saying something that could have been said with a single verb (W, 649; Adam, 102; Irons, 541; Zerwick et al., 701). The perfect tense is an extensive perfect (W, 577): "has committed" (NASB NRSV NIV ESV NET CNT; cf. KJV ASV). The emphasis is on sins committed in the past but recognizes that sins continue in the present.

5:15d ἀφεθήσεται: This structural marker is a third person singular future passive indicative of ἀφίημι that conveys releasing a person from a legal or moral obligation or consequence and may be rendered "cancel," "remit," or "pardon" (BDAG, s.v. "ἀφίημι" 2, p. 156). **Syntactically**, it is the main verb of this independent asyndeton clause. It serves as the apodosis of the dependent κἂν clause, with "sin" as its implied subject mentioned in the protasis. Because of the dative pronoun, the literal impersonal rendering is "it will be forgiven to him" (ASV), but we have preferred the more functional rendering "he will be forgiven." **Semantically**, the future tense is a predictive future that indicates something that will take place (W, 568). It will happen: "he will be forgiven" (NIV ESV NET CNT). The context of this conditional sentence makes it clear that there can be no confident assumption that there *must* be some sin committed by the sick person that needs divine forgiveness.

5:16a οὖν: This structural marker is a conjunction that may be rendered "therefore" (BDAG, s.v. "οὖν" 1a, p. 736). **Syntactically**, it identifies the clause as an independent conjunctive clause, "therefore confess sins to one another" (ἐξομολογεῖσθε οὖν ἀλλήλοις τὰς ἁμαρτίας) and appears in a post-positive position. **Semantically**, it is an inferential conjunction that introduces the result or deduction from what was said previously (Adam, 103): "therefore" (NASB NRSV NIV ESV CNT) or "so" (NET), though some leave it as unrendered (KJV NLT). James is drawing a deduction, conclusion, or summary about sin and how to deal with it in the congregation.

ἐξομολογεῖσθε: This Greek word is a second person plural present middle imperative of ἐξομολογέω that conveys the idea of making an admission of wrongdoing and may be rendered "confess" or "admit" (BDAG, s.v. "ἐξομολογέω" 2, p. 351). **Syntactically**, it is the main verb of this independent conjunctive clause with the readers as the subject assumed in ἐξομολογεῖσθε. The verb's direct object is ἁμαρτίας. **Semantically**, the present tense imperative is an imperative of command (W, 485–86). The second person imperative is typically rendered "confess *your*" (KJV ASV NASB NRSV NIV ESV NET NLT CNT), though we render the imperative as merely "confess."

Semantical Nugget: What does it mean to ἐξομολογεῖσθε οὖν ἀλλήλοις τὰς ἁμαρτίας in James 5:16? First, the verb ἐξομολογεῖσθε is also used in the LXX both for professing the Lord and for praising him (see

Gen. 29:35; 2 Sam. 22:50; 1 Chron. 16:4; 2 Chron. 5:13; Ps. 6:6; Jer. 40:11; Dan. 3:25). The act of confessing one's sins is firmly rooted in Judaism, whether for individuals (Lev. 5:5; Num. 5:7; Ps. 38:8) or for groups (Lev. 16:21; 26:40; Deut. 9:4–10). Second, the verb ἐξομολογεῖσθε is used in the NT mostly for "professing" (Matt. 11:25; Luke 10:21; Rom. 14:11; 15:9; Phil. 2:11). Apart from this passage, it is used for public confessing of sins in the NT only in Matthew 3:6; Mark 1:5; and Acts 19:18. Early Christian communities also understood this in a communal sense. In the Didache 4.14, the young convert is commanded to "confess [ἐξομολογήσῃ, same verb as in James 5:16] your sins in an assembly [ἐν ἐκκλησίᾳ])." "Communal confession of sin remains important for the life and health of the community, even if our own sins have not had obvious physical consequences in our lives" (Blomberg et al., 245).

5:16b καί: This structural marker is a conjunction meaning "and" (BDAG, s.v. "καί" 1b, p. 494). **Syntactically**, it introduces an independent conjunctive clause. **Semantically**, it is a coordinating conjunction often rendered "and" (NET ESV NASB NRSV etc.) that adds to James's description about the person who sins who is in need of prayer.

εὔχεσθε: This Greek word is a second person plural present middle imperative of εὔχομαι that conveys the idea of speaking to or making requests of God and may be rendered "pray" (BDAG, s.v. "εὔχομαι" 1, p. 417). **Syntactically**, it is the main verb of this independent conjunctive clause with the readers as the subject. The intransitive verb is followed by the prepositional phrase ὑπὲρ ἀλλήλων. **Semantically**, the present tense imperative is an imperative of command (W, 485–86). The link between sin and illness, forgiveness, and salvation is continued from the preceding verse. Here it is not only the elders who are encouraged to intercede on behalf of the sick, but the entire assembly (ἐκκλησία) is to constitute a community of mutual prayer. We are all exhorted to confess our sins to one another and to pray for one another.

5:16c ὅπως: This structural marker is a conjunction meaning "in order that" (BDAG, s.v. "ὅπως" 2b, p. 718). **Syntactically**, it introduces a dependent conjunctive clause. **Semantically**, it is a conjunction that indicates purpose (NET ESV NASB NRSV etc.), namely, the purpose of prayer. Despite the typical rendering "so that" (NASB NRSV NIV NET NLT CNT), we stay with the lexical rendering "(in order) that" with the subjunctive (cf. KJV ASV ESV).

ἰαθῆτε: This Greek verb is a second person plural aorist passive subjunctive of ἰάομαι that conveys the idea of delivering from a variety of ills or conditions that lie beyond physical maladies and may be rendered "restore" or "heal" (BDAG, s.v. "ἰάομαι" 2b, p. 465). **Syntactically**, it is the main verb of this dependent conjunctive clause of purpose (ὅπως). **Semantically**, the aorist tense is a constative aorist that depicts spiritual healing as a whole (W, 557–58). The plural verb again stresses the communal character of this passage.

5:16d ἰσχύει This structural marker is a third person singular present active indicative of ἰσχύω that conveys the idea of having requisite personal resources to accomplish something and may be rendered "have power" or "be able" (BDAG, s.v. "ἰσχύω" 2a, p. 484). **Syntactically**, it is the main verb of this independent asyndeton clause with "prayer" (δέησις) as its subject. **Semantically**, the present tense customary present conveys action that happens regularly (W, 521–22). Translations render it as "can accomplish much" (NASB), "is powerful" (NIV CNT; cf. NRSV), and the preferred "has great power" (ESV NLT).

5:16e ἐνεργουμένη: This structural marker is a nominative singular feminine present middle participle of ἐνεργέω that conveys the idea of putting something into action and may be rendered "work," "be active," "be effective," or "operate" (BDAG, s.v. "ἐνεργέω" 1b, p. 335). **Syntactically**, it introduces a dependent participial clause that functions adverbially, modifying the verb "has power" (ἰσχύει). It is placed under ἰσχύει to show its grammatical dependence on the independent clause. **Semantically**, the participle is a temporal participle (W, 623–24) *"when* active." The present tense is a customary present that conveys something that happens regularly about prayer when put into action (W, 521–22). This indicative clause has the appearance of an aphorism, which James often appends to the end of his paragraphs. It not only rounds off what he has just written, but also points forward to Elijah, the shining exemplar of the righteous praying person.

5:17a ἦν: This structural marker is a third person singular imperfect active indicative of εἰμί that conveys the idea of the subject and predicate being in close connection and may be rendered "is" (BDAG, s.v. "εἰμί" 2a, p. 283). **Syntactically**, it is the main verb of this independent asyndeton clause with "Elijah" (Ἠλίας) as its subject and "human being" (ἄνθρωπος) as predicate nominative (W, 43–44). **Semantically**, the imperfect tense is a stative imperfect (W, 548).

Lexical Nugget: What is the meaning of ἄνθρωπος and ὁμοιοπαθής in 5:17a? First, the noun ἄνθρωπος literally means "man." Many translations reflect the more formal-equivalent rendering of "man" (NIV ESV). Yet, due to context the noun is more idiomatic for a member of the human race and frequently rendered "human" (NLT) or "human being" (NET). This is more gender neutral and has a focus on human limitations (BDAG, s.v. "ἄνθρωπος" 2a, p. 81; cf. Bateman[2], 147). This rendering is supported due

to the second term: ὁμοιοπαθής. The adjective ὁμοιοπαθής is defined
as "pert. to experiencing similarity in feelings or circumstances, *with the
same nature* τινί *as someone*" (BDAG, s.v. "ὁμοιοπαθής," p. 706). The
word's only other NT occurrence is in Acts 14:15. The message is that the
great prophet was made of the "same stuff" of which both the readers and
the author (ἡμῖν) were made.

5:17b καί: This structural marker is a conjunction meaning "and" (BDAG, s.v. "καί"
1b, p. 494). **Syntactically**, it introduces an independent conjunctive clause.
Semantically, it is a coordinating conjunction often rendered "and" (NET
ESV NASB NRSV etc.) that adds to James's description about Elijah who as a
human being also prayed.[5]

προσηύξατο: This Greek word is a third person singular aorist middle indicative of προσεύχομαι that conveys the idea of petitioning deity and may
be rendered "pray" (BDAG, s.v. "προσεύχομαι," p. 879). **Syntactically**, it is
the main verb of this independent conjunctive clause with "he" as the subject assumed in προσηύξατο but referring back to Ἠλίας. **Semantically**,
the aorist tense is a constative aorist that describes the action as a whole (W,
557–58): Elijah prayed. Furthermore, the verb's use with a "cognate dative"
direct object adds to the semantic force "to emphasize the action of the verb"
(W, 168–69; Adam, 104; Irons, 541). The sense would be that "he prayed ear-
nestly" (KJV NASB NET NLT NIV CNT) or "fervently" (ASV NRSV ESV).

Grammatical Nugget: What is the significance of the aorist indicative
mood for "he prayed" (προσηύξατο) in James 5:17b? The simple indicative affirmation about the human nature of the prophet is followed by four
indicative statements about his specific deeds related to prayer, and the
paragraph concludes with two indicative statements about the results of
his praying. The nontypical (for James) parataxis of these six clauses, with
five consecutive uses of καί, is the most prominent linguistic feature of
this compact narrative section. It recalls, therefore, the narrative context
of this exemplar, drawn entirely from the text of 1 Kings.

5:17c τοῦ μὴ βρέξαι: This negated (μή) structural marker is an aorist active infinitive of βρέχω that conveys the idea of raindrops falling and may be rendered
"rain" (BDAG, s.v. "βρέχω" 3, p. 184). **Syntactically**, it is the main verb of
this dependent infinitive clause that is functioning adverbially modifying "he
prayed" (προσηύξατο). The genitive articular infinitive (τοῦ βρέξαι) following "he prayed" (προσηύξατο) is probably a Hebraism because it appears

---

5.   Elijah is the fourth significant exemplar in James. Elijah, according to Foster (pp. 165–91), is an exem-
      plar of prayer. He points out (p. 190) that James departs from Jewish tradition in stressing the prophet's
      human frailty rather than his superhuman feats (cf. 5:17a; Sir 48:1–10)."

after a verb that normally takes the simple complementary infinitive—a grammatical anomaly overlooked by most commentators. **Semantically**, the negated (μή) infinitive (τοῦ + infin.) is that of purpose (W, 591; Adam, 104). Thus, the intention of Elijah's prayer was to prevent rain.

5:17d καί: This structural marker is a conjunction meaning "and" (BDAG, s.v. "καί" 1b, p. 494). **Syntactically**, it introduces an independent conjunctive clause. **Semantically**, it is a coordinating conjunction often rendered "and" (NET ESV NASB NRSV etc.) that adds to James's description of Elijah praying for no rain and adds to the event recorded in 1 Kings.

οὐκ ἔβρεξεν: This negated (οὐκ) Greek word is a third person singular aorist active indicative of βρέχω that conveys the idea of raindrops falling and may be rendered "rain" (BDAG, s.v. "βρέχω" 3, p. 184). **Syntactically**, it is the main verb of this independent conjunctive clause with a supplied "it" as the subject of the verb, ἔβρεξεν. **Semantically**, the aorist tense is a constative aorist that describes the action as a whole (W, 557–58) about the lack of rain. The three-and-a-half-year drought is also found in the words of Jesus in Luke 4:25, so the time period has additional traction outside of James's writing.

> **Historical Nugget:** How do the three and a half years relate to the "three years" length in 1 Kings? The three-and-a-half-year drought is also found in the words of Jesus in Luke 4:25. A suggested source for this drought length usually is some unknown tradition or it is explained as an eschatological/apocalyptic reference (Daniel or Revelation). A better explanation is that James (and Jesus) simply displayed their knowledge of Judean agriculture with a reference to the early and later rains (5:7). It is well known among inhabitants of the Levant that after the later rains in the spring, there is a six-month drought before the early rains commence in the autumn. If Elijah's announcement of the drought was at the end of the six-month dry season, the additional three years of drought would then provide the total length of three and a half years mentioned by James and Jesus (Varner[1], 392–93).

5:18a καί: This structural marker is a conjunction meaning "then" (BDAG, s.v. "καί" 1bγ, p. 494). **Syntactically**, it introduces an independent conjunctive clause. **Semantically**, it is a coordinating conjunction conveying an expression of time and often rendered "then" (NASB NRSV ESV NET NLT CNT) that adds to James's description about the historical events about Elijah's praying.

προσηύξατο: This Greek word is a third person singular aorist middle indicative of προσεύχομαι that conveys the idea of petitioning deity and may be rendered "pray" (BDAG, s.v. "προσεύχομαι," p. 879). **Syntactically**, it is the main verb of this independent conjunctive clause with "he" as the subject assumed in προσηύξατο but referring back to Ἠλίας. **Semantically**, the aorist tense is a constative aorist that describes the action as a whole (W, 557–58): Elijah prayed "again" (πάλιν).

5:18b καί: This structural marker is a conjunction meaning "and" (BDAG, s.v. "καί" 1b, p. 494). **Syntactically**, it introduces an independent conjunctive clause. **Semantically**, it is a coordinating conjunction often rendered "and" (NET ESV NASB NRSV etc.) that adds to James's description about Elijah who as a human being also prayed.

ἔδωκεν: This Greek word is a third person singular aorist active indicative of δίδωμι that conveys the idea of causing something to happen especially in reference to physical phenomena and may be rendered "produce," "make," "cause," or "give" (BDAG, s.v. "δίδωμι" 4, p. 242). **Syntactically**, it is the main verb of this independent conjunctive clause with "heaven" (οὐρανός) as its subject and "rain" (ὑετόν) as its direct object. **Semantically**, the aorist tense is a constative aorist that describes the action as a whole (W, 557–58) about the coming of rain. The clause, "the heaven gave rain" (ὁ οὐρανὸς ὑετὸν ἔδωκεν), was a popular form of expression, as is seen in Acts 14:17.

5:18c καί: This structural marker is a conjunction meaning "and" (BDAG, s.v. "καί" 1b, p. 494). **Syntactically**, it introduces an independent conjunctive clause. **Semantically**, it is a coordinating conjunction often rendered "and" (NET ESV NASB NRSV etc.) that adds to James's description about Elijah who as a human being also prayed.

ἐβλάστησεν: This Greek word is a third person singular aorist active indicative of βλαστάνω that conveys the idea of causing something to grow and may be rendered "produce" (BDAG, s.v. "βλαστάνω" 1, p. 177). **Syntactically**, it is the main verb of this independent conjunctive clause with "earth" (γῆ) as the subject and "fruit" (καρπόν) as the direct object. **Semantically**, the aorist tense is a constative aorist that describes the action as a whole (W, 557–58) about the earth's production from the coming of rain.

> **Lexical Nugget:** Is there any significance in the mention of "fruit" again in James 5:18c? The word "fruit" recalls the description of wisdom from above in 3:17–18 with its promise there that the "fruit of righteousness is sown in peace for those who make peace." There is also a possible connection with James 5:7b, where we read that the farmer awaits the precious fruit of the earth (καρπὸν τῆς γῆς), which is always given after the first and then the second rain. The renewal of the earth by its fruit also establishes a parallel with the sick person mentioned in James 5. The refreshing

of the parched land through the praying of the righteous Elijah points to the refreshing of the weary and sick person through the praying of a righteous elder.

5:19a ἐάν: This structural marker is a conjunction meaning "if" (BDAG, s.v. "ἐάν" 1aα, p. 267). **Syntactically**, it is a dependent conjunctive clause. The entire clause, "*if* anyone among you" (ἐάν τις ἐν ὑμῖν), functions adverbially. It modifies the verb "let him know" (γινωσκέτω). The entire ἐάν clause is placed above the verb γινωσκέτω to visualize its grammatical dependence. **Semantically**, it introduces a third-class conditional clause: "if" (cf. KJV NASB ESV NIV NET etc.). It introduces the first of two hypothetical situations for the sake of the discussion (W, 696–99; Adam, 105). The situation is not necessarily describing a scene that has taken place in their assemblies. The scene that is portrayed in their "synagogue" *may* have taken place.

πλανηθῇ: This Greek word is a third person singular aorist passive subjunctive of πλανάω that conveys the idea of proceeding without a sense of proper direction and may be rendered "go astray," "be misled," or "wander away" (BDAG, s.v. "πλανάω" 2cβ, p. 821d). It is in the subjunctive because ἐάν takes its verb in the subjunctive (W, 470–71). **Syntactically**, it is the main verb of this independent conjunctive clause—the first of two predicates in the protasis of a third-class conditional sentence—with the indefinite pronoun τις as its subject. **Semantically**, the aorist tense is a constative aorist that describes the action as a whole about the final stage of returning the sinner (W, 557–58; 697): "errs" (KJV ASV), "wanders" (NRSV NIV ESV NET NLT CNT), or "strays" (NASB).

Theological Nugget: What is the significance of James's concern about people in the congregation in 5:19? James expresses concern about one of their "own" (ἐν ὑμῖν) who has been "turned" or "led astray" from the truth. This is a hypothetical member of the community considered to be among the "brothers" who was led astray, probably by a false teacher. Drawing from other references in the NT, this being led away by someone even to apostasy was a very real problem in the early church (Acts 20:29–30; 2 Tim. 3:1–9; Heb. 6:4–6; 2 John 7–8; Jude 3–4). Embedded in this verb's LXX usage are idolatrous ideas (Prov. 14:8; Isa. 9:15; Jer. 23:17; Ezek. 33:12). Satan is also portrayed as the ultimate deceiver, and thus "the deceived one," like this individual, could be under just such satanic influence.

5:19b καί: This structural marker is a conjunction meaning "and" (BDAG, s.v. "καί" 1b, p. 494). **Syntactically**, it introduces an independent conjunctive clause. **Semantically**, it is a coordinating conjunction often rendered "and"

(NET ESV NASB NRSV etc.) that adds to James's discussion about people who wander from the truth.

[ἐάν]: This Greek word is a conjunction meaning "if" (BDAG, s.v. "ἐάν" 1aα, p. 267). **Syntactically**, the bracketed [ἐάν] is an ellipsis that introduces a dependent conjunctive clause. The entire clause, "*if* someone brings him back" (ἐάν ἐπιστρέψῃ τις αὐτόν), functions adverbially. It modifies the verb "let him know" (γινωσκέτω). The entire ἐάν clause is placed above the verb γινωσκέτω to visualize its grammatical dependence. **Semantically**, it introduces a third-class conditional clause: "if" (cf. KJV NASB ESV NIV NET etc.). It is a second hypothetical situation for the sake of the discussion (W, 696–99; Adam, 105). So, the hypothetical situation is not necessarily describing a scene that has taken place in their assemblies. The scene that is portrayed in their "synagogue" *may* have taken place.

ἐπιστρέψῃ: This Greek word is a third person singular aorist active subjunctive of ἐπιστρέφω that conveys the idea of causing a person to change belief or course of conduct (spiritual or moral) and may be rendered "turn" (BDAG, s.v. "ἐπιστρέφω" 3, p. 382). It is in the subjunctive because the bracketed [ἐάν] takes its verb in the subjunctive (W, 470–71). **Syntactically**, it is the main verb of this independent conjunctive clause—second of two predicates in the protasis of a third-class [ἐάν] conditional sentence—with the indefinite pronoun τις as its subject. Although the second τις is its subject, the identity of this indefinite pronoun is not the one led astray but another person leading him back. **Semantically**, the aorist tense is a constative aorist that describes the action as a whole about the final stage of returning the sinner (W, 557–58; 697): "someone turns" (NASB NET; Irons, 541), "someone brings him back" (ESV CNT; cf. NRSV NLT), or "someone converts" (KJV ASV). Those who have been led astray need someone to bring them back or to "return them."

Lexical Nugget: What is "the truth" (τῆς ἀληθείας)? The noun is not limited to Christian doctrine in the theological sense but more broadly to all that is involved in the gospel and its way of life. The truth is something that is to be done as well as believed (Ps. 51:6; Gal. 5:7; 1 John 1:6). The "conversion" language of 5:19 is well known in both testaments (Isa. 6:10; Ezek. 33:11; Acts 3:19; 9:35; 2 Cor. 3:16). This command to motivate others to concern is rooted also in the OT (Lev. 19:17; Ps. 51:13; Ezek. 3:17–21; 33:7–9) and echoed strongly elsewhere in the NT (Matt. 18:12–15; 1 Thess. 5:14; 2 Thess. 3:15; 2 Tim. 2:25; 1 John 5:16; Jude 23). As Paul also urged in Galatians 6:1, James exhorts concerned brothers in the community who see a person in error in proper humility to turn him back to the way of the truth.

5:20a γινωσκέτω: This structural marker is a third person singular present active imperative of γινώσκω that conveys the idea of arriving at a knowledge of someone or something and may be rendered as "know," "know about," or "make acquaintance of" (BDAG, s.v. "γινώσκω" 1b, p. 200). **Syntactically**, it is the main verb of this independent clause with "him" as the subject assumed in the γινωσκέτω. **Semantically**, the present tense imperative is an imperative of command (W, 485–86): "let him know" (KJV ASV NASB ESV CNT) or "you should know" (NRSV NIV; cf. NET). Thus, it is a general admonition. The imperative imparting of knowledge is followed by a ὅτι substantival clause.

ὅτι: This structural marker is a conjunction meaning "that" (BDAG, s.v. "ὅτι" 1c, p. 731). **Syntactically**, it introduces a substantival dependent conjunctive clause: "*that* whoever brings back a sinner . . ." (ὅτι ὁ ἐπιστρέψας ἁμαρτωλὸν . . .). The entire clause functions as the direct object of the verb: "know" (γινωσκέτω). The clause is placed in parentheses in order to visualize its contribution to the independent clause. **Semantically**, it is an indirect discourse: "that" (KJV NASB ESV NET etc.). The entire ὅτι clause provides the content of the reader's mental perception (W, 456; con. Adam, 106). Yet, the specifics are found in the next verb.

ὁ ἐπιστρέψας: This Greek word is a nominative singular masculine aorist active participle of ἐπιστρέφω that conveys the idea of causing a person to change his belief or his course of conduct in a spiritual or moral sense and may be rendered "turn" (BDAG, s.v. "ἐπιστρέφω" 3, p. 382). **Syntactically**, it is a substantival participle in the content clause and is the subject of the following σώσει. The direct object of the verbal is ἁμαρτωλόν. **Semantically**, the aorist participle functions as a constative aorist, viewing the action as a whole (W, 557–58). The verb is repeated from 5:19 and carries the responsibility that was shown in the comments on that verse.

σώσει: This Greek word is a third person singular future active indicative of σώζω that conveys the idea of preserving from a transcendent danger and may be rendered "save" or "preserved from eternal death" (BDAG, s.v. "σώζω" 2aβ, p. 982). **Syntactically**, it is the first main idea of the dependent conjunctive ὅτι clause with "whoever brings back a sinner from his straying" as the subject. Its direct object is ψυχήν. **Semantically**, the future tense is a predictive future that indicates something that will take place (W, 568). It will happen: "will save" (NASB NRSV NIV ESV NET NLT CNT). The soul will be saved if the person is turned from error. The meaning of the verb here is unlike its earlier use in 5:16 where the meaning was being saved from sickness. Here the "salvation" is spiritual and eschatological, as witnessed by what the person is saved from, i.e., death.

Text-Critical Nugget: What is the correct reading for αὐτοῦ in James 5:20? Although the presence of αὐτοῦ is supported by the early papyrus P[74] and the fourth-century uncials ℵ and B, Metzger assigns it a "C" rating (Metzger[1], 615), but only because of a disagreement in the committee as to *where* to place the αὐτοῦ, not about its inclusion. An earlier committee for the textual variant rated the reading a "D" (cf. Metzger[2], 686). Nevertheless, Greek texts from Wescott and Hort to the NA[28], the SBL Greek NT and the Tyndale House GNT all include it. The omission of αὐτοῦ in later manuscripts is likely due to a scribal attempt to clear up the ambiguity as to whose soul will be saved: the converter's or the converted's (Varner[2], 396).

5:20b καί: This structural marker is a conjunction meaning "and" (BDAG, s.v. "καί" 1b, p. 494). **Syntactically**, it introduces a dependent conjunctive clause. **Semantically**, it is a coordinating conjunction often rendered "and" (NET ESV NASB NRSV etc.) that adds to James's discussion about wrongdoing.

καλύψει: This Greek word is a third person singular future active indicative of καλύπτω that conveys the idea of being covered in some physical way and may be rendered "cover up" or "remove from sight" (BDAG, s.v. "καλύπτω" 2a, p. 505). **Syntactically**, it is the second main idea of this dependent conjunctive ὅτι clause with an assumed subject, "whoever brings back a sinner from his straying," that parallels with the previous σώσει. Its direct object is πλῆθος ἁμαρτιῶν. **Semantically**, the future tense is a predictive future that indicates something that will take place (W, 568). It will happen: "will cover" (NASB NRSV NIV ESV NET CNT). It refers to overshadowing or smothering the effect of wrongdoing (Zerwick et al., 702).

Theological Nugget: Is James alluding here to a similar statement in Proverbs 10:12? Neither the LXX nor the Hebrew texts of Proverbs agree exactly with the wording in James, who shifts to the future tense (καλύψει) and uses the noun πλῆθος to magnify the sins. While it is true that God tells Ezekiel that if he warns the wicked and they do repent, then he will save himself as well (Ezek. 3:16–21; 33:9), the most consistent grammatical way of approaching 5:20 is that the benefits accrue to the converted, not to the converter. To James, the most *loving* act of all is to warn sinners from the error of their way and cover over their potential future sins. This future focus on the "converted" or "loved" one is consistent with its usage both in Proverbs 10:12 and in 1 Peter 4:8 (Davids, 201; Blomberg et al., 249).

James's Letter Translated

CHAPTER ONE

¹ James, a slave of God and of the Lord Jesus Christ, to the twelve tribes who are in the Diaspora: Greetings.

² Consider it pure joy, my brothers *and sisters*, whenever you encounter all types of trials, ³ because you know that the testing of your faith produces endurance. ⁴ And endurance should bring about its perfect work, in order that you may be perfect and complete, lacking in nothing.

⁵ Now, if any one of you is lacking wisdom, he should ask from God, the one who gives without reservation and does not reproach, and it will be given to him. ⁶ But he should ask in faith, doubting nothing, for the one who doubts is like a wave of the sea tossed and turned by the wind. ⁷ For that person should not expect that he will receive anything from the Lord. ⁸ A double-minded individual is unstable in everything he pursues.

⁹ Now, the lowly brother *and sister* should rather boast in his exaltation, ¹⁰ but the rich in his humiliation, because like a flower of wild grass he will pass away. ¹¹ For you see the sun rises along with its scorching heat and dries out the wild grass, and the flower falls to the ground, and its beautiful appearance perishes; so also, the rich man will fade away in the midst of his pursuits.

¹² Blessed is the person who remains steadfast under a trial, because after he has stood the test he will receive the crown of life, which he has promised to those who love him. ¹³ Let no one say when he is tempted, "I am being tempted by God," for you see, God cannot be tempted with evil things, and he himself tempts no one. ¹⁴ But each person is tempted by his own desire when he is lured and enticed. ¹⁵ Then when desire has conceived it gives birth to sin, and when sin is fully grown it gives birth to death.

¹⁶ Do not be deceived, my beloved brothers *and sisters*. ¹⁷ Every good act of giving and every complete gift is from above, coming down from the Father of the lights with whom there is no variation or shadow due to change. ¹⁸ When God decided, he gave birth to us by the Word of Truth, so that we should be a first portion of his created beings.

¹⁹ Know this, my beloved brothers *and sisters*; so, every person must be quick to hear, slow to speak, slow to anger; ²⁰ for you see a man's anger does not

produce the righteousness of God. [21] Therefore put away all filthiness and rampant wickedness, then accept with meekness the implanted Word, which is able to save your souls.

[22] But become doers of the Word, and not hearers only, deceiving yourselves. [23] Because if anyone is a hearer of the Word and not a doer, this one is like a man who looks intently at his natural face in a mirror. [24] For he looks at himself and he goes away and at once he forgets what he was. [25] But the one who looks carefully into the perfect law of liberty, and continues in it, by not relating to a forgetful hearer but by relating to one who does the deed, this one will be blessed in his doing.

[26] If anyone thinks he is religious while not bridling his tongue but deceiving his heart, this person's religion is worthless. [27] This is a pure and undefiled religion before God the Father: namely, to visit orphans and widows in their affliction, namely, to keep oneself unstained from the world.

Chapter Two

[1] My brothers *and sisters*, you must not hold to the faith of our glorious Lord Jesus Christ while committing acts of partiality. [2] For suppose a man enters into your synagogue wearing a gold ring in fine clothing, and a poor man in shabby clothing also enters, [3] and you pay attention to the one who wears the fine clothing and you say, "You sit here in a good place," and you say to the poor man, "You stand over there," or "Sit down at my feet," [4] have you not made discriminations among yourselves and have you not become judges with evil thoughts?

[5] Listen, my beloved brothers *and sisters*, has not God chosen those considered poor in the world to be rich *with respect to* faith and heirs of the kingdom that he promised to those who love him? [6] But you have dishonored the poor person. Do not the rich oppress you, and do they not drag you into courts? [7] Do they not blaspheme that honorable name which has been pronounced over you?

[8] If you really are obeying the royal law according to the Scripture, "You shall love your neighbor as yourself," you are doing well; [9] but if you are showing partiality, you are committing sin and as a result are convicted by the law as transgressors.

[10] For whoever observes the whole law but he stumbles in one point is accountable for all of it. [11] For he who said, "Do not commit adultery," said also, "Do not murder." Now if you do not commit adultery but you commit murder, you have become a transgressor of the law. [12] So speak and so act as those who are to be judged under the law of liberty. [13] For judgment is merciless to one who has shown no mercy. Mercy triumphs over judgment.

[14] What is the benefit, my brothers *and sisters*, if someone claims to have faith but he does not have accompanying deeds? Is that kind of faith able to save him? [15] If a brother or sister is poorly clothed and is lacking in daily food, [16] and one of you says to them, "Go in peace, keep yourself warmed and filled," and yet, without giving them the things needed for the body, what is the benefit? [17] So also, that kind of faith, if it is not accompanied by actions, is dead by itself.

[18] But someone will say, "You have faith, but I have deeds." Prove to me your faith apart from your deeds, and I will prove to you my faith by my deeds. [19] Do you believe that God is one? You are doing well. The demons even believe that God is one, and they shudder!

[20] But do you want to understand, O vain person, that faith without deeds is useless? [21] Was not Abraham our father vindicated by deeds when he offered up his son Isaac on the altar? [22] You see that faith was working together with his deeds, and faith was completed by means of his deeds. [23] In this way the Scripture was fulfilled that says, "Now Abraham believed God, and it was counted to him as righteousness"—and he was called "friend of God."

[24] You see that a person is being vindicated by means of deeds and not by means of faith alone. [25] And in the same way, was not also Rahab the prostitute vindicated by means of deeds when she welcomed the scouts and when she sent them out by another way? [26] You see just as the body apart from the spirit is dead, so also the faith that is not accompanied by deeds is dead.

Chapter Three

[1] Not many of you should become teachers, my brothers *and sisters*, because you know that we who teach will receive a stricter judgment. [2] You see, we repeatedly stumble in many ways. If anyone does not stumble in what he says, this one is a perfect man, who is able also to bridle his whole body.

[3] Consider that we put bridles into the mouths of horses so that they obey us and we guide their whole bodies. [4] Consider also ships! Although they are so large and though they are driven by strong winds, they are guided by a very small rudder wherever the will of the pilot directs. [5] So also, the tongue is a small member, yet, it boasts of great things. Consider a small fire; it sets ablaze a great forest!

[6] And the tongue is a fire. The tongue has been made the sum total of iniquity among our members, staining the whole body, and setting on fire the entire course of life, and is itself set on fire by hell. [7] Now every kind of beasts and birds, of reptiles and sea creatures, is tamed and has been tamed by mankind, [8] but no one is able to tame the tongue. It is an unstable evil, full of deadly poison.

[9] With it we repeatedly bless our Lord and Father, and with it we repeatedly curse people who are made in the likeness of God. [10] Does blessing and cursing come from the same mouth? My brothers *and sisters*, these things ought not to be so. [11] Does a spring pour forth from the same opening both fresh and bitter [*water*]? [12] Is it possible, my brothers *and sisters*, for a fig tree to produce olives, or a grapevine figs? Neither is it possible for a salt pond to produce fresh water.

[13] Who is wise and understanding among you? He should prove it by good conduct in actions with the gentleness of wisdom. [14] But if you have bitter jealousy and selfish ambition in your hearts, stop boasting and stop lying against the truth. [15] This is not the wisdom that comes down from above, but it is earthly, unspiritual, demonic. [16] You see, where jealousy and selfish ambition exist, there is disorder and every vile practice. [17] But the wisdom that comes from above is first pure, then is peaceable, gentle, open to reason, full of mercy and good fruits, impartial, sincere. [18] And a harvest of righteousness is sown in peace by those who work for peace.

Chapter Four

[1] What causes quarrels and what causes fights among you? Is it not from your passions that are at war in your members? [2] You desire and you do not own and so you murder. Likewise, you covet and are not able to obtain things and so you fight and quarrel. You do not own because you do not ask. [3] You ask and yet, you do not receive, because you ask wrongly, so that you might spend it on your pleasures. [4] Adulteresses, do you not know that friendship with the world means enmity with God? Therefore, whoever decides to be the world's friend makes himself God's enemy.

[5] Do you think that the Scripture speaks to no purpose? Does the spirit whom God has caused to dwell in us long enviously? [6] But God gives more grace. Therefore, it says, "God opposes proud people, but gives grace to humble ones."

[7] Therefore, submit yourselves to God, but resist the devil, and he will flee from you. [8] Draw near to God and he will draw near to you. Cleanse your hands, you sinners, and purify your hearts, you double-minded. [9] Grieve and mourn and weep. Your laughter must be turned to mourning and your joy to gloom. [10] Humble yourselves before the Lord, and he will exalt you.

[11] Do not slander each other, brothers *and sisters*. The one who slanders a brother or condemns his brother, slanders the law and condemns the law. But if you condemn the law, you are not a doer of the law but a judge. [12] The lawgiver and judge is one, who is able to save and to destroy. But who are you, who condemns your neighbor?

[13] Now listen, you who say, "Today or tomorrow we will go into such and such a city and will spend a year there and will trade and will make a profit." [14] Whoever you are you do not know what will happen tomorrow. What is your life? *Your lives are like smoky vapor*, namely, that your life appears for a little while and then *your life* vanishes. [15] Instead of your saying, you say, "If the Lord wills, we will both live and accomplish this or that." [16] As it is, you boast so arrogantly. Such arrogant boasting is evil. [17] Therefore, whoever knows to do the right thing and does not do it, it is sin to him.

CHAPTER FIVE

[1] Now listen, you who are rich, burst into weeping by howling with grief because of your miseries that are coming. [2] Your wealth is rotten, and your clothes are moth-eaten. [3] Your gold and silver are corroded, and the corrosion will be evidence against you and will eat your flesh like fire. It is in the last days that you have hoarded wealth. [4] Consider how the wage of the laborers which you have stolen from those who mowed your fields cries out against you, and the cries of the harvesters have reached the ears of the Lord of *Sabaoth*. [5] You have lived for pleasure on earth and you have lived in luxury. You have fattened your hearts for the day of slaughter, [6] you have condemned, you have murdered the righteous person. Does God not oppose you?

[7] Therefore, be patient, brothers *and sisters*, until the coming of the Lord. Consider how the farmer waits for the precious fruit of the earth, by being patient about it, until it receives the early and the late rains. [8] You also, be patient, establish your hearts, because the coming of the Lord is at hand. [9] Do not grumble against one another, brothers *and sisters*, in order that you may not be judged. Consider how the judge at the gate judges. [10] As an example of patient suffering, brothers *and sisters*, take the prophets who spoke in the name of the Lord. [11] Consider how we call blessed those who have endured. You have heard of the endurance of Job, and you have seen the Lord's outcome, that the Lord is compassionate and merciful.

[12] And above all, my brothers *and sisters*, do not swear an oath, neither by heaven nor by earth nor by any other oath. But your "yes" should be yes and your "no" no, in order that you do not fall under judgment.

[13] Is anyone among you suffering? Let him pray. Is anyone cheerful? Let him sing praise. [14] Is anyone among you sick? Let him call for the elders of the church, and they should pray over him, *by* anointing him with oil in the name of the Lord. [15] And the prayer of faith will save the one who is sick, and the Lord will raise him up. And if he has committed sins, he will be forgiven. [16] Therefore, confess sins to one another, and pray for one another in order that you may be healed. The prayer of a righteous person has power when active. [17] Elijah was

a human being with a nature like ours, and he prayed fervently in order that it might not rain, and for three years and six months it did not rain on the earth.[18] Then he prayed again, and heaven gave rain, and the earth bore its fruit.

[19] My brothers *and sisters*, if anyone among you is misled from the truth and *if* someone brings him back, [20] let him know that whoever turns a sinner from his straying will save his soul from death and will cover a multitude of sins.

Further Reading for Developing Exegetical Skills

Bateman IV, H. W. 2013. *Interpreting the General Letters: An Exegetical Handbook.* Handbooks for New Testament Exegesis. Edited by John D. Harvey. Grand Rapids: Kregel.

> *Interpreting the General Letters* consists of eight chapters covering genre, background, theology, interpretation, and communication of the general letters in the New Testament. Of particular significance is Bateman's step-by-step approach to interpretation of the letters.

Bock, Darrell L., and Buist M. Fanning, eds. 2006. *Interpreting the New Testament Text: Introduction to the Art and Science of Exegesis.* Wheaton, IL: Crossway.

> *Interpreting the New Testament Text* consists of two parts: exegetical methods and exegetical examples. The first examines numerous areas of interpretation: grammar, clausal layouts, word studies, biblical theology, the use of the Old Testament in the New, and genre studies. The second part provides case studies of the interpretive process.

Fee, Gordon D. 2002. *New Testament Exegesis: A Handbook for Students and Pastors.* 3rd ed. Louisville: Westminster John Knox Press.

> Fee provides an excellent guide for exegeting the New Testament. One of his greatest strengths is his explanation of "sentence flow analysis." This is a method that goes beyond traditional diagramming and illustrates the importance of the clausal analysis of any text.

Selected Clause-by-Clause Commentaries

Blomberg, C. L., and M. J. Kamell. 2008. *James*. Zondervan Exegetical Commentary on the New Testament. Grand Rapids: Zondervan.

This book is an excellent example of a commentary based on the analysis of clauses that enables the thought in a sentence to flow smoothly.

Davids, P. 1982. *The Epistle of James*. New International Greek Testament Commentary. Grand Rapids: Eerdmans.

The standard commentary on the Greek text for more thanw thirty years.

Varner, W. 2011. *The Book of James: A New Perspective: A Linguistic Commentary Applying Discourse Analysis*. The Woodlands, TX: Kress Biblical Resources.

This book is a holistic approach to the text built on the clausal layouts in the online Open Text analysis of the Greek NT text. It is an example of a thorough discourse analysis of James.

Figures of Speech in James[1]

FIGURES OF SPEECH INVOLVING COMPARISON

1. <u>Simile</u>, or resemblance: a declaration that one thing explicitly (by the presence of "like" or "as") resembles another.

   James 1:6 "for the one who doubts is <u>like</u> the surf of the sea,"

   James 2:26 "For <u>just as</u> the body apart from the spirit is dead . . ."

   James 5:17 "Elijah was a person with a nature <u>like</u> ours"

2. <u>Metaphor</u>, or Representation: a declaration that one thing is or represents another.

   James 3:6 "And the <u>tongue is a fire</u>"

   James 3:8 "It [the tongue] <u>is a restless evil</u>, full of deadly poison."

3. <u>Proverb</u>: a saying in common use, a specific illustration to signify a truth of life.

   James 4:17 "Therefore, whoever knows the right thing to do and fails to do it, for him it is sin."

4. <u>Personification</u>: the giving of human characteristics to inanimate objects, ideas, or animals.

   James 1:15 "when <u>desire has conceived</u> . . . and <u>sin . . . gives birth</u> to death"

   James 3:17 "But the <u>wisdom</u> that comes from above is first pure, then peaceable, gentle, open to reason, full of mercy and good fruits, impartial, sincere." (Recalls the personification of Wisdom in Proverbs 8)

   James 4:1 "Is it not from your passions <u>that are waging war</u> in your members?"

   James 5:4 "The wages which you defrauded from the laborers who mowed your fields <u>are crying out</u> against you. . . ."

---

1. This list is not exhaustive but is representative of the many figures of speech that James employs.

5. <u>Anthropomorphism</u>: the representation of God in the form of or with the attributes of man.

> James 4:4 "friendship with the world means <u>enmity</u> with God . . . the world's friend becomes God's <u>enemy</u>."

> James 5:9 "The judge <u>stands</u> before the gates."

6. <u>Idiom</u>: a fixed expression that cannot be understood grammatically from its component parts, but it has an understood and set meaning.

> James 5:16 "The prayer of a righteous person has great power <u>as it is working</u>."

FIGURES OF SPEECH INVOLVING SUBSTITUTION

1. <u>Metonymy</u>: the change of a word naming an object for another word closely associated with it.

> James 1:21 "receive with meekness the implanted Word which is able to save your <u>souls</u>."

> James 4:4 "<u>Adulteresses</u>, do you not know that friendship with the world is enmity with God?"

2. <u>Synecdoche</u>: an expression where the part stands for the whole or the whole for the part.

> James 2:7 "Name" is a synecdoche for the person

> James 4:13 "Today or tomorrow we will go into such and such a city and spend a <u>year</u> there. . ."

3. <u>Hendiadys</u>, or Two for One: two formally coordinate terms express a single concept in which one of the components defines the other.

> James 1:27 "A religion pure and undefiled before <u>God and the Father</u>" (God the Father)

> James 5:10 "As an example of <u>patience and suffering</u>" (patient suffering)

4. <u>Euphemism</u>: the substitution of an inoffensive or mild expression for an offensive one.

James 1:9 "The brother of <u>humble circumstances</u>" (a poor brother)

5. <u>Hyperbaton</u>, or Fronting: the placing of a word out of its usual order in the sentence for the sake of emphasis.

James 1:1 Literally "James, <u>of God and of the Lord Jesus Christ</u>, a slave."

James 1:21 "<u>with meekness</u> receive the implanted Word"

6. <u>Symbol</u>: a material object substituted for a moral or spiritual truth.

James 1:18 "so that we would be a kind of <u>first fruits</u> among his creatures" (early Jewish believers)

James 1:27 "to keep oneself unstained from <u>the world</u>" (mankind opposed to God)

James 2:20 "Do you wish to know, O <u>empty</u> (vain) man (person) . . ."

James 3:6 "The tongue has been made the world among our members" (the sum total of iniquity)

James 3:6 "setting on fire the <u>wheel of nature</u>" (entire <u>course of life</u>)

James 3:7 "and [*every kind of beasts and birds, of reptiles and of sea creatures*] has been tamed by man" (mankind or humankind)

James 4:4 "<u>Adulterers</u>, do you not know that friendship with the world is enmity with God?"

James 4:8 "<u>Cleanse</u> your hands, you sinners, and <u>purify</u> your hearts, you double-minded."

7. <u>Irony</u>: the expression of thought in a form that conveys its opposite.

James 2:8 "'You shall love your neighbor as yourself,' <u>you are doing well</u>."

James 2:19 "You believe that God is one? You are <u>doing well</u>!"

James 4:11 "But if you condemn the law, you are not a doer of the law but a judge." We who are condemned by the law end up condemning the law when we utter slanderous speech!

FIGURES OF SPEECH INVOLVING ADDITION OR AMPLIFICATION

1. <u>Chiasm</u>: a form of parallelism in which there is the inversion of terms in the second half of the verse or the passage.

> James 3:7:
> > A for every <u>nature</u> of beasts
> > > B is <u>tamed</u>
> > > B' has been <u>tamed</u>
> > A' by human <u>nature</u>

> James 4:2
> > A You <u>desire and you do not have.</u>
> > > B You <u>murder</u> and you <u>covet</u> and are not able to obtain.
> > > B' You <u>fight</u> and <u>quarrel.</u> You do not have because you do not ask.
> > A' You <u>ask and do not receive</u>

2. <u>Alliteration</u>: the repetition of the same letter initiating words in a passage.

> James 1:2 <u>π</u>ειρασμοῖς <u>π</u>εριπέσητε <u>π</u>οικίλοις ("when you encounter all types of trials")

> James 3:5 <u>μ</u>ικρὸν <u>μ</u>έλος ἐστὶν καὶ <u>μ</u>εγάλα αὐχεῖ ("the tongue is a small member, and yet it boasts of great things")

3. <u>Homoioteleuton</u>: the repetition of exact endings in successive words in a passage

> James 4:1 πόθ<u>εν</u> . . . πόθ<u>εν</u> . . . ἐντεῦθ<u>εν</u> ("What causes quarrels and what causes fights among you?")

> James 4:9 ταλαιπωρή<u>σατε</u> καὶ πενθή<u>σατε</u> καὶ κλαύ<u>σατε</u>. ("Be wretched and mourn and weep.")

4. <u>Anaphora</u>: the repetition of key words or lines at the beginning of successive predications.

> James 1:15 "Then when <u>that desire</u> has conceived . . ." (the article ἡ before ἐπιθυμία recalls the word ἐπιθυμία in 1:14)

> James 2:14 "What good is it, my brothers, if someone says that he has faith but he does not have accompanying deeds? Can <u>that kind of faith</u> save him?" (μὴ δύναται ἡ πίστις σῶσαι αὐτόν)

5. Inclusio: device in which a literary unit begins and ends with the same (or similar) word, phrase or clause. It is a framing device, stressing the theme.

> James 1:12 and 25 ("<u>blessed</u>"). The use of Μακάριος ἀνὴρ to introduce the section and οὗτος μακάριος to end the section

> James 4:7 and 10 Where the similar command frames the paragraph:
> "<u>Submit</u> therefore to <u>God</u>" (4:7)
> "<u>Humble</u> yourselves before the <u>Lord</u>" (4:10)

6. Polysyndeton: the repetition of the conjunction, instead of using subordinate clauses.

> James 5:17–18: "Elijah was a man with a nature like ours, <u>and</u> he prayed earnestly that it would not rain, <u>and</u> it did not rain on the earth for three years and six months. <u>And</u> he prayed again, <u>and</u> the sky poured rain <u>and</u> the earth produced its fruit."

7. Anabasis, or Gradual Ascent: an increase of sense in successive lines.

> James 1:14–15
> But each one is tempted
> when he is carried away
> enticed by his own lust.
> lust has conceived,
> gives birth to sin;
> sin is finished,
> brings forth death.

8. Hyperbole: exaggerated theme for the purpose of emphasis or heightened effect (more is said than is literally meant).

> James 2:15 "If a brother or sister is <u>naked</u> (γυμνοὶ) . . ."

> James 3:8 "<u>no human being</u> can tame the tongue."

> James 4:2 "you <u>murder</u>"

FIGURES OF SPEECH INVOLVING OMISSION OR SUPPRESSION

1. Ellipsis: the omission of any element of language that technically renders a sentence to be "ungrammatical" yet, the sentence is usually understood in context. The italic words in brackets below are examples of ellipsis in James.

James 3:2, 6, 8, 15, 16, 17 are examples where James omits [ἐστιν].

James 3:7 "and [*every kind of beasts and birds, of reptiles and of sea creatures*] has been tamed by mankind,"

James 3:11 "Does a spring pour forth from the same opening both fresh and salt [*water*]?"

James 3:12 "Neither [*is it possible for*] a salt [*pond*] to produce fresh water."

James 3:14 "and [*stop*] lying against the truth."

2. <u>Erotesis</u>, or Rhetorical Questions: the asking of questions without expecting an answer (to express affirmation).

James 2:4 "have you not made discriminations among yourselves, and have you become judges with evil thoughts?"

James 2:14 "What good is it, my brothers, if someone claims to have faith but he does not have accompanying deeds? Is that kind of faith able to save him?"

James 2:16 ". . . what is the benefit?"

James 2:21 "Was not Abraham our father vindicated by deeds when he offered up his son Isaac on the altar?"

James 3:11 "Does a spring pour forth from the same opening both fresh and salt [*water*]?"

James 3:12 "Neither [*is it possible for*] a salt [*pond*] to produce fresh water."

James 3:13 "Who is wise and understanding among you?"

James 2:14 "What good is it, my brothers, if someone claims to have faith but he does not have accompanying deeds? Is that kind of faith able to save him?"

James 4:1 "What is the source of quarrels and conflicts among you?"

James 5:6 "Does he not oppose you?"

3. <u>Anacoluthon</u>, or Non-sequence: a change from a construction which has been begun already, which appears ungrammatical.

> James 4:13 "Now listen (singular) you who say . . ." (plural)

> James 5:1 "Come now (singular) you rich ones" (plural)

4. <u>Merism</u>: a conventional phrase that enumerates several of its constituents or traits.

> James 2:21–25 The combination of patriarch Abraham (2:21–24) and prostitute Rahab (2:25) also form a merism—the two characters point to one reality. In this case the reality is justification by works.

> James 4:8 "Cleanse your hands, purify your hearts"

Bibliography

Adam, A. K. M. 2013. *James: A Handbook on the Greek Text*. Waco, TX: Baylor University Press.

Aland, K., et al. 2012. *Novum Testamentum Graece*. 28th ed. Stuttgart: Deutsche Bibelgesellschaft.

Aristotle. 1944. *Politics*. Translated by H. Rackham. Loeb Classical Library. Cambridge, MA: Harvard University Press.

Baker, W. R., and T. D. Ellsworth. 2004. *Preaching James*. St. Louis: Chalice.

Balz, H., and G. Schneider. 1990–93. *Exegetical Dictionary of the New Testament*. 3 Volumes. Grand Rapids: Eerdmans.

Bateman IV, H. W. 2013. *Interpreting the General Letters: An Exegetical Handbook*. Handbooks for New Testament Exegesis. Edited by J. D. Harvey. Grand Rapids: Kregel.

———. 2016. "Review of Robert J. Foster, *The Significance Exemplars for the Interpretation of the Letter of James*." *Journal of the Evangelical Theological Society* 59.1, 199–201.

Bateman IV, H. W., and A. C. Peer. 2018. *John's Letters: An Exegetical Guide for Preaching and Teaching*. The Big Greek Idea Series. Grand Rapids: Kregel.

Bateman IV, H. W., and S. W. Smith. 2021. *Hebrews: A Commentary for Biblical Preaching and Teaching*. Kerux Commentaries. Grand Rapids: Kregel.

Bauckham, R. 1998. "The Tongue Set on Fire by Hell (James 3:6)." In *The Fate of the Dead: Studies on the Jewish and Christian Apocalypses*. Supplements to Novum Testamentum 93. Leiden: Brill.

Bauer, W., F. W. Danker, W. F. Arndt, and F. W. Gingrich. 2000. *A Greek–English Lexicon of the New Testament and Other Early Christian Literature*. 3rd ed. Chicago and London: University of Chicago Press.

Blass, F., A. Debrunner, and R. W. Funk. 1961. *A Greek Grammar of the New Testament and Other Early Christian Literature*. Translation and revision of the 9th–10th German edition, by Robert W. Funk. Chicago: University of Chicago Press.

Blomberg, C. L., and M. J. Kamell. 2008. *James*. Zondervan Exegetical Commentary on the New Testament. Grand Rapids: Zondervan.

Bock, D. L., and B. M. Fanning, eds. 2006. *Interpreting the New Testament Text: Introduction to the Art and Science of Exegesis*. Wheaton, IL: Crossway.

Bullinger, E. W. 1986. *Figures of Speech Used in the Bible: Explained and Illustrated*. 10th ed. Grand Rapids: Baker.

Campbell, C. R. 2008. *Basics of Verbal Aspect in Biblical Greek*. Grand Rapids: Zondervan.

Davids, P. 1982. *Commentary on the Epistle James*. New International Greek Testament Commentary. Grand Rapids: Eerdmans.

Deppe, Dean. 1989. *The Sayings of Jesus in the Epistle of James*. Chelsea, MI: Bookcrafters.

deSilva, D. A. 2000. *Honor, Patronage, Kinship & Purity: Unlocking New Testament Culture*. Downers Grove, IL: IVP Academic.

Dibelius, M. 1976. *Commentary on James*. Translated by Michael Williams. Hermeneia. Philadelphia: Fortress Press.

Epictetus/Arrian. 1925. *Discourses*. Translated by W. A. Oldfather. Loeb Classical Library. Cambridge, MA: Harvard University Press.

Fanning, B. M. 1990. *Verbal Aspect in the New Testament*. OTM. Oxford: Clarendon.

Foster, R. J. 2014. *The Significance of Exemplars for the Interpretation of the Letter of James*. Wissenschaftliche Untersuchungen zum Neuen Testament. Tübingen, Germany: Mohr Siebeck.

Guthrie, G. H., and J. S. Duvall. 1988. *Biblical Greek Exegesis: A Guided Approach to Learning Intermediate and Advanced Greek*. Grand Rapids: Zondervan.

Hengel, M. 1974. *Judaism and Hellenism: Studies in Their Encounter in Palestine during the Early Hellenistic Period*. Translated by J. Bowden. Philadelphia: Fortress Press.

Herodotus. *The History of Herodotus*. Translated by A. D. Godley et al. 4 vols. Loeb Classical Library. Cambridge, MA: Harvard University Press, 1921–28.

Hodges, Z. C. 1994. *The Epistle of James*. Irving, TX: Grace Evangelical Society.

Hodges, Z. C., and A. L. Farstad. 1985. *The Greek New Testament According to the Majority Text*. 2nd ed. Nashville: Nelson.

_____. 2007. *The Apostolic Fathers: Greek Texts and English Translations.* 3rd edition. Baker Academic. See "Polycarp," "Didache," "The Shepherd of Hermas," 272–309, 334–69, 442–685.

Holmes, M. W. 2010. *The Greek New Testament SBL Edition.* Atlanta, GA; Bellingham, WA: Society of Biblical Literature; Logos Bible Software.

Irons, C. L. 2016. *A Syntax Guide for Reading the Greek New Testament.* Grand Rapids: Kregel.

Isaac, E. 1985. "1 (Ethiopic Apocalypse of) Enoch." Pages 1:5–89 in *The Old Testament Pseudepigrapha.* Edited by J. H. Charlesworth. New York: Doubleday.

Josephus. 1978. *Jewish Antiquities, Books I–IV.* Vol. 4. Translated by H. St. J. Thackeray. Loeb Classical Library. Cambridge, MA: Harvard University Press.

_____. 1978. *Jewish Antiquities, Books V–XIII.* Vol. 5. Translated by R. Marcus. Loeb Classical Library. Cambridge, MA: Harvard University Press.

_____. 1978. *Jewish Antiquities, Books IX–XI.* Vol. 6. Translated by R. Marcus. Loeb Classical Library. Cambridge, MA: Harvard University Press.

_____. 1989. *The Jewish Wars, Books I–III.* Vol. 2. Translated by H. St. J. Thackeray. Loeb Classical Library. Cambridge, MA: Harvard University Press.

_____. 1990. *The Jewish Wars, Books IV–VII.* Vol. 3. Translated by H. St. J. Thackeray. Loeb Classical Library. Cambridge, MA: Harvard University Press.

Kittel, G., ed. 1983. *Theological Dictionary of the New Testament.* 10 vols. Translated and edited by Geoffrey W. Bromiley. Grand Rapids: Eerdmans.

Louw, J. P., and E. A. Nida, eds. 1989. *Greek-English Lexicon of the New Testament: Based on Semantic Domains.* 2nd ed. New York: United Bible Societies.

MacDonald, W. G. 1979. *Greek Enchiridion: A Concise Handbook of Grammar for Translation and Exegesis.* Peabody, MA: Hendrickson.

Mayor, J. B. 1900. *The Epistle of St. James: The Greek Text with Introduction, Notes, and Comments.* 3rd ed. London: MacMillan & Co.

McCartney, D. G. 2009. *James: An Exegetical Commentary on the New Testament.* Grand Rapids: Baker.

Metzger, B. M. 1971. *A Textual Commentary on the Greek New Testament.* Stuttgart, Germany: Biblia–Druck.

_____. 1994. A *Textual Commentary on the Greek New Testament.* 2nd ed. Stuttgart, Germany: Biblia–Druck.

_____. 1992. *The Text of the New Testament: Its Transmission, Corruption, and Restoration.* 3rd enlarged ed. New York: Oxford University Press.

Metzger, B. M., and R. Murphy, eds. 1991. *The New Oxford Annotated Apocrypha: The Apocryphal/Deuterocanonical Books of the Old Testament*. New York: Oxford University Press.

Montanari, Franco, ed. 2015. *Brill Dictionary of Ancient Greek*. 2 vols. Leiden: Brill.

Moo, D. J. 2000. *The Letter of James*. Pillar New Testament Commentary. Grand Rapids: Eerdmans.

Moule, C. F. D. 1984. *An Idiom-Book of the Greek New Testament*. 2nd ed. Cambridge: Cambridge University Press.

Moulton, J. H., and G. Milligan. 1930. *The Vocabulary of the Greek Testament*. Grand Rapids: Eerdmans.

Mounce, W. D. 1996. *A Graded Reader of Biblical Greek*. Grand Rapids: Zondervan.

The Oxyrhynchus Papyri. Translated by B. P. Grenfell and A. S. Hunt. 15 vols. Cornell University Library Historical Monographs Collection. Reprinted by Cornell University Library Digital Collections.

Philo. *Philo*. Translated by F. H. Colson and G. H. Whitaker. 9 vols. Loeb Classical Library. Cambridge, MA: Harvard University Press, 1929–62.

Plato. *Plato*. Translated by Christopher Emlyn, William Preddy, H. N. Fowler, W. R. M. Lamb, Paul Shorey, and R. G. Bury. 12 vols. Loeb Classical Library. Cambridge, MA: Harvard University Press, 1935–52.

Polybius. *Histories*. Translated by W. R. Paton, F. W. Walbank, and Christian Habink. 8 vols. Loeb Classical Library. Cambridge, MA: Harvard University Press, 1967–2011.

Porter, S. E. 1994. *Idioms of the Greek New Testament*. 2nd ed. Sheffield: JSOT Press.

_____. 1994. "Jesus and the Use of Greek in Galilee." Pages 123–54 in *Studying the Historical Jesus: Evaluations of the State of Current Research*. Edited by B. D. Chilton and C. A. Evans. New Testament Tools and Studies 19. Leiden: Brill.

Robertson, A. T. 1934. *A Greek Grammar of the Greek New Testament in the Light of Historical Research*. London: Hodder and Stoughton.

_____. 1982. *Word Pictures in the New Testament*. 6 vols. Grand Rapids: Baker.

Robinson, M. A., and W. G. Pierpont. 2005. *The New Testament in the Original Greek: Byzantine Textform*. Southborough, MA: Chilton.

Spencer, A. B. 2020. *A Commentary on James*. Kregel Exegetical Library. Grand Rapids: Kregel.

Sevenster, J. N. 1968. *Do You Know Greek? How Much Greek Could the First Jewish Christians Have Known?* Novum Testamentum Supplement 19. Leiden: Brill.

Taylor, M. 2006. *A Text-Linguistic Investigation into the Discourse Structure of James*. London: T&T Clark.

Trench, R. C. 1880. *Synonyms of the New Testament*. London: Macmillan and Co.

Turner, N. 1980. *Style*. Vol. IV of A *Grammar of New Testament Greek*. Edited by J. H. Moulton. Edinburgh: T & T Clark.

Varner, W. 2010. *The Book of James: A New Perspective: A Linguistic Commentary Applying Discourse Analysis*. The Woodlands, TX: Kress Biblical Resources.

_____. 2017. *James: A Commentary on the Greek Text*. Dallas: Fontes Press.

Wallace, D. B. 1996. *Greek Grammar Beyond the Basics: An Exegetical Syntax of the New Testament*. Grand Rapids: Zondervan.

Witherington III, B. 2007. *Letters and Homilies for Jewish Christians*. Downers Grove, IL: IVP Academic.

Xenophon. *Anabasis*. Translated by Carleton L Brownson, E. C. Marchant, W. Miller, and G. W. Bowersock. 7 vols. Loeb Classical Library. Cambridge, MA: Harvard University Press, 1979–86.

Zerwick, M. 1963. *Biblical Greek: Illustrated by Examples*. Translated by Joseph Smith. SubBi 41. Rome: Pontifical Biblical Institute.

Zerwick, M., and M. Grosvenor. 1981. *A Grammatical Analysis of the New Testament: Unabridged Revised Edition in One Volume*. Rome: Biblical Institute Press.

Nugget Index

GRAMMATICAL NUGGETS

Syntactical Nuggets

Semantical Nuggets

Lexical Nuggets

THEOLOGICAL NUGGETS

Text-Critical Nuggets

Structural Nuggets

INTERPRETIVE ISSUE

FIGURE OF SPEECH

HISTORICAL NUGGETS

LITERARY NUGGET

QUOTATION NUGGETS

BACKGROUNDS NUGGET